THE BUMPER BOOK OF RESOURCES

ADVENT
CHRISTMAS
EPIPHANY

EDITED BY JOHN COX

kevin mayhew

www.kevinmayhew.com

kevin
mayhew

First published in Great Britain in 2015 by Kevin Mayhew Ltd
Buxhall, Stowmarket, Suffolk IP14 3BW
Tel: +44 (0) 1449 737978 Fax: +44 (0) 1449 737834
E-mail: info@kevinmayhew.com

www.kevinmayhew.com

9 8 7 6 5 4 3 2 1 0

ISBN 978 1 84867 788 3
Catalogue No. 1501483

Cover design by Justin Minns
© Images used under licence from Shutterstock Inc.
Edited by John Cox
Typeset by Chris Coe

Printed and bound in Great Britain

CONTENTS

SERVICES

SERMON IDEAS

CHRISTMAS

PRAYERS

RESOURCES

EPIPHANY

PRAYERS

SERVICES

SERMON IDEAS

ALL-AGE SERVICES

RESOURCES

ABOUT THE CONTRIBUTORS

FOREWORD

This Bumper Book (together with its two companion volumes) draws together material from a wide range of sources and a number of top authors to create an invaluable resource for anyone seeking help with prayers, services, sermon ideas and illustrative material both for general and all-age worship.

The three volumes cover the major festivals of the Christian year:

Volume 1: Harvest, All Saints, All Souls and Remembrance

Volume 2: Advent, Christmas and Epiphany

Volume 3: Holy Week, Easter, Ascension and Pentecost

Each volume is accompanied by a CD-ROM providing activity sheets and illustrations that can be reproduced to enliven learning and interactive worship.

ADVENT

PRAYERS

From the Lectionary

Matthew 25:1-13

Lord Jesus Christ,
prepare our hearts to meet you in this time of worship
and when you return in glory to establish your kingdom.
Confront, instruct and enable us by your Spirit,
so that we will be awake and alert,
equipped to live each moment
as though the day of your coming has dawned,
and ready to welcome you whenever it might be.

Nick Fawcett

Luke 1:39-55

Gracious God,
reminded at this season of your awesome gift in Christ,
we want to respond,
to offer something in return
as a sign of our gratitude for all you have done and continue to do.
We would bring you our worship –
not just well-intentioned thoughts and words
but our wholehearted adoration and joyful thanksgiving.
We would bring you our lives –
not just token deeds or outward show,
but hearts consecrated to your service,
embodying your love for all,
your care and compassion for everything you have made.
Receive, then, this time set aside for you
as a small yet sincere way of acknowledging your goodness,
and through it equip us to live as your people
this and every day.

Nick Fawcett

Mark 1:1-8

Redeemer God,
as we prepare to celebrate the birth of your Son,
speak through all we share together now:
the singing of hymns,

the reading of Scripture,
the preaching of your word,
the offering of prayers –
these and so much more.
Break through all that separates us from you and him:
over-familiarity,
indifference,
self-will,
disobedience, narrowness of vision, weakness of resolve.
Move among us through your Spirit – inspiring,
instructing,
revealing,
renewing –
so that we may be equipped now
to worship and always to serve.

Nick Fawcett

Luke 1:26-38

Almighty God,
we recall at this joyful season how,
through her willingness to hear your word
and commit herself to your service,
you were able to use Mary to fulfil your purpose,
entering our world,
inaugurating your kingdom
and bringing closer that day when sorrow and suffering,
darkness and death
will be no more.
Help us, then, as we gather now to worship,
to hear your word
and to respond with similar obedience,
prepared to be used as you see fit.
Through our discipleship,
weak and feeble though it might be,
may your grace be revealed,
your love made known
and your world enriched.

Nick Fawcett

We Come to Worship

Lord Jesus Christ,
we have come to worship you in this glad season of Advent,
a season of expectation,
of celebration,
and, above all, of preparation.
We come now, because we want to be ready –
ready to give thanks for your coming,
to recognise the ways you come to us now,

and to welcome you when you come again.
Open our hearts as we worship you,
so that all we share may give us a deeper understanding of this season
and a fuller experience of your love.
In your name we ask it.   *Nick Fawcett*

Advent 1

Lord Jesus Christ,
we come today yearning to welcome, worship, meet and greet you,
but conscious also that,
just as many were not ready to receive you
when first you entered our world,
so we too can be less prepared than we think,
our narrow expectations or misplaced assumptions
closing our minds to your presence among us.
So we ask that, as we draw near to you,
you will draw near to us,
stirring our hearts and capturing our imagination.
Prepare us to recognise you afresh at work in our lives and our world,
and so make us ready to serve you,
today and always.   *Nick Fawcett*

Advent 2

Father God,
just as you sent your servant John into the wilderness
to prepare the way of the Lord
and make ready your people to receive him,
so prepare us now to respond afresh to the gift of Christ
to all that you offer us through him.
Give us a readiness truly to listen, learn, worship and respond,
receiving the forgiveness he extends
and the renewal he makes possible,
and giving back in return our heartfelt gratitude
expressed in true commitment and faithful service.
In his name we pray.   *Nick Fawcett*

Advent 3

Lord,
as you spoke through John the Baptist,
and through the prophets before him,
speak now through this time of worship,
and through all who will share in leading it.
Behind the voices we hear,
the words we read and the message we listen to
may we hear your voice,
calling, confronting,

leading, loving,
enthusing and enabling.
Open our ears, our minds and our souls to your word of truth,
the Word made flesh,
Jesus Christ our Lord.

Nick Fawcett

Advent 4

Lord Jesus Christ,
born to Mary,
coming to our world through her,
be born afresh in us
that we might be born again through you.
Touch now this time of worship
that the message of your birth,
so familiar and well loved,
will speak afresh with new power and clarity,
thrilling our hearts
and filling us with joy and gratitude.
Draw close to us now,
that through welcoming you into our lives
and opening ourselves once more to your renewing power
you may reach out through us to the world,
bringing hope and healing,
light and life,
to the glory of your name.

Nick Fawcett

Advent Praise

Gracious God,
we praise you for this season of Advent,
this time for rejoicing and celebration,
praise and worship,
exulting in your goodness.

We praise you for coming in Christ,
bringing in a new kingdom
and anticipating an era of peace and justice
when the poor will have plenty,
the hungry be fed,
and the lowly be lifted up.

We praise you that you want us to be a part of that,
not just to share in it
but also to play a part
in bringing it to pass.
Forgive us that we sometimes lose sight of your purpose
and underestimate your greatness.

Open our eyes to the breadth of your love,
the wonder of your mercy
and the extent of your goodness,
and so may we give you the worship
and adoration that is due to you,
this and every day,
through Jesus Christ our Lord.

Nick Fawcett

The assurance of Advent

Loving God,
we rejoice in this season of good news and good will,
we celebrate once more the birth of your Son,
our Saviour Jesus Christ,
the Prince of Peace
the Lord of lords,
the Word made flesh,
and we praise you for the assurance of his final triumph.
As you came through him,
so you shall come again.

For coming among us through Jesus,
for bearing our flesh and blood,
for living our life and sharing our humanity,
for entering our world,
loving God, we praise you!
As you came through him,
so you shall come again.

For suffering and dying among us,
for your victory over death,
your triumph over evil,
and your promise that the kingdom will come,
loving God, we praise you!
As you came through him,
so you shall come again.

For the wonder of this season,
for its message of love and forgiveness,
its promise of peace and justice,
and the gift of life everlasting of which it speaks,
loving God, we praise you!
As you came through him,
so you shall come again.

Loving God,
we rejoice again in this season of good news and good will,
and we look forward to that day
when the Jesus of Bethlehem will be the Lord of all.
As you came through him,
so you shall come again.

In Christ's name we praise you!

Nick Fawcett

Receiving the word

Gracious God,
we praise you today for the power of your word,
the way you have spoken to so many people throughout history.
You called the universe into being – heaven and earth,
night and day,
the sea and the dry land,
life in its multitude of manifestations.
You spoke,
and it was done,
our world and our very existence owing to you.
For your word of life,
we praise you.

You called Abraham, Isaac and Jacob,
Moses and Joshua,
judges, kings and prophets,
Apostles, disciples, preachers and teachers –
a great company of saints,
each testifying to your sovereign purpose,
your awesome power
and your merciful love;
each hearing your voice and responding in faith.
For your word of life,
we praise you.

You came in Jesus Christ, the Word made flesh,
identifying yourself with our humanity,
sharing our joy and sorrow,
experiencing our life and death.
You came in fulfilment of your promises of old,
revealing the extent of your love
through everything he said and did,
demonstrating your gracious purpose for all.
For your word of life,
we praise you.

You speak still through the pages of Scripture;
through their record of your involvement in history
and their testimony to your will for the world.
You speak through dialogue between Christians,
through the witness of your Church and personal testimony,
through study and reflection,
and through the sharing of fellowship.
You speak through the grandeur of the universe
and the wonder of life,
your still small voice breaking into our experience
to challenge and inspire.
For your word of life,
we praise you.

Gracious God,
we rejoice at the ways you have spoken to us in the past
and the way you continue to speak today.
We receive your word with joyful thanksgiving,
and we pray for strength to make it so much a part of us
that your voice may be heard through all we are and do,
to the glory of your name.
For your word of life,
we praise you.

Through Jesus Christ our Lord.   *Nick Fawcett*

Thanksgiving

Loving God,
we thank you for this glad time of year,
this Advent season which reminds us of so much,
and which reveals so wonderfully the extent of your love.
For your coming and coming again in Christ,
we thank you.

This is a time for looking back
and remembering the birth of your Son,
light into our darkness;
a time for looking forward and anticipating his coming again,
as he returns to establish your kingdom and rule in your name;
but above all a time for the present moment,
for examining our lives, searching our hearts,
exploring your word, and renewing our faith;
a time for recognising more fully
that Jesus is with us each moment of every day,
now and always.
For your coming and coming again in Christ,
we thank you.

Loving God,
you came to our world in humility,
born of Mary in a stable.
You will come once more in glory,
through the risen and ascended Christ.
You are with us now even as we speak,
here through your Holy Spirit making Jesus real!
We praise you, the great truth of Advent.
For your coming and coming again in Christ,
**we thank you,
in his name.**   *Nick Fawcett*

Heavenly Father,
during this Advent season
we thank you for feeding us
in body, mind and spirit.   *Susan Sayers*

The world moves round into the light of the day
and we thank you, Father, that we are alive in it.
In this Advent season of watching and waiting,
keep us attentive to you, throughout the day,
ready to listen, ready to learn and ready to love.

Susan Sayers

John the Baptist

God, we thank you for Zechariah and Elizabeth
and for the birth of their son, John the Baptist.
We give thanks that he prepared the way
for the coming of Jesus.
Grant that we who are baptised
may be ready for the coming of our Lord.
You are their God and our God:
you are their Father and our Father.
Help us to know that as you came to them you come to us.

David Adam

Your presence

Lord our God, we give you thanks
and rejoice in the great love that you have for us:
we rejoice in your presence and in your peace.
We pray for your whole Church
as it prepares for the Christmas season.
May it encourage people to come before you
in joy and in celebration.
Bless all who preach and all who teach the faith:
may they show the joy of knowing you and your love.

David Adam

Joseph

Lord God, we give you thanks for Joseph
and for his courage to do your will.
Help us to bring in your kingdom
by our obedience to you this day and always.
May we show that we dwell in you and you in us.

David Adam

Mary

God, we thank you for the obedience of Mary
and for all who help to bring in your kingdom
by seeking to do your will.
We give thanks
for your faithful people throughout all ages.
Lord, guide your Church
that it may know your will and serve you faithfully.

David Adam

Confession

Rediscovering the word

Sovereign God,
we thank you for your word –
recorded in Scripture
and handed down over countless generations;
heard through reading, preaching, fellowship and worship;
glimpsed in the beauty of our world and the mysteries of life;
brought to life through prayer and meditation,
embodied through Jesus Christ, the Word made flesh.

Speak again now,
and give us ears to hear.

Forgive us that we are sometimes slow to listen.
We do not make time to read the Scriptures as we should,
allowing instead the pressures and responsibilities of life,
our many interests, pleasures and concerns,
to crowd out the time we spend with you.

Speak again now,
and give us ears to hear.

We become casual or complacent in our worship,
no longer expecting you to challenge us,
no longer moved to a sense of awe,
no longer hungry for spiritual food.

Speak again now,
and give us ears to hear.

We neglect the opportunity for fellowship,
turning in on ourselves,
imagining we know all there is to know of you,
more concerned with our own insights
than those we can gain from others.

Speak again now,
and give us ears to hear.

We grow deaf to your voice in creation,
our senses dulled by over-familiarity;
no time to pause and ponder,
to reflect on deeper, eternal realities.

Speak again now,
and give us ears to hear.

We believe we have listened and responded,
but our focus is on the written word
rather than the Word made flesh,
the letter rather than the spirit of your revelation in Christ.

Speak again now,
and give us ears to hear.

Sovereign God,
speak afresh through the pages of Scripture,
through the worship that we share,
the experience and insight of other Christians,
and, above all, through the inner presence
of the living Christ in our hearts.
Teach us, when your voice seems silent,
to listen again more carefully,
and to rediscover your word.

Speak again now,
and give us ears to hear.
Through Jesus Christ our Lord.

Nick Fawcett

Advent omission

Loving God,
the great festival of Christmas is drawing nearer
and we are busy preparing for it –
choosing presents,
writing cards,
planning get-togethers,
buying food –
so much that has become an accepted
and expected part of this season.
Yet, in all the bustle, we so easily forget
the most important thing of all:
responding to the wonderful gift of your Son.

You have come to us in Christ:
forgive us when we fail to receive him.

We tell ourselves that we are different –
that we will be worshipping you Sunday by Sunday,
sharing in services of lessons and carols,
hearing again familiar and well-loved verses of Scripture,
but we know that this isn't enough in itself,
for these too can become
just another part of our traditional celebrations,
washing over us
rather than communicating
the great message of the Gospel.
We become so concerned with the wrapping
that we fail to recognise the gift concealed underneath.

You have come to us in Christ:
forgive us when we fail to receive him.

Forgive us for relegating Jesus
to the periphery of our celebrations,
rather than placing him at the centre where he belongs;
for turning this season into a time for material extravagance,
rather than an opportunity for spiritual fulfilment;
for doing so much to prepare for Christmas on the surface,
yet so little to make ourselves ready within.

You have come to us in Christ:
forgive us when we fail to receive him.

Loving God,
open our hearts now to hear again your word,
to welcome the living Christ,
and to reflect on our response to his call.
May this Advent season teach us
to welcome him afresh into our lives
and to rejoice in his love not just at Christmas but always.

You have come to us in Christ:
forgive us when we fail to receive him.
We ask it for his name's sake.

Nick Fawcett

Intercessions

The hope of Advent

Lord Jesus Christ,
we remember today
how so many looked forward to your coming,
but we remember also
how it became harder to go on believing
as the years went by;
how hope started to splutter and dreams began to die until, finally, you came –
the fulfilment of prophecy,
the culmination of God's purpose,
the definitive expression of his love.
Lord of all,
the Word made flesh,
bring hope to your world today.

We remember with gladness
how you brought hope throughout your ministry,
a sense of purpose to those for whom life seemed pointless –
the poor, sick, outcasts and broken-hearted –
light shining in their darkness,
joy breaking into their sorrow,
new beginnings in what had seemed like the end.
Lord of all,
the Word made flesh,
bring hope to your world today.

Hear now our prayer for those caught today in the grip of despair –
those for whom the future seems bleak,
optimism seems foolish,
and trust seems futile.
Reach out in love,
and may light shine into their darkness.
Lord of all,
the Word made flesh,
bring hope to your world today.

Hear our prayer for those whose goals in life have been thwarted,
whose dreams have been shattered,
who have grown weary, cynical and disillusioned.
Reach out in love,
and rekindle their faith in the future.
Lord of all,
the Word made flesh,
bring hope to your world today.

Hear our prayer for those who mourn,
or who wrestle with illness,
or who watch loved ones suffer.
Reach out in love,
and grant them your strength and comfort.
Lord of all,
the Word made flesh,
bring hope to your world today.

Hear our prayer for those whose lives are blighted by injustice,
crushed by oppression, poverty, hunger,
and encourage all who work against the odds
to build a better world.
Reach out in love,
and grant the assurance of your coming kingdom.
Lord of all,
the Word made flesh,
bring hope to your world today.

Lord Jesus Christ,
we remember your promise to come again in glory,
the culmination of God's purpose,
the ultimate victory of love.
May that conviction bring new faith,
new vision,
and new purpose wherever life seems hopeless.
Lord of all,
the Word made flesh,
bring hope to your world today.
In your name we pray.

Nick Fawcett

Come, Lord Jesus

As we begin another Church Year
let us give thanks to God that he has made us,
that he loves us and that he comes to us.

O God, you are our Maker:
you give us life, you give us love,
you give us yourself.
Help us to give our lives,
our love and ourselves to you.
Keep us alert and aware of your presence,
that we may meet you each day
and know that you come to us in grace and in love.

Lord, as you come to your Church,
help us to reveal your glory.
Grant that we may show your grace
and your goodness in our lives.
We thank you for the grace and goodness
revealed in Jesus Christ
and that we are enriched in him.

We remember churches that are struggling
against the darkness of evil, of opposition, of apathy.
We remember especially
Christians who are being persecuted for their faith.

Silence

Come, Lord Jesus;
come, our Saviour and our God.

As we pray for your world,
we remember those who are seeking
to bring peace and goodwill among all.
We pray for those involved in war or the threat of war.
We think of those caught up in earthquakes, famine or flood.

Silence

Come, Lord Jesus;
come, our Saviour and our God.

Lord, let your presence be known in our homes and our actions.
May people be thankful for us
and our care of all that is around us.
We pray that you will show yourself to us
through our loved ones and friends.

Silence

Come, Lord Jesus;
come, our Saviour and our God.

We remember all whose lives are darkened by pain and distress;
all who are struggling with doubt and despair;
all whose faith is shaken by what is happening around them.
We pray for members of our community and friends
who are ill at this time.

Silence

Come, Lord Jesus;
come, our Saviour and our God.

God our Father, your grace has been given to us,
in the gift of eternal life and in your abiding presence.
We pray for all who are departed from us,
for friends and loved ones
in the fullness of your eternal kingdom.
We rejoice with them in the gift of life and your love.

Silence

Merciful Father,
accept these prayers
for the sake of your Son,
our Saviour Jesus Christ.   *David Adam*

Keep alert

Keep alert, because much is demanded of those to whom much is entrusted.

When the pressures of the day fragment our peace,
keep us watchful and alert,
both for ourselves and for the world.

Silence for prayer

For who is God but the Lord:
who is our rock but our God?

When false values are paraded among the true,
keep us watchful and alert,
both for ourselves and for our young.
Silence for prayer

For who is God but the Lord:
who is our rock but our God?

When our tight schedules leave no time for being merely available,
keep us watchful and alert,
both for ourselves and for those who need a listener.

Silence for prayer

For who is God but the Lord:
who is our rock but our God?

When the injustice of the world laughs at our insignificance,
keep us watchful and alert,
both for ourselves and for all who rely on our solidarity with them.

Silence for prayer

For who is God but the Lord:
who is our rock but our God?

When we begin to take the wonder of your creation for granted,
keep us watchful and alert,
both for ourselves and for every person you cherish.

Silence for prayer

Merciful Father,
accept these prayers
for the sake of your Son,
our Saviour Jesus Christ.   *Susan Sayers*

Be prepared

Be prepared for the coming of the Lord. John the Baptist was the promised forerunner to Christ, and his teaching inspired many to turn back to God's ways, making them receptive when Jesus began his ministry. We, too, need to renounce sin and prepare for the time when Christ will come again in glory.

Let us bring to God our loving Father
all the cares that weigh on our hearts,
knowing that he understands us better
than we understand ourselves.

Father, we bring the daily work
of those who labour
to spread the good news of Christ
amid apathy, ridicule or prejudice;
may they be encouraged and strengthened.

Silence for prayer

Father, hear us:
and prepare us to meet you.

Father, we bring our daily work,
with all the pressures, monotony,
enjoyment and mistakes;

help your world
to recognise your presence
and trust in your love.

Silence for prayer

Father, hear us:
and prepare us to meet you.

Father, we bring all our loved ones
with their hopes and disappointments,
their struggles and their successes;
may they be guided and nurtured by your love.

Silence for prayer

Father, hear us:
and prepare us to meet you.

Father, we bring all those
whose lives seem to them bleak,
painful or empty of meaning;
please release them,
unburden them,
and fill them with your gift of joy.

Silence for prayer

Father, hear us:
and prepare us to meet you.

Father, we commend to your unfailing love
all who have died,
especially . . .

Silence for prayer

Father, hear us:
and prepare us to meet you.

Filled with thankfulness for all
your many blessings to us,
we offer you our praise.
May we never forget your generosity.

Silence for prayer

Merciful Father,
accept these prayers
for the sake of your Son,
our Saviour Jesus Christ.

Susan Sayers

Your will be done

After years of waiting, the Lord is very near.

Father, we thank you
for raising up leaders and ministers in your church,
and we pray for them now.

Silence for prayer

In your way, Lord:
let your will be done in us.

Father, we thank you
for all that is good in our society
and pray now for all in positions of authority.

Silence for prayer

In your way, Lord:
let your will be done in us.

Father, we thank you
for our homes and families,
for our friends and neighbours.

Silence for prayer

In your way, Lord:
let your will be done in us.

Father, we thank you
for those who care for the sick,
the distressed and the dying.

Silence for prayer

In your way, Lord:
let your will be done in us.

Father, we thank you
for all those who worked with you,
in your plan of salvation for us.
Work also in us for the good of your world.

Silence for prayer

Merciful Father,
**accept these prayers
for the sake of your Son,
our Saviour Jesus Christ.**

Susan Sayers

Open our eyes and our hearts

Blessed are you, Lord God of Israel,
for you come to your people and set them free.
Through the light of Christ
you deliver us from darkness and the shadow of death
and guide us into the way of peace.

As we remember John the Baptist and all the prophets,
we give thanks for men and women of vision through the ages.
We ask you to guide and bless
all preachers of the word and ministers of the sacraments,
all who teach the faith and all who influence our daily lives.
We pray for all who are struggling for freedom in their faith
and for those who are imprisoned because of their beliefs.

Silence

Lord, open our eyes to your presence
and our hearts to your coming among us.

We give thanks for those who do research,
all scientists and biologists,
for all responsible for our health and well-being.
We ask your blessing upon all doctors and nurses.
We pray for the World Health Organisation
and for all who strive to free us from disease and illness.

Silence

Lord, open our eyes to your presence
and our hearts to your coming among us.

Lord, help us to know your presence in our homes.
We ask you to protect and guide our loved ones
into the ways of peace.
We remember before you all who suffer
from oppression or violence in their homes.

Silence

Lord, open our eyes to your presence
and our hearts to your coming among us.

We give thanks for your love and healing power
and ask your blessing upon all who are suffering,
who long for freedom
and all who are caught up in debt.
We pray for any who have lost their homes
or their work at this time,
especially any who have been separated from loved ones.

Silence

Lord, open our eyes to your presence
and our hearts to your coming among us.

We give thanks
that you have delivered us from the darkness of death
and offered us the light of life eternal.
We rejoice in the fellowship of all your saints
and we pray for friends and loved ones
who are departed from us.

Silence

Merciful Father,
accept these prayers
for the sake of your Son,
our Saviour Jesus Christ.   *David Adam*

The coming Christ

My brothers and sisters in Christ,
as we watch together for his coming,
let us pray together for the Church and for the world.

Lord, strengthen and guide your Church
in its mission to the world;
that sinners may be alerted to repentance
and many may be brought to the joy
of living in your love.

Silence for prayer

Lord, come to us:
live in us now.

Lord, we pray for the whole created world
and its peoples;
that no evil may thwart your will,
but that rather your kingdom may be established
and your will done.

Silence for prayer

Lord, come to us:
live in us now.

Lord, bless this community
and all who serve it;
that we may strive each day
to align our lives with the life of Christ
who saves us from sin.

Silence for prayer

Lord, come to us:
live in us now.

Lord, we pray for all who suffer –
mentally, physically and spiritually;
for those who see no comforts,
and do not realise their spiritual poverty.

Silence for prayer

Lord, come to us:
live in us now.

We commend to your love
all who have completed their life on earth,
that they may rest in your peace
and share your risen life.

Silence for prayer

Lord, come to us:
live in us now.

Thank you, Lord,
for the richness of your companionship;
for the joy and peace
your constant presence gives.

Silence for prayer

**Lord, we bring these prayers
in the name of Jesus Christ, your Son.**

Susan Sayers

Proclaiming God's word

Loving God,
we thank you today for the Scriptures,
and the opportunity we have each day
of reading and studying them for ourselves.
Hear now our prayer for all those denied that privilege.
We pray for those who have not heard the challenge of the Bible,
who do not possess a copy of it in their own language,
or who are denied the right to own a Bible or study it freely.
Lord, in your mercy,
hear our prayer.

We pray for those who have heard but closed their minds,
for those who read but do not understand,
and for those who have read the Bible so often
that it fails to challenge as it used to.
Lord, in your mercy,
hear our prayer.

We pray for those who work to make the Scriptures
known and available to all –
those who translate the Bible
into modern language and other tongues,
who print and distribute it across the world,
who strive to open its message afresh
to each and every generation;
and who preach from it,
witnessing to Christ from its pages.
Lord, in your mercy,
hear our prayer.

Loving God,
may your word be made known
with clarity, wisdom, faithfulness and power,
so that many hear its challenge
and respond in faith to your loving purpose.
Lord, in your mercy,
hear our prayer.

Through Jesus Christ our Lord,
the Word made flesh.   *Nick Fawcett*

Advent mission

Loving God,
accept our glad thanksgiving for all you have given us,
and hear now our prayers for your world.
We pray for those for whom there is no celebration –
the poor and the hungry,
the homeless and the sick,
the lonely and the bereaved,
the oppressed and the persecuted.
Lord, you call us to respond to their need:
help us to reach out in love.

We pray for all those whose celebration is marred by fear –
those who are anxious for themselves or a loved one,
who see no hope in the future,
or who live under the constant threat of danger.
Lord, you call us to respond to their need:
help us to reach out in love.

We pray for all who wrestle with grief –
those whose lives have been broken by tragedy,
who live each day in perpetual shadow,
crushed by the burden of sorrow.
Lord, you call us to respond to their need:
help us to reach out in love.

We pray for all who feel isolated –
those who feel unloved, unwanted,
who find it hard to show love towards others,
or whose relationships have been broken
by cruelty, discord, division.
Lord, you call us to respond to their need:
help us to reach out in love.

Loving God,
may your light reach into the darkest places of the world,
so that there may be hope rather than despair,
joy rather than sorrow,
and love rather than hatred.
Come now to our world through Jesus Christ,
to bring good news to the poor,
release to the captives,
recovery of sight to the blind,
and to let the oppressed go free.
Lord, you call us to respond to their need:
help us to reach out in love.

In his name we pray.   *Nick Fawcett*

Advent service

Loving God,
we thank you for the hope you have given us in Christ,
the meaning and purpose,
joy and fulfilment you bring us through him.
Hear now our prayer for those who find it hard to hope,
those for whom life is hard.
Reach out to them in their need,
and may the light of Christ break into their darkness.

We think of those we label as the Third World –
the hungry and undernourished,
homeless and refugees,
sick and suffering –
human beings just as we are,
deprived of their dignity in the desperate struggle for survival.
Reach out to them in their need,
and may the light of Christ break into their darkness.

We think of those who are caught up in war –
overwhelmed by fear and hatred,
their homes and livelihoods destroyed,
each day lived under the threat of violence.
Reach out to them in their need,
and may the light of Christ break into their darkness.

We pray for those who feel overwhelmed by life –
lonely,
frightened,
sad,
weary –
many dreading what the next day might bring.
Reach out to them in their need,
and may the light of Christ break into their darkness.

Loving God,
may the message of hope which Advent brings
burst afresh into our world,
bringing help, hope and healing.
And may we, as those who profess the name of Christ,
play our part in showing his love,
displaying his care,
and fulfilling his purpose,
so that he might come again this Christmas
to all who have lost hope.
Reach out to them in their need,
and may the light of Christ break into their darkness.

For his name's sake.   *Nick Fawcett*

Advent 1

Lord of light,
alert us to the hope of banishing darkness
so that we may be open to the coming of your Son.
May we also have our eyes opened to the end time,
ready and expectant, always prepared.
Let the energy of your mighty power
dazzle and refresh us,
as you bring us your love and peace,
mercy and grace, expectation and anticipation.
Lord, in your mercy
hear our prayer.

We pray for your Church
in its long journey in the light of Christ.
Shine your love into any dark corners,
prepare us for the glories to come,
and help us to sustain our worship and wonder.
As we look forward to the birth of your Son,
let us look back in penitence and humility,
committing ourselves anew to do your will
and to deepen our faith through worship and prayer.
Lord, in your mercy
hear our prayer.

As we put on the armour of light, this Advent,
broaden our vision so that
we can see the gifts and needs of others.
In serving you, may we serve the needs we see,
giving as much as we receive,
of our time, our talents, and ourselves.
And in your world today we pray especially for . . .
Equip those who are on the ground
with purpose and authority,
as we ask them to make a difference for your sake.
And may we provide what we can
in resources and prayer.
Lord, in your mercy
hear our prayer.

In our own community we pray for . . .
Lord, in your mercy
hear our prayer.

Let the sick and the suffering know your presence.
May those who care patiently,
and listen actively, feel your strength,
as we pray especially for . . .
Lord, in your mercy
hear our prayer.

We remember the names and lives
of those who have died . . .
We pray that those who mourn are comforted
and that friends and neighbours
support families who grieve at this time.
Merciful Father,
accept these prayers
for the sake of your Son,
our Saviour Jesus Christ.

Rupert Bristow

Advent 2

We pray for the capacity to wait, purposefully and actively.
Just as you are patient with us,
may we show patience in understanding your time.
We give thanks for the ministry of John the Baptist,
and we ask that we can respond to his call for repentance,
confident in the good news of Jesus Christ.
Prepare us in holiness and godliness for all that lies ahead,
generous and comforting God.
Lord, in your mercy
hear our prayer.

We pray for a Church which can be prophetic and pastoral,
a Church which is worthy of being the body of Christ,

which can inspire and challenge, nurture and teach.
As the world cries out for leadership,
as the world shows its need for spiritual space,
let the Church lift up the example of your Son,
sharing his message with those who will listen,
both within and beyond our congregations.
May the heralding of the birth of Jesus
be an inspiration for the Church in the world
to be a standard-bearer for you.
Lord, in your mercy
hear our prayer.

We pray that your promises to humanity,
given through the patriarchs and the prophets,
are heard by those who struggle in the world
as well as by those who wield power and influence.
We pray especially for places and people in turmoil,
remembering the current difficulties in . . .
We also ask that you watch over those we never hear about,
yet who are facing extreme hardship and hopelessness.
Let them know you are with them,
as you always stand by the oppressed.
Lord, in your mercy
hear our prayer.

In our own community we pray for . . .
Lord, in your mercy
hear our prayer.

We remember the sick and the distressed, especially . . .
Lift the spirits of carers and cared for,
and bring hope where this is absent, we ask, loving Lord.
Lord, in your mercy
hear our prayer.

We pray for those who have died, remembering . . .
May they rest in peace in your eternal kingdom
and may loved ones hold on to fond memories in their loss.
Merciful Father,
accept these prayers
for the sake of your Son,
our Saviour Jesus Christ.

Rupert Bristow

Advent 3

God in our midst,
we thank you for the extraordinary in the ordinary,
the way you ask us to do well what is expected of us,
the way you require us to be humble in duties small and large.
Send us, we pray, the gift of perseverance

in everything that honours you,
everything that brings us into your presence.
Let the light that is to come
inform our lives, inspire our imagination.
Lord, in your mercy
hear our prayer.

We pray for the confidence of the Church.
Through good leadership and prayerful support
may the many gifts of our church leaders
shine out to the wider world in the coming season of goodwill.
Let us communicate clearly how the original gift of your Son,
heralded by the patriarchs, the prophets and John the Baptist,
enters the world of your creation
to restore our relationship with you, our loving God.
Lord, in your mercy
hear our prayer.

What a wonderful world you have given us.
Help us always to remember the responsibilities
we have to be good stewards and wise guardians
so that future generations will benefit
from a faith passed down and a world passed on,
through small steps and bold strategies.
May we never let you down in this enterprise,
firm in the hope of your kingdom here on earth
and your glory in heaven.
Lord, in your mercy
hear our prayer.

In our own community we pray for ...
Lord, in your mercy
hear our prayer.

Let the suffering have relief from pain,
and may the skills of the health professionals and medical staff
bring the hope of recovery and the care they deserve.
We remember especially the sick
in urgent need of our prayers at this time ...
Lord, in your mercy
hear our prayer.

We pray for the souls of the departed,
remembering especially ...
May the peace they know in your presence
be felt by those who mourn
and may the memories of loved ones be a thanksgiving.
Merciful Father,
accept these prayers
for the sake of your Son,
our Saviour Jesus Christ.

Rupert Bristow

Advent 4

God of surprise and hope,
you have shown what is possible in faith,
as you gave to Elizabeth the chance to have a child
and entrusted to Mary the motherhood of your Son.
We pray that the essential story of humility and trust
is told and retold in home and church, school and street,
so that good news is shared and passed on
and we are prepared for Jesus' ministry amongst us.
Bestow on us the gift of insight
and the grace of understanding.
Lord, hear us.
Lord, graciously hear us.

Stepping out in faith was the task of the early Church.
Embolden your Church today to walk and talk
the message of Christmas,
as the waiting nears and the shepherds gather,
as wise men ponder and sages wonder.
Inspire our own church in its preparation and celebration
so that the community feels the energy and senses the significance.
Lord, hear us.
Lord, graciously hear us.

May the proud be scattered in the path of the powerless
and the rich show their generosity to the poor,
while the meek get ready to inherit the earth
and all prepare to bow down before the Christ who is Emmanuel.
Let nations and peoples in the midst of hardship and strife
set aside differences and seek renewal of the spirit of life
through encounter with a baby in Bethlehem,
vulnerable, holy, shining a light of hope through history, even to today.
Lord, hear us.
Lord, graciously hear us.

In our own community we pray for . . .
Lord, hear us.
Lord, graciously hear us.

Give to the afflicted and infirm, the distressed and the sad,
the hope that brings comfort and the will to carry on.
We remember especially those in urgent need of our prayers . . .
Lord, hear us.
Lord, graciously hear us.

Let your perpetual light shine on those
who have passed from this life to the next
and are now at peace with you, remembering . . .
We ask for your compassion to be felt by those who mourn.
Merciful Father,

accept these prayers
for the sake of your Son,
our Saviour Jesus Christ.

Rupert Bristow

Petition

Advent witness

Loving God,
we remember today how prophets foretold the coming of Christ –
how they declared their faith in your purpose,
their confidence in your love,
their assurance of your final victory.
They did not keep their faith to themselves;
they shared it with others:
teach us to do the same.

We remember how shepherds responded
to the message of the angels –
how they hurried to Bethlehem
and found the baby lying in a manger,
and how they went on their way praising and glorifying you
for everything they had seen and heard.
They did not keep their faith to themselves;
they shared it with others:
teach us to do the same.

We remember how John the Baptist
prepared the way of Christ in the wilderness –
how he proclaimed a baptism of repentance,
a new beginning,
the coming of one far greater than he could ever be.
He did not keep his faith to himself;
he shared it with others:
teach us to do the same.

We remember how you came to us in Christ –
how he brought light into our darkness,
hope into our despair,
joy into our sorrow.
He did not keep his faith to himself.
He did not live his life for himself;
he shared it with others:
teach us to do the same.

In his name we pray.

Nick Fawcett

The challenge of Advent

Lord of all,
you tell us to wait and pray for that time
when Christ shall come again to establish his kingdom;
that time when your purpose shall be fulfilled
and your name made known and worshipped on all the earth!
You challenge us to live in the light of that promise –
help us to respond.

Teach us, we pray, never to lose sight of your purpose,
never to stop believing that you are at work,
never to lose confidence in your kingdom.
Teach us that, as Christ came, so he shall come again.
You challenge us to live in the light of that promise –
help us to respond.

But teach us also not to waste the present moment,
not to place all our hope in the future,
or to imagine that you are unconcerned
for us and your world now!
Teach us to recognise that Christ is with us always,
by our side to the end of time.
You challenge us to live in the light of that promise –
help us to respond.

Help us to live and work for you always,
rightly and responsibly enjoying your many gifts,
and seeking to do your will and follow your ways.
Help us to live each day
as though Christ were coming back at that moment,
until that day when he returns in glory
and you are all in all.
You challenge us to live in the light of that promise –
help us to respond.

For his name's sake.

Nick Fawcett

Come among us

Lord Jesus Christ,
as you came once so you shall come again
to establish your kingdom
and to fulfil the purpose of the one who sent you.
Help us to learn from your first coming –
to remember that, despite the long years of expectation
and the desire of so many to see you,
there were few who found room for you when you finally came.
Save us, then, from complacency,
and teach us to live each day to your glory,

happy at each moment to stand in your presence,
and ready to welcome you
on the day of your return.
In your name we pray.   *Nick Fawcett*

Come, Lord Jesus, draw near; come, Lord:
come among us.
Come as our Saviour; come, Lord:
come among us.
Come as our Friend; come, Lord:
come among us.
Come as the Light; come, Lord:
come among us.
Come and we shall be saved; come, Lord:
come among us.   *David Adam*

Jesus, Word made flesh.
Maranatha.
Come, Lord, dwell among us.
Jesus, born of the house of David.
Maranatha.
Come, Lord, dwell among us.
Jesus, born of the blessed Virgin Mary.
Maranatha.
Come, Lord, dwell among us.
Jesus, from the realm of glory.
Maranatha.
Come, Lord, dwell among us.   *David Adam*

Come, my Lord, my light, my way;
come, my lantern, night and day;
come, healer, make me whole.
Come, my Saviour, protect my soul;
come, my King, enter my heart;
come, Prince of Peace, and never depart.   *David Adam*

Awaken us, O God, to your coming.
Open our eyes that we may see you.
Open our ears that we may hear you.
Open our lips that we may talk about you.
Touch our hearts that we may love you.
Come, Lord, come among us.   *David Adam*

Lord, as you come to your Church,
help us to reveal your glory.
Grant that we may show your grace
and your goodness in our lives.

We thank you for the grace and goodness
revealed in Jesus Christ
and that we are enriched in him.

David Adam

Come, Lord, be known among us.
As you came to earth, born of Mary,
come into our hearts and homes.
As you became a little child,
help us to grow in awareness of you.
As you walked this earth,
help us to walk and work with you.
May the bright light of Christ
enlighten our hearts,
shine in our minds,
direct our journeying,
and scatter the darkness from the world.

David Adam

Morning star of God

Leader
Morning star of God,
rising in beauty from the ashes of our night,
encourage us your servants who walk in darkness
and need the loving touch of your light
to lift us into joy.

All
Be gracious to us
for without your light
we are left in our darkness for ever.

Leader
Morning star of God,
clothed in unattainable glory,
enfold us in your robes of light,
that we may stand in gladness before you
in the beauty of your presence.

All
Be gracious to us
for without your light
we are left in our darkness for ever.

Leader
Morning star of God,
our joy and our desiring,
come to us we beseech you,
shine upon us once again
for life is cold without you.
Our bodies, minds and spirits ache with longing
for the glory of your light.

All
Be gracious to us
for without your light
we are left in our darkness for ever.

Mary Hathaway

Preparing for Christmas

O God, as we prepare for Christmas
may we be ready for your coming to us.
As we make space for friends and relatives
may we make room in our lives for you.

In our daily living let us seek to do your will
and help to bring in your kingdom.
Through the working of the Church,
through obedience to you,
through reaching out in mission,
through the proclaiming of the Gospel,
your kingdom come:
your will be done.

Through our striving for peace,
through our caring for the poor,
through our desire for justice,
through the ways we seek to improve your world,
your kingdom come:
your will be done.

Through our love in our homes,
through our honesty and sensitivity,
through our relationships and friends,
through our hopes and our ambitions,
your kingdom come:
your will be done.

Through the healing of the ill,
through looking after the lonely;
through our compassion and care,
your kingdom come:
your will be done.

We remember especially today
any who have asked for our prayers
or who are in trouble or danger.
We ask that we may share with them
in the fullness of your kingdom.

Silence

Merciful Father,
accept these prayers
for the sake of your Son,
our Saviour Jesus Christ.

David Adam

Another Advent has begun.
Lord our God,
lead us in the way of truth and love,
kindness and mercy.
As we get ready for Christmas,
may we learn more about loving you and loving one another.
Give us courage to keep asking
the big questions about life and death,
knowing that you are in our past, our present and all our future.
You know us completely and you love us completely.
Thank you, Lord God, for making us,
and for coming to be born among us as a baby.
May we worship you with our whole lives.

Susan Sayers

Living for God

As we share in Mary and Elizabeth's joy
at the coming of our Saviour,
we quieten and still ourselves
in the presence of you, God.
Heavenly Father, we can only marvel
at the way you are happy to work with us.
We want you to know
that we are willing to be used.

Susan Sayers

Blessed are you

Blessed are you, Lord my God,
for you sent messengers and prophets
to tell of your coming.
You sent John the Baptist
to help us to prepare your way.
Help me to show your presence
in my daily life and in my work.

David Adam

Blessed are you, Lord our God,
for you are our Creator
and you have called us to know you
and proclaim your love.
Help us to be aware
that you speak to us through the Scriptures
and through those who tell
of your presence and power today.

47

Blessed are you, Father, Son and Holy Spirit.
God, we thank you for the prophets
who told us of your love and salvation.
We give thanks for Isaiah and Amos, Jeremiah and Malachi,
Ezekiel and John the Baptist.
You are their God and our God:
you are their Father and our Father.
Help us to know that as you came to them you come to us.   *David Adam*

Blessed are you, Lord our God,
for you send your messengers and prophets
to tell of your coming.
As John the Baptist was a burning and shining light
in the darkness,
help us to show your presence in our daily life.   *David Adam*

Blessed are you, Lord God of all creation,
to you be praise and glory for ever!
Your messenger, John the Baptist,
was a shining and burning light in the darkness.
He spoke the words of a prophet
and proclaimed forgiveness and the kingdom.
He prepared the way for the coming of the Lord.
May we share in his witness to the light
that true Light come into the world,
and rejoice that the Christ dispels our darkness.   *David Adam*

Blessed are you, Lord God of all creation.
To you be praise and glory for ever!
In the darkness of this passing age your light has shone out.
You have not forced yourself upon us,
but you only come if we so will it.
As we rejoice in the obedience of Mary, the blessed Virgin,
may we accept you into our lives and homes,
knowing that you have come to dwell among us.   *David Adam*

SERVICES

Advent Service

The bidding

We are a chosen people,
a people belonging to God,
who has called us out of darkness
into his wonderful light.
In his name we come together
to celebrate once again
the coming of God's Kingdom among us,
and to wonder afresh
at the mystery of his loving purposes for us.

Let us confess our sins and failings to God
in penitence and faith:
words spoken without sensitivity;
actions lacking in compassion;
attitudes rooted in selfishness.
May we seek his pardon
for our divisions and disunity,
our failure to live in his light,
and receive with joy his forgiveness and peace.

Silence

Let us listen with open ears and minds
to the good news of God's kingdom
and receive it into our hearts and lives.
May we gladly celebrate
the birth of our Saviour,
and willingly respond to the message of peace on earth
and goodwill to all people.

Silence

Let us commit ourselves anew to serving God faithfully
as we pray for those in need –
the vulnerable and exploited,
the anxious and fearful,
the unloved and lonely,
the grieving and hopeless.
May we demonstrate in our lives
the reality of God's love
as seen in Jesus Christ,
and reflect the justice and peace of his kingdom.

Silence

Let us express the Christian hope
of eternal life in our praise and worship,
as we remember those
who have gone before us
in the faith of Christ;
as we serve him day by day
in the power of his Spirit;
as we look forward with confidence
to that day when we will see him
face to face.

Silence

Lord, guide us in the ways of peace,
lead us in your righteousness,
and set our hearts on fire with love for you,
now and for ever.

The sharing of the light

Jesus said,
'I am the light of the world.
Whoever follows me
will not walk in darkness,
but have the light of life'.

As each person passes the light to another:
The light of Christ
As each person receives the light from another:
Thanks be to God.

During this, a Taizé chant could be sung softly; 'The Lord is my light' is especially suitable.

Hymn

Make way, make way,
or Thou, whose almighty Word

Confession and absolution

We bring all our sins to Christ,
the Light of the World,
confessing them openly and honestly.

Lord Jesus,
you call us to be good stewards
but often we fail you.
You call us to use your gifts
for the wellbeing of others,

**but we stockpile them
for our own comfort.
You call us to show compassion
to the stranger and the prisoner,
but we think only of our own interests.
You call us to be merciful to others
as you are merciful to us,
but we harbour resentment and jealousy
in our hearts.
We repent of our sins and wrongdoing
and ask you to forgive us.
Strengthen us to serve and obey you,
and prepare our hearts
for the day of your coming in glory.**

May God in his mercy
pardon and cleanse us,
keep us faithful in his service,
and make us ready to stand before him
and hear him say 'Well done',
through Jesus Christ our Lord.

Hymn

O come, O come, Emmanuel

The following readings are associated with each of the commonly sung verses of this hymn, and could be read in between them:

Isaiah 11:1-4 ('O come, thou Rod of Jesse . . .')
Numbers 24:15b-17 ('O come, thou Dayspring . . .')
Isaiah 22:21-23 ('O come, thou Key of David . . .')
Exodus 3:1-6 ('O come. O come, thou Lord of Might . . .')

Reading

Isaiah 52:7-10

Hymn

How lovely on the mountains

Reading

Romans 13:11-14

Anthem

There is probably as much music for church choirs to sing at Advent and Christmas as there is for the rest of the year! Choice of material will depend largely on the standard of the singers and the amount of time available for rehearsal, though the anthems beloved of Anglican choirs won't always sit easily in a multi-denominational setting. One of the following choral pieces would be effective as part of an Advent Sunday act of worship with a choir drawn from the participating churches:

4-part anthems:
'O thou the central orb' (Wood)
'How beauteous are their feet' (Stanford)
'Light of the world' (Elgar)
'The shepherd' (Mawby)
'Great Father of light' (Mawby)

Reading
Matthew 25:31-46

Hymn
Heaven shall not wait

Address or meditation

Song
You are the King of Glory

Intercessions
Creator God,
you made this world out of nothing
and saw that all of it was good.
How it must grieve you
to see how we have abused and spoiled
its riches and beauty!
We pray for those who work to look after it
and ensure its resources
are distributed more fairly among all people.

Father in heaven,
Hear our prayer.

Emmanuel, God with us,
you came to share our human life
that we might share your eternal life.
How you must weep
over the bitterness and hatred,
the selfishness and lack of care
which afflict our society.

We pray for those
on the margins of the community:
the lonely and unloved,
the homeless and helpless,
the abused and vulnerable,
the anxious and depressed.

Father in heaven,
Hear our prayer.

Holy Spirit, Comforter and Enabler,
you are the presence of God within us,
our conscience, encourager and guide.
How you long for us to be more open
to your teaching and leading!
We pray for your Church throughout the world,
and especially here in . . . ,
that we may be united in worship and witness,
and dedicate ourselves
to bringing the light of Christ
to all whom we meet.

Father in heaven,
Hear our prayer.

**Holy and loving God,
fill us with joy and hope
as we work for the coming of your kingdom
and look forward to that day
when we will see you face to face,
through Jesus Christ our Lord.**

Our Father . . .

**Come and bring light
to dispel our darkness.
Come and bring hope
to drive out our fear.
Come and bring joy
to banish our sorrow.
Come and bring love
to fill our longing hearts,
that through us the whole world
may come into your light.**

Hymn

Hills of the north, rejoice,
or We will cross every border

Blessing

May God our Father,
the Creator and Sustainer of all,
give us a fresh vision of his kingdom.

May Christ his Son,
the Saviour and Redeemer of all,
cleanse us from all sin
and open up for us
the way of eternal life.

May his Holy Spirit
fill us with divine love,
empower us to live for his glory,
and make us ready
for the day of his coming.

Final prayer

Come among us
and dwell with us, Lord Jesus.

Hymn

Lo, he comes with clouds descending,
or Lord, the light of your love

Stuart Thomas

Advent 1

Abraham and God's faithful people

Advent is a time when we rejoice in the coming of Christ into our lives, that he came at Christmas, and that he comes again to be our Lord and King. Advent celebrates that our God comes to us again and again.

Begin in the dark. If the room is not dark, close your eyes.

Welcome the light

The people who walked in darkness have seen a great light; they who lived in a land of deep darkness, on them the light has shined.

Isaiah 9:2

Candle-lighting

On the first Sunday in Advent we light one candle to say with all faithful people:
The Lord comes to us.
He abides with us.

When our lives are darkened it is necessary to celebrate God's presence that comes to us and the light that God gives us.

Light one Advent candle.

Jesus Christ is the Light of the World:
Eternal Light, shine in our hearts.

Blessed are you, Lord our God, for you have called us out of darkness to be children of Light. The bright light of your presence scatters the darkness and we remember your love towards us; through Christ our Lord.

Reading
Genesis 18:1-15

Hymn
The God of Abraham praise (third verse)

Special intention – in the light of God
When this world is as dark as night,
you are the one we call the Light.
Come, Lord Jesus.
When we are tempted to go astray,
you are the one we call the Way.
Come, Lord Jesus.
When the storms of life increase,
you are the one we call our Peace.
Come, Lord Jesus.
When troubles to our lives bring harm,
you are the one who brings us calm
Come, Lord Jesus.

Almighty God, give us grace to cast away the works of darkness and to put on the armour of light, now in the time of this mortal life, in which your Son Jesus Christ came to us in great humility; so that on the last day, when he shall come again in His glorious majesty to judge the living and the dead, we may rise to the life immortal; through Him who is alive and reigns with you and the Holy Spirit, one God, now and for ever.
Common Worship Collect for Advent 1

Closing prayer
Lord of Life, of Light, of Love,
come that I may fully live;
come that I may walk in the light;
come that I may burn with your love.
Come Lord this day,
I welcome you.
David Adam

Advent 1

The time is now

Introduction

We like to think, don't we, that we live in a moral universe; that, despite the way life may sometimes seem, justice will finally be done. But how many of us actually believe that? How seriously do we take the prospect of a day when we will be asked to account for the way we have lived our lives? The idea carries with it difficult and disturbing issues, yet it is one that featured strongly in the teaching of Jesus, and not least in his parables, more of which are devoted to this theme than to any other. The exact details of what he meant are open to debate but the broad thrust is clear enough: a time of judgement will come. Here is a message which brings both promise and challenge – the assurance that good will finally triumph but, alongside that, the question: on which side will our lives tip the scales? Have we used our gifts wisely? Have we thought of others as well as ourselves? Have we been honest and above-board in all our dealings? Have we offered forgiveness in the way God has repeatedly forgiven us? Have we responded to the call of Christ in the poor, the weak and the hungry? The warning is of a future day of reckoning but the response Jesus is looking for concerns the here and now. The day will come when we must answer before God. Is it time to take a long hard look at our lives to see if anything needs changing? And, if it does, isn't it time we did something about it?

Hymn

Rejoice, the Lord is King
At the name of Jesus

Prayer

Lord of all,
you are not a God who delights to judge,
remote and uncaring,
eager to punish wrongdoing.
You are a God rich in mercy, always looking to forgive,
extending chance after chance
to acknowledge our mistakes and start again.
Yet, ultimately, you cannot turn your back on evil,
for you know the havoc and misery it can cause –
its power to hurt, corrupt and destroy,
to despoil life and deny your love.
So you act in human history
to overthrow injustice and confront oppression.
You act in human hearts
to stir consciences and challenge evil.
And you tell us that the time will come
when you will act once and for all,
a day of judgement
when you will weigh every life in the balance
and deliver your verdict.
Teach us then to live today in the light of tomorrow,

to make known your love and seek your will,
where we fail, grant your mercy on us and all,
through Jesus Christ our Lord.

Reading

14:16-24

Meditation of a guest dining with Jesus and Simon the Pharisee

Turn down the chance of a feast!
Can you see that happening?
I can't!
It's possible, I suppose, that one or two wouldn't be able to make it –
a pressing engagement, perhaps,
an unavoidable commitment –
but the majority would move hell and high water to be there,
not just for the chance of a free meal, though that's reason enough,
but for the whole occasion,
the fun, frivolity, friendship,
everything an event of that sort symbolises.
Would people really turn their backs on that,
let alone respond with open hostility?
No, I'm sorry, but it just doesn't ring true,
the prospect not only ridiculous but, quite frankly, incredible.
And yet, isn't that precisely why Jesus told the story,
to bring home how foolish it is
to turn down the invitation he brings,
to turn our backs on the joy, blessing and fulfilment
he so longs for us to share in?
It should be incredible, shouldn't it?
But sadly it's not,
time and again his love rejected,
his offer of new life thrown back into his face.
We all do it, if we're honest,
even though we may think we're committed.
We've time enough for him when it's convenient,
when it suits us to make time,
but we're only too ready to thrust him aside
when 'more pressing' concerns raise their head,
his call then relegated to second place.
Not now, we say,
tomorrow will do,
but, all too often, tomorrow never comes.
Thank God he's ready to make allowances –
only don't push it too far
and certainly don't go counting any chickens,
for the invitation may not hold for ever,
not even for us.
If we're too busy to respond, there are others ready,

others only too conscious of their need
and the privilege extended to them.
Delay too long,
and you may find your place at table taken,
your seat occupied,
the banquet God had in store for you consumed by another.
Think about those words of his,
that message he tried to put across.
It's not just about others;
it's about you –
the response you've made,
the response you continue to make.
The guest list is made up,
but it can easily be changed.
Don't say you haven't been warned!

Silence or Hymn

At your feet we fall, mighty risen Lord
And can it be that I should gain

Meditation of a typical nominal Christian

Not ready!
What's he trying to say? Of course I'm ready,
prepared for the coming of the kingdom whenever that might be –
no way you'll catch me on the hop!
All right, so I've not done anything about it,
not yet, anyway,
but I will when I need to, you mark my words.
What's the hurry, though, that's what I say –
there'll be time for change later –
live a little first while you have the chance,
let your hair down,
push the boat out,
enjoy today and let tomorrow take care of itself.
Oh, you may tut and shake your heads,
but there'll be ample opportunity to make amends, you'll see.
Don't think I'm stupid,
I'll be watching for the signs as well as any,
and if it's ever clear that my time's up,
the writing on the wall either for me or this world of ours,
I'll make my peace with God soon enough.
But all that's for later,
no point worrying about it now.
I've got years left in me yet, haven't I? – haven't I?
Lord, what's going on . . . help . . .
I never thought . . .
never imagined for a moment! Lord . . .
are you there . . .
are you listening? Oh Lord!

Silence or Hymn

Give me oil in my lamp, keep me burning
O when the saints go marching in

Reading

Luke 12:35-48

Meditation of Simon the Zealot, one of the twelve disciples

We thought the waiting was over.
After all those years looking forward to the dawn of the Messiah,
we dared to hope the moment had arrived,
the day when God's kingdom would at last be established
and his servant would rule over all.
But apparently not,
for here he was,
our friend Jesus, whom we had looked to with such confidence,
such anticipation,
telling us to be dressed for action,
prepared once again for his coming.
It left us bemused, bewildered,
for why did he have to leave us?
Why not simply stay and claim the kingdom now?
It wasn't that simple, unfortunately,
a time apart needed before we could truly be together,
and it came as a bitter blow.
It had been hard enough for those before us to keep faith,
to hold on to the belief that the Messiah would come
despite centuries of disappointment,
and now here he was talking of another long delay in store,
no telling how long it might be before his return;
even, indeed, whether we might see it in our lifetime.
It takes courage to go on trusting then;
a special kind of faith to keep hope fresh
and the flame burning as brightly as the day it was lit.
We may think we're ready and waiting,
but it doesn't take long for carelessness or complacency to set in.
He will come, we tell ourselves, but not today
not tomorrow,
and probably not the next day; so relax,
take it easy,
plenty of time for more serious discipleship.
He will come, but there's no sign of it yet,
not even the slightest indication that the day is near;
so, for the moment at least,
let's accommodate the way of the world,
a little pragmatism to balance faith.
Do you see what I'm getting at?
We say we believe,
that our faith is as vibrant as the day it was born,

but it no longer makes any difference to our lives,
its life-giving breath slowly anaesthetised
by habit and familiarity.
Don't let that happen to you.
Don't be caught short when the day finally dawns.
I know his promise seems a long time ago
and it's fulfilment equally as far away,
and I know how easy it is
to feel like those who waited so long for the Messiah's coming
yet never saw it.
The difference is that we've seen him for ourselves,
we've watched as he dwelt among us,
lived, breathed, suffered and died;
and we know now, despite everything that may seem to deny it,
that, as he came, so he shall come again.

Silence

Prayer

Sovereign God,
we know that our faith is poor and our service is weak.
Have mercy upon us.

We want to be different,
striving each day to live more faithfully,
but we are weak and foolish,
swift to ignore your guidance,
so easily led astray.
Have mercy upon us.

We try to begin afresh,
uplifted by your grace, renewed by your love;
yet, despite our resolve,
we continue to let you down,
both in the things we do
and the things we leave undone.
Have mercy upon us.

Sovereign God,
we have sinned against you
in thought and word and deed,
and we know we deserve only punishment,
but we ask you again for pardon,
for help and time to learn from our mistakes
and to amend our lives.
Deal kindly, we pray,
and, in your mercy,
redeem, remake and restore us,
Jesus Christ our Lord.

Hymn

Lo, he comes with clouds
Restore, O Lord, the honour of your name

Blessing

Nick Fawcett

Advent 2

People of vision

Advent is a time when we rejoice in the coming of Christ into our lives, that he came at Christmas, and that he comes again to be our Lord and King. Advent celebrates that our God comes to us again and again. Today is the Second Sunday in Advent when we remember the prophets and give thanks for all people of vision.

Invitation to worship

With all the prophets and people of vision
we rejoice in the grace and goodness of God,
Father, Son and Holy Spirit.

The Lord is here.
His Spirit is with us.

Hymn

Be thou my vision, O Lord of my heart

Silence

Candle-lighting

On the Second Sunday in Advent we light two candles,
one for all of God's faithful people
and one for men and women of vision.
When our lives are darkened
it is necessary to celebrate
the presence that comes to us
and the vision that is given to us.

The Lord comes to us.
He abides with us.

The lighting of the two Advent candles.

Jesus Christ is the Light of the World:
eternal light, shine in our hearts.
Lord, open our eyes to your presence.
Come, Lord of light.
Lord, open our ears to your call.
Come, Lord of light.
Lord, open our hearts to your love.
Come, Lord of light.
Lord, open our lives to your guiding.
Come, Lord of light.

Blessed are you Lord God for you open the eyes of the blind. You gave vision and insight to the prophets. We thank you for Amos and Hosea, for Isaiah, Jeremiah and Ezekiel and all the prophets, and for all people who have extended our awareness through their vision. You are their God and our God, their Father and our Father. Help us to know that as you came to them you come to us.
Blessed be God for ever.

Silence

Reading
Isaiah 9:2, 3, 6, 7

Hymn
Come, thou long-expected Jesus

The Gospel
Luke 10:23, 24

Sermon

Silence

Hymn
Long ago the prophets knew

Creed

Confession

Thanksgiving

Praise and thanks to you, Lord our God, for you give us sight and insight, eyes to see you and hearts to love you. We thank you for the beauty of the world and the glory of creation. We praise you for the many colours of nature and for the brightness of the sun. We thank you for all who have looked deeply and been aware of you and your working: we thank you for the prophets and all people of vision.

Intercessions

Good and gracious God,
open our eyes to your presence
and our hearts to your love.

Bless all who seek to know you and proclaim you.
We remember all who study the scriptures
and all who seek to be still before you.
Lord, guide all who would lead us to a deep awareness of you.
We ask your blessing upon all ministers and preachers
and all who teach religious studies.
Lord, open our eyes to your presence
and our hearts to your love.

Lord, direct all who seek to influence our lives
and our thoughts through their own vision.
Bless all who are doing research
and all who are seeking to conserve what is good.
We remember before you all politicians,
scientists, musicians, artists and craftspeople,
and all who through their vision are enriching our lives.
Lord, open our eyes to your presence
and our hearts to your love.

Strengthen and bless all who are striving
to enhance and uphold family life.
Help us to see where we can increase our love and care.
We remember before you all who feel neglected or lonely.
May we prove to be good neighbours where we can.
Lord, open our eyes to your presence
and our hearts to your love.

We give thanks for all who have used their insight
for healing and medical research.
We ask your blessing upon all doctors, nurses
and all involved in healing and wholeness.
We bring before you friends and loved ones
who are ill or struggling at this time.
Lord, open our eyes to your presence
and our hearts to your love.

Lord, extend our vision that we may know your presence
and see our life as in your hands.
Bless all our loved ones who are departed from us
and grant that they may enjoy the vision of your glory.
Merciful Father,
accept these prayers
for the sake of your Son,
our Saviour Jesus Christ.

Collect

God be in my head, and in my understanding.
God be in my eyes, and in my looking.
God be in my mouth, and in my speaking.
God be in my heart, and in my thinking.
God be at my end, and at my departing.

Sarum Book of Hours (1514)

The Lord's Prayer

Silence

Hymn

God has spoken – by the prophets

Blessing

The Lord grant you a vision of his presence,
an awareness of his love,
a sensitivity to his guiding,
and the blessing of God Almighty,
the Father, the Son and the Holy Spirit
be upon you and your loved ones
this day and for always.

David Adam

Advent 2

Judging

Introduction

Life isn't fair. How often have you told yourself that? And, of course, it's perfectly true. We live in a society riddled with inequality and in a world scarred by injustice on a truly monumental scale. Some go hungry through no fault of their own, while others enjoy fantastic wealth purely by dint of luck or birth. While we may like to think that hard work is rewarded, honesty bears fruit and good ultimately triumphs, in this life at least the cold facts say otherwise.

It is one thing, though, to make such an observation, quite another to move from it to presume that we can judge the rights and wrongs of things – that prerogative belongs to God. We may imagine we know all the ins and outs of a situation; the reality is that we don't. We may assume we understand the motives behind people's actions; the truth is that we can only guess at them. There is always more to circumstances than meets the eye – a fact we are swift to emphasise when it concerns us but all too ready to forget when it relates to others. Here, at least in part, is the message that Jesus was looking to get across in his parables concerning the last judgement. They were not, as we might imagine, simply warnings concerning some distant and hazy future time; they were equally, if not more, a stern reminder of the danger of judging others now and, in so doing, of judging ourselves in turn.

Hymn

Your kingdom come, O God
Who would true valour see

Prayer

Sovereign God,
we thank you that you judge not by the outside
but by the person underneath;
not simply by our faithless actions
but by our underlying desire to serve you.

Where we are swift to condemn,
you are looking to forgive;
where we are eager to find fault,
you are willing to make allowances.

You do not condone our mistakes,
but you are always ready to show mercy;
to believe in our potential
rather than dwell on our past record.

Save us from interpreting your judgement
in terms of our own narrow horizons,
from attributing to you a strictness
which reflects our own intolerant attitudes
and denies your grace.

Teach us to forgive as you have forgiven us,
and to leave final judgement in your hands
where it belongs.
Through Jesus Christ our Lord.

Reading

Matthew 13:47-50

Meditation of James, fisherman and one of the twelve disciples

So, you think you can escape, do you?
You actually imagine that, while others will be caught,
you can somehow slip through the net?
Well, take it from me, you can't!
I've been a fisherman all my life
and I know from experience
that when you're out for a catch
you finally get it.
Not the first time, perhaps,
nor even the second,
but eventually, through sheer perseverance,
you'll get what you're looking for.
If that's true of our efforts,
how much more so of God,
the one who sees what we presume to be hidden,
who reaches out to the furthest corners of the world,
whose power is without limit
and whose purpose extends before and beyond all.
Do you seriously believe you can avoid his judgement?
Don't be fooled.
It may not come now
or even in your earthly span,
for, in his eyes, our lifetime is but a drop in the ocean,
but the day of reckoning will come
and, when it does, there'll be no wriggling off the hook,
no burying ourselves in the sand.
We will all face his searching gaze,
each be revealed for what we are,
and what verdict will he pronounce then,
what fate will the future hold?
The warning is given,
the choice is yours:
continue to swim against the tide,
or accept his guidance,
follow his way,
and, when the net is drawn in,
enter into the joy of his kingdom.

Silence

Reading

Matthew 13:24-31

Meditation of Thomas, one of the twelve disciples

Wheat and weeds,
good and evil –

it all sounds so simple, doesn't it? –
so straightforward;
the distinction between them as clear as it's possible to be.
And we'd like to think it is, wouldn't we:
ethical issues, moral decisions,
black and white,
right and wrong,
true or false?
It's so much easier that way,
for we know precisely where we stand:
no need to argue or debate things,
no need even to think –
the correct course is prescribed for us
and woe betide anyone who dares suggest otherwise.
But is that what Jesus was saying?
I'm not so sure,
for, look more carefully,
and you'll see that you can't always separate
the one from the other,
not in this life, anyway.
There is good and evil, of course,
sometimes starkly apparent,
but the reality is that there's a bit of each in all of us,
everyone capable of rising so high or falling so low.
It's not for us to point the accusing finger,
to sort out the wheat from the weeds,
much though we'd occasionally like to.
Judge not, lest you be judged –
isn't that what Jesus told us?
And we ignore that message at our peril,
for we may well find ourselves in the dock
should we pursue our case too far.
No, the advice is simple enough:
look not to others but yourself,
your own words,
your own deeds,
and ensure that the seed which was sown
is the one that is growing;
that the final crop lives up to expectations.
Judgement will come in God's good time;
our lives weighed in the balance and the harvest assessed –
will your life prove to have been fruitful?

Silence or Hymn

You've got to walk that lonesome valley
Somebody's knocking at your door

Reading

Mark 13:32-37

Meditation of Matthew, one of the twelve disciples

The time is coming, they tell me:
the day of the Lord's return,
when we shall stand before him
and he will separate the sheep from the goats,
the wicked from the righteous.
So forget about the present,
think instead of the future,
for that's what matters –
our final destiny,
the life to come –
nothing else.
Well, I'm sorry, but have I missed something?
For that's not the way I heard it,
not what I thought Jesus was saying at all.
Keep alert, he warned, certainly,
for the day will dawn as God has promised,
but when that will be we've no idea;
today, tomorrow or far beyond,
who can say?
It's not the 'when' of his coming that should concern us,
but the fact that he will,
and the difference that makes
not to the future
but to the here and now,
to the way we live every moment of every day.
We've a job to be doing,
a broken world out there
needing to hear his word
and know his love;
and that's what will concern him when he comes,
not whether we've been looking forward eagerly to his kingdom
but whether we're doing something to make it happen,
to help build heaven on earth.
So what will he find in you?
A life dedicated to his service,
continuing his ministry where he left off,
or an obsession about the future so strong
that you've forgotten about the present?
A life lived for others,
committed to bringing light where there is darkness,
joy where there is sorrow,
or a preoccupation with yourself,
with securing your own salvation?
Don't think I doubt his promise.
The time is coming, just as they say,
a day when we will be called to account,
made to answer for the way we've lived our lives.
But if I were you I wouldn't dwell on that too long:
I'd get down to the business of discipleship,
to walking the way of the cross,
or otherwise you may find,

when the moment comes
and judgement is pronounced,
that the verdict is very different
from the one you had in mind.

Silence

Reading

Matthew 25:31-46

Meditation (of two Christians on the day of judgement)

(To be read by two voices, alternately)

I wasn't much of a Christian, the way I saw it.
(I wasn't a bad Christian, the way I saw it.)
Test me on doctrine and I'd be lost completely,
(Test me on doctrine and I'd have a ball,)
the complexities of theology a mystery to me.
(the niceties of theology a delight to me.)
My prayer life?
(My devotional life?)
That wasn't much better,
(That was spot on,)
the words somehow never seeming to flow,
(the words coming so easily,)
discipline hard to achieve.
(discipline coming naturally.)
It was the same with the Bible, I'm sorry to say;
(It was the same with the Bible, I'm glad to say;)
I found most of it a closed book.
(I knew it inside out.)
I tried hard enough, heaven knows,
(I hardly had to try,)
but, let's face it, it's not the easiest of books to read,
(for, let's be honest, it's such a wonderful book to read,)
so many passages serving to puzzle rather than inspire.
(every passage seeming to leap out and speak to me.)
And as for obedience, well, the less said about that the better,
(And as for obedience, well, I'm not one to boast,)
for I kept slipping back into my old ways,
(only it was as though my old self had died completely,)
temptation catching me unawares,
(temptation brushed aside,)
my relationship with God a shadow of what it should have been.
(my relationship with God everything it could be.)
So you can see what I mean, can't you? –
(So you get my point, don't you? –)
not much of a Christian, all told,
(not a bad Christian, all told,)

and as I stood there before Jesus, I feared the worst,
(and as I stood there before Jesus, I had no fears whatsoever,)
uncertain of his verdict, to say the least.
(confident of his verdict, to put it mildly.)
You can imagine my relief, can't you?
(You can imagine my shock, can't you?)
'Come, you that are blessed by my Father.'
('Depart from me . . . you that are accursed.')
I couldn't believe my ears!
(I thought I was hearing things!)
What had I done to deserve such blessing?
(What had I done to deserve such punishment?)
When had I ever put myself out for Jesus?
(When had I ever let Jesus down?)
Yet I had, time and again, without ever realising it.
(Yet I had, day after day, without ever realising it.)
When I reached out to the needy,
(When I turned my back on the needy,)
when I responded to the poor,
(when I ignored the poor,)
when I visited the sick,
(when I recoiled from the sick,)
I was serving Jesus,
(I was failing Jesus,)
easing his pain,
(adding to his pain,)
expressing his love.
(denying his love.)
I'm not much of a Christian, I still think that,
(I wasn't a bad Christian, I really believed that,)
yet, happily, I got one thing right –
(yet I got one thing hopelessly wrong –)
I responded to others,
(I put myself before others,)
I showed I cared,
(I didn't care,)
and now love brings its own reward.
(and now I must pay the price.)
God moves in mysterious ways.
(God have mercy on me, a sinner.)

Silence

Prayer

Almighty God,
we have set ourselves up in your place so often,
presuming we have a right to judge others.
We know it is wrong,

and we try to stop ourselves,
but time and again we fall into the same trap,
pointing the accusing finger in condemnation.
Forgive us,
and help us to change.
Teach us to see the best rather than the worst,
to look for good rather than evil,
to build up rather than destroy.
Teach us that you will judge
in your own way and time,
and may we be happy,
when that moment comes,
for your response to us to be based
on the way we have responded to others.
In the name of Christ we ask it.

Hymn

O day of God, draw near
Christ, triumphant, ever reigning

Blessing

Nick Fawcett

Advent 3

People immersed in God

Advent is a time when we rejoice in the coming of Christ into our lives, that he came at Christmas, and that he comes again to be our Lord and King. Advent celebrates that our God comes to us again and again. Today is the Third Sunday in Advent, a day when we remember John the Baptist and all who turn towards God to serve him.

Invitation to worship

With John the Baptist and all God's faithful
we immerse ourselves in the love,
light and leading of God,
Father, Son and Holy Spirit.

The Lord is here.
His Spirit is with us.

Hymn

Hark! a thrilling voice is sounding

Silence

Candle-lighting

On the Third Sunday in Advent we light three candles, one for all of God's faithful people, one for men and women of vision, and one for John the Baptist and all who immerse themselves in the love and presence of God.

When our lives are darkened
it is necessary to celebrate the presence that comes to us
and the light that is given to us.
The Lord comes to us.
He abides with us.

The lighting of the three Advent candles.

Jesus Christ is the Light of the World:
eternal light shine in our hearts.
Father you created us by your love and for your love.
May we abide in you and you in us.
Jesus you redeemed us by your love and for your love.
May we abide in you and you in us.
Spirit of God you guide us by your love and for your love.
May we abide in you and you in us.
Holy and Blessed Three your love enfolds and surrounds us.
May we abide in you and you in us.

Blessed are you, Lord our God,
for you sent your messenger John the Baptist
to prepare the way and make ready for your coming,
that we may be prepared and ready
to receive and welcome you into our lives and homes.
As you come to us in love may we abide in your love
and in your presence this day and for ever.
Blessed be God, Father, Son and Holy Spirit.
Blessed be God for ever.

Silence

Reading

Isaiah 40:1-11

Hymn

On Jordan's bank the Baptist's cry

The Gospel
Matthew 3:1-12

Sermon

Silence

Hymn
The advent of our King

Creed

Confession

Thanksgiving
O God, we give you thanks and praise for all who have prepared the way for us to know you and to love you. We thank you for John the Baptist, that he prepared the people for the coming of Jesus. We remember in thanksgiving those who have taught us the faith by word and by example and all who have led us to you by art, music and writings. We give thanks for our baptism and the knowledge that we dwell in you and you in us. To you, O Lord our God, be praise and glory now and for ever.

Intercessions
Holy and Mighty God,
as we give thanks for John the Baptist,
we ask your blessing upon all who prepare the way
for others to know you and to love you.
Guide with your wisdom
all who prepare people for baptism or confirmation.
We remember all who lead worship or study groups
and all who speak of your presence and your power.
Lord, may we witness
that we dwell in you and you in us.

Holy and Mighty God,
we give thanks for all who prepare young people
to live their lives fully.
We ask your blessing upon
all who are involved in education,
and all who influence our minds through the press,
the media and their words and their actions.
Guide with your wisdom all that are called to govern
and to make decisions about the future of our world.

Lord, may we all be prepared to live simply
that others might simply live. May we all work for justice,
righteous dealing and for freedom.
Lord, may we witness
that we dwell in you and you in us.

Holy and Mighty God,
we ask your blessing upon our homes and our loved ones.
We remember all who are preparing for the Christmas season
and pray that they may make in their lives a place for you.
We remember all who will feel lonely or neglected at this season.
Lord, may we witness
that we dwell in you and you in us.

Holy and Mighty God,
we give thanks for the grace of forgiveness
and the opportunity to turn to you and your love.
We ask your blessing upon all who are consumed with guilt
or who cannot allow forgiveness for themselves or others.
We remember all who are in prison
and those who are suffering for their faith and their witness to you.
Lord, may we witness
that we dwell in you and you in us.

Holy and Mighty God,
we remember before you all who are terminally ill
and are being prepared for death. May they find in you courage and hope
through the promise of life eternal.
Merciful Father,
accept these prayers
for the sake of your Son,
Jesus Christ our Lord.

Collect

O Lord Jesus Christ,
who at your first coming sent your messenger
to prepare your way before you:
grant that the ministers and stewards of your mysteries
may likewise so prepare and make ready your way
by turning the hearts of the disobedient
to the wisdom of the just,
that at your second coming to judge the world
we may be found an acceptable people in your sight;
for you are alive and reign with the Father
in the unity of the Holy Spirit,
one God, now and for ever.   *Common Worship Collect for Advent 3*

The Lord's Prayer

Silence

Hymn

We are marching in the light of God

Blessing

The love of the Father strengthen you,
the love of Jesus surround you,
the love of the Spirit guide you,
and the blessing of God Almighty,
the Father, the Son and the Holy Spirit
be upon you and your loved ones
this day and for always.

David Adam

Advent 3

Promise

Introduction and lighting of Advent candles

We are here to look back. We are here to look forward. We are here to remember Jesus, born in a stable. We are here to worship Christ who shall come again in glory. We come to listen again to the words of Scripture that speak of God's promise. We come to rejoice in the Word made flesh. We come recalling the voice in the wilderness preparing the way of the Lord. We come to hear God's voice speaking to us. Open your ears, open your eyes, open your hearts, open your minds, and may God fill your souls with the living presence of Jesus Christ.

Prayer

Loving God,
you promised Abraham
that through his offspring all the earth would be blessed –
and it was.
You promised through your prophets
that the Messiah would come –
and he came.
You promised Mary
that she would give birth to a son –
and she did.
You promised the disciples
that death would not be the end –
and it wasn't.
You promised your followers
that they would receive the Holy Spirit –
and it happened.
Loving God,

you promise that when two or three are gathered in the name of Christ,
he will be there among them.
Help us, remembering the faithfulness you have always shown,
to trust in that promise too –
to know you are here and to meet with you now.

Hymn

Earth was waiting, spent and restless

Music

Sinfonia (Messiah) Handel, during which Luke 1:5-7 is read

Meditation of Zechariah

I didn't believe it was possible, not any longer,
not after all those years of trying.
There had been so many disappointments,
so many false alarms, and we'd given up, ages ago.
It still hurt occasionally, of course it did.
We love children, both of us;
and we'd have given anything to see that little crib occupied,
that lovingly embroidered shawl wrapped around our little baby.
We shouldn't have tempted fate –
it was stupid, we know that now –
but at the time we never anticipated any problems,
and we just couldn't help looking forward,
planning for the future:
two bright-eyed young things with so much before us,
or so we thought.
She used to cry, Elizabeth,
after her hopes had been raised only to be dashed again.
And although I'd try manfully to comfort her,
assure her next time it would be different,
all the while my heart was breaking as much as hers.
But then she started to torture herself,
feeling she'd failed me somehow,
that it was all her fault,
even God's punishment for some unrepented sin.
I don't need to tell you she was wrong,
but it was hard work making her see that –
so much extra heartache
before she finally accepted it was just one of those things.
But then I had this dream –
at least I think that's what it was.
I was in the temple
and suddenly a man appeared
telling me we were to have a child,
ordained by God and consecrated to his service, so he said.

Well, I dismissed it, of course;
a cruel trick of the mind, that's what I thought.
But the next thing I knew, there was Elizabeth,
a look of wonder in her eyes,
blurting out the news that she was expecting!
Well, you could have knocked me down, you really could!
I honestly thought she was having me on,
that the strain had finally got to her. But I couldn't tell her –
I'd been struck dumb since that dream of mine.
So I just stood there, trying to humour her.
I'm glad now I couldn't speak, pour scorn on the idea,
for she was right.
A child, at our time of life!
I still marvel every day I see him,
our wonderful little boy.
And I know now never to lose hope for with God nothing is impossible.
Yet we were the lucky ones, I realise that, and for every one of us
there's another still enduring the pain,
still waiting, hoping and praying for a miracle.
I don't know why God lets that happen
any more than I know why he chose to bless us.
It's a mystery to us both.
But there's an odd twist I have to mention,
for though our baby brought us joy,
more than words can ever express,
somehow Elizabeth seemed even more excited
by the birth of her cousin's boy –
Jesus the name was –
always claimed he was more of a miracle than John,
though I can't think why.
She's no nearer understanding this crazy world of ours than I,
but when she looks at Jesus
sometimes I get this strange feeling it's in him,
rather than John,
that she's looking for an answer;
he she hopes will one day make sense of it all.

Music

O magnum mysterium, Victoria, during which Matthew 1:18-19 is read

Meditation of Joseph

I didn't know what to think,
not when she first told me –
my sweet innocent Mary, pregnant!
I suppose I should have been angry, and I was later,
extremely!
But that wasn't my first reaction;
it was shock, more like, disbelief,

an inability to take it in.
You see, I just couldn't see her playing around,
deceiving me behind my back –
not Mary.
Other girls perhaps,
but she wasn't like them;
I'd have trusted her with my life if necessary.
So when she started chattering on about this angel,
about being with child by the Holy Spirit,
do you know what?
I listened!
No, honestly, I really did! Maybe that does sound daft,
but I just couldn't believe she was making it all up,
inventing an excuse to get her off the hook.
And, let's face it, if it were an excuse it was a pretty lame one;
I mean, when's the last time you saw an angel? Precisely.
But if I took it calmly at first,
it wasn't long before the doubts set in,
the questions that couldn't be answered,
the niggling voices that wouldn't go away.
And in no time suspicion had grown into something worse –
resentment,
bitterness,
condemnation.
I'd have called off the engagement,
there's no doubt about that;
much as I liked the girl,
there was simply no way a man in my position
could countenance going through with it,
not if I wanted to keep any semblance of respectability.
She was tarnished, according to the Law anyway,
her purity soiled;
and if I took no notice
the village gossips would soon put their heads together
and decide I had done the tarnishing –
too impatient to wait until the goods had been paid for.
So that was it.
My mind was made up.
It was just a question of finding the right words and the right time,
breaking it to her as gently as I could. Only then I had this dream,
almost a vision you might say it was, looking back,
so powerfully did it speak to me.
Suddenly it was *me* seeing angels, not Mary,
it was *me* hearing the voice of God instead of her;
and it was the same message,
the same story –
this child she carried,
born of God,
his gift to humankind,
the one who would at last redeem his people.
Did I believe it?

Well, I suppose I must have done, in a way.
I married her after all,
despite the snide remarks,
the wagging tongues.
Maybe, of course, I wanted to marry her anyway,
or just didn't want to hurt her.
Maybe I simply liked the thought of being a dad,
and wanted to believe that story of hers,
incredible though it seemed.
To be truthful
there were probably all kinds of reasons behind my decision;
yet perhaps it's through such things as those,
our everyday thoughts and feelings,
just as much as through dreams and visions,
that God chooses to speak to us.
Perhaps through those most of all.

Music

Glory to God (Messiah) Handel, during which Luke 1:39-43 is read

Meditation of Elizabeth

My baby jumped for joy, I swear it!
Oh I know you often feel them kicking,
and you may well say it was only shuffling about in the womb,
but this was different, I'm positive.
It was the first time I'd ever felt it move for a start,
a wild lurch as Mary approached,
almost as if it knew even then
she was carrying the child who would shape its life.
Yes, I know that sounds ridiculous,
and I wouldn't have given it another thought myself –
I'm not usually given to romanticising.
But you see, when I saw Mary coming,
I knew something special had happened,
something quite out of the ordinary.
I realised she was pregnant for one thing,
but then we women do spot those things, don't we?
Not that it was showing yet, mind you,
but it was there in her eyes,
in her expression,
in the spring in her step,
just as it had been in mine a few months earlier.
I knew, and I ran to embrace her,
sharing her joy.
Yet there was more to it than that,
I could feel it in my bones even before she began to speak.
I could sense that her child would be different,
not just from mine but from every child, born to set us free,

the fulfilment of our hopes,
the answer to our prayers.
You think that's over the top?
Well, I may have over-reacted, I accept that,
let my imagination run away with me.
I'd been a bit on edge, it's true,
ever since that queer business with Zechariah –
that day before I conceived when he came back from the temple,
eyes staring, shaking his head in disbelief,
unable to say a word until after John was born.
It got me down, I don't mind admitting it,
and yes, perhaps I was a little overwrought,
perhaps just plain excited.
But I still say it,
despite what anyone may think –
my child leaped in my womb, positively jumped for joy!

Hymn

Meekness and majesty

Music

The angel Gabriel Basque carol, during which Luke 1:26-38 is read

Meditation of Mary

Why me?
That's what I kept on asking myself.
Why me?
I mean, it was obvious what people were going to say, wasn't it?
The sly looks,
the knowing grins,
the wagging tongues.
And Joseph?
Well, he really hit the roof.
Furious he was, and who can blame him?
If we'd been married it would have been different,
but engaged – it was bound to cause a scandal.
And it hurt, more than anyone will know;
I never realised people could be so cruel.
I didn't even want a baby, that's what made it worse;
it was the last thing on my mind.
I was still young,
not ready for that kind of responsibility,
wanting to enjoy life a little.
I could have done without those sleepless nights,
the endless washing,
the countless extra demands.
And believe me, it didn't get any easier.

Well, it never does, does it?
I'll never forget how he disappeared like that
on the way back from Jerusalem –
a right old panic he had us in.
But was he sorry?
Well, if he was he had a funny way of showing it.
'You should have known where to find me,' he said –
'My Father's house, where else?'
Cheeky monkey!
And then, just when life was plodding along nicely,
back on an even keel,
he went swanning off into the wilderness to be baptised.
Oh, I know he had to make his own way, don't get me wrong,
but I couldn't help feeling
he was getting mixed up in something dangerous.
And so it proved.
We could all see it coming,
all except him apparently.
He said the wrong things
to the wrong people
in the wrong places,
and there could only be one result.
It nearly broke my heart to watch it –
my beautiful boy, broken and bleeding,
struggling with that cross,
hanging in agony.
But then he looked down, not at the rest of them but at me.
And in his eyes was such love, such care,
such tenderness!
I saw suddenly the eyes of God looking at me
through the eyes of my child,
and I asked myself then,
as I'd asked so many times before,
yet differently this time, so very differently:
Why me? Why me?

Reading

John 19:25-27
… Meanwhile, standing near the cross of Jesus were his mother, and his mother's sister, Mary the wife of Clopas, and Mary Magdalene. When Jesus saw his mother and the disciple whom he loved standing beside her, he said to his mother, 'Woman, here is your son.' Then he said to the disciple, 'Here is your mother.' And from that hour the disciple took her into his own home.

Music

But who may abide the day of his coming? (Messiah) Handel, during which Matthew 25:31-33 is read

Meditation of Matthew

He told us he would come again,
that as he had departed so he would return.
And we believed him, totally,
without reserve or hesitation.
It was what kept us going, that promise,
the one thing that gave us strength to battle on through thick and thin.
Yet sometimes,
just occasionally,
I catch myself wondering whether we should look forward;
whether it will all be so cosy,
so comfortable,
as we sometimes seem to imagine.
You see, I can't help remembering those words of his,
about the sheep and the goats,
about the final judgement –
so simple,
so straightforward,
yet so chilling in their implications:
'I was hungry, and you fed me,
thirsty, and you gave me a drink,
a stranger and you welcomed me,
naked, sick, imprisoned, and you were there to help.'
That's what he said – through serving these,
even the very least of them, you serve me.
It sounds good, doesn't it?
The sort of message we like to hear.
Yet sometimes those words disturb me,
for I can't help asking, 'Which am I?'
Oh, I know which I'd like to be, stands to reason!
And I know which I should be, all too well.
But if I'm honest,
really truthful with myself,
I fear I'm more often a goat than a sheep.
I saw the plight of the hungry,
but it was me I worried about feeding.
I heard the cry of the thirsty,
but it was my own need I satisfied.
I spotted the loneliness of the stranger,
but wasn't sure I could trust them.
I was told about the naked,
but it was I who got the new clothes.
I glimpsed the despair of the sick,
but was afraid to risk infection.
I knew some were denied their freedom,
but was reluctant to get involved.
Not now, I told them;
next time I'll do something, next time I'll help –
God will understand.
But will he, that's the question?

I've been good at talking,
good at preaching,
good at praying,
and in faithfulness at worship I have few peers.
Yet when I recall those words of Jesus
and measure them against his life,
sometimes I find myself almost hoping he doesn't come back,
for if he does and judgement comes,
even though I've called him Lord,
it may be me at whom he points the finger,
and me he says he never even knew.

Prayer

Living God,
through Jesus Christ you have taught us to pray,
'Thy kingdom come, thy will be done.'
We look forward to the day when that prayer is answered –
a day when there shall be no more night,
no more tears,
an end to mourning and crying and pain –
an end to death itself.
Sustain us, we pray, through all the uncertainties
of our fleeting lives
with that sure and certain hope,
and help us live each day in the knowledge that one day
you will be all and in all.

Hymn

Hark the glad sound, the saviour comes

Nick Fawcett

Blessing

Advent 4

The Blessed Virgin Mary

Advent is a time when we rejoice in the coming of Christ into our lives, that he came at Christmas, and that he comes again to be our Lord and King. Advent celebrates that our God comes to us again and again.

Begin in the dark. If the room is not dark, close your eyes.

Welcome the light

In him was life, and the life was the light of all people. The light shines in the darkness, and the darkness did not overcome it.

John 1:4, 5

In Christ Jesus the darkness is defeated:
his light has come into the world.
Emmanuel, God is with us.

In Christ Jesus a new day has dawned:
his light has come into the world.
Emmanuel, God is with us.

In Christ Jesus is our hope and joy:
his light has come into the world.
Emmanuel, God is with us.

In Christ Jesus life is eternal:
his light has come into the world.
Emmanuel, God is with us.

Candle-lighting

On the fourth Sunday in Advent we light four candles, one for all of God's faithful people, one for men and women of vision, and one for John the Baptist and all who immerse themselves in the love and presence of God. The fourth candle is for the Blessed Virgin Mary and all who give themselves to God in love.

When our lives are darkened
it is necessary to celebrate the presence that comes to us
and the light that is given to us.
The Lord comes to us.
He abides with us.

Light four Advent candles.

Jesus Christ is the Light of the World;
eternal light, shine in our hearts.

Blessed are you, Lord our God, for in the fullness of time you shared in our humanity, being born of the Blessed Virgin Mary. You came down to lift us up; you became human that we might share in the divine. As we rejoice in Mary doing your will and so welcoming you into her life may we abide in you and know that you abide in us.
Blessed are you Father, Son and Holy Spirit.
Blessed be God for ever.

Reading

Isaiah 7:10-14

Hymn

Hark the glad sound

Special intention – in the light of God

We bring before you, O Lord,
all whose lives are darkened.
We remember the poor and the homeless,
all who are ill and suffering,
those who are approaching death,
and all who have lost loved ones.
Lord be known to them, come as the light,
let your peace fill them and your love enfold them.
We ask this for you love and mercy's sake.

Closing prayer

O Light that lightens our way,
let us not fear the darkness of this day.
To open to you is to welcome the Light.
To walk in your light is to know eternal life.
Come, Lord Jesus,
be known to all who walk in darkness.
Come, Lord Jesus,
you are our light and our salvation.
Come, Lord of life.

David Adam

Advent 4

Expectation

Introduction and lighting of Advent candles

'Come, thou long-expected Jesus.' 'O come, O come Emmanuel.' So we sing year after year at Advent. But do we mean it? Are we really looking forward to the coming of Christ? Do we truly believe one day he will return? And if so, what will it all mean? It is questions such as these that Advent puts to us, for above all this is a season of expectation, a season which reminds us of the promise Jesus gave to come again in glory. Soon we shall be celebrating once more the coming of Jesus in a stable in Bethlehem – a coming his people had looked forward to for so long yet which, when it finally happened, they failed to recognise. It is with that sobering truth in mind that we ask ourselves today: 'What do *we* expect? And what *should* we expect?'

Prayer

Lord Jesus Christ,
we are here just a short time away from Christmas –
that great festival which we know and love so well –
which perhaps we know and love too well!

We have heard the stories and sung the hymns so many times
that there is a danger of the medium
becoming more important than the message.
We come today wanting to avoid that,
eager instead to reflect on the meaning of your coming –
for yesterday, for today, for tomorrow.
So now,
through readings,
through music,
through meditations,
we come to worship you.
Speak to us through it all, we pray,
so that this season of Advent may not simply be a part
of our build-up to Christmas, but a time in its own right
which deepens our faith
and strengthens our commitment.
Lord Jesus Christ,
meet with us now,
and speak your word.

Hymn

How lovely on the mountains are the feet of him

Music

Glory to God (Messiah) Handel, during which John 1:1-5, 9, 14, 18 is read

Meditation of John the Apostle

There's only one word for it,
one word that gets anywhere near the truth,
that sums up the wonder of it all,
and that's 'Jesus'.
Trust me, I know,
for I've spent a lifetime trying to find the right words.
Since I followed Jesus all those years ago,
since I sat with the apostles in that upper room,
since we went out teaching and preaching in the Master's name,
I've been looking for ways in which to describe my experience,
and I've used words,
masses of them,
more than I can begin to count . . .
When I stood and preached to the multitudes,
when I nurtured believers in their new-found faith,
when I prayed for the sick,
when I led times of worship,
when I reminisced with friends,
when I witnessed to strangers,
words, words, words.

But they've never been sufficient,
never begun to express what I really want to say.
And now more than ever I find that's true,
sitting here trying to record the good news as revealed to me.
I've written so much,
page after page,
my own words and his,
woven together as best I can into a tapestry of his life.
I've told of the beginnings and the ends, of his signs,
of his teaching,
of his actions.
I've spoken of those lesser-known characters,
the ones Matthew, Mark and Luke missed out,
and I've given details of those private moments,
when it was just us and Jesus together
as the end drew near.
I've tried,
I've really tried to get it across,
to tell you what Jesus meant to me and to so many others.
But there's so much more I could still write,
so much I've had to leave out.
I could go on to the end of time
and still not do justice to all I want to tell you.
That's why I say there's only one word,
one word that says it all,
because Jesus was the fulfilment,
the embodiment,
the personification of God's word.
The Law and the Prophets spoke of him.
The wisdom of the teachers spoke of him.
The universe in all its glory speaks of him.
And if you want to listen,
if you want to hear,
if you want to understand what life is all about,
then take my word for it,
the only way is to know him for yourself,
the word made flesh!

Music

O come, O come, Emmanuel, during which 2 Peter 3:1-4, 8-15a is read

Meditation of Peter

'How much longer?' they keep asking.
'When will the waiting be over and the kingdom arrive?'
Well, how should I know?
In all honesty why should I have any more idea than the rest of them?
But they just don't get it.
They think because I was with Jesus,

close to him for those three years,
that I must have some special knowledge, inside information,
a hotline to heaven.
If only I had!
At least then I could shut them up and get a bit of peace.
At least I could give some answers
instead of telling them yet again to be patient. Patient!
Why should they be?
I'm not!
I'm consumed with frustration,
chafing at the bit,
desperate for something to happen,
for it's hard, I can tell you, being a Christian today.
There are informers everywhere, looking to make a quick penny.
There's the Pharisees spitting poison.
There's the rest of them, our own kin, intent on destroying us.
And there's Caesar, mad Caesar, delighting in cruelty,
any way of using us for sport.
We've seen brothers and sisters in Christ
tortured,
flogged,
stoned;
we've heard their screams, their groans, their sobs,
listened to their cries for mercy, their pleas for help;
and they want to know, who can blame them, when it will all end.
It's made worse by what Jesus told us –
all that stuff about not seeing death before he comes.
If he hadn't said that, not raised our hopes, it might have been easier –
we'd certainly have felt different –
so what was he thinking of, making such a promise?
Yet maybe that's not fair,
for he told us after all not to speculate about the future,
to imagine we can ever be certain,
not even to concern ourselves with dates or times.
'Leave it to God,' that was his advice.
'Trust in him and get on with living.
It may be hard,
it may be costly,
but you've a job to do, here and now.'
I'm not saying that answers everything,
but the more I think about it, the more it does help.
for, of course, he has come, through his Spirit,
and his kingdom is here, all around us,
if only we have eyes to see it.
He will return in person too, I've no doubt about that;
sometime he will finally reign supreme.
But what matters is not when that happens;
it's living each moment in the confidence that it will.
And if I'm really truthful, most of the time,
when we're not facing danger,
when we're not running for our lives,

I'm quite happy with that,
for I love this life in so many ways and am in no hurry for it to end.
Is that wrong? I don't know.
All I can say is, 'In your time, Lord.
In your own time.'

Hymn

Come, thou long-expected Jesus

Music

But who may abide the day of his coming (Messiah) Handel, during which Matthew 25:31-33
is read

Meditation of Matthew

He told us he would come again,
that as he had departed so he would return.
And we believed him, totally,
without reserve or hesitation.
It was what kept us going, that promise,
the one thing that gave us strength to battle on through thick and thin.
Yet sometimes,
just occasionally,
I catch myself wondering whether we should look forward;
whether it will all be so cosy,
so comfortable,
as we sometimes seem to imagine.
You see, I can't help remembering those words of his,
about the sheep and the goats,
about the final judgement –
so simple,
so straightforward,
yet so chilling in their implications:
'I was hungry, and you fed me,
thirsty, and you gave me a drink,
a stranger and you welcomed me,
naked, sick, imprisoned, and you were there to help.'
That's what he said – through serving these,
even the very least of them, you serve me.
It sounds good, doesn't it?
The sort of message we like to hear.
Yet sometimes those words disturb me,
for I can't help asking, 'Which am I?'
Oh, I know which I'd like to be, stands to reason!
And I know which I should be, all too well.
But if I'm honest,
really truthful with myself,
I fear I'm more often a goat than a sheep.

I saw the plight of the hungry,
but it was me I worried about feeding.
I heard the cry of the thirsty,
but it was my own need I satisfied.
I spotted the loneliness of the stranger,
but wasn't sure I could trust them.
I was told about the naked,
but it was I who got the new clothes.
I glimpsed the despair of the sick,
but was afraid to risk infection.
I knew some were denied their freedom,
was reluctant to get involved.
Not now, I told them;
next time I'll do something, next time I'll help –
God will understand.
But will he, that's the question?
I've been good at talking,
good at preaching,
good at praying,
and in faithfulness at worship I have few peers.
Yet when I recall those words of Jesus
and measure them against his life,
sometimes I find myself almost hoping he doesn't come back,
for if he does and judgement comes,
even though I've called him Lord,
it may be me at whom he points the finger,
and me he says he never even knew.

Music

Rex Tremendae (Requiem) Mozart, during which Revelation 21:1-4 is read

Meditation of John

One day we'll see him again.
Don't ask me when,
don't ask me how,
but one day
when all this struggle is over –
all the pain,
all the grief,
all the fear,
all the doubt –
then he will return to establish his kingdom.
I know that's hard to believe sometimes.
When you keep on battling against the odds and nothing seems to change,
when you stand up for what is good yet evil seems to triumph,
when love is met with hatred,
gentleness with violence,
truth with falsehood –

of course you start to wonder.
When you're faced with suffering,
sickness,
death;
when greed and corruption are rewarded with plenty
and justice is trampled underfoot;
when the poor get poorer
and the world goes by uncaring –
it's impossible not to ask yourself, day after day,
why is it allowed to happen?
But he will come, I'm certain of it –
not just because he promised to,
though that's important, of course;
not simply because he came back before,
cheating death of its victory,
triumphing over the grave,
though that's more vital still;
but because he *has* to return if anything is finally to make sense,
if faith is to be anything more than a grand delusion.
And it *is* more; it *has* to be.
These goals we strive towards,
this life revealed in Christ,
the promises he made,
the truths he taught,
everything he lived and died for –
they're real, I know that,
for they have turned my life around,
sustained me through my darkest moments,
lifted me beyond my highest thoughts,
and given me a joy that knows no bounds.
So though now we see but do not understand,
though faith is sometimes hard and Christ seems far away,
we'll hold fast to hope,
waiting for a time when there will be an end to tears and pain and death,
a time when God will live among his people
in a new and beautiful kingdom;
and we shall see him again, our Lord Jesus Christ,
crowned in glory and splendour,
King of kings,
Lord of lords,
all in all,
yet one with us!

Reading

Revelation 22:1-5, 20

Then the angel showed me the river of the water of life, bright as crystal, flowing from the throne of God and of the Lamb through the middle of the street of the city. On either side of the river is the tree of life with its twelve kinds of fruit, producing its fruit each month; and the leaves of the tree are for the healing of the nations. Nothing accursed will be found there any more. But the throne of God and of the Lamb will be in it, and his servants will worship him; they will see his face, and his name will be on their foreheads. And there will be no more night; they need no light of lamp or sun, for the Lord God will be their light, and they will reign for ever and ever.

The one who testifies to these things says, 'Surely I am coming soon.' Amen. Come, Lord Jesus!

Prayer

Loving God, we praise you
for fulfilling your age-long purpose
through the birth of Jesus.
We thank you
that your promises are not simply empty words like so many of ours,
but pledges we can rely on,
knowing they will always be honoured.
Teach us, then, to read the Scriptures as Matthew read them,
hearing your word revealed in Christ
and trusting in the promise of new life
you have given us through him.

Hymn

Lo! he comes with clouds descending

Blessing

Nick Fawcett

SERMON IDEAS

Advent 1

End times?

Unlike heaven and earth, which will end, my words will never pass away. But as to the day or hour that this world will end, nobody except the Father knows it, not even the angels in heaven or the Son. (Mark 13:31, 32)

I've been in a hurry to get things done this week for, according to a preacher from Oakland, California, the end of the world is just around the corner: to be exact, due tomorrow at 6pm. Actually, of course, I've not been in any hurry at all, for I pay no credence whatsoever to this kind of drivel. People have been predicting the end of the world with depressing regularity since time immemorial, and no doubt they will continue to do so for years to come, which is all very strange when you consider the words of Jesus above, in which he makes it quite clear that nobody but God knows when the end times will be. Elsewhere, he stresses that we should not concern ourselves with such things, but should instead get on with the daily business of life and service.

   Certainly we are called to look forward to his coming again and to ensure that we are ready to greet him when he does finally return. But when that will be, where and how it will happen, what it will involve and so forth are not for us to concern ourselves with. What Jesus was saying to his disciples is that, come what may, we must keep faith. Heaven and earth may pass away, and so too may we, but though *this* life may end, our hope is in things unseen, a kingdom beyond this world. That's what matters: faith in the future shaping the present, so that instead of fretting about what's to come we live now as he would wish. Don't brood on tomorrow. Rejoice today, and trust in him. We may pass *on* before he comes, but, like his words, we will never pass *away*.

Nick Fawcett

Rise and shine

You are well aware of the times we're living in. It's high time for you to awake, for the day of our salvation is closer than when we first came to faith . . . Wake up to what righteousness is all about; keep your lives free from sin. Some of you – and I say this to your shame – have no knowledge of God. (Romans 13:11; 1 Corinthians 15:34)

Few of us like getting up in the morning, but of course we have to, and for those who need to rise early an alarm clock is essential, it being the only thing guaranteed to arouse them from their slumber in readiness for another day. I have an alarm clock at home that is particularly special. Bought for me by my wife at Christmas many years back, it features an early photograph of my two children and a message from them both recorded when they were both at primary school age. What better sight and sound could I hope to wake up to? Though I still groan with dismay when the alarm goes off, my reluctance to wake up is tempered by their well-loved voices.

Advent offers an alarm clock of a different sort. Far more than a prelude to Christmas, it reminds us of the central themes of the gospel – of what God has done, is doing and will yet do – and as such it serves as an annual wake-up call to hear and respond. The above words of Paul to the Romans and Corinthians perfectly capture that sense of urgency: 'awake, for the day of our salvation is closer than when we first came to faith'. Here, in other words, is a summons to rouse ourselves and hear again the message of Christ; to shake off our lethargy and commit ourselves afresh to his service. Do we still hear his voice and answer his call? Or have we metaphorically rolled over and dozed off in our discipleship? Take time, this Advent, to listen to what God is saying to you, and to respond.

Nick Fawcett

Year A

Thought for the day
We are to wake up and make sure we stay ready for the second coming.

Readings
Isaiah 2:1-5
Psalm 122
Romans 13:11-14
Matthew 24:36-44

The Church begins its new year on Advent Sunday with the alarm clock jerking us out of sleep. There isn't even a snooze button. There is rather a sense of urgency as we listen to the readings.

First we have the vision seen by Isaiah of the last days, with the holy hill of Jerusalem a centre of pilgrimage for people from every nation. It is a picture of two-way traffic; the pilgrims streaming towards the city from all directions in order to understand and know God better, and the Word of God pouring out from Jerusalem in all directions to teach, explain and transform lives.

From our position in time we can appreciate the typical and extraordinary nature of such prophecy, since in Jesus the Word of God has indeed been pouring out from Jerusalem to the rest of the world, and to the rest of time during this last age before the end of all. And it is to him that the people come in every generation to have their lives transformed.

The Isaiah passage ends with a summons and an invitation to walk in the light of the Lord, and Paul takes this up in his letter to the Romans. The armour of light that will protect us from evil is the life of love spelt out by Jesus both in teaching and example. So, as we begin our preparation for Christmas, we are reminded of Jesus' humility in coming to live among us and show us the Way, and also of the future, when he will return in glory as righteous judge.

In the Gospel we have Jesus' own teaching about the last days, and discover that one thing we can be certain of is that the second coming cannot be predicted. No last-minute revision will be possible, then, and the regular coursework format is a more helpful model. We have to live our lives in constant readiness so that we are not taken by surprise. This is partly so that we can be prepared for death or the second coming, and partly so that we can enjoy that quality of eternity which means God is constantly coming to us even while we live out our earthly lives. We need to be ready to receive him at every moment of every day.

Susan Sayers

Year B

Thought for the day
Be alert and watchful; keep yourselves ready.

Readings
Isaiah 64:1-9
Psalm 80:1-7, 17-19
1 Corinthians 1:3-9
Mark 13:24-37

There is a sense, in the reading from Isaiah, that, but for God's mercy, we are in a hopeless situation. Even as we beg for God's help, recognising that he has proved himself to be the one and only real God, we know that our behaviour has been a rejection of all God is and values. So what point can there be in asking for help from the One we spend so much time ignoring, rejecting and dismissing?

Yet there is hope; the prophet clings on to the fact that we are of God's making. Perhaps his love and affection for us will, even now, move God to show mercy to his wayward creation of humankind. Psalm 80 echoes this pleading for rescue and restoration, undeserved as it is. Both these readings from the Old Testament give us a flavour of the generations of longing and yearning for a saviour, often from the pit of human experience and in a very candid recognition of the human condition.

In contrast, the reading from Paul's letter to the Christians in Corinth is written after the coming of Jesus, the promised Saviour. It is full of the confidence which comes from knowing that, though we cannot save ourselves and our weaknesses are as weak as ever, the life of Jesus in us has power to keep us strong to the end and uphold us in what is right and good. God has indeed acted with an outpouring of unearned and undeserved love and generosity, simply because it is God's nature to act with grace and mercy. Since God is utterly faithful, we can trust him even with the worst of ourselves; his power in us is always going to be sufficient.

Today's Gospel is Jesus speaking to us of real and serious things. Never does Jesus pretend to us; never does he gloss over costs or dangers. Treating us with respect, he warns us so as to prepare us, and we need to take notice of what he is saying. He is speaking of great cosmic turmoil, and disturbing self-appointed leaders with power to attract and lead many astray. We are warned against gullibility and fashion-chasing where truth is concerned. Even Jesus is not in possession of the exact times and dates, but he is concerned to pass on to his followers, with considerable urgency, the need to be alert and watchful, so that whatever time the end comes we will be ready and prepared.

Susan Sayers

Year C

Thought for the day
The gathered hopes of generations remind us to get ourselves ready, so that Christ's return will be a day of excitement and great joy.

Readings

Jeremiah 33:14-16
Psalm 25:1-10
1 Thessalonians 3:9-13
Luke 21:25-36

Today is filled with a sense of expectancy. It's rather like knowing that when you come of age you'll inherit a fortune, or that in another few years your ISA account will mature. Only this is rather more mind-blowing than mere financial hope. The promise is there and stands secure, and God, being faithful, will keep that promise. Eventually, when the time is ripe, he will gather up all the goodness and honour and patience and long-suffering that has been grown throughout the ages, and bring things to completion.

This week's readings speak to the deep-seated longings of humanity for right and justice to triumph. They speak to our yearning for a final end to all the cruelty and misery of our world, some of which we all know from first-hand experience. Of course, it is serious and sombre stuff to be considering the winding-up of all the created universe as we know it, and it is very necessary to be reminded of our need to be ready by the lives we are leading. Yet running through the readings is a clear, bright shaft of strong and exhilarating hope, which we can catch and make our own. God is familiar with our world. He too hears the cry, generation by generation, of those who find faith in a good God impossible because they are overwhelmed by the sorrows and tragedies screaming at them. But ultimately, as Christ has already shown us on the cross, and in his risen life, it is good that triumphs, and God's harvesting at the end of time will be a glorious celebration of all that is just, right and loving. This is not wishful thinking but hope, in all its integrity.

Susan Sayers

Waiting for God

Aim

To make people more aware that Christ comes to them today.

Reading

Mark 13:35

Illustration

It was near Christmas and in the Advent season, and Peter waited for God to come. He prayed every day, 'God, show me your face and I shall be saved.' Peter had tried to live a good life; he was now old and looked forward to the coming of God. He continued to work in his paper shop, where he had worked most of his life. Here he heard all sorts of conversations and met many people. A single mum was telling a friend how she did not have enough money to buy presents for her child. When everyone else had gone, Peter said to her, 'I heard what you said. I have a few toys on the shelves; they are not selling very well, go and pick anything you would like.' She could hardly believe it for there were some wonderful things on the shelves. As she went away with her arms full, Peter was delighted. His reward was her smile.

Later that day, he caught a young lad stealing a magazine from the shelves. He was on the way out with the magazine up his jumper when Peter stopped him. He could have called the police or told the boy's parents. He saw the boy was poor and afraid, and he felt sorry for him. 'If you want a magazine, and have no money, talk with me,' he said. 'Magazines are soon out of date; I can always find one to give you. You must not just help yourself. Take the magazine for free and ask me another time.' The boy's face changed from a look of fear to a beaming smile. He thanked Peter and ran from the shop.

An old man came into the shop and was saying how lonely he was since his wife died. This would be his first Christmas on his own – he was not looking forward to it. Peter said, 'We were expecting a friend to come for Christmas, and he has said he cannot make it. We have prepared for his coming. Would you come to us instead? We would love to share Christmas with you.' The old man's face lit up in a beautiful smile and he said, 'You have made me feel so wanted, and I would love to come.'

That night Peter prayed his Advent prayer, 'Show me your face and I shall be saved.' In a dream God spoke to him and said, 'Peter, today I came to you, and three times you made me smile. Grace and peace be upon you.'
(Apologies to Tolstoy!)

David Adam

Advent 2

Keeping faith

When John heard in prison what the Messiah was doing, he sent word by his disciples and said to him, 'Are you the one who is to come, or are we to wait for another?' Jesus answered them, 'Go and tell John what you hear and see: the blind receive their sight, the lame walk, the lepers are cleansed, the deaf hear, the dead are raised, and the poor have good news brought to them.' (Matthew 11:2-5)

Christmas crackers are invariably disappointing, aren't they? They look so full of promise stacked neatly in the box, but when you come to pull them it's always to find the same old tat inside. They're all show and no substance. And that sense of anticlimax rather describes how John the Baptist must have felt as he languished in prison following his arrest by Herod. He'd begun his ministry full of anticipation, believing that the kingdom of God was at hand, but now he found himself confined to a prison cell. Understandably, he started to question, wondering if God was at work in Christ after all. If so, why was Herod still in control? Why did evil continue to prosper? Why did nothing appear to have changed?

We can feel the same, when we look at our world. Has anything really changed for the better? Have we changed? Is the gospel really able to make a difference to life, or is it simply wishful thinking? For John, the answer came in reports concerning Jesus. Despite the fact that he, too, was experiencing hostility and rejection, people were being transformed by his touch – healed, renewed, restored, forgiven. Yes, there was still evil, injustice, sorrow and suffering, but the kingdom of God was nonetheless starting to grow. And, for all that remains wrong in the world today, lives continue to be changed. In peace discovered, hope reborn, strength gained, love shown, faith kindled, joy experienced and meaning found, God continues to bring new beginnings in Christ. Keep faith, for despite everything that frustrates his purpose and obscures his love, he is still at work, and the kingdom is growing among us.

Nick Fawcett

Believing the impossible

An angel of the Lord appeared to [Zechariah], standing on the right-hand side of the altar of incense. On seeing him, Zechariah was awestruck and paralysed by fear, but the angel said to him, 'Don't be frightened, Zechariah, for your plea has been heard. Your wife Elizabeth will bear you a son, and you are to call him John. He will bring you joy and gladness, and many will rejoice at his birth, for he will be great in the eyes of the Lord. He will turn many of the people of Israel to the Lord their God, and he will go out in the spirit and power of Elijah to turn the hearts of parents to their children, and those who have gone astray to the wisdom of the righteous – to prepare people so that they are ready for the Lord.' Zechariah said to the angel, 'How can I know this is true? For I am an old man, and my wife also is getting on in years.' The angel replied, 'I am Gabriel. I stand in God's presence, and he has sent me to tell you this good news, but now, since you have not believed my words, which in due course will be fulfilled, you will be struck dumb, rendered mute until the day these things happen.' (Luke 1:11-15a, 16-20)

'Impossible! It can't be done!' That was the response of Zechariah to the news that his wife Elizabeth was to give birth to a son. Whether she was beyond childbearing years is not clear, but there is no doubt that any hopes the couple might have had of her conceiving were long since gone. They were reconciled to their disappointment, so to be told that a child was to be born to them after all must have seemed too good to be true. From a human point of view, it was a perfectly understandable response, but here we are talking about God. That is what Zechariah failed to account for, and that is what made all the difference, for with God all things are possible.

Do we believe that? There will be times when we find God's promises hard to accept; times when we look at our life or the life of the world and feel that both are beyond redemption. Humanly speaking, that again is perfectly understandable, but once more it fails to account for God – the God who lived and died among us in Christ, raising him from the tomb; the God who has repeatedly shown that nothing is beyond him, however much it may seem beyond us!

Nick Fawcett

Year A

Thought for the day
Get the road ready for the Lord!

Readings
Isaiah 11:1-10
Psalm 72:1-7, 18-19
Romans 15:4-13
Matthew 3:1-12

Before any real changes can take place in our spiritual development, we have to come to the point of recognising where we are and wanting it to be better. All addicts and their families are painfully aware of the necessity to acknowledge the addiction and find it unbearable, before there is any real hope of kicking the habit. It is at the point when a situation finally becomes intolerable that we are galvanised into taking action to change things.

Living in exile, the people of Israel became acutely aware of their nation's need for good leadership, justice, integrity and peace. In today's passage from Isaiah we sense their longing, as they look forward to God providing what they know they need. Typically, the prophecy was fulfilled in far greater measure, since the kingdom of justice, peace and love – the kingdom of God proclaimed by Jesus – is still growing throughout the entire world.

John the Baptist's message of repentance once again recovered the urgency for people sorting their lives out, since the coming of the Messiah was imminent and they wanted to put things right and be ready, much as we might rush round clearing up the house just before guests are due to arrive – especially those guests we want to impress, or those who we know will notice the clutter! Often the clearing will be something we know has needed doing for ages; the arrival of guests simply reminds us that it has to be done.

So what about all that spiritual clutter and grime which we know needs sorting? Today the Gospel helps to nudge us into urgent action, recognising that we don't want things to stay as they are, and the effort of changing whatever needs changing is well worth it. God comes and knocks at the door of our hearts all the time – not just at the end of the world.

Susan Sayers

Year B

Thought for the day

John the Baptist prepares the way for the coming of the Messiah by helping the people to realign their lives.

Readings

Isaiah 40:1-11
Psalm 85:1-2,8-13
2 Peter 3:8-15a
Mark 1:1-8

Mark's Gospel bursts straight in with the dynamic claim that we are hearing about nothing less than the Messiah, the Son of God, entering into the realm of ordinary human life. Just as the prophet Isaiah had foretold, this event would require some drastic preparation work, and here is John (we are given no other introductory details about him) suddenly fulfilling the old prophecy and urging people to get their lives and attitudes sorted out and cleaned up. He is using the effective symbolism of baptismal washing as a sign of washed lives. If you are willing to step into the river, publicly, confess your sins and be pushed down under the water as a sign of your repentance, you are quite likely to mean what you say, and emerge from the experience full of new, fresh enthusiasm for walking God's way.

This is exactly the thorough kind of repentance we all need regularly. Perhaps we should use every shower and bath time as an opportunity for such spiritual washing. Then we would experience daily the fresh start and openness provided by God's forgiveness of acknowledged and confessed sin.

Along with John's call to thorough repentance and baptismal washing was the message he preached, directing his followers to look for the powerful person of great honour who would be coming shortly and whose baptism would be not with water but the Holy Spirit of God. Just imagine standing dripping and cleansed by the Jordan as you hear about someone who will drench and immerse you in the holiness of the Spirit of God. It must have triggered in many the deep longing and expectant thirsting for God which allows lives to be shaken, hearts to be softened and the kingdom to come.

The same is true now. It is as an expectant people, thirsty for God and longing for a total immersing in his life, that we prepare during the season of Advent for the festival of Christmas. The extent to which we respond to John's call across the centuries will determine how open and receptive we are to welcoming Jesus and allowing him into our lives. The life which Peter describes – of harmony, repaying even evil with blessing, and doing good regardless of the consequences – is a direct result of living immersed in the Holy Spirit of God.

Susan Sayers

Year C

Thought for the day

It had been prophesied that there would be a messenger to prepare the way for the coming of the Messiah. Now John the Baptist appears with his urgent message of repentance.

Readings

Malachi 3:1-4
Canticle: Benedictus
Philippians 1:3-11
Luke 3:1-6

Today we read one example of many references from the prophets to a messenger who will prepare people for the coming of the anointed one, the long-awaited Messiah or Christ. It is typical of God's provision for his people. All teachers and builders know the necessity for thorough preparation and the way this so often involves chipping back to the solid foundations and making good. Anyone in advertising knows that people may need telling the same thing several times before they are likely to do anything about changing their favourite product.

So God, knowing human nature affectionately and realistically, tells us beforehand what he will do, and then provides John who himself points towards someone else. Hopefully there will be those who, having heard the prophecies, will already be waiting expectantly, ready to latch on to what the messenger is saying. There will be those who, through John's urgent message, will be sorting their lives out so that when Jesus' ministry begins, their hearts will already be attuned to receive what he has to say and eventually to recognise who he is.

And what about us? Paul's prayer, similar to that in the letter to the Thessalonians last week, is rather like the image of carrying a very full mug of tea from the kitchen back to bed, carefully holding it so that nothing spills and nothing is lost on the way. We are in the privileged position of having read the prophesies, seen them fulfilled in John the Baptist, and having met Jesus through the Gospels and his living presence. So in a sense we are like the full mug of tea. What we now have to do is make the journey to death and the second coming without losing a drop of what we have been given.

At another level is the recognition that it isn't enough to hear John's message once. It does us all good to use each Advent as a fresh chance to look at our lives and habits, and sort them out; to be ruthless about anything which is impairing our walk with God.

Susan Sayers

Stir-up Sunday

Aim

To show we need to prepare for the coming of our Lord.

Reading

Mark 1:3

Illustration

The Sunday before the beginning of Advent used to be called 'Stir-up Sunday' for two reasons. The prayer for the Sunday begins, 'Stir up, O Lord, the wills of your faithful people'; a wonderful prayer that wants us to 'bring forth the fruits of good works'. It is by what we do that we will be known, so it is important that our works are good, important that we do something.

Traditionally 'Stir-up Sunday' was also the time when the Christmas cake was made. Mother would get all the ingredients – the flour, the fruit, the eggs – and mix them together. Everyone in the house had a stir of the cake before it went into the oven. All this was part of the preparations before Christmas.

We now often spend weeks preparing for this one day. How much time do we spend preparing for the coming of God to us? If someone is coming to stay, we will make sure there is room for them, that we have time for them, that we will give them some attention. Our God comes and seeks room in our lives; he wants us to be aware of him, for us to give him some of our time and attention. Are you prepared for this?

David Adam

Advent 3

A continuing response

In the distant past God spoke in various ways through the prophets to our ancestors, but latterly he has spoken to us through his Son, whom he chose to inherit all things and through whom he created the universe. Reflecting God's glory, he is the precise imprint of God himself, his mighty hand upholding all creation . . . So then, let us pay heed to what we have heard, so that we do not stray from it. (Hebrews 1:1-3a; 2:1)

'Will you still love me tomorrow?' So runs the haunting refrain of the 1960s hit song by The Shirelles. It's a question that Jesus might equally pose in relation to Christmas, a time when, unlike any other, our churches will be full to bursting as people gather for candlelight carol services, midnight mass, nativity presentations and the like. For a short time, faith resurfaces and the message of the gospel strikes a chord with the general public. But how many will be in church the following week? How many will spare Jesus a thought the rest of the year? How many will see faith as a matter of commitment rather than an occasional response? The answer, sadly, is precious few.

We, of course, will be among those few . . . or will we? We may profess the name of Christ and worship him week by week, but does the message of the gospel touch our lives in the way it once did? Is our faith as alive as the day we first pledged ourselves to his service? Do we still see discipleship in terms of an ongoing relationship, a continuing journey? Or has our commitment become more a matter of dutiful routine than joyful response? Responding to Jesus is not a one-off affair, done once and then able to take care of itself. It's something we must go on doing, working at our relationship, building up our faith if it is to stay strong. We may have loved Christ yesterday. We may still love him today. But will we still love him tomorrow?

Nick Fawcett

Fulfilment in Christ

'She will bear a son, and you are to call him Jesus, for he will save his people from their sins.' All this took place so that what was spoken of the Lord by the prophet might be fulfilled. (Matthew 1:21, 22)

Read the Gospel accounts of the life, death and resurrection of Jesus and one thing will leap out at you: the constant references to events taking place in order to fulfil the Scriptures. In the opening four chapters of Matthew alone there are four instances, and so it continues through the remainder. Prophecies of old are seen to point beyond their original context to the person of Christ, finding there a deeper relevance.

Is this what we mean by the fulfilment of God's word? In part, yes, but Jesus saw himself as far more than the realisation of ancient promises. He came, he said, to fulfil not only the words of the prophets but the law also, that which lay at the heart of his people's faith. Everything this had attempted to do, he said – putting us right with God, bridging the gap that keeps us apart – was accomplished through him. The law prescribed outward observance; he brought inner change. The law called for sacrifice; he made that sacrifice once and for all. The law consisted of various commandments; he summed them up in a single command: to love one another. In him we see fulfilled not simply the occasional prophecy but God's entire purpose, his will for all. No wonder, then, that we are able to find fulfilment through him in turn.

Nick Fawcett

Year A

Thought for the day

Great expectations. Jesus fulfils the great statements of prophecy.

Readings

Isaiah 35:1-10
Psalm 146:5-10 or Canticle: Magnificat
James 5:7-10
Matthew 11:2-11

John the Baptist's task had been to prepare people for the coming of the Messiah, and that placed him, with all the prophets before him, in the age before the coming of the kingdom. We recall how John had urged people to sort out their lives, stressing the possibility of judgement as the all-seeing God came among his people in person, and it is easy to see how John's enthusiasm had polished his hopes into a specific shape. This is something we are all prone to do.

While it helped the urgency and focus of John's message, the side effect was that when Jesus' ministry started to look different from his expectation John began to wonder if he'd been mistaken. The frustration and suffering of his imprisonment must have added to the undermining negatives.

What Jesus does is hold up the Isaiah prophecy as a checklist. If these signs of the kingdom are indeed happening, then John can trust that the promised Saviour is indeed at work, even if the style of his ministry is different from what he had imagined. It's all to do with our expectations. If we get into the way of fleshing these out completely through our imagination, we may find that we don't recognise the real thing when we see it. So it is as well to stay flexible, holding on to what we do know for certain and keeping our minds open about the details. This is true for us when we try to imagine God, heaven, or the end of all things. They may look like the paintings and frescoes of the Old Masters, and they may not. We mustn't let our expectations become stunted or narrowed by a particular artist's impression. That is what happened when people expected the astronauts to see God above the clouds and were disappointed. Our great expectations of God will be fulfilled far in excess of anything we might imagine and entirely in keeping with his nature.

Susan Sayers

Year B

Thought for the day

In Jesus, God will be fulfilling the Messianic prophecies about the promised Saviour.

Readings

Isaiah 61:1-4, 8-11
Psalm 126 or Canticle: Magnificat
1 Thessalonians 5:16-24
John 1:6-8, 19-28

Advent almost engulfs us with its spirit of urgent preparation. Everyone writes lists and tries to organise food, apt presents and thematic decorations; the store cupboard fills with things no one is allowed to touch yet, and tops of wardrobes become hiding places for bulky secrets. The Church's season of Advent is a kind of spiritual equivalent of all this, not just because we are rehearsing Christmas carols and Nativity plays, but because we are standing alongside the people of Israel in their period of waiting and preparation for the coming of the promised Saviour. In these four weeks we can sense something of their generations of waiting and longing.

It is the Messiah's Advent that we journey through at this time of year, and here too we find checklists and plans, secrets and mysteries, half-seen puzzles, and truths which have yet to be unpacked and savoured. The Isaiah reading for today is a case in point. We are given a kind of checklist of pointers to look out for in the promised Saviour, which will ensure that we recognise him when he comes. It is a wonderful checklist, full of hope and freshness, the overturning of negatives and the victory of good over evil.

Hearing either Psalm 126 or the Magnificat from the standpoint of the Isaiah passage is like having a peep into the wrapped future, and sensing that on Christmas morning we shall not be disappointed. And, of course, the Incarnation of Christmas morning is indeed the unwrapping of that promised secret. Even as John the Baptist was teaching by the river Jordan, he knew that the Christ was already there among them, though still hidden, since his public ministry had not yet begun. It would not be long before those qualities on Isaiah's list could be checked out and validated by the people, provided they had eyes open to recognise in Jesus all that the prophets had foretold.

But at the moment we are still in the waiting place, and all that is in the future. For now, we sense the expectancy of the faithful people of Israel, and also recognise our own place of waiting for that final coming of total accomplishment at the end of time. We live with our hopes and our questions, our puzzles and our trust in the faithful God. We know that in God's way all the checklists of qualities and characteristics both for the first and the second coming will hold good.

John the Baptist finds the authorities trying to do a full story on him, mistakenly homing in on the messenger instead of the coming King. He describes himself, in the words of the prophet, as simply a voice – not to be curiously interviewed, but heard, with the heart as well as the ears. We can make this Advent such a time of listening to the real message, rather than being sidetracked by all the less important things. The reading from Thessalonians gives us sound, practical ideas for this.

Susan Sayers

Year C

Thought for the day
Our period of preparation shifts from repentance and forgiveness to the freed exhilaration of hope, as the momentous truth of God's immanence begins to dawn on us.

Readings
Zephaniah 3:14-20
Canticle: Isaiah 12:2-6
Philippians 4:4-7
Luke 3:7-18

Over the first two weeks in Advent we have been focusing our attention on putting our lives straight, and this may well have been a very challenging and painful task. We may still be wrestling with its implications.

The shaft of hope has always been present in all this. But now it is as if the forgiveness we are receiving, resulting from real repentance, has enabled that shaft of hope to flood us with unexpected light and joy. From the viewpoint of forgiveness, the coming of Christ, both as we look back to Bethlehem and forward to the last day, is not something to fear, but to anticipate with great delight and enthusiasm.

There is Zephaniah's image of light-hearted and liberated singing and dancing, with something of the flavour of the street parties which celebrate peace after war. And there is Paul's signing-off message as he draws to a close his letter to the Christians at Philippi, the sense of God's closeness throbbing through the words. Everything is going to be all right; they can rejoice and go on rejoicing, whatever the immediate sufferings, because God has them ultimately safe.

And the people are enthusiastically taking up John the Baptist's challenge, and throwing themselves into giving up the behaviour they'd probably always known was wrong, but which they had never had the desire to address before.

In the gathering momentum some of them get over-enthusiastic, and how easily John could have been tempted to go along with their misguided assumptions. Thankfully his own rigorous self-awareness keeps him humble, and he is able to use their questions to point their expectations in the right direction – towards the Christ.

Susan Sayers

Ready for Christmas

Aim

To show God's kingdom comes when his will is done.

Readings

John 2:11
Luke 2:7

Illustration

Are you ready for Christmas? Have you sent all your cards? Bought presents? Got the food ready? What will you do on Christmas Day? Will you make room for Jesus: make sure Christ is in Christmas?

It was Jessie's birthday and she looked forward to it. She lived in an old people's home and had friends around her – but she was invited to her daughter's for her birthday. She would be with the family, including the three children. They made sure there was a nice room ready for her and the house was warm. Her daughter had bought the food she liked. All was ready.

On the first night her daughter had an evening class, the children were out with friends, and her son-in-law decided to go to the pub. On her birthday the children had other things to do and so would be out all day – football, swimming and netball are important. Jessie's son-in-law spent the day in the garage tinkering with his car, and her daughter decided to do some last-minute shopping on her own. Again Jessie was left alone. They had a meal together in the evening, then the children went on the computer and the others watched television. Jessie was glad to go back to the home where people had time to talk to her and give their attention to her.

Will we make time for Jesus on his birthday, or will we be too busy doing other things?

David Adam

Advent 4

Faithful to his promise

Then Mary said, 'My soul magnifies the Lord, and my spirit exults within me in God my Saviour, for he has looked on the lowliness of his servant. He has honoured his promise to our forebears and come to his servant Israel's assistance. He has remembered to show mercy to Abraham and to all his descendants for ever!' (Luke 1:46-48a, 54, 55)

'Ronseal', we're told, 'does what it says on the tin.' There's a clever reverse psychology in that advert, for the implication, though never explicitly stated, is that most products don't do what they're meant to – that their claims are bogus, their promises false. And that, sadly, is the way many people have come to view promises in general: to be taken with a generous pinch of salt. Pledges made by politicians prove to be spin rather than substance; guarantees and warranties turn out to be worth less than the paper they're written on. The fact is that, from earliest times, promises have been made only to be broken.

Perhaps that, more than anything, explains why so few people were ready to welcome Jesus when he came – simply because they'd given up expecting, their hopes in the promise of a

Messiah having been dashed by years of disappointment. And yet come he did, the one anticipated for so long taking flesh and entering our world. As Mary put it in her song of celebration: 'He has honoured his promise to our forebears and come to his servant Israel's assistance.' Faith was not, after all, in vain: the waiting was over, the day had dawned, for in the child she carried not only was the Messiah to be born, but also everything God had pledged was to be realised, the truth of his word and faithfulness of his purpose finally vindicated. What God says he will do, he does do – that is the triumphant message of Advent. It may take time, it may not be in our lifetime, but ultimately his promises will be honoured, his purpose fulfilled.

Nick Fawcett

Light of the world

Then Jesus spoke to them again, saying, 'I am the light of the world: whoever follows me will not walk in darkness, but will have the light of life.' (John 8:12)

The winter solstice is a time many approach with mixed feelings. On the one hand it takes us to the shortest day of the year, a time when the hours of darkness extend for their longest, but on the other it means that we've turned the corner and can start looking forward again to the evenings drawing out as we move first into spring and then into summer. No wonder, then, that the solstice has found its way into the rituals of so many ancient religions, for at a time when life is literally at its darkest it offers the promise of new light, new life, new beginnings.

As Christians, we celebrate light of a different sort: that which came into the world through Christ. The theme permeates numerous biblical texts associated with this season: 'The people who previously walked in darkness have witnessed a great light; light has shone on those who dwelt in a place of deep darkness' (Isaiah 9:2). 'A new dawn will come from heaven, and the sun will shine on those sitting in darkness and in the shadow of death' (Luke 1:78, 79a). 'Suddenly, an angel of the Lord appeared before them, and the Lord's glory shone round about them' (Luke 2:9a). 'The star that they had seen rise went ahead of them until it finally stopped over the place where the child was' (Matthew 2:9b). 'In him was life, and that life was the light of all. The light shines in the darkness, and the darkness could not overcome it' (John 1:4, 5). That's what we celebrate at Christmas: not lighter evenings to come but lighter lives now, light that goes on shining in life's darkest moments, even the shadowed valley of death. Whether it's spring, summer, autumn or winter, it makes no difference, for this is a light that illuminates our path today, tomorrow and every day.

Nick Fawcett

Year A

Thought for the day
Through the willing participation of Mary and Joseph, God is poised to come among his people as their Saviour.

Readings
Isaiah 7:10-16
Psalm 80:1-7, 17-19
Romans 1:1-7
Matthew 1:18-25

Matthew, writing for a Hebrew audience, is keen to show the Jewish people that Jesus is indeed the promised Messiah. He draws attention to Isaiah's prophecy spoken to King Ahaz, and sets out Jesus' credentials. Through Joseph, Jesus is a descendant of King David; through Mary, this son, born to a virgin, fulfils the ancient prophecy and turns out to be 'Immanuel' or 'God with us'.

It is not unusual for prophecies about short-term, immediate events to turn out to have resonances far in excess of their original meaning. One familiar example is the call to St Francis to 'repair my Church, which is in ruins'. It was far more than one stone chapel which was eventually 'repaired'; the whole Church of God became refreshed and invigorated.

The expectant atmosphere of today's readings attunes us to God's way of orchestrating events and working in co-operation with his people. The stage is set, the timing is right, and the focused light of all the hopes and longings of generations is about to shine out in the person of Jesus. Typically, we find God delighting in using the ordinariness of good people so that extraordinary things can be accomplished. Typically, he allows individual people to know their own part in the action exactly as and when they need to know it.

It is because Joseph is expecting God to be God that he is prepared to alter his sensible and considerate plan to make no loud accusations about Mary when divorcing her for assumed unfaithfulness. Whatever that dream was, it made him think again. Perhaps Mary had tried to tell him the truth and he hadn't been able to believe her before. We can only guess at how Mary felt before Joseph changed his mind.

God will still speak to us through our dreams, memories and feelings, if only we take the trouble to notice. They can often be our own personal parables, able to put us in touch with our true selves; enabling us to recognise God's ways forward which we haven't been able to see before.

Susan Sayers

Year B

Thought for the day
God's promised kingdom, announced both to King David in ancient times and to Mary by the angel Gabriel, will go on for ever.

Readings
2 Samuel 7, 1-11, 16
Canticle: Magnificat or Psalm 89:1-4, 19-26
Romans 16:25-27
Luke 1:26-38

When King David is filled with enthusiasm for building a great and holy temple to house the ark of the covenant, his offer is turned down, but the graciousness of his attitude very much accepted by God. Through the prophet Nathan, God points out to David that the seeming permanence of a grand building is nothing to be compared with the real permanence of the eternally present God. With such a nature there is no problem with flexibility; eternal Presence can move wherever the people go, untied by structural foundations.

Having assured King David that the building idea will be taken up by his son, God reveals his own blueprint for an everlasting kingdom, and the coming of a reign within the royal House of David which will eventually spread throughout the whole world. It was out of this promise that the hope of God's Messiah was born, particularly in the dark years following the collapse of the monarchy. Gradually the understanding of this Messiah became less tied in people's minds with temporal ruling power and more with a priestly kind of kingship which would bring worldwide blessing and hope.

So when we find Gabriel visiting Mary with a message that her son will reign on the throne of his ancestor, David, and his kingdom will never end, we are listening in on a gathering together of all the hopes and longings of generations, right back to King David himself. By this time, the overtones of a Messianic, priestly kingship will be there, and through Mary those hopes and plans can be accomplished for the saving of the whole world.

The passage from Romans gives us a glorious sense of a crescendo as the full spread of God's kingdom builds to completion. John Ellerton's well-loved hymn *The day thou gavest, Lord, is ended* puts it like this:

So be it, Lord; thy throne shall never,
like earth's proud empires, pass away;
thy kingdom stands and grows for ever
till all thy creatures own thy sway.

Our amazing privilege is to be part of the building.

Susan Sayers

Year C

Thought for the day
When we co-operate with God amazing things happen.

Readings
Micah 5:2-5a
Canticle: Magnificat or Psalm 80:1-7
Hebrews 10:5-10
Luke 1:39-45 (46-55)

It is not only Mary and Elizabeth who are pregnant in today's readings. The whole atmosphere this week is full of expectancy and the sense that what we are looking forward to has already begun to be fulfilled. It may be hidden but it leaps within us.

The prophet Micah speaks of events far greater than he imagines, and we, with our knowledge of the Gospel, can pick up on the image of a shepherd saviour being brought to birth and establishing a reign of peace. The writer of the letter to the Hebrews reminds us not just of Christ's birth but also of his death. As an unborn child already has the DNA pattern for the potential adult, so we are given here a kind of spiritual antenatal scan of Jesus, stretching back into the longing and forward to the sacrificial giving which secures our future.

There is enormous strength in the capacity to set aside something precious to you in order that a greater good may be enabled to happen. We marvel at Jesus laying aside his glory; laying aside his garments to wash the disciples' feet; laying aside the law – all in obedience and out of love. It is a hallmark of true godliness.

So when we find human beings like Mary willing to lay aside so much in obedience and out of love, we are watching the most real and beautiful of human nature; God and humanity co-operating together for the good of the world.

Today we are given the chance to press the pause button as Mary and Elizabeth meet, with their unborn children within them, and wonder at what can happen when we allow God to work in us and with us for the good of the world.

Susan Sayers

God's gift

Aim

To rejoice that Jesus Christ has come into the world.

Reading

John 3:16

Illustration

Mother and Father had wrapped up the present in beautiful paper with tinsel and bows. The present was in a big box. For a long time it remained unopened as if their child was frightened of it. Then the paper was taken off and folded up carefully, the present was taken out of the box, and the child played the whole day with the box. The child enjoyed having the box and playing with it. Mother and Father hoped that their child would soon realise what a wonderful present had been given to her . . .

I knew an old lady who was uninterested in presents. Whenever she was given a present, she was very grateful. She always remembered to say, 'Thank you'. But she did not open the gift. In her house I saw a pile of unopened gifts and I felt it was rather strange and sad.

Today I would like to give you all a present of a cheque for one million pounds. But you can only have it on one condition: you are to frame it, to show how generous I am, but not cash it.

Let us get behind the tinsel and the wrappings today and discover God's greatest gift. He gives himself to us. Let us come and give ourselves to him.

David Adam

ALL-AGE SERVICES

Advent 1

For pre-school age to 5 years – Year A

Thought for the day
We are to wake up and make sure we stay ready for the second coming.

Readings
Isaiah 2:1-5
Psalm 122
Romans 13:11-14
Matthew 24:36-44

Aim
To learn the importance of being alert to God all the time.

Starter
Play this version of 'musical bumps'. Tell the children that when you show the red sign they stand still. Whenever the music stops they sit down. This will mean that they have to keep watching, as well as listening, while they jump up and down.

Teaching
Praise everyone for watching and listening so well in the game. It was because they were watching and listening so well that they knew when to stop and when to sit down. Explain that Jesus told his friends to watch and listen carefully – he will be pleased to see how well the children at (your town) can do it already!

Explain that you are going to tell them a story. Every time they hear the word 'Jesus', they put their hand up.

Now tell them this story.

The world God had made was very beautiful. It had blue sea and green grass, and flowers of red and yellow and pink and purple. There were furry animals, and shining fish, birds which sang songs, and frogs which croaked. There were people. There were clouds. There was sunshine and rain and snow. God loved the world he had made. But he saw that people were spoiling the world; they were choosing to hate one another instead of loving one another. Sometimes they chose well and were happy. Sometimes they chose to be selfish and made themselves and each other very unhappy.

'The people I have made need saving and rescuing,' thought God. 'I will come to save and rescue them.'

He got his people ready. 'Watch and listen carefully!' he told them. 'Then when I come to save you, you will recognise who I am.'

Some of the people kept listening and watching. As they grew old they passed the message on to their children. And they passed it on to their children – 'Keep watching and listening. One day God will come to us to save and rescue us.'

At last, God kept his promise and came among his people in person to save and rescue them. The people had been expecting a rich and powerful king, but God came among his people as a tiny baby, who was born in a stable and put to bed in the animals' hay. This baby, whose name was Jesus, was God's Son, who had come into the world to save and rescue us.

Not everyone recognised him, because he wasn't what they were expecting. But the ones who were used to listening out for the loving words of God, and the ones who were used to watching out for the loving kindness of God – they knew exactly who Jesus was, and they were very pleased to meet him!

Praying

Dear God,
the world is full of your love. *(trace big circle)*
Help us to listen out for it. *(cup ears)*
Help us to watch out for it. *(shade eyes and look around)*
Thank you for all the goodness and love
that we can hear and see.

Activities

On the worksheet they can draw small and big things they enjoy seeing and hearing. These can all be cut out and stuck on to a group picture, or hole-punched and hung on to a coat hanger mobile, like this:

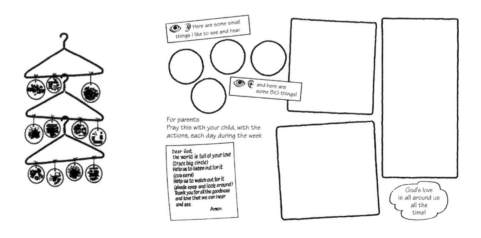

Susan Sayers

For pre-school age to 5 years – Year B

Aim

To prepare for the coming of Jesus.

Readings

Isaiah 64:1-9
Psalm 80:1-7,17-19
1 Corinthians 1:3-9
Mark 13:24-37

Teaching

This is Advent Sunday and it tells us someone is coming soon. Who is coming? When do we remember that Jesus is coming? Do you know how many Sundays there are in Advent? (Show the Advent Candles or hold up four fingers.) What happens after four Sundays?

When Jesus came, the night was dark. There were stars shining in the sky. If you looked out on the hills you could see shepherds guarding their sheep in case there were wolves or robbers. One young shepherd had to keep the light burning to scare away the darkness and the dangers. He liked to keep a great big fire burning. What do you think he put on the fire?

He put on a big piece of wood, a log – and he threw it on to the fire. He did not get too close because fire burns. Now he watched the sparks fly upwards like bright lights in the dark. They flew higher and higher right up into the sky. Joel – that is his name – watched the sparks rise into the night. He thought that they would go up higher and then go out, but he saw that they were getting brighter. The sky was being filled with light. It wasn't sparks he was watching; it was God's angels of light coming down from heaven. He began to hear them singing. The shepherds were nearly all asleep, they would miss the angels and their song – so Joel woke them up. Wake up! Wake up! The shepherds jumped up for they thought a wolf was coming. But they got a big surprise. Joel pointed upwards and they heard and saw angels in the sky. The angels were singing a beautiful song: 'Glory be to God in the highest and peace on earth.' Then the angels told them Jesus is coming and he is coming to Bethlehem. The shepherds were very excited and all of them wanted to go to Bethlehem and see Jesus.

Activities

We are going to make some shepherds to take into church, and later they will go and see Jesus. (Next week the children will make an angel; the third week, Mary and Joseph; and the fourth week, the baby Jesus and a star.) The figures can be coloured in and stuck to a piece of kitchen roll tube to make them stand. Each child should end up with a nativity group.

We will also colour in one candle to remind us that Jesus is coming and he comes to us.

Prayer

O God, you are always with us, even in the dark.
You come to us because you love us.
As you told the shepherds about Jesus,
help us to learn about his coming and his love for us.

Song

Jesus bids us shine

David Adam

For pre-school age to 5 years – Year C

Thought for the day

The gathered hopes of generations remind us to get ourselves ready, so that Christ's return will be a day of excitement and great joy.

Readings

Jeremiah 33:14-16
Psalm 25:1-10
1 Thessalonians 3:9-13
Luke 21:25-36

Aim

To help them understand getting ready for Christmas in terms of getting ready to meet Jesus in person.

Starter

Stop . . . Get ready . . . Go! Starting always from standing still in a space on their own, on the word 'Go!' the children do whatever the leader calls out (e.g. hop like rabbits, swim around like fish, slither like snakes). When the leader calls 'Stop!' the children stop and at 'Get ready!' they go to the starting position again.

Teaching

Draw their attention to the way they had to get ready for the game each time. Christmas is coming – whose birthday is it at Christmas? How are we going to get ready for Christmas?

Jesus told us that one day he would come back. We will be able to see him, either then or when we die, whichever happens first.

How can we get ready to meet Jesus? What would he like to see us doing?

During the discussion, make simple drawings of the way they think Jesus would like to see them living.

Praying

The children find a space on their own again. Taking the ideas they have come up with, lead the children to pray: 'Jesus, we want to be ready to meet you. Please help us to . . . (share our toys/forgive each other/be kind to our brothers and sisters, etc.)' and everyone mimes the activity. Then call out 'Stop!' and the children go back to their space for the next prayer.

Activities

Use the worksheet to reinforce the idea of getting ready for Christmas being linked with getting ready to meet Jesus.

Susan Sayers

For 6 to 10 years – Year A

Aim

To show the importance of looking and watching.

Readings

Isaiah 2:1-5
Psalm 122
Romans 13:11-14
Matthew 24:36-44

Teaching

(Start with the Activity.) Whenever we go anywhere we need to know the direction, so we have a map or a compass. Ask how these help with a journey. If we have been there before, we might not need these. But even when we go somewhere we know we have to watch where we are going and look out for traffic and anything dangerous.

The key is for the car. If you drive, you have to be very watchful. You cannot close your eyes or look away when you are driving. What sort of things do you have to look out for?

The watch is so that we know the time. There are some things that depend on us being on time and if we are too late, we will miss out. See if the children can give examples.

Mr Magoo is a comic character who never looks where he is going and gets into all sorts of dangers but just escapes. He walks out of a high window because he is not looking but a girder is being slowly lifted and he walks across it and lands on an opposite building. He steps on a hole in the ground and would have fallen in but the head of someone is coming out of the hole and Mr Magoo steps on it and goes on safely. He is so funny to watch because he does not look where he is going, but in real life he would be dangerous.

We all need to look where we are going. Some time someone will say to us, 'Look out' or 'Watch where you are going'. We need to use our eyes and be aware of what is around us.

Today is Advent Sunday. Who knows how many Sundays there are in Advent? It is the same every year. Advent is the beginning of the Church year and it is also the four Sundays before Christmas. Let us count them backwards together and then say: 'Christmas': '4, 3, 2, 1, Christmas.' Advent reminds us that it is soon time to celebrate that Jesus came to earth. Who was his mother? Who was her husband? Where was Jesus born (the name of the town and the place in that town)?

Advent means 'coming'. It reminds us that Christmas is coming but it also tells us God comes to us, Jesus comes to us and wants to be our friend. Too often we fail to meet Jesus because we do not look for him; we do not fix a time to be with him in prayer. We need to give more attention to the fact that God comes to us and that he loves us. Here is a special prayer for you to say each day, so that you can invite Jesus into your life and home:

Come to my heart, Lord Jesus, there is room in my heart for you.

Activity

Tell the children that we are to pretend we are going on a journey but we cannot begin until we find certain things. Tell them of the things you have hidden and ask them to find them: a watch, a map, a compass and a key. Ask them to look for them but not to touch them or to tell anyone else. Let each come to you when they know where the four things are. The last ones can be helped a little. Once all have seen the objects, get four people to bring the different things.

Prayer

Lord God, open our eyes to your presence,
open our ears to your call,
open our hearts to your love,
that we may be aware of you
and your coming to us.

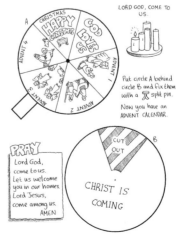

Susan Sayers

For 6 to 10 years – Year B

Thought for the day
Be alert and watchful; keep yourselves ready.

Readings
Isaiah 64:1-9
Psalm 80:1-7, 17-19
1 Corinthians 1:3-9
Mark 13:24-37

Aim
To know that Jesus will be coming back in glory.

Starter
Get ready to . . . Each time the children crouch in the 'get ready' position, and when you show a symbol of a particular activity, they have to mime it until the whistle blows for the 'stop and get ready' stage again. (Possible items might be a football, tennis racket, swimwear and goggles, a horse shoe and a paintbox.)

Teaching
Prepare the signs and symbols right to be placed on the floor during the teaching.

Explain that Advent means 'coming' and the person we're waiting and preparing for is Jesus. Now place down the '1st' rosette as you tell them about the first time Jesus came to earth. (Involve them and use what they already know.) As you discuss that first coming, place down the picture of the Nativity.

As you display the '2nd' rosette, tell them that the manger at Bethlehem wasn't the only time for Jesus to come to our earth. We are told in the Bible, by the prophets and by Jesus himself, that he will be coming again one day. Place down the 'When?', 'Where?', and 'How?' cards, and read excerpts from today's Gospel to find out the clues we have been given. Go over these in discussion, displaying the big question mark as you draw the clues together and establish that there is still lots we don't know (and even Jesus didn't know) about exact times and dates. What we do know is that it will happen, and we need to make sure we keep ourselves alert, so that we'll be ready for Jesus when he comes in glory.

Praying

Jesus, get us ready to meet you
when you come again in glory,
so that we can welcome you
when we see you face to face.

Activities

During Advent the children will be making a four-stage pop-up model which can eventually be a table centrepiece or a crib at home. Instructions and outlines are given for stage one on this week's worksheet. You may like them to mount the sheet on thin card to make it all stronger. They will need scissors that really work, and colouring materials. Try paints with thin brushes for a change. For younger children you could enlarge the sheets during Advent to A3.

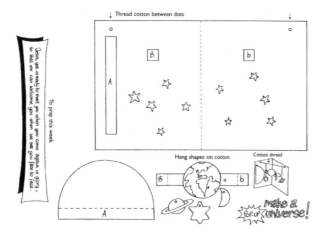

Susan Sayers

For 6 to 10 years – Year C

Aim

To look at the God who comes.

Readings

Jeremiah 33:14-16
Psalm 25:1-9
1 Thessalonians 3:9-13
Luke 21:25-36

Teaching

Who can tell me what we mean by past, present and future? Tell me something that has happened in the past; now something that is in the present; now something that is in the future. Who knows the words for the past and the future if the word for the present is 'is'? 'Was' is for the past and will 'be' is for the future. Because our God has always been and always will be, we can say, 'God was, God is, God will be'. Let us say that together. Now I will tell you about God in the past the present and the future:

Once upon a time, in the past, there was a man called Moses and God asked him to do some very hard things to get his people free. Moses had to take them across a big desert (check they know what a desert is); they had to go through burning hot land where there was no water. Then they had to walk through the sea. Moses was afraid that he was not strong enough but God said to him, 'Do not be afraid because I am with you.' God said he would not leave Moses on his own and this gave Moses strength.

Can you tell me of other people in the past who have known God was with them? (Encourage them to tell Bible stories and other stories.)

God has promised that in the future, whatever happens, he will be with us. Even when there are troubles in the world, even when the way is dark, God promises he will go with us and will care for us.

What is good to know is that God is always with us. He is with us now and we can speak to him. God loves us and wants us to love him.

Activity

Make a Christmas card with Joseph and Mary travelling towards Bethlehem. Look at the maze and help the travellers on their journey.

Prayer

God, you have always been ready to help your people.
You will be with us whatever happens.
Help us to know you are with us now.
Hurrah for the Lord is here:
his Spirit is with us.

Song

Learn at least the chorus of 'Do not be afraid'.

David Adam

Get ready!

Resources

- Music and words
- A flip chart or two large sheets of card. On the first sheet: *'Getting ready for Christmas – Things to do.'*
  On the second sheet: *'Getting ready for Jesus – Things to do.*
  1. Live our lives God's way. 2. Share God's good news.'
- Some marker pens
- A small bare tree branch with twigs
- Sticky tack
- 24 clean jam jars or glass tumblers
- Red, orange and yellow tissue paper
- Diluted PVA glue, poured into shallow dishes
- Baby wipes for sticky hands
- 24 tea lights
- Matches and tapers
- Fig tree illustration (*see note 1*)
- Timeline (*see note 2*)
- Numbers 1–24, cut out of paper (*see note 3*)

Leaders

Minimum: 1
- Leader

Optimum: 6

- Leader (Introduction and Conclusion)
- Storyteller
- Music Leader
- Explorer
- Activity Leader
- Prayer Leader

Suggestions for additional music

- Lo, he comes with clouds descending
- Great is the darkness

Service

Welcome

As people arrive, invite them to add items to your giant list: 'Getting ready for Christmas – Things to do.' For example, 'Write Christmas cards' and 'Order turkey'.

Introduction

Today is the first Sunday of Advent. Who has an Advent calendar at home? (Invite responses.) The countdown to Christmas is beginning, and as we can see from our long list of things to do, we have a lot of preparations to make. In our Advent services, as we look forward to Christmas, we think about waiting for Jesus and preparing for his arrival. Jesus' message in today's story is: get ready! Let's hear what he said.

Storytelling

Before Jesus died, he made a promise. He said that a lot of bad things would happen in the world, but that he would come back one day and put everything right: he would make sure that everything was done God's way. He called this the kingdom of God and said he would come in power and glory to establish it. He told his disciples that they had to be ready! He couldn't say when God's kingdom would come, so they had to look for the signs. This is how he explained it. *(Invite a volunteer to hold up the bare branch.)* 'It's like this fig tree. It is bare all winter – then leaves start to appear. *(Stick on the seven leaves with sticky tack, one by one, leaf-side outwards.)* When you see the leaves sprouting, you know that summer is on its way.' *(Invite another volunteer to hold up the picture of the sun.)*

Jesus said, 'It will be like this when I come back to earth. There will be signs that it's nearly time: *(Turn over each leaf in turn to show the words.)* there will be fighting in Jerusalem; there will be wars; there will be earthquakes; there will be hunger, illness and unhappiness. People will be worried and afraid. When you see all these things happening, you will know that the kingdom of God is near and I am on my way. *(Turn over the sun to show Jesus returning in glory.)* So get ready!'

Music

God is working his purpose out

Exploring

When Jesus knew he was going to die, he told his disciples what would happen in the future. He promised that he would come back, but that in the meantime, lots of things would go wrong – and these would all be signs that God's kingdom was just around the corner. Ever since, Christians have looked at the signs of the times and thought, 'This is it! Things are looking bad – Jesus must be coming back soon.' For example, when Jerusalem was destroyed by the Romans in AD 70, Christians at the time must have expected Jesus to come back then – but he didn't. An English Archbishop, (Wulfstan, Archbishop of York in the *Sermon of the Wolf to the English*) predicted Jesus' return when he preached a sermon about all the bad things around him: violent crime, dishonest people in power, high taxes and unusually bad weather. England was fighting a war and people had been killed. This could have been a sermon from last week – but in fact it was preached in 1014, and the war he was talking about was against the Vikings.

So if Christians throughout the last 2000 years have seen signs that Jesus is on his way, isn't it time he was here? If we are going to think about this question, we need to think about time. The earth is four thousand six hundred million years old. Let's make this huge amount of time easier to imagine by picturing the earth as 46 years old. Its life has been this long.

Invite two volunteers to unroll the timeline and hold it out so that you can point to the different years as you mention them.

It has taken all this time for the earth to become the place we know, full of forests, seas, deserts and mountains. The earth was 11 when the first microscopic blobs of life appeared. The simplest animals – such as worms – arrived when the earth was 40. Dinosaurs didn't exist until the earth was over 45 years old. In this version of earth's life, human civilisation began only two hours ago! Put like this, the time between Jesus' death and now is the blink of an eye. *(I am indebted to Arundhati Roy for this wonderful comparison: she compared the earth to a 46-year-old woman. This Earth Woman idea and the related facts and figures can be found in her book, The God of Small Things (Flamingo, 1997).*

We are certainly living in the time before Jesus returns, but we don't know how long that time will last. Only God knows, and from his point of view a few hundred or a few thousand years must look pretty much the same. In the meantime, Jesus left clear instructions about what we should do: be ready! He told his disciples to be prepared for his return by living good lives and spreading God's good news. So at this time of year, as our Advent calendars count us down to Christmas and we rush to make all our preparations for the big day, let's not forget that we need to get ready for the biggest day of all: the day when Jesus comes back in power and glory. Our 'To do' list for this is short and easy to remember: *(Flip over the Christmas 'To do' list to reveal a second, shorter list: 'Getting ready for Jesus – Things to do.')* We need to live our lives God's way and share God's good news, not just during Advent, but every day.

Activity

Getting ready for Jesus is often described as preparing the way. Today we will make special Advent candle holders, which we will use to light a pathway.

Invite people to gather round the craft tables and decorate the 24 plain glass jars or tumblers with flame-coloured tissue paper and a number for each one. Tear the tissue paper roughly into pieces and soak them in the diluted PVA – they will stick to the outside of the glass in colourful, overlapping layers. Stick the numbers on last, in the same way. As each glass is finished, place an unlit tea light inside it. Ask people to hold their Advent lights and move so that odd-numbered lights are on one side of the aisle and even-numbered ones on the other. Light the candles with a taper.

Now let's lay a path of Advent lights, as a reminder that we need to make way for Jesus in our lives.

Prayer action

Turn off the lights in church. Encourage people to lay down their Advent lights in order, 1–24, on either side of the aisle as it leads up to the altar.

As we look at this path of lights leading us through the days of Advent, let us pray with a simple Taizé chant: 'Wait for the Lord'.

Sing the chant together.
O Lord, show us your way.
Guide us in your truth.

Music
Lord of the future

Conclusion

Lord of the past, present and future,
may we remember your birth,
look forward to your coming
and know your presence with us now.

Notes

1. Fig tree illustration

Print the double-sided leaves on green card and cut out. Print the double-sided sun picture on white card and cut out. You may like to enlarge these visual aids to A3.

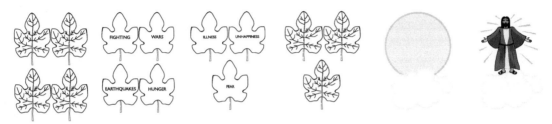

2. Timeline

You will need a 5m long roll of paper – lining paper is ideal. Draw a horizontal line along the length of the paper and mark it at 10cm intervals. Label the marks from 1-46.

3. Numbers 1-24, cut out of paper

Print on white paper and cut out.

Claire Benton-Evans

Advent 2

For pre-school age to 5 years – Year A

Thought for the day

Get the road ready for the Lord!

Readings

Isaiah 11:1-10
Psalm 72:1-7, 18-19
Romans 15:4-13
Matthew 3:1-12

Aim

To think about getting ready for Jesus at Christmas.

Starter

Ready, steady, go! Give the children different tasks to do (such as running to the back wall, jumping round a chair, hopping to a leader). Having explained the task, they have to wait until you say, 'Ready, steady, go!' before they start.

Teaching

Talk about getting ready for Christmas, and all the things going on at home and in the shops. Everyone has long lists of jobs to do and cards and presents to make or buy. Show some of your own scribbled lists. How can we get ourselves ready for Christmas? Show the children an Advent calendar, with a week of windows already opened, and then open today's window. The Church calls this time before Christmas 'Advent', which is another way of saying 'coming'. We can use this time to work on something we find hard to do, like sharing our toys, going to bed when we're told to, or remembering to help at home. (Talk over the ideas with the children.) We can do this as a present to give Jesus at Christmas.

Praying

Dear Jesus,
when I open today's window
in my Advent calendar
I remember the present
I am getting ready to give you.
Please help me to do it well.

Activities

Give each child some modelling clay to make the shape of them doing what they are working at during Advent. Here are some suggestions to help the children think of their own:

- Praying every day
- Helping at home in some way
- Telling the truth
- Sharing without getting cross
- Going to bed at the right time
- Feeding/cleaning out a pet

Next week the children will be making a box to put their model in, and the week after it will be wrapped up so that all the gifts can be part of the offering at Christmas.

Susan Sayers

For pre-school age to 5 years – Year B

Aim

To prepare for the coming of Jesus.

Readings

Isaiah 40:1-11
Psalm 85:1-2, 8-13.
2 Peter 3:8-15a
Mark 1:1-8

Teaching

Have you ever been sent with a message or been asked to go somewhere and get something? It is important that messengers carry the right message and don't get it wrong. If you were sent to the kitchen for a biscuit and brought back some soap, it would be wrong.

God has often sent messages to people and he makes sure they get the right message. God calls his messengers 'angels'.

Once, long ago, God sent a messenger – one of his angels – to a little town called Nazareth, to the house of a young woman called Mary. The angel knew exactly which house to go to. Mary had been outside in the garden working, looking after plants. Now she was having a quiet time in the house, waiting until her mother came home. Suddenly she saw God's messenger in the room. The door was open and she did not hear the messenger knock or come in, but suddenly he was there. Mary was frightened and hid her eyes. But the angel said to her, 'Do not be afraid, Mary. I come from God and God is very pleased with you. God knows that you love him and try to do what he wants. He now wants you to do something special; he wants you to have a baby that you will call Jesus.'

Mary was not really sure what the angel meant and asked him. Meanwhile, God and the messenger waited for her answer. (If possible, show a picture of Mary with the angel.) The angel told Mary that God would make it happen and that she would be the mother of Jesus.

Mary said, 'I will do what God wants.' The angel was very happy and went back to God to say he had delivered the message. And all the angels rejoiced.

Activity

We are going to pass on a message from one to another. I will whisper it and pass it on. 'God loves you.' See if we get it right.

We will colour in an angel for our Christmas crib – let it be gold and silver, if possible. Do you remember whom the angel came to last week?

How many candles are there to colour in?

Prayer

God, we thank you
that you sent the angel messenger to Mary
and that she let Jesus be born into the world.
We will try to do what you want us to do
because we know that you love us.

Song

Jesus bids us shine

David Adam

For pre-school age to 5 years – Year C

Thought for the day

It had been prophesied that there would be a messenger to prepare the way for the coming of the Messiah. Now John the Baptist appears with his urgent message of repentance.

Readings

Malachi 3:1-4
Canticle: Benedictus
Philippians 1:3-11
Luke 3:1-6

Aim

To understand that John was the messenger helping people get ready for Jesus.

Starter

Call and change. Sit round in a circle. One person calls someone else's name and these two change places. The one who was called becomes the next caller. This game helps build the group together, and is an acting-out of what John the Baptist was doing.

Teaching

Find out if any of the children have cousins, and what their names are. Point out that they may not live with you but they are members of your family.

Tell them that one of Jesus' cousins was John. And God had a job he needed John to do. When John was grown up God asked him to go and get people ready for Jesus.

How could he do that? First he went off on his own to pray. Then he started talking to the people. He said to them, 'Listen, I've got a message for you!'

'A message for us?' asked the people. 'What message have you got for us?'

'Well,' said John, 'we all need to get ready. Soon God will be coming to us, and we aren't ready for him yet.'

'How exciting!' said the people. 'You are right, we must be ready to welcome him. But what can we do?'

John said, 'God will want to find that we are kind and loving and being fair to one another.'

'Oh dear!' said the people. 'I'm afraid we're not always like that. Some of us have bad tempers and some of us are greedy and some of us want our own way all the time. But we do want to be ready. Please help us get ready.'

'All you have to do,' said John, 'is to be sorry about those things and want to put them right.'

'We are sorry,' said the people. 'We don't want to be bad tempered and greedy and wanting our own way all the time. We want to make God happy when he comes.'

'In that case,' said John, 'I will wash you in the river as a sign that your bad temper and greediness and wanting your own way all the time are washed away and you are forgiven.'

The people felt happy and free. They went back home to enjoy loving and sharing and being fair. It would not be easy, but they were determined to do their best.

Praying

Ask the children to sit with their hands closed up as if they are hiding something inside. Imagine that one hand holds something for which you want to thank God that you are good at. As you open that hand, think of showing the thing you are good at to God. Everyone says, 'Thank you, God, for making me good at this.' Imagine that in the other hand you are holding something you would like to be better at (telling the truth/being a good friend/helping at home). As you open this hand, think of showing God and say, 'Please, God, help me to be better at this.'

Activities

Use the worksheet to continue getting the crib ready for Christmas – today is the manger – and reinforce the teaching about John the Baptist.

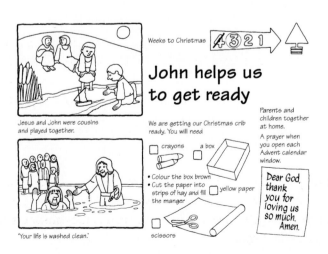

Susan Sayers

For 6 to 10 years – Year A

Aim

To learn about John the Baptist and the need to prepare.

Readings

Isaiah 11:1-10
Psalm 72:1-7, 18, 19
Romans 15:4-13
Matthew 3:1-12

Teaching

Who knows the motto of the Scouts? 'Be prepared'. Throughout our lives we need to prepare for various things. Every day meals need to be prepared – and there's special preparation for parties. We have to prepare for school and for any sport we will take part in. If we are going on a journey, we need to prepare – the car will need petrol, we may need tickets and passports, and we also need to know where we are going. What other preparations can you think of?

In the times of Jesus and John the Baptist, if a king was going on a journey, one of his main preparations was to send someone down the road before him. Because the roads were often just dirt tracks, this man had to make sure there were no dangerous holes in the road or big bumps. He had to ensure that the road was as level as possible for the coming of the king. Then he had to visit the places where the king was going and warn the people in advance. Then they could not say they did not know he was coming, and at the same time they could prepare for the coming of the king.

Before Jesus began his work John the Baptist tried to prepare the people for the coming of Jesus. He told them they were going in the wrong direction to meet the king and they should turn around. The word he used was 'repent'. That meant they should be sorry for the wrong things they were doing and seek to do what is right. John told them to be ready because Jesus was coming soon and Jesus was more powerful than John. A lot of people came to John and were baptised by him in the river Jordan. They were plunged into the river to show that their sins were washed away. He wanted people to be ready, to be prepared, for the coming of Jesus.

Which Sunday in Advent is this? It is the second Sunday. How many more Sundays are there until Christmas? Christmas is when we celebrate the coming of Jesus into the world and his coming into our lives. When Jesus came people were not ready for him; there was no room. So, where was he born?

You might have got all your cards written out, you may have bought your presents – who has? – but are you ready also to let Jesus into your life and your home? Are you prepared for Jesus coming and for him wanting to be friends with you? John the Baptist said, 'Prepare the way of the Lord.' Will we remember those words and get ready for Jesus?

Activity

Play 'In the river, on the bank'. Let the children stand in a circle and when you say, 'In the river', they have to jump forward. You can repeat it. If you say, 'On the bank', they have to jump backwards. If you say, 'On the river' or 'In the bank', they are not to move at all. Anyone who does the wrong thing is out.

Prayer

Jesus, we are getting ready
to celebrate your birthday.
Let us make sure we make room for you that day.
As you come to us in love,
may we come to you
and give you our love.

Song

Jesus, come among us
with your glorious light.
Jesus, come among us;
help us do what's right.

Jesus, come among us,
come now and every day.
Jesus, come among us;
hear us as we pray.

(Tune: Caswall, 'Glory be to Jesus')

David Adam

For 6 to 10 years – Year B

Thought for the day

John the Baptist prepares the way for the coming of the Messiah by helping the people to realign their lives.

Readings

Isaiah 40:1-11
Psalm 85:1-2, 8-13
2 Peter 3:8-15a
Mark 1:1-8

Aim

To hear about John the Baptist and his teaching about watching closely.

Starter

What's different? Get into pairs. Take it in turns for one to hide their eyes while the other changes something about the way they are standing or what they are wearing. See if the difference is recognised, then swap roles. Ideas for differences: cross arms in different way, hair tucked behind other ear, shoelace undone/done up, ring on different finger.

Teaching

Sometimes we don't notice things that we are used to seeing. Today we are going to look at someone who got people noticing things they had stopped looking at. (Have two people in conversation for this.)

What was his name?
His name was John. One day no one had heard of him and the next, there he was out in the wild desert outside Jerusalem, drawing huge crowds of people because of what he was saying. They felt he was telling them what they knew they needed to hear. They didn't come because what he said was easy – in fact, it was very challenging – but he made them feel they wanted to go for it with everything they had.

Go for what?
Sorting their lives out. They started to look closely at how they were really thinking and behaving – John helped them notice their own bad habits and the unloving, discontented way they were living. They suddenly wanted to put those things right. John told them it was like road-building.

Road-building?
Yes. He said they needed to build their lives like a good road ready for God to come to them, a road that was straight and true with no mountains of greed or empty pits of cruelty and grumbling. And they needed to start building it straight away.

Why?
Because John said it wouldn't be very long before God's Messiah was coming to live among them, and they all wanted to be ready for that.

So what did they do about their road-building?
Well, like I said, they had a good look at themselves, saw what needed to be changed, told God about it and then John washed them.

Washed them?
Yes, they waded into the local Jordan river, and when they confessed their sins John dipped them right under the water as a sign that their lives were being washed clean.

That's a good idea. You'd really feel you were making a fresh clean start if you were dipped right under water in a flowing river. Now they would feel they'd done what they could to be ready for the Messiah.

Yes, that's right. And we can do the same, you know.

We can?
Oh, yes. If we take a look at how we speak to people, and what we do for them, and what we don't do for them, we'll soon see which bits of our road need changing. Then we can tell God we've noticed them and are sorry.

What will God do?
He'll forgive us and give us a fresh start.
Perhaps we could do that in the bath or shower?
Good idea.

Praying

Loving God, open my eyes to see
what needs changing and putting right
in my thinking, speaking and doing,
because I want to turn away from sin
and turn towards you.

Activities

The children will be making Stage
Two of the Christmas pop-up model.
There are instructions and outlines
for this on the sheet. You may like
them to mount it all on thin card for
extra strength. As with all the Advent
sheets, younger children may find it
easier if it is enlarged to A3 size.

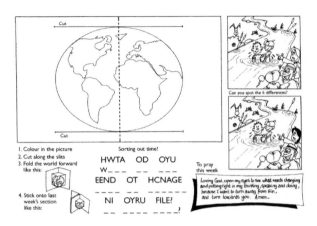

Susan Sayers

For 6 to 10 years – Year C

Aim

To tell the story of Zechariah and the birth of John the Baptist.

Readings

Baruch 5:1-9 or Malachi 3:1-4
Canticle: Benedictus – Luke 1:68-79
Philippians 1:3-11
Luke 3:1-6

Teaching

Who knows the name of the mother and father of John the Baptist? His mother's name was Elizabeth. Do you know anyone with this name? Elizabeth was married to Zechariah. That is a harder name to remember – let us say it together.

Zechariah and Elizabeth had no children. They would have liked to have had a son so that he could follow in the work of his father. Now they were getting old and did not think that they would ever have children.

Zechariah was a priest and often went to the Temple for services. At home he helped in the services of the synagogue (explain). He hoped that one day he might be asked to do something special at the Temple in Jerusalem and he was asked. He was asked to offer incense to God as a sign of worship and love. Only one person was allowed to do this for all the people, so he was in that part of the Temple by himself. Zechariah prayed to God that he might do the work properly and with love.

While he was making the offering, which caused a lot of smoke, he was surprised to see someone there in the room with him. He thought he would be on his own. Then he realised this was no ordinary person: this was a messenger from God. Do you know what a messenger from God is called? Yes, it was an angel. Zechariah began to shake with fear. But the angel said, 'Do not be afraid, for your prayer has been heard and your wife Elizabeth will have a son and you will call him John.'

Zechariah was not sure about this and doubted what the angel told him. So the angel said, 'Because you have doubted, you will now be unable to speak until the time when the baby is born.' Suddenly the smoke of the incense moved and the angel was gone. Zechariah wondered if he had dreamt it all. But when he tried to speak he found he could not. He opened his mouth but the sounds would not come out.

People were waiting for him to come out and say a prayer. They wondered why he was so long. When he did come out he could not speak to them; he had to make signs. When he went home Elizabeth was worried about his voice. But he made signs and wrote that his voice would come back.

While he was unable to speak to *people*, Zechariah could still speak to God in prayer. At last, after being silent for nine months, Zechariah held in his arms his own son. When they wanted to know the baby's name, Zechariah had to write it down. He wrote, 'His name is John.' As soon as he did this he was able to speak again and he sang a song to God.

What the angel said to him had come true. He had a little boy and he also had his voice back. The little boy grew up to be John the Baptist.

Activity

See if the children can mime different jobs – a carpenter, a driver, a footballer, a singer, a teacher, a priest. Some may like to mime what a parent does as a job, or jobs done around the house like hoovering, sweeping, washing-up or cooking.

Prayer

God, we thank you for our voices,
that we can speak and shout and sing.
Let us remember every day to speak to you in prayer.

Song

Come on and shine

Zechariah and the Angel

What was the name of Zechariah's wife?

What was their baby called?

God, we thank you for the birth of John the Baptist and for our own life. Amen

David Adam

131

A library guide for Bible Sunday

Text

2 Timothy 3:16

What's the point

Let's try and give people a small insight into the sheer wonderful variety of literature that the Bible contains.

Preparation

You will need:

- a simple grid, drawn on, for example, a flipchart pad or whiteboard, dividing it into sections marked 'History' Romance' 'Law/Ethics' 'Poetry' 'Adventure' 'Politics'– you may want to think of different ones, and that's fine, but bear in mind whatever space constraints you have

- 'Books of the Bible' cards, about postcard size, each bearing the name of one of the books of the Bible. You probably won't want to use all of them, but ensure a good range of genres to fit in with your chart. You'll need enough for every group to have perhaps two or three, no more than that, because you want them to have time to discuss, not just plump for the obvious category. It doesn't matter if they're duplicated.

- Sticky tack or other fixings
- one or two children on hand to manage the display

Activity

Get the congregation into groups, and draw attention to your chart. Give each group a few 'Books of the Bible' cards – it's probably best not to have them handed out with the hymn books in this instance, or people may be tempted to spend the first part of the service pondering – or even talking about – them! Ask them to decide where each book belongs in the 'Library'. Should it be in the History section, the Romance section; maybe it should be under Politics or Adventure? If it seems just too obvious, they can make it more interesting by cross-referencing the same book to other sections – it may fit into several – but the principal task is to decide between themselves on just the main classification. After an appropriate time, let someone from each group tell you about their decisions. They may want to say something about the discussions that they had, since the book seemed to fit into several sections. Then stick their card to the chart, in the chosen section, but point out where appropriate that that's just its main heading. If this were a real library you'd have to cross-reference it to a number of sections. If some of the categories people choose for particular books seem really wide of the mark to you, don't make an issue of it – it just shows what a wonderful variety of reading there is in the Bible: something for everyone, of whatever age, background or taste. You can finish up by summarising the point that the Bible really does have something for everyone. Whatever kind of reading people are into, there's something in this library for them!

Reading

2 Timothy 3:10-17

Now, you've seen me, haven't you? – watched the way I've behaved, my lifestyle, my faith, my patience, my love, my persistence, my persecutions, and the way I endured the troubles that came upon me in Antioch, Iconium and Lystra. I mean, did they have a go at me, or did they have a go at me! But God got me through all that, didn't he? Well, of course, for anyone who tries to live a godly life in Christ, persecution goes with the territory. And all sorts of bad people will go from bad to worse, deceiving themselves and others – but as for you, well, just keep to what you've learned, and accepted. And if in doubt, just remind yourself who you heard it from in the first place. I mean, you studied the scriptures right from childhood, didn't you, and that's how you came to salvation through faith in Christ. Every passage of scripture comes by God's own inspiration. Useful for all kinds of things, it is: teaching, criticism, correction, and for learning right and wrong – so that the people of God can be properly skilled and equipped for all the good things God's calling us to do.

Michael Forster

The voice in the wilderness

Resources

- Music and words
- Lots of empty boxes and containers
- Several large, plain sheets
- *(Optional)* Some pebbles and stones
- The Peters Projection map. A large, laminated version is produced by Oxfam and available from amazon.co.uk. Mount it on a portable pin board for this service
- Map pins (or spot stickers, if preferred)

Leaders

Minimum: 2
- Leader
- Storyteller

Optimum: 5
- Leader (Introduction and Conclusion)
- Storyteller
- Music Leader
- Explorer/Activity Leader
- Prayer Leader

Suggestions for additional music

- On Jordan's bank the Baptist's cry
- Inspired by love and anger

Service

Welcome

As people arrive, invite them to create a wilderness landscape at the front of church: use lots of different boxes and empty containers to make rough terrain, then cover the whole thing with large, plain sheets. You may like to add some pebbles and stones on top.

Music

Long ago, prophets knew

Introduction

Our Advent story today takes us to the wilderness. This was a wild, empty place near Jerusalem, full of mountains and deep crevasses, rather like the landscape we have created in church this morning. It was home to John the Baptist. Let's hear his story from the Bible.

Storytelling

Storyteller   In the fifteenth year of the reign of Emperor Tiberius, when Pontius Pilate was governor of Judea, and Herod was ruler of Galilee, and his brother Philip ruler of the region of Ituraea and Trachonitis, and Lysanias ruler of Abilene, during the high-priesthood of Annas and Caiaphas, the word of God came to John son of Zechariah in the wilderness.

Leader   I'm sorry to interrupt, but there were a lot of old emperors, kings and rulers in that bit! I wonder if we could bring John's story a bit more up to date? And make it a bit more local?

Storyteller   In the second year of *Barack Obama's* presidency, when *Queen Elizabeth II* was on the throne and *David Cameron* was Prime Minister of Great Britain, and *Michael D. Higgins* was the President of Ireland, during the time when *Rowan Williams* was Archbishop of Canterbury, the word of God came to Zach's son, John, in the middle of *Bodmin Moor*.* He went into all the surrounding areas, proclaiming a baptism of repentance for the forgiveness of sins, as it is written in the book of the words of the prophet Isaiah:

'The voice of one crying out in the wilderness: "Prepare the way of the Lord,
make his paths straight.
Every valley shall be filled,
and every mountain and hill shall be made low,
and the crooked shall be made straight,
and the rough ways made smooth;
and all flesh shall see the salvation of God."'

Did you notice something when we updated the first part of John's story? There was a great long list of important people, but we passed by them all and ended up with a man on his own

---

*   Replace the italics with current leaders and the last with a local area which might be described as 'wilderness'.

in the wilderness who had no title and no power – yet the word of God came to him. John, a wild loner, was chosen to be God's spokesman.

Let's have a closer look at what God's spokesman said. He went around 'proclaiming a baptism of repentance for the forgiveness of sins' – he told people to say sorry for the things they had done wrong, get baptised and be forgiven. In other words, he told people to change, because Jesus was on his way. The Gospel writer says that John was fulfilling an old prophecy about a lone voice in the wilderness, crying out for change before the Saviour comes. The prophecy used a powerful image:

> Every valley shall be filled,
> and every mountain and hill shall be made low,
> and the crooked shall be made straight,
> and the rough ways made smooth.

This voice calls for a change so radical, so momentous, it would be like a reshaping of geography. Look again at the wilderness landscape we made earlier, with all its hills and valleys. Can we transform it into a flat plain? Come and help me move mountains!

Encourage everyone to come forward and rearrange the boxes and empty containers to make a level plain. Cover it again with the sheets.

This changed landscape gives us a picture of the kind of change John was calling for. He wanted people to transform their lives by leaving their old ways behind them and starting afresh, with their sights set on Jesus. This change would cause such an upheaval it would be like moving mountains – but it would be a change for the better. This hilly desert is now a flat plain, which is much easier to cross; John wanted people to change their lives so that they would be readier to follow Jesus.

John the Baptist gives us a clear picture of what a prophet is like. As our updated version of his story showed, he was an ordinary person with no political power – and yet God chose him to call for change. He spoke with authority, 'proclaiming' what people needed to do. So this prophet was an ordinary person who spoke with authority about the need for change. Does this description ring any bells? Prophets did not die out in biblical times: all around us today there are ordinary people protesting about the way things are and crying out for change. Not all these voices are true, but we need to listen to them to decide whether God is speaking through any of them. Some call us to stop relying on fossil fuels or capitalism, and changes like this would be as massive as turning a hilly desert into a flat plain.

Let's look at just one example which, coincidentally, concerns geography. Two ordinary men worked on ideas for a new map of the world. One was a clergyman called Gall and the other was an amateur historian called Peters. The map Peters produced, using Gall's ideas, presented all the countries of the world based on exact comparisons of their surface area. It looks like this.

Hold up the Peters Projection map.

On traditional maps, Greenland looks the same size as Africa. In fact, Africa is 14 times larger, so this map accurately represents that huge difference in size. Come and have a closer look at this new way of seeing the world.

Encourage people to come forward. Allow plenty of time for them to look and ask questions.

This new map has changed the way many people think, because it challenges our assumptions about wealth and power. The richest countries are not necessarily the biggest; the countries which dominate the map contain some of the largest populations and the poorest people. Many charities and political organisations now use this map to try and change the way people think.

This map is just one example of what we might call a modern prophetic voice, calling for change. So remember John the Baptist – the lone voice in the wilderness – and keep your eyes and ears open for other prophets. They will be calling for change, calling us to move mountains, calling us to change the world!

Prayer action

We regularly say prayers for the world: today we will use this new view of the world to help us picture it accurately as we pray for particular people and places. In a time of quiet, bring before God those individuals or countries for whom you would like to pray. Come forward and place a pin in the map to mark the subject of your prayer.

Place your own pin in the map and encourage others to do so during a period of silence.

Creator God,
you hold the world in your hands.
Hear our prayers
in Jesus' name.

Music

Make way, make way

Conclusion

Lord of the wilderness,
as we go out into the world,
may we hear the cries for change
and listen for the call of your Holy Spirit.

Claire Benton-Evans

Advent 3

For pre-school age to 5 years – Year A

Thought for the day

Great expectations. Jesus fulfils the great statements of prophecy.

Readings

Isaiah 35:1-10
Psalm 146:5-10 or Canticle: Magnificat
James 5:7-10
Matthew 11:2-11

Aim

To know that God is more wonderful than we can ever imagine, and to continue getting ready for Christmas.

Starter

Pass the parcel. Inside is a giant balloon, ready to be blown up, with the word 'God' written on it (OHP pens work well). During the game play or sing *Our God is so great.*

Teaching

Tell the children what it says on the balloon, and talk about how small the balloon and the word are at the moment. Is God really small and unimportant like this? No! God is the one who made the world and everything in it. (Start to blow up the balloon.)

Is that all? No! God is the one who knows and loves each of us by name. (Blow up the balloon some more.)

Is that all? What else do we know about the one true God? Collect their suggestions, making the balloon bigger with each one. Add other characteristics yourself:

- He's always ready to listen to us.
- Jesus came to show us how kind and loving he is.
- He helps us when we are sad or ill or frightened.
- He has always been alive and always will be.
- He helps us to be kind and loving and fair.

At each quality, inflate the balloon so that it is huge, and draw attention to how big God's name is now. Our God is more powerful and wonderful and loving and kind than we can ever imagine, and yet he wants to be friends with us! And he's the best friend you could ever hope to have, because he loves you, and is always there for you and will never let you down.

Praying

Our God is so big,
so strong and so mighty,
there's nothing our God cannot do!

Activities

Using the net below as a guide, cut out the shapes for the boxes from coloured paper. Help the children to assemble the boxes as shown, and place their models from last week inside, talking about what they represent and how their 'present' for Jesus is going. Encourage them in what they are doing.

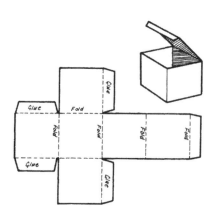

For pre-school age to 5 years – Year B

Aim
To continue with the Christmas story.

Readings
Isaiah 61:1-4, 8-11
Psalm 126 or the Magnificat
1 Thessalonians 5:16-24
John 1:6-8, 19-28

Teaching
Who can remember what we call God's messengers? The messengers were sent to the shepherds and to Mary. (If there is no reply, get them to look at the angels they have made.)

Mary told Joseph how the angel came to her and said that she would have a baby. Joseph wished the angel would come and speak to him. He looked for it all day but it did not come. Then at night, when it was dark and he was asleep, the angel came and spoke to him in a dream. The angel had a message for Joseph: 'Joseph, son of David, I want you to look after Mary and the baby she is going to have. You must call the baby Jesus because he will save his people.' When Joseph woke up he thought about his strange dream. He would look after Mary and call the baby Jesus.

Now Joseph had to get ready to go on a long journey and take Mary with him. They were going to go from Nazareth, where they lived, right down to Bethlehem to have their names written in a book. It was about 76 miles. If we had to go that far we would go by car or by train. Joseph would walk and Mary would walk with him or ride on their donkey. They would have to walk every day for a whole week. They would be very tired. Mary would be especially tired because her baby was soon to be born.

Near the end of the week they went past Jerusalem. There were lots of other people walking and riding camels, horses or donkeys. They had six miles to go and they were very slow because Mary could not go any faster. Joseph looked after her and helped her. At last they could see Bethlehem and they could see the fires in the hillsides where the shepherds were looking after their sheep.

It was now quite dark. Joseph looked up at the stars and said thank you to God that Mary had got safely to Bethlehem; it would be good if her baby was born there.

Activity
We are going to colour in Joseph and Mary and then we will colour in three candles for three Sundays in Advent. Do you know how many more Sundays there are in Advent?

Prayer
God, we thank you for the message of the angels
and for Mary and Joseph.
As we look forward to Christmas
help us to know that Jesus comes to us.

Song

Jesus' love is very wonderful

David Adam

For pre-school age to 5 years – Year C

Thought for the day

Our period of preparation shifts from repentance and forgiveness to the freed exhilaration of hope, as the momentous truth of God's immanence begins to dawn on us.

Readings

Zephaniah 3:14-20
Canticle: Isaiah 12:2-6
Philippians 4:4-7
Luke 3:7-18

Aim

To celebrate looking forward to Christmas as a time of God's love being shown to us.

Starter

I'm thinking of someone . . . Everyone sits in a circle and tries to guess who you are thinking of. Start with something that could refer to lots of children (he's a boy/wearing a sweater) and gradually get more specific (his shoes have green dinosaurs on the bottom) until lots of children know who you mean. Everyone says, 'God made Jack and God loves Jack.'

Teaching

Beforehand, get a good quality picture of the nativity (from a Christmas card) and put it in a box. Wrap the box in Christmas paper. We will use this during the teaching.

Get out some wrapping paper and scissors, and let the children guess what they are used for. Talk about why we give each other presents at Christmas, and establish that it isn't because we want something back but because we love the people and want them to see that we love them.

Now remind them of the starter activity and how God knows and loves each of us. Explain that at the first Christmas he gave the world the best Christmas present ever, not because he wanted anything back, but just because he loves us so much. Show the Christmas present. What was God's Christmas present to the world, to show he loves us? Open the present and let the children see that it is Jesus.

Praying

As you hold the Christmas present and then open it and hold up the picture, say this prayer together:

Thank you, God,
for loving the world so much
that you gave us Jesus
to be with us for ever.

Activities

Use the worksheet to continue getting ready for Christmas by making the crib – this week it's Mary, Joseph and Jesus. The present-wrapping activity will need a variety of small pieces of Christmas paper.

Susan Sayers

For 6 to 10 years – Year A

Aim

To show Jesus as the One who is to come.

Readings

Isaiah 35:1-10
Psalm 146:5-10 or Canticle: Magnificat
James 5:7-10
Matthew 11:2-11

Teaching

Who remembers last week's story? It was about John the Baptist. Can you tell me what he said to people and what he did? He wanted people to do what God wanted, to do what was right and not wrong. He told people when they were going the wrong way and asked them to turn around. He also took them to the river and dipped them in the water to show how God made them clean.

This week we hear that John the Baptist is a prisoner in a castle. He had done nothing wrong but he had spoken against King Herod. John said the king had done wrong and wicked things. The king was angry with John for saying this about him and he locked him up in a castle. While John was there he wondered what was happening to Jesus and if Jesus was the special person God had promised. He sent some of his disciples to ask Jesus, 'Are you the One who is to come or do we look for another?' (What do you think he meant by this?)

Jesus sent a message back. He told John's disciples, 'Tell John what I am doing. He will understand that I am doing what is expected from the Promised One. Tell him that the blind receive their sight, the lame walk, lepers are cleansed, the deaf hear, the dead are raised up and the poor have the good news brought to them.' Not everyone could do the things that Jesus was doing. The wonderful things Jesus did pointed to the fact that he was God's Chosen One: the One who people were waiting for. John would know that these are the things that the Christ would do. Can you tell me any of the other wonderful things that Jesus did?

We do not know what John said when his disciples told him of all that was happening but he must have felt pleased to know that God's work was being done and that Jesus was God's Promised One.

Activity

The worksheet looks at the question John asked and then gets the children to act like detectives and look at the evidence.

Prayer

Jesus, help us to know you as our friend
and as our Saviour and our God.
We thank you for all the wonderful things you do.
Help us to know your power and your love.

Song

What a wonderful Saviour is Jesus

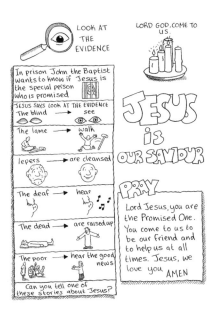

David Adam

For 6 to 10 years – Year B

Thought for the day

In Jesus, God will be fulfilling the Messianic prophecies about the promised Saviour.

Readings

Isaiah 61:1-4, 8-11
Psalm 126 or Canticle: Magnificat
1 Thessalonians 5:16-24
John 1:6-8, 19-28

Aim

To know that the prophets foretold the coming of Jesus, and Jesus fulfilled these prophecies.

Starter

The next object is… Have a number of objects hidden from view. Give out a short description of an item, such as: 'This object is black and white and re(a)d.' The children raise their hand when the item matching the description is shown. Show several other items before showing a newspaper, which fits the description, even though it may be slightly different from what was expected. Here are some other ideas:

- The next object has a face all the time (a clock)
- The next object is for the heads of li(e)rs (a pillow)
- The next object is to play with when you get round to it (a ball)
- The next object is put up at the down times (an umbrella)

Teaching

Talk about how we knew what to look out for in that game, so we could recognise the object when it appeared. And sometimes we understood the description better after we'd seen the object.

Today we are looking at some of the things the prophets said to describe the coming Messiah, long before Jesus was born. When Jesus did appear on earth, those things came true, and people found they understood them better than they had before.

On a large sheet of coloured paper, draw an outline of Jesus, his arms stretched out in welcome, based on the picture right, and lay this on the floor. On top of it have a sheet of the same size but different colour, which has been cut into sections. On each section have written out the different section of Isaiah's prophecy. Across all these lay a title on white paper which says 'Messiah' on one side and 'Christ' on the reverse. It should all look like this:

Tell the good news to the poor	Comfort the broken-hearted
Set free those feeling imprisoned	Announce the time when God would show his merciful judgement
Give people clothes of praise and joy to replace their sadness	Be fair to everyone
Make what is right grow strong	Put wrong things right

Explain how the prophets were sent by God to prepare the people for the coming of his chosen one. The Hebrew word for this anointed, chosen person was 'Messiah'. The Greek word was 'Christ'. (Turn the title over and back as you say this. Leave it on the Messiah side.) As the Old Testament is written in Hebrew, we'll stick with their word, Messiah, while they are waiting for him to come.

In order to help the people get ready, God spoke through the prophets to tell them what the Messiah would be like when he came. That way they could recognise him, and be ready for him. Let's look at some of the things they said about this Messiah. Lay the Messiah title at the side, and look at the sections, one by one, with all the readers reading them out. In turn take each section off and lay them all around the emerging picture. Gradually we can see that all these descriptions fit the Jesus we know from the Gospels. And as the New Testament was written in Greek, we'll use the Greek word for him: the Christ. (Reverse the title.)

Praying

Jesus, Jesus, we have come to see
that you must really be
the Son of God our Father.
We've been with you and we all agree
that only in your service
can the world be truly free!

Activities

On the sheet the preparations continue for the third stage of the Christmas pop-up model. Instructions and outlines are provided, but you may wish to strengthen the models with thin card. Also, if time permits, look at how the Bible is split into Old and New Testaments, and look at the names of the prophets, flicking through the Old Testament to find the books of Isaiah, Jeremiah and the others.

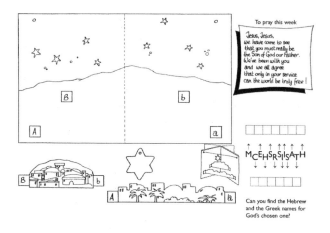

Susan Sayers

For 6 to 10 years – Year C

Aim
To begin the Christmas story with the journey to Bethlehem.

Readings
Zephaniah 3:14-20
Canticle: Isaiah 12:2-6
Philippians 4:4-7
Luke 3:7-18

Teaching
Who has ever gone on a long walk? What is the longest distance you think you have ever walked? You may have been on a walking holiday and camped out each night.

Before the days of cars the fastest people could travel would be on a horse. A donkey was often used but it did not go so fast. Most people walked to wherever they were going.

I want you to imagine how long it would take you to walk to . . . (give an example of a well-known place about 80 miles from home). What would you need for the journey? You would certainly need some food. You may need to have a tent or some money to stay in a hotel. You might like to take a first-aid kit. Let us pretend we are setting off. We have a pack on our back and a stick in our hand. We will go around the room marching and singing, 'We are marching in the light of God'. Let us first stand still and practise singing.

Now that we have marched around the room, I will tell you of a journey. (If possible, show a map of the Holy Land.) We are going to go from Nazareth to Bethlehem. Can someone come and show me where Nazareth is and where Bethlehem is? It is not far on a map – our fingers could walk it very quickly. But it is as far as (name a place) is from here.

Now this was the journey that Joseph was getting ready to go on. He had put some food on the donkey and some water. He put a blanket on the donkey for Mary and a small rolled-up tent on the back. Joseph would walk all the way. After they left Nazareth they would go down by the hills of Samaria, travelling near the river Jordan. They would then pass by the edge of Jerusalem. There were lots of people on the road: many were walking, some were on donkeys, camels or horses. The road was very busy and at night there were many tents and campfires. Because Mary was soon going to have her baby she was very tired.

Not long after Jerusalem, Joseph and Mary had only six miles to go but Mary was very slow. She was frightened that the baby might be born on the journey. Joseph looked after her very carefully until at last they reached Bethlehem. As they entered the city it was getting quite dark. The shepherds had already lit fires on the hillsides. Joseph said a big thank-you to God for they had arrived safely.

Activity
March around the room to the music 'We are marching'. When the music is turned down, the last one to stop is out, as is anyone who stops marching when the music is playing.

Prayer
God, we thank you that wherever we go you are there.
You never leave us
and are always ready to help us and hear us.

Song

We are marching in the light of God

David Adam

Love in action

Resources

- Advent wreath, votive candles and matches
- A Christmas parcel
- Toy animals, some with bandages, eye patches etc.
- Any *Doctor Who* prop or sound effect, such as a Sonic Screwdriver, a snatch of the theme tune or the distinctive sound of the TARDIS
- A scarf and a walking stick, to plant on volunteers
- Fur/animal skin for John
- Chains for John
- Dark robe for Disciple
- White robe for Jesus
- Copies of the heart puzzle *(see note)* and envelopes
- Pens and pencils
- Music and words
- A long piece of elastic *(at least 4 m)*, with the ends firmly knotted together

Leaders

Minimum: 5
- Leader/cast member
- Cast/Storytellers x 4

Optimum: 9
- Leader (Introduction and Conclusion)
- Three Storytellers (John, Disciple and Jesus)
- Music Leader
- Explorer
- Prayer Leader
- Cast x 5 (may also be Storytellers)

  The Postman/woman, wearing a navy jacket and a big bag

  The Vet, wearing white or green

  Doctor Who, wearing anything recognisable as the current Doctor

  The Scruff/Doctor, wearing messy or unexpected clothes (such as a hippy, biker or goth outfit)

  Injured person

Suggestions for additional music
- Tell out, my soul
- We have a gospel to proclaim
- Will you come and follow me

Service

Welcome
Light a votive candle each and then the Advent Candle.

Introduction
This Sunday in Advent we remember John the Baptist, God's messenger who was sent to prepare the way for the Messiah. John knew this was his purpose in life, but how did he know that Jesus was the One? How could he be sure that Jesus was the Son of God he had spent his life preparing for? Today we will be thinking about how we can know this, too. We will start with a sketch about a different kind of messenger who is looking for someone.

Activity

Postman	*(Addressing the congregation)* Excuse me, I'm trying to deliver this Christmas present. It says here it's for the Doctor, but the address has been torn off. So I need to look for someone who might be a doctor. Here's someone now . . .

Vet walks on, surrounded by toy animals – many in bandages.

Postman	Well, this person certainly looks kind, and they obviously know how to use bandages. Excuse me, are you the Doctor?
Vet	Sorry – I do help the sick, but I'm a vet. I only look after animals.
Postman	Oh. Never mind, here's someone else. Who's this?

Doctor Who walks on. Someone shouts, 'Doctor Who!'

Postman	Doctor – who? So he's the Doctor I'm looking for! Excuse me, sir, I think this Christmas present is for you.
Doctor Who	Christmas present? I wouldn't even be in this dimension if the TARDIS hadn't malfunctioned! Sorry – I don't think it can be for me.
Postman	Oh well – I thought, as your name was the Doctor – but never mind.

Scruffy person rushes on from the back and speaks to the people watching.

Scruff	Can I have that scarf? And that walking stick? And I'll need that chair.

Taking these items to the front, the Scruff then helps a hobbling person on, sits them down and proceeds to bandage their leg with a makeshift splint.

Postman	Well this person looks too much of a mess to be a proper doctor, and they've got no manners – fancy taking all your stuff like that! But they do seem to know what they are doing.
Injured person	Thank you, that feels so much better.
Postman	I wonder – are you the Doctor?
Scruff	Look at this: what do you think?
Postman	*(To the people)* What do you think? Is this the Doctor I've been looking for?
All	YES!
Postman	At last! *(Hands over parcel)* Then this is for you. Merry Christmas!

Music

Love came down at Christmas

Leader

Today's Bible story begins with John the Baptist. He has been thrown into prison because of everything he had been saying about the coming of the Saviour. This is what happened. *(After John's first question, the lines are taken directly from Matthew's Gospel (NRSV): you may prefer to use a different translation.)*

Storytelling

Jesus is unwrapping the leg of the injured person from the last scene and encouraging him/her to stand. The disciple is a little distance away, with John in chains.

John	Go on – ask him. Is he the One?

Disciple	*(To Jesus)* Are you the one who is to come, or are we to wait for another?
Jesus	Go and tell John what you hear and see: the blind receive their sight, the lame walk, the lepers are cleansed, the deaf hear, the dead are raised, and the poor have good news brought to them. And blessed is anyone who takes no offence at me.

(To the crowd) What did you go out into the wilderness to look at? A reed shaken by the wind? What then did you go out to see? Someone dressed in soft robes? Look, those who wear soft robes are in royal palaces. What then did you go out to see? A prophet? Yes, I tell you, and more than a prophet.

(Pointing at John) This is the one about whom it is written,
'See, I am sending my messenger ahead of you,
who will prepare your way before you.'
Truly I tell you, among those born of women no one has arisen greater than John the Baptist; yet the least in the kingdom of heaven is greater than he.

Exploring

In our sketch, the postman found who he was looking for not because of the Doctor's appearance or title, but because of what he/she actually did. Today's Bible story is all about actions speaking louder than words. John wants an answer: who is this Jesus? Is he the Messiah? Jesus says simply, 'Look at what I do: I heal the sick, raise the dead, bring good news to the poor.' He lets what he does explain who he is.

I wonder what our own actions say about us? In front of you, you will find a three-piece puzzle. Take the section labelled, 'Knowing ourselves' and on the back of it, write down anything you do which shows other people the best of you.

Allow a few minutes for everyone to do this. You may need to start people off by asking,
'Have you helped anyone? Done a kind thing? Sacrificed something for the sake of others?'

Now take the second section, 'Knowing others'. Do we judge other people by what they are or by what they do? On the back of this piece, write anything that other people have done for you which has shown you the best of them.

Allow a few minutes for everyone to do this. You may need to start people off by asking, 'Has anyone helped you? Done a kind thing? Sacrificed something for your sake?'

Now take the third section, 'Knowing God', and do the same thing. What has God done to show us the best of himself?

Allow a few minutes for everyone to do this.

God showed himself to us when he gave us his Son. Through Jesus and the things that he did, we know who God is: God is love. These pieces fit together to form a shape to remind us of this. What is it? *(Give everyone a moment to form the shape of a heart, then hold up your own fitted-together shape.)* This is what God is all about, and this is what the best part of each of us is all about, too. Love.

Take the big circle of elastic and invite volunteers to help you lay it out in the shape of a big cross on the floor.

Prayer action

In our prayers today, we will use this shape to help us understand who and what God is. God showed us himself in his Son, Jesus. Jesus loved us so much that he died for us on the cross.

(Then get everyone to move the elastic into the shape of a heart.)

This shows us what God is: God is love. And his love is so big and long and wide and stretchy that it includes us all.

(Invite everyone to step inside the heart shape, picking it up and stretching it out to reach round everyone.)

Loving God,
thank you for our love for each other.
Thank you for your love for us,
which surrounds us and includes us,
whoever and wherever we are.

Music

Wide, wide as the ocean

Conclusion

Love is the heart of the Gospel and we live out the Gospel most powerfully in our lives when we show people what love means, rather than merely telling them about it.

I leave with you the command which St Francis of Assisi gave to his followers: 'Go – preach the Gospel. If necessary, use words.'

Let us pray:

Lord Jesus,
John knew you
when he saw your love in action;
may we know you, too,
through the love in our lives.
As we look towards Christmas,
may we share the good news of your love
in all that we say and do.

Claire Benton-Evans

Note

Heart puzzle

Print out, copy onto A3 card or paper then cut out the heart shapes and the component pieces along the solid lines; place each puzzle in an envelope.*

Claire Benton-Evans

* This 'divided heart' idea was inspired by the Godly Play story, 'The Ten Best Ways'.

Advent 4

For pre-school age to 5 years – Year A

Thought for the day

Through the willing participation of Mary and Joseph, God is poised to come among his people as their Saviour.

Readings

Isaiah 7:10-16
Psalm 80:1-7,17-19
Romans 1:1-7
Matthew 1:18-25

Aim

To see that we can help God.

Starter

Have a selection of jigsaws and other puzzles that the children can work on together, with the leader encouraging everyone to help each other.

Teaching

Draw attention to the way we all helped each other, and how good that was. Talk about what people say when they are asked to help with something. Sometimes they say things like:

'No, I don't want to.'
'No, I'm too busy.'
'No, it's too hard.'

(You could use different toys or puppets to say these things.)

Sometimes when people are asked to help they say things like:

'Yes, I'd love to.'
'Yes, I'll do that for you.'
'Yes, it sounds hard but I'll do my best.'

God needed some help for his plan to save his people. He asked Mary to help him by being Jesus' mum. He asked Joseph to help him by looking after Mary and the baby Jesus. Mary and Joseph could have said, 'No, I don't want to' (and the other refusals). The children can join in, doing the thumbs-down sign each time. But they didn't say that! They said 'Yes!' (thumbs up). So God got the help he needed, and Jesus came into the world at the first Christmas to save us and set us free.

Praying

Dear God,
when you want someone to help,
ask me.
I don't want to say 'No!' (thumbs down)
I want to say 'Yes!' (thumbs up)

Activities

This week we are making the wrapping paper to wrap our present to God. Remind the children of their models, and print some paper with stencils or shapes dipped in paint. Wrap the box which can then be offered to God on Christmas Day. Encourage the children to keep up their resolution and offer God what they have tried their best to do. On the worksheet there is a picture to colour of Mary and Joseph going in to Bethlehem.

Susan Sayers

For pre-school age to 5 years – Year B

Aim

To enter into the joy of the coming of Jesus.

Readings

2 Samuel 7:1-11, 16
Magnificat or Psalm 89:1-4, 19-26
Romans 16:25-27
Luke 1:26-38

Teaching

Can you remember last week when Joseph and Mary set off to walk to Bethlehem? Well, they have walked all week except Saturday, the Sabbath, when they worshipped in the synagogue (church). Every day, Monday to Friday, they walked miles. When Mary was tired she sat on the donkey but she walked a good bit of the time. Now she was very tired – and the donkey was tired. They were walking more slowly than most other people, and it would be getting dark when they arrived in Bethlehem. The stars were coming out in the sky and they could see the fires the shepherds had lit in the hills to frighten away wild beasts. Joseph wished Mary would go a little faster but knew she could not for she was soon to have her baby. When they got to Bethlehem all the inns were full of people. At the last place they tried, Mary could hear the noise and the singing, the place was crowded; she prayed that she could have somewhere quiet.

Joseph brought the innkeeper to see Mary. He explained that there was no room, but he had a quiet cave behind the inn. If Mary did not mind sharing it with the cow and the hens, she could make herself comfortable there. How pleased Mary was: this was better than a noisy inn. Now she could settle down.

As she rested she listened to the cow munching hay and the hens quietly clucking.

She knew the time had come: the baby Jesus was to be born in the stable. She was so happy. There in the quiet, with Joseph looking after her, the baby Jesus came, and Mary and Joseph gave him their love. Mary hugged the baby and said, 'Hello, Jesus.'

Activity

We know that Jesus was born on Christmas Day. Let us colour in the picture of Jesus lying in the cradle of hay. Then we will put all our nativity figures together so that we can take them into church (or take them home). Some of the figures could be used on Christmas Day. If there is time, let the children talk about the crib figures.

Prayer

God, we thank you
for the coming of Jesus into the world
and for loving us.

Song

Away in a manger

David Adam

For pre-school age to 5 years – Year C

Thought for the day

When we co-operate with God amazing things happen.

Readings

Micah 5:2-5a
Canticle: Magnificat or Psalm 80:1-7
Hebrews 10:5-10
Luke 1:39-45 (46-55)

Aim

To understand that Mary was happy to work with God.

Starter

Working together. Ask the children to help you do various jobs as you get ready for the session. If you have access to a parachute, play some parachute games which need everyone to work together (such as 'mushroom', 'roll the ball' or tent making). Alternatively have everyone helping to make a 'Happy Christmas' frieze for the church.

Teaching

Point out how we all worked together in that activity. What jobs do they help with at home? Each time emphasise the co-operation that gets the job done well.

Use rag dolls or cut-out figures to tell the story.

God needed a very important job done. He needed someone to bring Jesus into our world and look after him. So he looked around and saw just the right person: Mary. He didn't choose her because she was rich or pretty or clever. He chose her because she was ready to work with God. She was already friends with him. She talked to him and listened to him in her prayers each day, and tried to live as God wanted her to. (How was that?)

So one day God told her he had chosen her to be the mother of Jesus. Mary was very surprised. It was such an important job, and she knew it would be a hard job to do well. What do you think – did she say yes or no?

Mary said 'Yes!' and went off to visit her cousin Elizabeth who lived in another town. Elizabeth was going to have a baby, too. You remember John the Baptist we met last week? Well, it was him, only he hadn't been born yet when Mary went to see his mother.

As soon as they met they hugged and kissed, and John started leaping about inside his mum because he was so excited! (Have you ever felt a baby moving about inside your mum? It's a funny feeling.)

Mary didn't need to tell Elizabeth her news. Elizabeth seemed to know already, and they sang and danced to praise God for being so wonderful.

Praying

Leader	Dear God, when you want us to be kind, help us to say
All	Yes!
Leader	When you want us to be honest, help us to say
All	Yes!
Leader	When you want us to help someone, help us to say
All	Yes!

Activities

The worksheet helps the children to complete their Christmas crib today, so these can be blessed in church and taken home. They are also going over the main points of today's story.

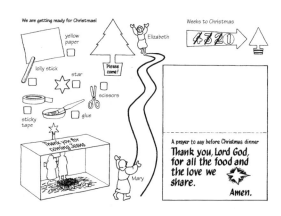

Susan Sayers

For 6 to 10 years – Year A

Aim

To look at the coming of Jesus through the eyes of Joseph.

Readings

Isaiah 7:10-16
Psalm 80:1-7, 16-18
Romans 1:1-7
Matthew 1:18-25

Teaching

Who can tell me how Mary discovered she could be the mother of Jesus? The angel Gabriel came from God and told her that if she was willing she would become the mother of Jesus.

At this time Mary was preparing to marry Joseph. In fact, everyone was already calling them man and wife. Joseph was looking forward to marrying Mary. But when he heard she was going to have a baby he was not so happy. It was not his baby, so why should he look after it? He was upset and decided to send Mary back home to her parents. Joseph thought they could have the job of looking after her and her baby. Though he planned to do this it made Joseph very sad. He did love Mary.

One night, after he had finished working in his carpenter's shop and gone to bed, Joseph had a dream. He remembered this dream for always. In his dream an angel came to him, just as an angel had come to Mary. The angel spoke to him and said, 'Joseph, son of David, do not be afraid to take Mary as your wife, for the child conceived in her is from the Holy Spirit.' So Joseph now knew what Mary had told him was true. The angel then said, 'She will bear a son and you are to name him Jesus, for he will save his people from their sins.' Joseph was not sure he understood all this but he did know he was to give the baby his name and so call him his own son. He knew that the baby was to be called Jesus and that is the same as Joshua and it means 'God saves'.

Joseph knew he would do what the angel had said. He would not send Mary away but he would love her and the baby Jesus.

Activity

On the worksheet there is a picture to make showing the angel appearing to Joseph. Using finger paints, the group could make a big banner that says 'GOD SAVES' and show the Christ child in a manger.

Prayer

God, we thank you for Joseph
and that he cared for Mary.
We are glad he did what you asked him to do.
Help us to do what you want us to do.

Song

The world was in darkness

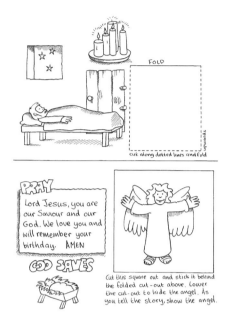

David Adam

For 6 to 10 years – Year B

Thought for the day

God's promised kingdom, announced both to King David in ancient times and to Mary by the angel Gabriel, will go on for ever.

Readings

2 Samuel 7, 1-11, 16
Canticle: Magnificat or Psalm 89:1-4, 19-26
Romans 16:25-27
Luke 1:26-38

Aim

To see how Gabriel's news to Mary fitted in with God's promise to King David.

Starter

Pass the ring. Thread a ring on a length of string. Everyone holds the string, passing it through their hands. One person stands in the middle of the circle. The ring gets passed secretly along the string from hand to hand. The person in the middle has to try and guess where it has got to. When they are right someone else takes over in the centre. Finish by giving a pack of sweets to whoever is holding the ring, and asking them to hand the sweets round to everyone, so that as the ring is revealed, everyone is given a gift.

Teaching

Explain that all through the hundreds of years before Jesus was born, God's promise had been passed on, from one generation to the next, sometimes seen and sometimes hidden from public view, until at the first Christmas, when Jesus the Christ was born, that message was seen clearly, and has been bringing blessing to everyone ever since.

But what was the message? Let's first go back in time to about 1000 BC – that's about three thousand years ago. We are in the city of Jerusalem, and this is King David. (Dress a child appropriately.) He is thinking deeply. (King David thinks deeply.) Then he has a good idea. (Turn on torch above his head.) He talks it over with Nathan the prophet. (Choose someone to be Nathan and give them both the script, *see CD-ROM.*) Then choose two children to be Mary and Gabriel, and give them the second script.

Praying

Once in royal David's city
stood a lowly cattle shed,
where a mother laid her baby
in a manger for a bed.
Mary was that mother mild,
Jesus Christ her little child.

Activities

Today the pop–up model will be completed, using the drawings and instructions on the sheet, strengthened with thin card. Also discuss with the children how God's promise to King David was fulfilled when Mary said yes to God. Jesus' kingdom is still growing today.

Susan Sayers

For 6 to 10 years – Year C

Aim

To discover how much the children know of the Christmas story.

Readings

Micah 5:2-5a
Canticle: Magnificat or Psalm 80:1-8
Hebrews 10:5-10
Luke 1:39-45 (46-55)

Teaching

Last week we talked about the journey from Nazareth to Bethlehem. Can you remember how far they travelled? By the end of the week Mary would be very tired. They were travelling very slowly because Mary's baby was due to be born. This meant that by the time they got to Bethlehem the places that put people up were full. An eastern khan (the nearest to a hotel) was really a common place where everybody slept together with little privacy. People did not remove clothes to sleep and they shared a fire or fires on which they cooked their own food. The khan was often very noisy, especially when friends and relatives were meeting there. Do you think Mary would have liked her baby to be born among all those crowds and the noise? I think she was pleased when the innkeeper said she could use the stable. The stable might have been a separate building or a cave in the hillside. What would you find in the stable? Hay, donkeys, cows, hens and maybe a camel. They would spend the night with the animals. They had a blanket but what would Mary and Joseph use to make themselves more comfortable? They would use the straw that the animals also used for bedding. Here Jesus would be born.

Activity

Let us pretend we are making a film of the scene. What do you want to show in the stable? What would Joseph be doing? There is no nurse, or helper for Mary, only Joseph. Do you think he might be a little worried? Once the baby is born, how could we show the joy of Mary and Joseph?

Joseph would help to see that Jesus was clean and wrapped in swaddling bands. (See if the children can explain what these are.) Once Mary is asleep, where does Joseph put Jesus? (Make sure they know what a manger is.) Now let us have a Joseph and Mary and act it out.

Prayer

God, we thank you for our parents,
for all the love and care they show for us,
and we thank you for the love and care
that Mary and Joseph gave to the baby Jesus.

Draw in the shepherds and colour the picture. It could be cut out and used as a Christmas card.

Song

See him lying on a bed of straw

Jesus my Lord,
I you adore.
O help me love
you more and more.

David Adam

Newborn

Resources

- Advent wreath, votive candles and matches
- Three 'stations' around the church or cafe-style seating
- On a whiteboard or OHP: a large outline of a new baby *(see note)*
- Drywipe markers
- At each station or on each table: A4 pieces of paper with the outline of a new baby *(see note)*; pens or pencils
- Music and words
- Small pieces of paper with the outline of a new baby *(see note)*
- Pens or pencils

Leaders

Minimum: 2

- Leader
- Additional Storyteller

Optimum: 7

- Leader *(Introduction and Conclusion)*
- Activity Leader
- Storytellers x 2
- Music Leader
- Explorer
- Prayer Leader

Suggestions for additional music

- The Virgin Mary had a baby boy
- The angel Gabriel from heaven came
- For Mary, mother of our Lord

Service

Welcome

Light a votive candle each and then the Advent Candle.

Introduction

This last Sunday of Advent is dedicated to Mary. We remember her, waiting patiently and faithfully, for the birth of her son who would change the world for ever. Her particular experience was unique, but all of us who have become parents know how the birth of a child changes lives: a new life begins, and our lives will never be the same again. Today we will be thinking about the new life that Mary brought into the world.

Introduce the big outline of a baby on the whiteboard or OHP.

This is a new baby. This child could grow up to be or do anything – but at the moment of birth, everything is an unexplored possibility, like a blank sheet of paper. Imagine this is a new baby, born today. What could he/she be when he/she grows up? What things could he/she do?

Ask for and give suggestions to start the ball rolling: a good friend, a footballer, funny, a dentist, artistic, a daredevil, a parent . . .

Gather round one of these blank outlines and fill it in with as many ideas as you can think of. What might this baby be or do when he or she grows up?

Allow plenty of time for people to fill the outlines with their ideas, then come together again.

In this Christmas season, we are thinking about one special baby in particular. Mary and Joseph knew more than most parents about what their baby would be when he grew up. Listen carefully to this bit of the Christmas story, and pay attention to what the angel tells Joseph about Mary's baby. If you hear something that Mary and Joseph could fill in on a blank outline like this, wave your hand in the air. So listen carefully . . .

Storytelling

Read Matthew 1:18-25 with two voices: the narrator and the angel. Encourage the waving!

Who heard something that Mary and Joseph could fill in on a blank outline like this? Even before he was born, Mary and Joseph knew their baby would be . . . what?

Elicit these points and write them inside the baby outline on the whiteboard or OHP.

- a boy
- called Jesus
- Son of God the Holy Spirit
- Saviour – he would save people from their sins

During the following hymn, wipe these points and use a different colour to fill the baby outline with messy, scribbled words – taken from the opening activity – and some negative words such as 'angry', 'impatient', 'disappointed', some of which are crossed out.

Music

Infant holy

Exploring

Let's look again at these baby outlines which we filled in earlier. *(Show one of the filled-in A4 outlines.)* Here is a brand-new life, full of possibilities: the problem is, as we get older, we can start to feel a bit like this:

Show your whiteboard/OHP baby outline full of scribbled words and crossings-out.

There are lots of things we are and still lots that we can be – but there are also quite a lot of things we wish we weren't, and things we have failed to be. This person wishes she wasn't quite so angry – but she is. This person is never going to be the completely perfect, ever-patient parent he planned on being.

Indicate the baby outlines from the opening activity.

Gather round one of these outlines again and this time, add things which a person might not want to grow up to be or do – things they might regret or feel sorry for. Fill it in with as many ideas as you can think of and cross each one out as you write it, as if you are trying to make it go away. What might this baby not want to be or do when he or she grows up?

Allow plenty of time for people to fill the outlines with their ideas, then come together again. Return to your whiteboard/ OHP baby outline full of messy, scribbled words.

God understands that we are not perfect, and that our lives can become like this – rather messy and full of mistakes as well as possibilities. That is why he gave us his son, Jesus. What Jesus offers us is the chance to start again – to say sorry, to be forgiven and to have a fresh start *(rub out all the words and scribble)* just like a newborn baby.

Prayer action
Hand out small baby outlines and pens.

Take a fresh outline of a new baby and as you look at it, think about fresh starts and new beginnings. Perhaps you know a new baby; perhaps you know someone older who is trying to make a fresh start. Perhaps you are beginning something new, or perhaps there are things in your life that you'd like to put behind you, so that you can start afresh. Whoever or whatever it is, write or draw it on this picture of a newborn baby, then offer it to God as your prayer for a new beginning.

Allow enough time for people to think and complete their prayers. Then invite people to come and lay their prayers on the altar, or perhaps at the foot of the crib if your church has a large Nativity scene. When all the prayers have been offered, call for a moment of quiet in which to bring them before God.

Lord Jesus,
you came here as a new baby and grew up among us.
We offer you our own prayers for new beginnings
in your name,

Music
Away in a manger

Conclusion
Living Lord,
may we, like Mary,
give ourselves body and soul
to the service of your life-giving love.

Note

Baby

Print out, copy onto A4 paper and cut along the straight solid lines for the activity; enlarge and trace or copy by hand for the whiteboard/OHP.

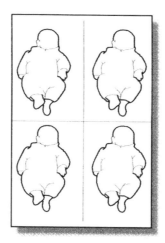

Claire Benton-Evans

Action Prayers

Hopes and fears

Resources

- A large pin board covered with the outline of the 'mystery Messiah' (on CD-ROM – *see note*)
- Small blank cards, plus two labelled 'Hopes' and 'Fears'
- Pens and pencils
- Drawing pins

Leader

Remember the carol, 'O little town of Bethlehem'? In the opening verse, we sing that 'the hopes and fears of all the years' were met in Bethlehem on the night of Jesus' birth. The Jewish people had been waiting through the centuries for God's chosen one, the Messiah, to unite their people and restore their fortunes. *(Indicate the 'mystery Messiah' outline.)* No one knew who this mystery Messiah would be or when he would come, but the hopes and fears of an entire nation were pinned on him.

Pin the cards labelled 'Hopes' and 'Fears' onto the outline of the Messiah, covering the question mark.

As we wait excitedly for Christmas, we remember all the people who pinned their hopes and fears on the coming Messiah. We know the Son of God who fleshed out this outline, and soon we will celebrate his birth. We can continue to bring our hopes and fears to him in prayer. In a moment of quiet, let's call to mind all those people and situations we would like to bring before God.

Pause.

When you are ready, come forward and write or draw your prayer, then pin it to this outline of Jesus, the Messiah.

Prayer action

Allow plenty of time for people to complete their prayers.

Closing words

Father, we bring you our hopes and fears
in the name of Jesus, our long-awaited Saviour.

Note

Mystery Messiah outline

Print out one copy and enlarge by hand or with a photocopier. Make it as large as possible.

Claire Benton-Evans

Crib service – starlight

Resources

*   Gold star shapes (on CD-ROM, *see note*)
*   Lengths of ribbon for hanging the stars on the tree
*   Pens and pencils

Leader

Jesus is the light of the world. When we pray, we can ask him to shine the light of his love wherever there is darkness. For our prayers today, let's remember all those people who are most in need of love this Christmas. We think of those we love; people we know; people we don't like; those who may have no one to pray for them. (Pause.) Let's each take a gold star shape and write or draw our prayers on it. When you have finished your star prayer, come and add it to the branches of the Christmas tree.

Prayer action

Allow plenty of time for people to complete their prayers. If the church is packed, it may be easier to collect the stars and bring them forward in collection plates, then invite a couple of helpers to hang them on the tree.

Closing words

Jesus, Light of the world,
we offer these prayers in your name.
Shine like a star in the darkness
and guide us all closer to you.

Note

Gold star shapes

Copy on A4 gold card or paper and cut out. Use a hole punch for the hole.

Claire Benton-Evans

Preparing the way

Resources

- Nativity scene, stable or crib
- Pieces of paper shaped like footprints (about the size of a child's foot – see CD-ROM for photocopiable sheet)
- Pens and pencils.

Leader

Advent is all about waiting. Jesus' people waited for the birth of their king and saviour, Mary waited for her child to be born and every year we count down the days which lead to Christmas. In our prayers today we remember all those who waited for the arrival of that baby in the stable, and pray for people we know who are waiting. Perhaps you are impatient for the Christmas festivities; maybe you know someone who is waiting for an operation, or for a new job, or for something in their lives to improve. Whatever your prayer is, write or draw it on one of these footprints and lay a path to the stable door.

Prayer action

As people complete their prayers, place the first footprints by the church door and start to lay a path to the stable.

Closing words

Living Lord,
as you took shape in your mother's womb
so we begin our journey through Advent,
towards Christmas.
May you guard and guide us all as we wait
and meet us at our journey's end.

Note

Footprints

Copy onto A4 paper and cut around the prints.

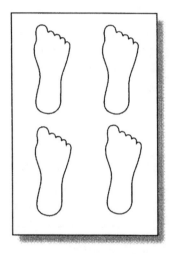

Claire Benton-Evans

Talk Ideas

Advent 1 – Waiting in hope

Beforehand get a kitchen timer, and one of those automatic timers which you fix on a lamp.

Begin by explaining how you are going to set the timer for X minutes, at which time the talk should be finishing. You are also setting the light to come on halfway through the talk. (Do this.)

Talk about the way things seem to take ages coming, because we want them so much – like birthdays, Christmas, holidays, pension day or tea time. Other things seem to come too fast – like telephone bills, exams or dentist appointments – because we aren't looking forward to them at all.

The early Christians were really looking forward to Jesus coming back in glory, and it seemed to be taking for ever. People who expected it to happen before they were 16, grew to 75 and died, and still Jesus hadn't come. It has been about 2000 years now, and he still hasn't come.

Now as soon as we start measuring the time for something, it seems to make us impatient. 'A watched pot never boils', they say. Because you know this talk will end when the ringer goes, you are probably all waiting for it to ring at any moment, especially as the light will remind you that it's all being timed. Peter told the people not to think God was slow in coming; he was just patiently waiting for the right time, and that might be any time. That's still true –

Jesus could come again at any moment, on any day. All we know for certain is that he is definitely going to return in glory, and we can't give an exact time and date to it.

Meanwhile, we can live our lives to the full, living the life of love that God shows us, and keeping in close contact with him through prayer and worship, so that we are ready when he does appear.

Susan Sayers

Advent 1 – Expect the unexpected

Matthew 24:36-44

If any of us were to say that we weren't just the teeniest bit interested in what the future holds then they've either got life totally sorted and know how to sort out every global problem (answers on a postcard, please) or they're too busy writing their autobiography to care. Life is unreliable. No matter how we look at life or how much we look at the clock and complain about the monotony of our existence, anything, and everything, can change within a split second.

Lots of people spend money and time trying to predict their future and what it holds for them. The question is, does knowing what is going to happen in a few days', months' or even years' time change the way we think and live now?

Just say, for instance, that someone read your palm and said you were going to win a fortune. So, you go and live according to that prediction and use every bit of credit and hire purchase that you can lay your paws on. And . . . the bills arrive quickly followed by a solicitor's letter suggesting that you'd better pay the money back, with mega-large interest, asap. Alternatively, you might decide that if life is so unpredictable and that it could end quite unexpectedly, then you should live life to the full, right now, this instant or even sooner and ignore everyone in the pursuit of pleasure. Pretty soon you've got no friends, no money and no idea how much more of this pleasure trip you can take.

In reality, most of us don't live as if nothing and no one matter. We have people we care for and hope that they care for us. We try and save some money for the future or have an insurance policy as a protection against the unexpected. We are urged to make the most of our future by putting money into a pension scheme just so that we can enjoy our retirement (that is if we aren't too wasted to enjoy it). But the nagging thoughts still continue, 'Is this it?', 'What are we here for?', 'Have I missed the bus?'

As Jesus chats with his disciples, he tells them that at some point he wants to come back. The disciples must have thought he was barking mad but only Jesus knew that his time on earth was limited and the purpose of his human life was soon to be made painfully obvious. Jesus suggests that people will forget or ignore what he's said and done and live as if they weren't accountable to anyone. But, Jesus reminds them, the 'Son of Man' will return when people least expect it. This isn't used as a threat but as a promise that soon evil will become subject to the authority of Heaven, and that Jesus' return will signal the time when the ravages of evil will be put right.

No one knows when all that Jesus said will actually happen. All we do know is to expect the unexpected!

Pete Townsend

Advent 1 – When will it happen?

Luke 21:25-36

It doesn't seem as if a week goes by without reports of something happening in the sky, news of tidal waves or treacherous storms at sea, or even the threat of asteroids hitting the earth! Earthquakes, tornadoes, flash floods cause many people to be frightened and panic. There is a problem. Weather forecasts and predictions try to warn us of what may happen, but if they are so accurate, why do so many people get caught out?

Guessing what the weather will do can be a tricky business. It's no joke walking in a crowd of people when you're dressed in waterproof coat, wellington boots, plastic bags wrapped around your legs and a bucket on your head, and everybody else is wearing short sleeves and sunglasses. So, you ignore the weather forecast of torrential rain, go out in short sleeves and sunglasses and promptly get soaked. Sometimes you just can't win.

But, let's be honest, most of us would prefer to know what to expect rather than be kept guessing. Some surprises are OK, such as a birthday or Christmas, provided you've given everyone enough hints.

In the Bible reading, Jesus said that there would be lots of warnings and signs about his return but no one will know for sure when it's going to happen. Some of the things that Jesus referred to happen very frequently, almost too frequently. For instance, people in San Francisco, America, know they live in a major earthquake area. Earthquakes have happened before and occasionally earth tremors hint at what may be to come. But no one knows exactly when 'the big one' will happen. They prepare for it, they rehearse possible scenarios and plan how they may react to a major earthquake. But still no one knows when.

Even if you know it's going to happen sometime, isn't it possible that you can become a bit bored with wondering when it's going to happen? Rather like having a fire drill – the alarm sounds and you evacuate the building . . . eventually. Well, it's only a rehearsal, isn't it?

In San Francisco, they know history is going to repeat itself and another major earthquake will hit the city. They can't live every day in fear and they can't live every day ignoring the evidence. They watch, wait and prepare. Pretty much just what Jesus asks of us.

Pete Townsend

Advent 2 – The Word

If you prefer to emphasise God's word there are several ways in which you can illustrate its impact. You'll need to prepare an appropriate warning sign and a familiar advertising slogan to a scale that can be seen by the whole congregation.

1) *Words convey information,* which is easily demonstrated by holding up an encyclopaedia. We find this everywhere – in books, magazines and in the broadcast media. The Bible also gives us knowledge about certain people and situations, but it goes much further than useful historical facts. It also tells us how to apply that knowledge in our daily lives so that we can live as God means us to.

2) *Words sometimes carry a warning.* At this point display a triangular road sign with an exclamation mark in the middle. It's fairly obvious that there's some danger or hazard ahead, but we need some words to indicate what it is – a flood, an accident or long traffic queues. God's word also contains warnings about the consequences of wrong behaviour or attitudes, and of going our own way instead of following him.

3) *Words also encourage us.* Here you could hold up a familiar advertising slogan which encourages us to buy a particular product. However, you should go on to stress that God's word isn't a sales pitch. God uses his word to encourage us to keep going with the Christian faith when we feel like giving up, to take risks for the sake of his kingdom, to open our lives to his guidance. Through it the Holy Spirit persuades us of the truth, and enables us to act on it.

Stuart Thomas

Advent 2 – Repentance

Thought for the day
Let's make a clear road to get ourselves ready for welcoming Jesus.

Reflection on the readings
Isaiah 11:1-10
Psalm 72:1-7, 18-19
Romans 15:4-13
Matthew 3:1-12

Today Paul reminds us of the teaching and encouragement we are given through the Scriptures, so that we maintain our hope. By the end of the passage he's talking about us overflowing with hope, once we've got into the habit of being constantly topped up by God, who is, after all, the ground of all hope. And with the hope come all kinds of other good things, like joy and peace and a life of faith in the Spirit's power.

Hope is linked with longing: longing for all the good things we sense life was meant to be like, but which it so often falls short of. 'One day ...,' the prophet dreams in our first reading from Isaiah; one day it will be as we all long for it to be, with righteousness and real justice, and no conflict or cruelty.

Is it just a dream? Almost like an alarm clock, John the Baptist bursts into our longings and starts shaking us into action. It is the action of thorough, deep-seated repentance, so that we may be prepared and ready for Jesus to save us and make the dream kingdom a practical reality. So that we are ready to come when he says follow; so that we actually notice him calling us.

Every time we come to the Eucharist we need to prepare ourselves to meet with Jesus, which is why we start off the service with a time of confession. How can we best use this provision? Clearly real repentance is far less likely to happen if we just read through the words on a Sunday without thinking much about them. The truth is that every time we realise we are thinking, acting or speaking unlovingly, bitterly, destructively, dishonestly or unfairly, we need to repent immediately and make ourselves right with God, whose love and truth our living has insulted. Then, when we gather as the community of faith at the Eucharist ... we shall be making a communal act of real repentance.

Discussion starters
1. Why do we need to repent and confess our sins when we gather to worship God and receive Communion?
2. Read through the words of the General Confession below, looking at what it suggests we should be sorting out in our lives. Have we become calloused to any of these, so we no longer count them as needing repentance?

3. As the church community here, what things do we perhaps need to repent of together? Are there any long-standing blocks (such as wrong attitudes, misplaced priorities) on the road which we've stopped noticing because we are so accustomed to them? Get rid of them now by repenting together of them . . .

Almighty and most merciful Father,
we have wandered and strayed from your ways like lost sheep.
We have followed too much the devices and desires of our own hearts.
We have offended against your holy laws.
We have left undone those things that we ought to have done;
and we have done those things that we ought not to have done;
and there is no health in us.
But you, O Lord, have mercy upon us sinners.
Spare those who confess their faults.
Restore those who are penitent,
according to your promises
declared to mankind in Jesus Christ our Lord.
And grant, O merciful Father, for his sake,
that we may live a disciplined, righteous and godly life,
to the glory of your holy name.

Susan Sayers

Advent 2 – Matthew 3:1-12

Can you imagine what image John the Baptist would have made? Just think, here's a bloke dressed in a camel-hair suit, a leather strap wrapped around his waist and dipping grasshoppers into a pot of honey and popping them into his mouth! In between mouthfuls he gives the crowd a load of verbal about their antics and suggests they have a lot in common with snakes. He then goes on to give them some tips on gardening and hints that they all could do with a dunk in the river. You can just hear the mutterings of 'Been in the sun too long' or 'What can you expect from someone who wanders around the desert all day?' Quite a few folk would have been making gestures indicating that John was a few grains short of a sandcastle.

John the Baptist was a man who had turned his back on the comforts that most people enjoyed and had given himself to reading and meditating about God. Despite his odd appearance and behaviour, John was recognised as a messenger. His message was that all the people should '. . . Get the road ready for the Lord . . .' (Matthew 3:3). This wasn't such a strange thing to say as you might imagine. During, and before, biblical times the roads were almost non-existent. Those tracks that did exist were in a terrible condition and most people who travelled were warned to sort out all their legal affairs and say goodbye to their family because there was no guarantee that you would get to your intended destination safely.

The few good roads that did exist were built for a special purpose. King Solomon built a road of black basalt (a volcanic rock which often contained crystals). These special roads were constructed to reflect the wealth of the king. These roads were built by the king and mainly for the benefit of the king. They were often referred to as 'The king's highway'. Before the king began his travels a message was sent out telling the people to get the roads repaired and looking good in preparation for the king's arrival.

John's message was just the same, the only difference being that the road to be prepared wasn't made of basalt but of flesh and blood, the human heart and mind. John was preparing the people to hear the words of Jesus and the words wouldn't reach their destination if the 'road' wasn't ready to receive a message from the King.

John was concerned that the people were too occupied with their own comforts and had forgotten who God was! The rulers, politicians and religious leaders were too busy building

ADVENT – ALL-AGE SERVICES

their own little kingdoms to listen to the message of the 'King'. John was determined that when Jesus began his journey the people had at least been warned of his coming.

Pete Townsend

Advent 3 – Matthew 11:2-11

John the Baptist was in prison (he'd got on the wrong side of Herodias, who was the wife of Herod and had previously been the wife of Herod's brother Philip, but that's another story). John had heard a great deal about Jesus and what he was saying. His curiosity aroused, John sent some of his followers to find out who exactly Jesus was. In fact, John told his followers to ask Jesus whether he was the one who they were looking for or were they to expect someone else.

Can you imagine a couple of guys going up to another guy and saying 'Are you the one we're supposed to be looking for or not? 'Cos if not, then we're to look for some other geezer.' This wasn't really meant to sound crazy, it just sounded like it! The problem was that John was expecting the Christ to come and act like a judge, telling people what they'd done wrong and what would happen to them if they continued behaving that way (Jesus did say words to this effect later on). So when John heard what Jesus was saying and doing, it confused him a little bit.

Jesus' reply to the odd question simply reminded John of some predictions from the Old Testament:

Isaiah 29:18-19

The deaf will be able to hear whatever is read to them; the blind will be freed from a life of darkness. The poor and the needy will celebrate and shout because of the Lord, the Holy God of Israel.

and

Isaiah 61:1

The Spirit of the Lord God has taken control of me! The Lord has chosen and sent me to tell the oppressed the good news, to heal the broken-hearted, and to announce freedom for prisoners and captives.

Jesus wanted John to know that what God had promised would happen was now happening.

John wasn't accused of doubting or lacking faith in God. All Jesus wanted to do was to open John's eyes to everything that God wanted to do. No one expected John, or anybody else, to immediately recognise who Jesus was and what he had come to say and do. Unfortunately, John had difficulty seeing and hearing much more about Jesus, Herod cut his head off! Fortunately, the disciples and the rest of the population of Israel had a bit more time to get to know Jesus.

For us, getting to know Jesus isn't a snap of the fingers and we know it all and more. Getting to know Jesus is all about a relationship, one which takes time to grow. A lot of the relationship is simply taking the time to chat and experience the day-to-day with Jesus. Another aspect of the relationship is getting to know Jesus through the Bible and accepting that exactly what he said is exactly what he will do. It all takes time but there again, time is all it takes. In other words, enjoy the experience of getting to know Jesus and don't give yourself a headache purely because it doesn't happen overnight.

Pete Townsend

Advent 4 – Matthew 1:18-25

Joseph had a dream . . . a great, stonking, technicolour, 3-D, front row sort. Imagine, here's a bloke who's just found out that the woman he was engaged to is pregnant! You know how it is, take it in your stride, no problem, happens every day. Wrong!

The Jewish tradition was for the marriage to be taken in three stages. First was an engagement, often announced while the couple were still children, their engagement having been arranged by the children's parents. Second was the 'betrothal'. This was the official bit which lasted a year and could only be called off if the female was unwilling to go ahead before the formal agreement had been announced. To break off the 'betrothal' was only possible by divorce. The third part was the actual marriage ceremony, which occurred at the end of the year of betrothal.

Tradition had ruled that if a woman was pregnant before marriage then she was considered to be promiscuous and could, after a public trial, be stoned to death. Fortunately, at the time of Mary and Joseph's betrothal, stoning had become history (to a large cheer of relief from a percentage of the female population). It was now custom to conduct a 'secret' divorce and keep the problem as far from wagging tongues as possible. This was the action that Joseph had decided upon before the dream.

So, there he goes, off to bed with a cluttered head full of angry thoughts and feelings of rejection. Then, just as soon as his eyelids hit the cheeks, along comes a gold-framed dream direct from God. Can you imagine, God tells him that it's still OK to marry Mary, she may be pregnant but she hadn't been unfaithful to him and she was still a virgin! Having received all of this, Joseph turned over and carried on snoozing . . . no he didn't! Joseph listened to what he'd heard and did exactly as God had asked him to. He married Mary even though a lot of people would have suggested that he hadn't been able to wait until his marriage before starting a family or that he'd failed to follow customs of the Jewish law and walked in the opposite direction to Mary.

Joseph heard God, did as he was asked and kept faith in God's word. God had used a dream to get through to Joseph and the dream had packed a real punch. Joseph was to remember that dream many times during Mary's pregnancy and afterwards.

Is it possible that we too can hear from God, do exactly as he asks and stick with it even when the gossip suggests that we may be a few biscuits short of a packet? A few years ago, before crossing the road, children were encouraged to 'Stop! Look! And Listen!' Not a bad piece of advice especially when God wants to have a word in our ear.

Pete Townsend

Keep alert

Thought for the day
Keep alert, because much is demanded of those to whom much is entrusted.

Aim
To explore the practicalities for keeping alert for when Jesus comes.

What's in store

Characters

Manager, Assistant, Customer, Boss.

Provide a jacket and tie for the manager, various items of the store's produce and some authentic cardboard cartons. The manager and shop assistant are moving cartons from one place in the shop to another,

Manager	Easy does it, Fred.
Assistant	Yes, sir.
Manager	Always bend your knees, rather than your back.
Assistant	Yes, sir.
Manager	I take my responsibilities seriously, you know; and as a shop assistant your back is one of my heavy responsibilities.
Assistant	Yes, sir. These chocolate and nut cookies weigh a ton, don't they, sir?
Manager	Ah yes, more heavy responsibilities the boss left me with, eh ... ha, ha!
Customer	Hallo, Harold! The boss gone away and left you in charge, has he? How about a packet of chocolate and nut cookies for friendship's sake? I'll buy you a pint this evening at the Crown.
Manager	You owe me a pint as it is, you old skinflint! And anyway, what do you think the boss would think if he came back and found me dishing out his stock. He's left me in charge because he reckons I'll look after things properly for him.
Customer	I don't think you'll see the boss in a hurry. He's languishing in the sun somewhere I expect. Anyway, I'll have some chewing gum. (*He buys chewing gum, thanks the manager and leaves*)
Manager	What's that grinding noise, Fred?
Assistant	That's my stomach, sir. It seems a long time since breakfast. (*He strokes one of the packets of cookies*)
Manager	Yes, I'm rather peckish, myself. Oh, come on, let's split a packet of these between us! Bill's probably right – the boss won't be back yet. (*They do so and start eating*)
Boss	(*Comes in and stares amazed at what is going on. Then he coughs to get their attention*) So this is the man who was so sure I could trust him, is it?
Manager	(*Trying to hide biscuits*) Mr Taylor! . . . I wasn't expecting you!

Boss   Evidently. Mr Woodman . . .

Manager Yes, sir? You're fired.

Discuss and list suggestions for practical ways to stay alert and avoid falling into temptation.

Discussion starters

1. Obedience is something most of us find very hard. How is it linked to selfishness and what factors make it easier/more difficult for us to do?

2. When is obedience a matter of life and death? How can we practise obedience in little ways so we are ready for the Big event?

Susan Sayers

Christingle

Resources

- Ordinary Christingles, made in advance, enough for one each (see The Children's Society website for further details: www.childrenssociety.org.uk)
- Giant Christingle (visit www.childrenssociety.org.uk to download a useful guide on how to make these)
- Music and words
- Christingle costumes: at least three, but as many as you can manage. Each child will need:

 – a simple white tunic or extra-large white T-shirt

 – a flame headdress (*see note 1*)

 – a small bowl or basket of satsumas, clementines or mandarin oranges. You will need enough oranges for everyone
- A very large map of the world *(see note 2)*
- A wide red ribbon or strip of red fabric
- Several collection plates
- Matches and tapers
- Containers for orange peel

Leaders

Minimum: 1
- Leader

Optimum: 6

- Leader (Introduction and Conclusion)
- Activity Leader 1 and 2
- Music Leader

- Explorer
- Prayer Leader

Suggestions for additional music

- While shepherds watched
- Hark, the herald-angels sing
- Mary had a baby

Service

Welcome

As people arrive, invite some children to dress up as Christingle candles (as many as you have costumes). Explain that they will be helping you later on in the service.

Introduction

Welcome to our Christingle celebration. Everyone will have a chance to join in today's service: there will be things to look at, things to listen to and things to think about. Of course, there will also be treats to eat!

Music

Once in royal David's city

Exploring

Who has been to a Christingle service before? (Invite responses.)

I wonder if you can tell me what the different parts of the Christingle mean?

Hold up your giant Christingle. Invite children to come up and point to the different parts and tell you what they mean. Elicit the following answers, which you may like to repeat when the children have finished.

The familiar meaning of the Christingle is this:

- The orange represents the world.
- The sweets and fruit represent the fruits of creation – all the good things that God has given us.
- The red ribbon represents Jesus' love and the blood he shed for us.
- The candle represents Jesus, the light of the world.

We are used to this way of understanding the Christingle. However, there is another way. Could I have my volunteer Christingle candles, please?

Activity 1

Bring forward your volunteers.

The Christingle candle reminds us that Jesus is the Light of the world. Today's Bible reading looks forward to Jesus' birth, saying, 'the dawn from on high will break upon us, to give light to those who sit in darkness.' Yet Jesus told us that we are the light of the world, too. He said this to his followers: 'You are the light of the world . . . let your light shine before others, so that they may see your good works and give glory to your Father in heaven.' So my helpers here have dressed up as Christingle candles to remind us that each one of us is the light of the world. It's our job to show God's goodness to other people.

Now the Christingle candle stands in an orange, which represents the world. Here is another representation of the world for our living Christingle candles to stand on.

Show the map of the world and lay it down.

This reminds us that we live in the real world – we have our feet on the ground. We must show God's love in our everyday lives.

Invite your volunteers to stand on the map.

The Christingle has a red ribbon around the orange, representing Jesus' love. Here's a red ribbon for our living Christingles.

Lay the big red ribbon on the map.

Now this red ribbon looks as if it is marking out a path. Jesus' love shows us the way to go, because we have his loving example to follow.

Invite the volunteers to stand on the ribbon.

Finally, the Christingle has sweets and fruit sticking out of it, reminding us of the fruits of creation.

Hand the baskets or bowls of little oranges to your volunteers and encourage them to hold the fruit out at arm's length.

These living Christingles are holding out their tasty treats not for one person to munch, but for us all to share. Please keep your little oranges when you get them, because we will share them out later as part of our prayers.

Encourage your volunteers to move among the congregation, handing out the oranges, then return to their positions at the front.

So these living Christingles are here to remind us that we all have a job to do. We are shining lights who live in the real world. Our job is to follow Jesus' loving example and share the good things we have been given.

Give your volunteers a round of applause and ask them to sit down.

This Christingle service is raising money for The Children's Society, which helps vulnerable children and young people. Our living Christingles have reminded us to be the light of the world, to love others and to share what we have. Today we have a chance to do just that. However little money we have, let's share some of it with children who really need our help.

Take a collection for The Children's Society during the next hymn.

Music

It's rounded like an orange

Prayer Action

Today we will use these little oranges in our prayers. These sweet and tasty fruits are at their best at this time of year. They remind us of all the good things that God's creation produces for us to enjoy. We'll hold these oranges in our hands as we rest quietly in God's presence. Let's say thank you in our hearts for all the good things he has given us.

Pause.

Now let's peel the oranges.

Allow time for everyone to do this.

Before we eat our oranges, we remember what we have learnt today. Let's share! Please give a piece of your orange to the person next to you, then let's all enjoy this fruit.

People exchange pieces of orange and then eat. Pass round containers for the peel.

Let us pray.
God of all good things,
thank you for your great goodness.
Help us to share your gifts.

Activity 2

Distribute and light the Christingles according to your church's custom. Turn off the lights and sing the following carol by candlelight.

Music

Away in a manger

Conclusion

God of Love,
let us be living Christingles.
May we be the light of the world,
making a difference to people around us.
May we live in the real world,

keeping our feet on the ground.
May we be guided by your love,
following your way.
May we be thankful for your gifts,
sharing them with all.

Notes

1. A flame headdress

Cut flame shapes out of red and yellow card or paper and attach to a circlet of card, like this. Add a second flame to the back of the circlet and staple the points of the flames together, so that they stand up.

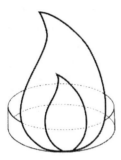

2. A very large map of the world

A great resource is the giant, brightly coloured, plastic floor mat in the children's game, *Globe Trotting*, produced by the Early Learning Centre. If you can't get hold of this, you could stick some large pieces of card or lining paper together and paint on the outlines of continents and countries with a thick brush.

Claire Benton-Evans

RESOURCES

Advent

Advent heralds the start of the Church's liturgical year and extends over the four Sundays before Christmas Day (25 December). Advent is an important season, yet it can so easily be squeezed out by the hurly-burly of Christmas and the tendency these days for that season's festivities to be celebrated before rather than over the 12 days following Christmas Day. So one of the challenges is to keep Advent special!

Advent takes its name from two Latin words: *adventus*, which means 'an arrival', and *advenire*, meaning 'to come to'. In Roman times, the 'Adventus Ceremony' marked the occasion of the Emperor's arrival at a city.

There is evidence that Advent was celebrated by the Western Church as early as the fourth century and was well established by the sixth century. Advent only became part of the tradition in the Eastern Church a couple of centuries later, where it takes a different pattern.

Coming immediately before Christmas, Advent is a time to prepare to celebrate Jesus' birth. But the roots of Advent lie not in a babe lying in a manger, but in the mystery of Jesus as Christ our Lord and King. Perhaps the best-known Advent carol is 'O come, O come, Emmanuel', based on the sequence of the Great 'O' antiphons that date back to the eighth century. These were sung before and after the Magnificat at Evening Prayer, one on each of the seven days leading up to Christmas Eve. The antiphons anticipate Christ's arrival as the One who will come and deliver God's people. Although the antiphons had mostly faded away, Common Worship in the Anglican Church readopted their use.

So whilst during Advent the Church gets ready to celebrate Jesus' birth, Christians also use this short period as preparation for their own deliverance from all that gets between us and God. Hence on the one hand Advent takes a triumphal theme, and on the other hand it has a sombre tone. Traditionally, this is reflected in the use of purple as the liturgical colour, symbolising both kingship and penitence. A preference in some churches today is to use blue during Advent, to differentiate this season from Lent, because blue symbolises the sky, where heralds announced Jesus' birth, and because the colour is associated with Mary, the mother of our Lord.

With the emphasis on expectation rather than penitence, Advent sermons on the Four Last Things – Death, Judgement, Heaven and Hell – are less commonly preached today. Likewise the penitential practice of fasting in Advent is perhaps less rigorously observed today than it should be! Traditionally, Advent also points to the four comings of Christ; hence the four Sundays in Advent. The first is his coming to us in the flesh, and the last is his second coming at the end of the world when he will judge the living and the dead. Advent also asks us to reflect on Christ's coming into our hearts and at his coming to us at our death.

Reflecting the fact that Advent stands at the beginning of the Church's year, Kenneth Stevenson writes, 'Advent marks a fresh start when the imagination is kindled to look forward to the coming of Christ, specifically at Christmas itself'.* Whatever our preference, or however we observe this season, a sense of 'alert watchfulness', as *Times and Seasons*** defines Advent, enriches this wonderful season as we pray 'Maranatha. Come Lord Jesus'. The season of Advent reminds us that through Christ's coming we ask, in the words of the Advent collect, for the 'grace to cast away the works of darkness and to put on the armour of light, now in the time of this mortal life'.

Simon Hill

---

* Kenneth Stevenson, *All the Company of Heaven* (Norwich, The Canterbury Press, 1998), p.9.

** *Times and Seasons* (Church House Publishing, 2006).

Advent Candles

Johann Wichern, a Protestant pastor, founded a mission school in Hamburg. During Advent the children would ask every day whether Christmas had arrived. So in 1839 he made an Advent wreath on which he placed 19 small red candles and four large white candles. On successive weekdays a red candle would be lit, and on Sundays a white candle, until the last candle was lit on Christmas Eve.

The Advent wreath familiar today has four candles around the ring, with a fifth in the centre. On the first Sunday of Advent, the first candle is lit. On the second Sunday, the first candle is relit, from which the second is lit, and so on until all four candles are lit on the Sunday before Christmas Day. The candle in the middle of the Advent wreath is lit on Christmas Day, generally at the first Communion of Christmas.

The lighting of the candles in the context of worship perpetuates the original practice of saying prayers around the Advent wreath. Traditionally, the four candles have been used to represent the prophets, John the Baptist, Mary the Mother of our Lord, and the People of God – illustrative of the Sunday readings in Advent. Recent liturgies, as in *Times and Seasons** for example, offer alternative themes, with appropriate prayers.

The custom of the use of different coloured candles has also grown. Traditionally, red candles are used for the four Sundays, to contrast with the white candle in the centre, the liturgical colour for Christmas Day. Some churches prefer violet candles for three of the four Sundays with a rose candle for the third Sunday of Advent, known as Gaudete Sunday, from the Latin 'to rejoice', which is the theme of the liturgy on that day. Others use blue candles in keeping with the Advent themes of hope and waiting.

Whatever the colour, Advent candles enrich and enlighten the liturgy as well as the countdown to Christmas Day.

Simon Hill

Advent Wreath

The invention of the wheel was a defining moment in humanity's civilisation. Wheels are taken for granted, but in a religious context they take on a whole new meaning. The wheel is a symbol of the Sun deities and represents the cycle of life: of birth, death and rebirth. It is commonly used in the practice of the occult. So perhaps it is surprising that the Church adopted the wheel as a symbol of faith. But the emerging Church commonly adopted pre-Christian festivals and customs and 'Christianised' them. The Advent wreath, or Crown as it is sometimes referred to, is an example of this practice.

Whilst its origin is uncertain, the Advent wreath can be traced to the sixteenth century. Its present form dates from the late nineteenth century when a pastor in the German Lutheran Church built a large wooden ring from an old cartwheel and fixed candles on the rim. Prayers were said around the ring as the candles were successively lit during Advent. The custom spread throughout Germany, and by the 1930s had reached the United States and Britain, probably through German Lutheran immigrants. Advent wreaths are widely used by churches today and grace many a home, as a focus for prayer during the season of Advent.

The Advent wreath encapsulates the eternal cycle of the seasons. It is generally decorated with various evergreens that, together with the lighting of the candles, symbolise the persistence of life in the midst of winter. Traditionally, laurel is used to symbolise victory over suffering, pine and yew for immortality, and cedar for strength and healing. Holly represents Christ's passion, and ivy God's faithfulness and eternity. There are other interpretations, but above all the Advent wreath is a ring with no beginning or end, a symbol of the everlasting life found in Christ, God with us, Emmanuel.

Simon Hill

** *Times and Seasons* (Church House Publishing, 2006).

Celtic Thoughts

Be prepared!

Psalm 66; Isaiah 40:1-9; Matthew 25:1-13

Prepare the way of the Lord.

Mark 1:3

In the wasteland may the Glory shine.
In the land of the lost may the King make his home.

For Celtic Christians the time before Christmas (known as Advent, which means the Coming) is a period of preparation, as we repent and wait in hope for the coming return of Christ. This period used to be known as a second Lent. Fasting was less severe, but people carved out time to go apart and wait on God. Could we make it our aim to dispel the spirit of restlessness and acquisition, and to instil the spirit of wonder, warning and waiting during this period?

What did those Celtic Christians focus their minds on during these weeks, and what should we focus our minds on? God prepared for the birth of Christ within his people, through prophets. Many of them lived in simplicity as a sign that they were waiting for God to fulfil his promises. As we meditate on their lives and words we, too, hear the call to live lives of simplicity as a sign. Then we think about the witnesses at the time of Christ's birth, Mary and Joseph, Elizabeth and Zechariah, Anna and Simeon, whose waiting was joyful and humble.

This is also a time for thinking about what the universe, humanity, and ourselves are coming to, and about the four last things of death, giving account, eternal bliss and separation.

At heart, this should be a time of waiting in contemplation of the presence of Christ within us; for we are called, like Mary, to be bearers of Christ now and into the future.

In the coming days the readings will focus on these things.

Calm us to wait for the gift of Christ;
cleanse us to prepare the way for Christ;
teach us to contemplate the wonder of Christ;
touch us to know the presence of Christ;
anoint us to bear the life of Christ.

Ray Simpson

We wait in the darkness

Psalm 17; Isaiah 42:14-23; Romans 8:31-39

You know my heart. You have come to me at night … reveal your wonderful love and save me.
Psalm 17:3, 7

We wait in the darkness, expectantly, longingly, anxiously, thoughtfully.
The darkness is our friend.

In the darkness of the womb,
we have all been nurtured and protected.
In the darkness of the womb
the Christ-child was made ready for the journey into light.
It is only in the darkness that we can see the splendour of the universe –
blankets of stars, the solitary glowings of the planets.
It was the darkness that allowed the Magi to find the star
that guided them to where the Christ-child lay.
In the darkness of the night, desert people find relief
from the cruel relentless heat of the sun.
In the blessed desert darkness Mary and Joseph were able to flee
with the infant Jesus to safety in Egypt.
In the darkness of sleep, we are soothed and restored,
healed and renewed.
In the darkness of sleep, dreams rise up. God spoke to Joseph and
the wise men through dreams. God is speaking still.
Sometimes in the solitude of the darkness our fears and concerns, our hopes and visions rise
to the surface. We come face to face with ourselves and with the road that lies ahead of us.
And in that same darkness we find companionship for the journey. In that same darkness we
sometimes allow ourselves to wonder and worry whether the human race is going to survive.
And then, in the darkness we know that you are with us, O God, yet still we await your coming.
In the darkness that contains both our hopelessness and our hope, we watch for a sign of
God's hope.
For you are with us, O God, in darkness and in light.

Presbyterian Church of Aotearoa, New Zealand (abridged)

O God of life, darken not to me your light,
O God of life, close not to me your joy,
O God of life, shut not to me your door,
O God of life, refuse not to me your mercy,
O God of life, soften to me your anger
and O God of life, crown to me your goodness.

Carmina Gadelica

Ray Simpson

O come from on high

Psalm 60; Isaiah 60:1-3; Luke 2:1-7

The one who is holy and true has the key of David, and when he opens a door no one can
close it; when he closes a door no one can open it . . . The great Son of David has won
the victory.

Revelation 3:7; 5:5

As Christians reflected over the centuries on the nature of the coming King, they were given
awesome insights. These were expressed in 'The Prayer of the Great O's', known as the Advent
Antiphons, which were said from 17 December. This prayer expresses two great truths about

Christ. First, that he was the eternal Son of God, the second person of the Trinity, the eternal Wisdom who had always been guiding God's people. Second, that the great representatives of God's people, such as Moses and King David, prefigured Christ. Jesus was perceived as living to the full what these characters lived in a measure. In the fourteenth century a monk from the Durham monastery became a hermit on the island of Farne, just as had their monastery's founding saint, Cuthbert. As this unknown hermit meditated on this vein, his imagination ran riot, and he wrote this prayer to Christ:

You are David who scattered with strong arm your foes
and shattered death's barred gates to free your own people;
you slew the giant vaunting
and the sons of Jacob taunting
though you had but a sling.
You like wormwood undermining,
armed and battle not declining
victory did nobly gain.
Philistinian ranks were saddened,
Saul and his retainers gladdened
by the trophies of the slain.
Warfare for us waging blithely
to the cross-top leaping lithely
hell's great might you overthrew.
Wondrous tones from your harp ringing
– your wounds were in painful stringing –
yield a tune folk did not know.
Kindest Jesus then uphold us
when death's darkness does enfold us
be our comfort and our stay.

A Monk of Farne

Give to us Christ's strength blithely to surmount life's ills.
Give to us, O God, strong love
and that beautiful crown of the King.   *Ray Simpson*

Winter solstice

Psalm 8; Isaiah 45:8-13; Luke 21:25-38

I will give you treasures from dark, secret places.

Isaiah 45:3

The darkest and the coldest time
is also the brightest time:
O Christmas Christ,
the radiance around the moon
is not as fair
as the radiance
around your head.

O Holy One,
the majesty of the winter sea
is not as glorious as your majesty.

At the departing times
the coldest times
of our lives;
at the times of excitement
and the times of expectancy;
at the times of intersection,
when hard choices have to be made,
be with us, Prince of Peace.

Kate McIlhagga

Now begin the 12 long nights of yule. One night soon will be born Jesus, Son of the King of Glory, creation's Joy. You will gleam to him moon and furthest star. You will gleam to him hills and housetops afar.

Lord of the solstice,
on this day of briefest light
help us to be at home with the treasures of the dark.
As the days have drawn in
help us to flow with the ebb tides of life.
At the turning of the year
help us to welcome the Dawn from on high.

Ray Simpson

The eve of the great Nativity

Psalm 47; Isaiah 62:10-12; Matthew 1:18-25

An angel of the Lord appeared to the shepherds, and the glory of the Lord shone round about them.

Luke 2:9

This night is the long night.
It will snow and it will drift.
White snow there will be till day,
white moon there will be till morn.
This night is the eve of the Great Nativity,
this night is born Mary Virgin's Son,
this night is born Jesus, Son of the King of Glory,
this night is born to us the root of our joy,
this night gleamed the sun of the mountains high,
this night gleamed sea and shore together,
this night was born Christ the King of greatness.
Ere it was heard that the Glory was come,
heard was the wave upon the strand.
Ere 'twas heard that his foot had reached earth,
heard was the song of the angels glorious;

this night is the long night.
Glowed to him wood and tree,
glowed to him mount and sea,
glowed to him land and plain,
when that his foot was come to earth.

Carmina Gadelica

Babe of Heaven, Defenceless Love,
in order to come to us
you have to travel far from your home.
Come to strengthen us
on our pilgrimage of trust on earth.
Your birth will show us
the simplicity of the Father's love,
the wonder of being human.
Help us to live fully human lives for you.

Ray Simpson

Reflections

Advent

Advent says Christmas is coming –
but it is more than a countdown,

and more than a warning
that the time is short
for all we have to do:

Advent is for preparing –
not only for Christmas
but for preparing ourselves;

Advent is for waiting
not only for Christmas to come
but for waiting 'on the Lord'
in stillness and in silence;

Advent is for watching
not only for the postman
but for Christ when he comes;

Advent believes that Christ is coming
and talks of hope at the end of time,
at the end of life.

And so, for generations,
in Advent, people looked to the future,
for the Second Coming
and the end of time.

And I believe that the End is Christ:

that when I come to the end of my time
Christ will be there;

that when human history comes to the end
Christ will be there.

Beyond that,
beyond what we can see,
or dare not hazard a guess
and I will not limit hope.

But Advent believes that Christ is coming,
not only at the end of time,
but now.

Advent is watching
to see what he is doing in the world
and watching for Christ coming to you,

you recognising and receiving him,
him bringing you peace and joy
and setting you free.

Ken Taylor

Hope

'What hope is there when...'
begin so many questions.

But always there is hope;
and where there's hope, there's life.

Hope cannot be defined –
that would restrict it straight away;

as soon as you say what you hope for
you limit the possibilities –
and hope has no limits.

Hope is realistic:
it faces squarely the enormity of evil
and the sin that disfigures every human life.

It has known failure, and disappointment,
suffering and despair,
and not been broken.

Hope is not optimism,
never that superficial, arrogant belief

that all will turn out well in the end
regardless of what we do.

Optimism is complacent, brash, insensitive,
and hope is none of these.

Hope is humble, trusting, vulnerable,
and quite invincible.

Hope is an open space,
it is room to manoeuvre,
to grow, develop, reach out,
and move forward.

Hope insists there is always a way forward,
a way out of the impasse;
but it is only a possible way forward:
we do not have to take it.

We do not have to move or change or grow;
we can stay exactly where we are if we wish –
denying hope, refusing life,
rejecting resurrection.

But hope believes that,
whatever happens,
we are never at the end of the road,
because just ahead of us is God,
opening up a way for us to follow:

'Hard pressed on every side,
we are never hemmed in;
bewildered, we are never at our wits' end;
hunted, we are never abandoned to our fate;
struck down, we are not left to die.'

There is certain and unlimited hope for you –

to be accepted and risked in faith,
responding to the beckoning of God.

Ken Taylor

A is for Advent

There are many words connected with the Advent season which begin with A. These 'A' words can be used as the basis for individual talks, in a series of assemblies or services, all together.

A – Anticipated

The birth of Jesus was anticipated in the writings and words of God's messengers many hundreds of years before. We can still read the anticipation in the words of the prophets Isaiah and Micah, telling of a new King who would be born, and even anticipating the town where the birth would take place, Bethlehem. Some people anticipated that the promised leader would be a strong warrior, while others thought he would be a man of peace.

A – Adventure

The whole experience was an adventure for the wise men. They had been used to power and control, and probably enjoyed real comfort and security. To leave all that behind because of some old writings and a strange star in the sky was quite an adventure. The adventure got stronger when they visited a confused and angry King Herod, and more exciting still when they found Jesus and knelt before him.

A – Aches

Have you ever been for a long walk on a dusty, stony track in the heat of the sun? Mary and Joseph had to walk for a few days to make their way from their home village of Nazareth to the town of Bethlehem so that Joseph could be added to the lists of people being counted at that time. They probably walked all the way, with Joseph carrying their clothes and bags with all that they could manage, and Mary struggling on, knowing that the baby was due at any time. There is little wonder that they were keen to rest their aching limbs in whatever place they could find, even the stable.

A – Astonished

That's just one of many words that could be used to describe the shocked and stunned surprise of the shepherds on the hillside. First it was the dazzling light, then the strange and powerful message of an angel who spoke to them. Then they were astonished by the choir, and astonished by finding this very special baby having just been born in a stable and wrapped in a cloth. The whole experience was Astonishing.

A – Angels

There are a number of angels in the Advent stories. There was the angel called Gabriel, who had the duty of telling Mary that she was to be the mother of the son of God. Then there was the angel who visited Joseph in a dream and encouraged him to stick with Mary, to care for her, and to love her and the special child Jesus. And then there were the amazing angels – perhaps too many to count – who visited the hillside above Bethlehem to tell the shepherds the good news about the birth of Jesus.

A – Awesome

What was it that made the wise men kneel at the side of the manger and leave precious, expensive gifts? The baby Jesus probably didn't look any different from any other new-born baby, yet for them this was an awesome sight and an awesome moment. They had been led there by a star in the sky, and they knew in their hearts that this little baby would change the world. For Mary and Joseph, as they welcomed the wise men and watched them worship their son, this was also quite awesome. Mary continued to wonder about it and think it all through.

A – And ...

And what now? We know the stories, we know that Advent is about getting ready to welcome Jesus again, and we know that God sent his Son to be born in that dirty, smelly place. And so it is up to us – we either let ourselves get all wrapped up in the fuss we all make over Christmas, or we are different and allow God to lead us, like the shepherds and wise men, to worship that awesome child.

Nick Harding

The Bible

(The reader should hold a large black Bible)

I do not love this book
because it is black enough to please Puritans,
holy enough to scare demons,
thick enough to stop bullets,
heavy enough to squash flies;
but because sometimes when I read it
I am moved
deeper than tears.

I do not love this book because
they say it is the very words of God,
and polish every dot and comma,
like golden ornaments
in an idolatrous temple;
but because sometimes when I read it
God speaks in a strange tongue
deeper than words.

I do not love this book
because the passionate preacher
beats the truth out of it
with his blunt fist
and sharp ideas,
(for some use the book
to support their opinions,
as others might use it
to support their tables).
But I do love this book
because sometimes when I read it
I am disturbed by a truth
deeper than thought.

And when I read of Jesus,
then I know,
that he is the Truth
that moves my soul –
the living Word of God.

Peter Dainty

Living in hope

Isaiah 11:1-10; Psalm 72:1-7; 18, 19

Hope is a strange land to live in;
for some, little more than a misty marshland
of wishful thinking;
for others, firm ground beneath the feet
and already the hint of gold on the horizon
heralding sunrise.

Israel,
finding it too hard
to hold on to their hope in an invisible God
found instead Saul;
why, you had only to look at him!
Head and shoulders above the rest of them,
surely Saul would deliver them
from the fear of their enemies,
surely Saul would be the king above all kings?
They lived in hope.

And when Saul failed them
as people are apt to do
(especially those we put on pedestals)
well, there was David,
the golden boy, the man after God's own heart:
surely he ... ?
And then Solomon,
munificent architect of that magnificent temple,
renowned for his wisdom and wealth:
surely he ... ?
They lived in hope.

But no.
The kingliness of the invisible God
proved too hot for mere mortals to handle and,
one after the other,
crowned heads were turned
by power, spun and crumbled into ruin
as the rot set in and the royal family tree
was finally felled:
hope grounded.

Until,
from the tree stump
a pale, brave, incongruous shoot
broke, almost unnoticed,
through the dark mouldy stuff.
What would become of it?

And we, we hopefuls, are we the same?
Finding it too hard
to hold on to any hope
we may ever have had in an invisible God,
do we count on a change of prime minister,
party or president –
or have we lost even that meagre hope,
reckoning 'politicians are all the same . . .'?
And do we then lower our sights,
hope for less:
that the children will pass their exams and find work;
that Dad's cancer will go into remission,
that it'll stay fine for the big match
and I'll find a nice coat in the charity shop:
is that too much to hope for,
God – is that too much to ask?

No. It is too little.
And yet – yes, maybe it is too much.

Come on, I want you to dig deep into your soul,
tell me what you *really* hope,
you know, 'If you could have three wishes . . .'
(True, I am not your fairy godmother
but I am, in fact, God.)
Tell me about your longing for peace,
for a world where those who have plenty are prodigal,
the poor belong to the past
and the future is free.
Tell me: I'm listening,
and your cry
echoes in my heart
echoes my heart.

And your lesser hopes,
nudged to the surface by the day's needs,
I hear them too;
they are part of that great cacophony,
my world sounding off,
from which I must distil a symphony.

The tree was felled:
but what of that maverick shoot?

First choice of route I cannot guarantee,
but safe arrival at your hoped-for destination, yes:
the shoot is the first planting
and the first seeding
of the new Eden:
anchor your hope in nothing less
than its good earth
and the certainty of its springing eternal.

For the peace, the perfection for which you hope is there,
though it lies on the other side
of judgement, and redemption:
will you walk through these?
For there are no easy answers,
no quick healing of my people's wounds,
no saying 'Peace!' where there is no justice,
no saying 'Hope!' where there is no willingness
to walk the way of the cross ...
To be free from persecution,
prejudice must welcome light;
greed must learn grace;
to be free from poverty,
wealth must be cast on the water;
fat cat and church mouse embrace;
to be free from abuse, anger must yield
without a fight and face down,

as our trees are felled
and the whole earth is judged
by that maverick shoot,
God's perfect King

equipped with the Spirit of God for an uncertain term
but that very Spirit personified;
until that day when the glory of God
puts the sun and the moon out of business
and we live not in hope
but there, in the hoped-for,
sufficient presence of God himself.

Sheila Walker

Meditation

Advent 1 – Mark 13:24-37

'But in those days, after that suffering, the sun will be darkened, and the moon will not give its light, and the stars will be falling from heaven, and the powers in the heavens will be shaken. Then they will see "the Son of Man coming in clouds" with great power and glory. Then he will send out the angels, and gather his elect from the four winds, from the ends of the earth to the ends of heaven ... Truly I tell you, this generation will not pass away until all these things have taken place. Heaven and earth will pass away, but my words will not pass away.'

Mark 13:24-27, 30, 31

Meditation of a modern-day Christian

The sun dark,
moon dull,
stars falling from heaven?

Well if that's happened, *I* haven't heard,
nor anyone else, come to that.
There's been the odd eclipse, of course,
meteors too,
but nothing to worry about,
no upheaval to shatter the cosmos
and signal the end of time.
So what did Jesus mean,
claiming his own generation would see such things?
Was he wrong,
deluded,
or could he have meant something else?
Do you know what: I think he did,
for he talked of heaven and earth passing away,
not *us* –
of his elect being gathered together
when these things happen to welcome him on his return.
This life may end, in other words,
but not the life to come,
our hope being in things unseen –
a kingdom beyond this world.
That's what matters:
faith in the future shaping the present,
so that instead of fretting about what's to come
we live now as he would wish.
I'm not saying it won't happen,
the end of life as we know it –
no doubt one day it will –
but his point was we have nothing to fear,
for he will be with us always,
faithful though all else may fail.
Don't brood on tomorrow.
Rejoice today,
and trust in him.
We may pass on before he comes,
but we will never pass away.

Prayer

Almighty God,
thank you for giving us joy in the present
and hope for the future;
the sure and certain knowledge that your love
not only surrounds us now,
but will continue to do so for all eternity,
nothing in heaven or earth,
life or death,
being able to separate us from it.
Deepen our faith in everything you hold in store,
and may that assurance shape every aspect of who and what we are.
Teach us to trust, serve and live for you,
today and always.

Nick Fawcett

Advent 2 – Mark 1:1-8

The beginning of the good news of Jesus Christ, the Son of God. As it is written in the prophet Isaiah, 'See, I am sending my messenger ahead of you, who will prepare your way; the voice of one crying out in the wilderness: "Prepare the way of the Lord, make his paths straight."' John the baptiser appeared in the wilderness, proclaiming a baptism of repentance for the forgiveness of sins.

Meditation of John the Baptist

You've heard of the Romans I suppose?
A decadent lot, to put it mildly –
but I'll say this for them:
they know how to build roads.
There are dozens everywhere,
even out here in the wilderness,
running straight and true, mile after mile,
and what a difference they've made,
journeys that once took a week now being a matter of days.
Not that Rome cares about us, of course.
They're thinking only of their armies.
One sniff of trouble,
let alone rebellion,
and they can be down on us now like a ton of bricks,
legions hurried in from across the world.
But you've got to admire their foresight –
how they're prepared, it seems, for anything.
I'm following their example, in a sense,
creating a road of a different sort,
into the wilderness of human lives,
for my task is to prepare the way of the Lord,
to make straight a path for his coming.
He'll be here soon, you see,
the day almost upon us,
but will you be ready receive him –
ready to hear his voice and meet his gaze,
to answer when he calls?
Oh, you may think so,
but don't be fooled,
for most of those who've come out to me here in the wilderness
aren't even close.
So take heed,
listen to my words,
and be prepared,
so that, whenever he comes, he may find the road clear,
a highway into your heart.

Prayer

Lord Jesus Christ,
prepare a way in our hearts
so that you may more fully enter in.
Break down the barriers of doubt and disbelief
that keep us from you –
faults and failings that deny your love
and obstruct your purpose.
Fill us with your love,
redeem us by your grace
and renew us by your power.
Make your path straight within us,
so that, consecrated to your service,
we, in turn, may help to prepare your way in the lives of others.

Nick Fawcett

Advent 3 – John 1:6-8, 19-28

This is the testimony given by John when the Jews sent priests and Levites from Jerusalem to ask him, 'Who are you?' He confessed and did not deny it, but confessed, 'I am not the Messiah.' And they asked him, 'What then? Are you Elijah?' He said, 'I am not.' 'Are you the prophet?' He answered, 'No.' Then they said to him, 'Who are you? Let us have an answer for those who sent us. What do you say about yourself?'

John 1:19-22

Meditation of John the Baptist

Who was I, they wanted to know,
and I knew full well what they were thinking:
that I was the Messiah,
the promised one of God,
come at last to set them free.
Why wouldn't they listen!
I'd spent weeks, months, out there in the wilderness,
pointing to the Christ,
preparing his way,
and still they'd made up their minds it was me.
Clearly I had to spell things out –
so that's what I did.
'Let's get this straight,' I said, 'once and for all:
it's not me!'
But still they kept on,
their minds, it seems, already made up.
I could have knocked their heads together,
such was my frustration,
but the misunderstanding wasn't entirely their fault,
much though I wish it were.
Somehow, despite my best intentions,
I'd put across too much of me
and too little of him.
Perhaps it was the camelhair clothes,

193

the diet of locusts and honey,
the desert lifestyle –
who can say? –
but, whatever it was, I'd obviously sent out mixed messages,
failing to point as unmistakably to the Christ as I imagined.
What about you?
Do you make the same mistake?
You may not think so,
but, take it from me, it's easily done,
what you say and do
and what you think you say and do
not necessarily the same.
So ask yourself this, prayerfully and honestly:
who does your life speak of –
you or Jesus?
The answer may surprise you,
as it did me.

Prayer

Remind us, Lord, that we are called to witness not to ourselves,
the Bible
or the Church,
but to you:
to what you said,
what you have done
and who you are.
Forgive us for losing sight of that,
unconsciously putting across a different message.
Forgive us for confusing incidentals with what really matters.
Help us to seek your glory before our own,
putting you first and self second,
so that, in all we do,
we may truly honour your name.

Nick Fawcett

Advent 4 – Luke 1:26-38

In the sixth month the angel Gabriel was sent by God to a town in Galilee called Nazareth, to a virgin engaged to a man whose name was Joseph, of the house of David. The virgin's name was Mary. And he came to her and said, 'Greetings, favoured one! The Lord is with you.' But she was much perplexed by his words and pondered what sort of greeting this might be. The angel said to her, 'Do not be afraid, Mary, for you have found favour with God.'

Luke 1:26-30

Meditation of Mary, the mother of Jesus

Don't be afraid, he said!
As though angels popping up out of the blue are two a penny,
no cause for concern.
Well I'm sorry, but I was petrified,

caught between the urge to run and scream.
And when he started on about being favoured by God,
blessed among women,
it only made things worse.
Who was *I* to be singled out, *I* to be chosen –
a nobody like me from Nazareth?
Whoever this guy was, he'd come to the wrong house,
and the sooner he was gone the better.
But he *didn't* go,
and somehow, despite myself, I listened,
my amazement growing by the second
as he talked of a child I would bear;
a saviour who would rule over the house of David
and whose kingdom would never end.
'How can this be?' I asked.
'For a start, I'm still a virgin!'
But he wasn't finished yet, not by a long way,
this child he spoke of to be not just my son,
but *God's* too,
conceived by his Spirit.
Well, if I was troubled before,
I'd more reason to be then,
for this was mind-blowing stuff,
certain to turn the world upside down
and change my life for ever.
Yet somehow I suddenly felt strangely calm,
happy to accept whatever was asked of me,
no questions asked.
Why?
Because, if God was really speaking,
and could actually use someone as ordinary as me,
then surely *nothing* was beyond him,
however impossible it might seem.
The future was in *his* hands, not mine,
and what better place could there be to leave it!

Prayer

Mighty and mysterious God,
for all kinds of reasons we don't find faith easy.
We consider what is asked of us,
the scale of your challenge,
and we feel small,
incapable of rising to it.
We come up against questions of faith,
and we struggle for answers,
so much seeming to defy explanation.
And though part of us longs to serve you,
another part rebels,
preferring to serve self instead,
resisting your call and turning from your way.

Help us, despite everything that fights against you,
that deflects us from the path of faithful discipleship,
to stay true nonetheless.
Give us the courage, confidence and conviction we need
to understand what you want from us
and gladly to respond.

Nick Fawcett

CHRISTMAS

PRAYERS

A Time of Worship

Loving God,
at this time of giving and receiving,
of showing our love and gratitude to others
through the exchanging of cards and presents,
we are reminded of the great gift you have given us in Christ
and of how little we have to offer in return.
You have blessed us in so much:
receive our worship.

Whatever we might bring, it can never repay you.
Whatever we might sacrifice,
it can scarcely begin to express our thanks,
but what we can offer and gladly bring
is our praise,
our homage,
our adoration,
offered in the name of Jesus.
You have blessed us in so much:
receive our worship.

Like the choir of angels on the night of his birth
we sing your praise and tell out the good news.
Like the shepherds, returning from the manger,
we give you the glory for all that we have heard and seen.
Like the magi, kneeling in wonder,
we offer our gifts as a token of our love and sign of our commitment.
You have blessed us in so much:
receive our worship.

Loving God,
at this time of giving and receiving
we do not have much to bring to you,
but we offer this time together –
our songs,
our reading,
our thinking, speaking and listening –
and we offer ourselves, such as we are,
in reverent praise and joyful celebration.
You have blessed us in so much:
receive our worship.
In the name of Christ.

Nick Fawcett

Loving God,
you have come to us in Christ.
So now we come to you,
to offer our worship,
to hear your word
and to reflect on your love.

David Adam

We rejoice with Mary and Joseph,
with the shepherds and the angels,
with the wise men,
with the Church in heaven and on earth.
We commend ourselves,
all peoples and the whole world
to your unfailing love.

David Adam

We come before the Christ child,
we kneel before the infant,
we adore with the shepherds,
we worship with the wise men,
we love him with Mary and Joseph,
we wonder at the 'Word made flesh',
we bow before the mystery.
We sing glory to God with the angels.
We will travel this day rejoicing,
glorifying and praising God.

David Adam

Praise and Thanksgiving

Loving God,
we thank you for this day and all it speaks of –
your promise of old to send a Messiah to your people,
the fulfilment of that promise through the sending of your Son,
the realisation of those long years of expectation,
the glad tidings proclaimed by the angels,
the wonder and mystery of that first Christmas.
For all this time means and will always mean,
we praise you.

We thank you for this season's power to move, inspire and challenge,
to gladden the hardest of hearts and most broken of spirits,
to stir our minds and capture our imagination.
For all this time means and will always mean,
we praise you.

We thank you for the special things we associate with Christmas –
the spreading of goodwill,
the sharing of friendship,
the longing for peace,

and the expressing of love.
For all this time means and will always mean,
we praise you.

But above all we thank you for the truth behind this day –
the message that you have come to us,
that you love us,
that you have shared our humanity,
and that you want us to share in your everlasting life,
For all this time means and will always mean,
we praise you.

Loving God,
accept our praise,
receive our thanksgiving,
bless our celebrations,
and may the wonder of the Gospel
come alive in our hearts this day,
through Jesus Christ our Lord.   *Nick Fawcett*

Father,
as we celebrate the birth of Jesus, your Word,
we thank you with our whole heart.
The bells and lights and presents and decorations
in church and in our homes
express our thanks to you, Lord,
for coming into the world in person.   *Susan Sayers*

Thank you
for being prepared to face the dangers and risks
of human mistakes and sin
in order to save us.   *Susan Sayers*

For all the many blessings of this past year
and for all the good that you have enabled us to do;
for the experiences that have taught us
humility and patience,
we thank you.   *Susan Sayers*

Father,
we can never thank you enough
for coming to rescue us,
and we praise you now and in our lives.   *Susan Sayers*

We thank you that through your love
we can receive so many joys and blessings in our lives.
We thank you especially for the relationships
which enrich our lives so much.   *Susan Sayers*

Lord God, thank you for healing me
with the blessing of your forgiveness.
Thank you for your generous, shining love
that changes crusted lives and broken spirits.
Thank you that you love us as we are
and are happy to enlist our help
in the lighting of dark places,
bringing hope and joy.
Blessed be God for ever.

Susan Sayers

Thank you for the holy family,
Mary, Joseph and the others.
May families reflect their dedication to put your will first;
may purity, love and trust grow strong in our household.

Ray Simpson

Confession – a time for receiving

Lord Jesus Christ,
we recall today how you entered your world
and the world did not know you;
how you came to your own people,
and they would not receive you;
how you were born in Bethlehem,
and there was no room for you in the inn.
From the beginning it was the same old story –
your love rejected,
your grace ignored.
Lord have mercy,
and teach us to receive you with gladness.

We remember that you came to set people free
and to offer a new relationship with God –
breaking down the barriers which keep us apart,
bearing the price of our disobedience,
opening up the way to life.
Yet we remember, too,
that though some listened for a moment,
few followed you to the end.
Time and again it was the same old story –
your love rejected,
your grace ignored.
Lord have mercy,
and teach us to receive you with gladness.

We know we are no better,
each of us guilty, day after day,
of spurning your guidance,

forgetting your goodness
and abandoning your way.
We talk of commitment,
but our faith is weak;
we speak of following you,
but follow only our own inclinations;
we claim to be a new creation,
but it is the old self that still holds sway.
Time and again it is the same old story –
your love rejected,
your grace ignored.
Lord have mercy,
and teach us to receive you with gladness.

Lord Jesus Christ,
we marvel that, despite it all –
the world's hostility and our own faithlessness –
still you reach out in love,
never giving up,
refusing to write us off.
We thank you that you are always ready
to offer a fresh start, a new beginning,
to anyone willing to receive it.
Come what may, it is the same old story –
you continue seeking us out,
however often we thrust you aside,
your love rejected,
your grace ignored.
Lord have mercy,
and teach us to receive you with gladness.

In your name we ask it.   *Nick Fawcett*

Intercessions

Christ, our Saviour, is born. Eternal God breaks into human existence to transform and redeem it.
In the darkness of night, God's majestic glory becomes a vulnerable newborn baby. The Creator of
all is entirely dependent on those he has created. Such is the measure of his infinite love.

As we gather to worship the Christchild,
born today,
let us pray trustfully
to our heavenly Father.
Father, we pray for all Christians
celebrating with us all over the world,
in all climates, times and seasons
as our planet turns.

Silence for prayer

Light of ages:
be born in our hearts.

Father, we pray for all areas of darkness
where your light is desperately needed
to bring peace, understanding,
sensitivity and compassion.

Silence for prayer

Light of ages:
be born in our hearts.

Father, we commend to you our homes,
families, neighbours and friends;
all children and young babies,
all being born today.

Silence for prayer

Light of ages:
be born in our hearts.

We pray for those who are hungry,
cold or homeless;
for all who are separated from their loved ones;
all who find the festivities of Christmas
emphasising their isolation and misery.

Silence for prayer

Light of ages:
be born in our hearts.

We thank you for all who have worshipped you
throughout the ages;
for the lives and examples of all
who shone with your light
and now rest in your peace.

Silence for prayer

Light of ages:
be born in our hearts.

Father in thankfulness we praise and worship you.
May Christ be born into the world in every generation
through those who love and serve him.

Silence for prayer

Merciful Father,
accept these prayers
for the sake of your Son,
our Saviour Jesus Christ.

Susan Sayers

Lord Jesus Christ,
born an outcast and refugee,
in weakness and frailty,
as we rejoice today hear our prayers
for all those who have no cause for celebration.
Lord, in your mercy,
hear our prayer.

We pray for the hungry and the homeless,
the poor and the unemployed,
the oppressed and the exploited,
the lonely and the downhearted.
Lord, in your mercy,
hear our prayer.

We pray for the sick and the dying,
the sorrowful and the bereaved,
victims of violence and war,
all whose lives have been shattered by tragedy and disaster.
Lord, in your mercy,
hear our prayer.

Lord Jesus Christ,
born to set your people free,
come again to our world,
bringing reconciliation where there is division,
and comfort where there is sorrow,
hope where there is despair,
and confidence where there is confusion.
Lord, in your mercy,
hear our prayer.

Come and bring light where there is darkness,
and love where there is hatred,
faith where there is doubt,
and life where there is death.
Lord, in your mercy,
hear our prayer.

Lord Jesus Christ,
come again to our world,
and bring that day nearer when your kingdom will come,
and your will be done.
Lord, in your mercy,
hear our prayer,
for we ask it in your name.

Nick Fawcett

As we recall the star that shone out above Bethlehem,
we thank you for the gift of your Son, the light of the world.
Let us join with people down the ages who have celebrated
this event and rejoice.
Lord, in your mercy
hear our prayer.

We pray for the Church worldwide at this special time,
remembering the places where worship is difficult or dangerous;
the places where worship is joyful but food is scarce;
and the places where the festive season
is mixed with worries about the future.
May your Son's birth bring hope to all communities
and may your Church be strengthened in all its work
to make you better known.
Lord, in your mercy
hear our prayer.

Lord, bring a new spirit of cooperation
and search for peace in our world.
May those who hold the key to progress
be encouraged to seek reconciliation and peaceful change.
And in our own land, may fairness and justice
guide those in local and national government.
Lord, in your mercy
hear our prayer.

In our prayers, let us remember all those who are on duty
over the Christmas period, while we celebrate your Son's birth.
We pray especially for the emergency services,
our armed forces and our hospitals;
for ships at sea, for charities offering relief to the homeless,
for the police and for clergy called to those in need of support.
Lord, in your mercy
hear our prayer.

In our own community we pray for . . .
Lord, in your mercy
hear our prayer.

We bring to you, Lord, all who are unwell in mind, body or spirit
and who need your comfort at this time.
In a moment of silence we remember those known to us
who are sick, lonely or depressed . . .
Help us and all those who are in a caring role
to make a difference this Christmas
and to bring some comfort and relief to those who suffer.
Lord, in your mercy
hear our prayer.

We remember fondly those who have died
and are now at peace with you.
You know, Lord, that the loss of a loved one, recently or long ago,
is difficult for us to cope with at Christmas.
May the memories we have be good recollections
of characteristics and events which have meant a great deal to us.
And may the story of Christmas renew our faith
in the hope of eternal life.
Merciful Father,
accept these prayers
for the sake of your Son,
our Saviour Jesus Christ.

Rupert Bristow

We pray for all the groups of Christians
who are celebrating Christ's birth today.

Silence for prayer

O God, we thank you
for loving us so much.

We pray for all babies,
that they may be given love and care.

Silence for prayer

O God, we thank you
for loving us so much.

We pray for all who are missing their loved ones,
and all who find Christmas difficult.

Silence for prayer

O God, we thank you
for loving us so much.

We pray for all those in pain
and those with debilitating illness.

Silence for prayer

O God, we thank you
for loving us so much.

We pray for those in prison
and for their families.

Silence for prayer

O God, we thank you
for loving us so much.

We pray for the homeless,
and all refugees.

Silence for prayer

O God, we thank you
for loving us so much.

We thank you for the joy of Christmas
and welcome you in our homes.

Silence for prayer

**Father,
accept these prayers
for the sake of your Son,
our Saviour, Jesus Christ.**

Susan Sayers

Jesus, your mother Mary in her simplicity and sincerity
was ready for your coming into our world.
We pray silently to be made ready for you to come again,
and for all our special needs.

Gerald O'Mahony

Based on Bible Texts

Luke 2:1-7

Sovereign God,
with Mary and Joseph gazing into the manger,
with shepherds hurrying to and from the stable,
with angels praising you on high,
with wise men kneeling before the Christ-child,
and with generations across the years
who have known and loved your Son,
experiencing his presence in their lives,
so now we join to marvel and celebrate,
offering you our heartfelt worship and joyful praise
for your gift beyond words,
Jesus Christ our Lord.

Nick Fawcett

Luke 2:15-21

Lord Jesus Christ,
like the shepherds of old
we come with hearts ablaze to celebrate your birth, to kneel in wonder,

to offer our thanksgiving
and to respond personally to you.
May we, like them, thrill to the good news of your coming, and go on our way rejoicing,
making known to those we meet
everything we have found to be true in you.
In your name we pray.

Nick Fawcett

Luke 2:25-36

Lord Jesus Christ,
come among us in this time of worship.
As you came in Bethlehem
and will come again in glory,
so, we ask, draw near now
and open our eyes to your presence among us here.
Speak your word,
impart your blessing,
grant your mercy
and renew our faith,
so that we may be ready at every moment
to welcome you and be equipped
to live more truly to your praise and glory.

Nick Fawcett

John 1:1-14

Loving God,
remind us that in taking flesh and being born as a baby,
you identified yourself fully with humankind,
not imposing yourself upon us
but drawing alongside,
inviting a response.
Remind us that you made yourself vulnerable,
exposing yourself to persecution and rejection from the beginning,
willingly bearing the price of love.
Open our hearts today to respond –
freely, gladly and reverently –
ready to risk something for you
who risked so much for us.

Nick Fawcett

Come and Abide with Us

Glory be to God in the highest,
to our God who has come among us
and taken upon him our flesh.
God, we give you thanks and praise
for your wonderful gift of yourself.
Help us to know your presence in our lives and in our homes.

We rejoice with the whole Church
as it celebrates your love for us.
We ask your blessing upon any churches
where there is oppression or persecution at this time.
We pray for all who will preach the word
and celebrate the sacraments
today and throughout this season.
We pray for those who will celebrate
in refugee camps and prisons
or completely on their own.
We remember those who would have liked
to have been with us in our worship.

Silence

Jesus, proclaimed by the angels, born of Mary,
come and abide with us.

We give thanks for the message of the angels
and we pray for peace on earth
and goodwill among all peoples.
We pray for all who are caught up in war or violence at this time.
We remember the world's poor, the homeless
and any who live in fear or anxiety.
We pray for all who feel neglected or unwanted.

Silence

Jesus, proclaimed by the angels, born of Mary,
come and abide with us.

We give thanks that our Lord was born into an ordinary family
and lived in an ordinary home.
We ask your blessing
upon all our loved ones and friends this Christmas:
may we know your presence in our joys and celebrations.
We remember all who have to spend this Christmas away
from their homes and loved ones.

Silence

Jesus, proclaimed by the angels, born of Mary,
come and abide with us.

We give thanks that Christ became human
that we might share in the Divine;
that through Christ is our salvation.
We pray for all who are ill or unable to enjoy life.
We remember those who are fearful for their future
or who are unable to cope with the present.
Lord, may they know your love and care for them.

Silence

Jesus, proclaimed by the angels, born of Mary,
come and abide with us.

We give thanks that you came to earth to lift us into heaven.
You took upon you our life
that life could be eternal.
We remember loved ones who have died this year
and those with whom we have spent Christmases past.
Lord, grant to them the gift of life and joy eternal.

Silence

Merciful Father,
accept these prayers
for the sake of your Son,
our Saviour Jesus Christ.   *David Adam*

Lord Jesus Christ,
come among us in this time of worship.
As you came in Bethlehem and will come again in glory,
so, we ask, draw near now
and open our eyes to your presence among us here.
Speak your word,
impart your blessing,
grant your mercy
and renew our faith,
so that we may be ready at every moment to welcome you
and be equipped to live more truly to your praise and glory.   *Nick Fawcett*

Lord Jesus, you have come among us,
to share in our lives and to let us share in yours.
As you give yourself to us today,
help us to give ourselves to you.   *David Adam*

Jesus Christ, you have come
to lift us into the fullness of your kingdom.
You, dear Lord, have become human
that we may share in your divinity.
You have come to live among us
that we may be your friends.
We give you thanks for Christmas,
for the gift of your presence and yourself.   *David Adam*

Every day can be a Christmas day,
for the Lord comes to us as he came to Bethlehem.
He seeks to be born in us,

he wants us to come to him like the shepherds,
he wants to live in and work through us,
he comes eternally and seeks room in our lives,
for the Lord comes to us as he came to Bethlehem.

David Adam

We give thanks for all who celebrate Christmas,
all who are worshipping in churches and in their homes,
all who acknowledge Jesus in their midst.

David Adam

Thank you, Jesus,
for being born
into our world.
Thank you for showing us God's love.

Susan Sayers

Son of the elements,
Son of the heavens,
Son of the moon,
Son of the sun,
Son of Mary of the God-mind,
Son of God, firstborn of all creation,
dwell with us today.

Ray Simpson

The True Meaning of Christmas

Loving God,
we thank you for this season of Christmas –
for all it has meant to so many over the years,
all it continues to mean to us,
and all it will mean in generations to come.
You have given us so much:
receive our praise.

We thank you for carols old and new,
for familiar and much-loved words of Scripture,
for all that speaks of your coming among us in Christ.
You have given us so much:
receive our praise.

We thank you for reunions with family and friends,
for the spirit of giving and receiving,
for the mood of goodwill and celebration.
You have given us so much:
receive our praise.

We thank you for all the good things we will enjoy –
good food,

good company,
good fun.
You have given us so much:
receive our praise.

Loving God,
help us in all of this to keep sight
of the heart of Christmas,
what it all really means –
to celebrate the birth of the infant Christ,
to worship him as joyfully and reverently
as shepherds and wise men long ago,
to welcome and follow him as faithfully
as those who left everything to be his disciples.
You have given us so much:
receive our praise.

Loving God,
forgive us if we have lost sight
of what this season truly means.
Forgive us if we have become over-familiar
with its simple yet wonderful message.
Forgive us if we have failed to make room for Christ
in our Christmas celebrations.
You have given us so much:
receive our praise.

Speak to us now
through all that we shall do and share,
all we shall sing and hear,
so that our lives may be touched
by the wonder of his presence.
You have given us so much,
**receive our praise
through Jesus Christ.**   *Nick Fawcett*

The Christmas Story

Help us through all we share today
to hear the story of Christmas speaking to us
as though for the first time.
May familiar and well-loved words take on new meaning,
so that we may share the elation of Mary,
the excitement felt by the shepherds,
and the wonder experienced by the wise men.
May what was news of great joy for them,
bring joy likewise to us,
this and every day,
through Jesus Christ our Lord.   *Nick Fawcett*

Remind us, Lord,
that after the stable came a cross,
after birth, death,
after celebration, sacrifice,
and after pleasure, pain,
each bound by a single stem:
the wonder of your love.
Help us to rejoice in all that this season means,
not just in part,
but in full.

Nick Fawcett

The world Jesus was born into
was the world we know.
Thank you for being prepared
to face the dangers and risks
of human mistakes and sin
in order to save us.

Susan Sayers

Sovereign God,
though we have heard it so many times before,
and though the words of readings and carols
we will share today are so familiar
we know them almost back to front,
that through the worship we bring you
our hearts may thrill again to the good news of Christ,
and our spirits soar at the message of his coming.
Grant us new insights and deeper understanding,
so that our faith may be enriched and our joy increased
as we celebrate the great gift of your Son –
glad tidings yesterday,
today
and every day.

Nick Fawcett

The Glorious Message

Gracious God,
we thank you for the glorious message of this season:
the glad tidings of great joy,
ever old yet ever new.
We thank you for the faith of Mary,
the commitment of Joseph,
the message of the angels
and the response of the shepherds –
the way you changed their lives that day in Bethlehem.
Above all, though,
we thank you that you have changed our lives too;
that the good news these heard and responded to long ago

is news still today –
as special now as then,
and for us as much as anyone!
Teach us never to forget that wonderful truth;
knowledge burn brightly in our hearts,
a constant source of joy and inspiration,
whatever life may bring.
In the name of Christ, we ask it.

Nick Fawcett

This Christmas we pray
that we may stop our noise,
chatter and arguing
long enough
to hear the angels
singing of hope and peace.

Susan Sayers

Birth Place

May we journey with you,
Jesus, Mary and Joseph,
to your birthplace at Bethlehem,
firm in the faith,
loyal to the truth,
obedient to your Father's will
along the path that leads to life.

Ray Simpson

Now is born Christ the king of greatness.
Glow to him stars and streets;
glow to him churches and trees.

Ray Simpson

Homes and the Homeless

We ask your blessing
upon all who do not celebrate this Christmas.
We remember all who will be homeless or lonely
and all who are poor or deeply in debt.
We pray that our homes
may be places of love and peace
where you, Christ, are welcome.
May we know that in the coming of others to us
you also come and seek our love.

David Adam

The Christmas story makes us reflect
how it should be in families,
each looking out for the other.
Holy Spirit of God, make our own families
to be a place where we feel at home.

Gerald O'Mahony

Many of us will be celebrating
with our families and friends.
We invite you to join us in all the festivities,
and ask you to teach us true loving.   *Susan Sayers*

We give thanks that our Lord was born
into an ordinary family
and lived in an ordinary home.
We ask your blessing
upon all our loved ones and friends this Christmas:
may we know your presence in our joys and celebrations.
We remember all who have to spend this Christmas
away from their homes and loved ones.   *David Adam*

As Christmas brings together
family members and friends,
and we make contact with those we seldom meet,
may all our relationships be nourished
with love and forgiveness,
and may we value one another more.   *Susan Sayers*

Jesus, born in a stable,
make here your home.
Jesus, born of a peasant girl,
make here your home.
Jesus, searched for by wise seekers,
make here your home.
Jesus, reared at a carpenter's bench,
make here your home.
Jesus, risen from the wintry ground of death,
make here your home.   *Ray Simpson*

Homemaker God,
who made yourself at home in a cowshed,
come to all who are sleeping rough.
May the light of the Bethlehem family
be a light for the homeless in our world.   *Ray Simpson*

Jesus Christ, Son of glory,
who for love comes among us,
bless to us this day of joy.
Open to us heaven's generous gates.
Strengthen our hope.
Revive our tired souls
till we sing the joys of your glory

with all the angels of heaven.
Hold also those who are sleeping rough,
those who feel shut out of society,
those who are cold and hungry,
and these we name before you now.

Ray Simpson

Many of us will be celebrating
with our families and friends.
We invite you to join us in all the festivities,
and ask you to teach us true loving.

Susan Sayers

The Shepherds

Lord Jesus Christ,
like the shepherds of old
we come with hearts ablaze to celebrate your birth,
to kneel in wonder,
to offer our thanksgiving
and to respond personally to you.
May we, like them, thrill to the good news of your coming,
and go on our way rejoicing,
making known to those we meet
everything we have found to be true in you.
In your name we pray.

Nick Fawcett

Holy Jesus, Son of God,
as we long to hear the songs of the angels,
may we keep our eyes and hearts fixed on your coming.
As we travel with the shepherds to Bethlehem,
may we bow before your beauty and your majesty.
When we return to our homes, fill our days with your glory,
that we may rejoice in your love and abiding presence,
Jesus Christ, our Saviour and our God.

David Adam

Lord, as we remember the shepherds
in the hills above Bethlehem,
open our eyes to your glory,
open our ears to the songs of angels,
grant to us the joy of the shepherds,
that we may come to your presence,
bow before you in love and adoration,
and go on our way rejoicing.
Through him who shared in our humanity,
even Jesus Christ, our Lord.

David Adam

Sharing Our Lives

Lord, we recognise our great need of your grace,
and give you thanks and praise
for making possible what would otherwise
be impossible.
Thank you, Lord Jesus,
for coming to share our human lives.
Dying, you destroyed our death.
Rising, you restored our life.
Lord Jesus, come again in glory.

Susan Sayers

Light of the World

Father, we rejoice and sing,
for you love us with a great love.
We give thanks to you for the coming of our Lord Jesus Christ
into our world and into our lives.
Let us enjoy your presence with us,
and the love you offer to us in Jesus our Lord.

We give thanks for all who celebrate Christmas,
all who are worshipping in churches and in their homes,
all who acknowledge Jesus in their midst.

Bless the outreach and the mission of your Church.
Give all your people the courage to tell the Gospel story
and proclaim your presence and love.

We remember all whose lives are darkened by fear,
those who have no faith,
those who doubt God and themselves.

Silence

Jesus, Light of the World,
come scatter the darkness.

We ask for peace on the earth
and good will among all peoples,
that we may learn to accept your peace,
share your peace and live your peace.
We remember before you
all who suffer from war or violence at this time, especially . . .

Silence

Jesus, Light of the World,
come scatter the darkness.

We give thanks for our homes
and the friends with whom we will celebrate this Christmas.
We remember absent friends and loved ones.
We remember all who are lonely
or feel rejected at this time.

Silence

Jesus, Light of the World,
come scatter the darkness.

We remember in your presence
all who are ill at home or in hospital,
all who are struggling in any way.
We pray for doctors and nurses
and everyone who will have to be at work today.

Silence

Jesus, Light of the World,
come scatter the darkness.

We give thanks that Jesus came down to lift us up,
that he lived that we might not die.
We remember loved ones departed
in the fullness of your kingdom.

Silence

Merciful Father,
**accept these prayers
for the sake of your Son,
our Saviour Jesus Christ.**   *David Adam*

We pray that the light of the world
may shine so brightly in our lives
that other people notice it
and are attracted to you
by the way we live and love.   *Susan Sayers*

Jesus, proclaimed by angels;
light up our darkness.
Jesus, worshipped by shepherds;
light up our darkness.
Jesus, adored by wise men;
light up our darkness.
Jesus, God who is with us now;
light up our darkness.   *Ray Simpson*

Jesus, you are the glory of eternity shining among us,
the tenderness of God here with us now.
Jesus, you are the Healing Person,
the pattern of goodness,
fulfilling among us the highest human hopes.
Jesus, you are the champion of the weak,
the counsellor of the despairing,
the brother of us all, who knows our every need.
Jesus, you are the splendour of the Father,
the Son of Mary,
our Bridge between Earth and the world beyond.

Ray Simpson

Prince of Peace

Child of Glory, Child of Mary,
at your birth you were proclaimed the Prince of Peace.
You came to remove the wall
that divides one people from another;
may walls of hostility and fear come tumbling down.

Ray Simpson

Word Made Flesh

May we make room with the innkeeper
and know the joy of the shepherds,
the message of the angels,
the seeking of the wise men,
the bliss of Mary,
the presence of the Christ-child; and may we rejoice
in the Word made flesh dwelling among us.

David Adam

As we celebrate Christmas,
when the Word of God became flesh,
we pray for the Church, the Body of Christ.
May we be so filled with God's loving life
that our actions touch the world with hope which lasts
even when Christmas decorations are put away.

Susan Sayers

This Day of Joy

Jesus Christ, Son of glory,
who for love comes among us,
bless to us this day of joy.
Open to us heaven's generous gates.
Strengthen our hope.
Revive our tired souls

till we sing the joys of your glory
with all the angels of heaven.

Hold also those who are sleeping rough,
those who feel shut out of society,
those who are cold and hungry,
and these we name before you now.

Ray Simpson

Sovereign God,
we can never repay your goodness
and never fully express our thanks,
but we bring you again today our praise and worship,
offered in the name of Jesus.
Like the choir of angels on the night of his birth,
we sing in adoration.
Like the shepherds,
returning from the manger,
we give you praise for everything we have experienced.
Like the magi,
kneeling in wonder,
we bring you our homage as a token of our love
and a sign of our commitment.
All we think, say, do and are
we bring to you in reverent praise and joyful celebration,
in the name of Christ.

Nick Fawcett

Mothers

O Saviour Christ,
you existed before the world began.
You came to save us
and we are witnesses of your goodness.
You became a tiny child in a cot
showing us the simplicity of our parents' love.
You chose Mary as your mother
and raised all motherhood to a divine vocation.
May all mothers be bearers of life and grace
to their husbands, their children
and to all who come to their homes.

Ray Simpson

Refugees

Thank you for the sanctuaries of Egypt
that were offered to the holy family,
for their acquaintance with God-honourers
of another land and religion,
for the hermits and holy people of the deserts.

We pray for God-honourers
who seek to welcome your servants
in Egypt, in Muslim lands and everywhere;
for refugees, for hermits and others who pattern
an alternative way to that of our acquisitive society.

Ray Simpson

Christmas Preparations

Here I offer you, Lord Jesus,
all my preparations for Christmas.
Teach me more about giving
and more about receiving.
Realign my priorities
in tune with your will,
and enable me to see more clearly
how best to celebrate your coming
as our Lord and Saviour.

Susan Sayers

Blessing of the Christmas Tree

Bless, O Lord, this Christmas tree,
all that goes on to it
and all that goes on around it.
May the needles that point upwards
lead us to worship the Creator
who came from heaven to be born as a child.
May the needles that fall to the ground
remind us of the needs of the poor
and those at the bottom of the social pile.
May the decorations that brighten this dark season
prompt us to celebrate it with thoughtfulness and joy.

Ray Simpson

A Grace before Christmas Dinner

Lord Jesus, born in Bethlehem
on the first Christmas Day,
welcome to this meal with us.
We give thanks to God for food on the table
and for the love and fellowship we share.
As we eat and drink to celebrate Christmas,
we know your love in our hearts.

Susan Sayers

A Christmas Blessing

God of Mary and Joseph,
God of the shepherds and the magi,
God of the baby lying in a manger,
God with us,
touch our hearts
with the living presence of Christ,
fill us with the love and joy
which he alone can bring,
and send us out to proclaim his kingdom,
glad tidings for all.
In his name we pray.

Nick Fawcett

SERVICES

Carol Service

This service follows a traditional pattern of lessons and carols, supplemented by meditations developing the themes of the readings. No visual material is recommended for this service.

Music

Sleep, holy babe (*Traditional Carol*)

Introduction

'Let us go now to Bethlehem and see this thing that has taken place, which the Lord has made known to us': the response of the shepherds to the good news of Christ's birth, and the beginning of a night which was to see them returning soon after 'glorifying and praising God for all they had heard and seen, as it had been told them'.

   We cannot, of course, see quite what they saw, even if we were able to go now to the Holy Land and visit the place where these great events unfolded, but we are here now to listen again to words of scripture which, familiar though they may be, still have the power to speak to us in new and unexpected ways. Let us step back then, and put ourselves in the shoes of those who were part of that extraordinary night of his birth, and let us hear afresh the good news of Jesus Christ, which God continues to make known to us today.

Lighting of Advent Candles

Carol

O come, all ye faithful

Prayer

Gracious God,
at this time of giving and receiving
we remember the greatest gift of all –
your coming to our world in Christ
to live and die among us,
your identifying with humankind
so that we might become your children
and know life in all its fullness.

Help us, as we hear again the Christmas message,
to understand more fully
the sheer magnitude of all you have given,

and as we celebrate this glad season
help us to receive Christ into our hearts,
and offer to you, through him,
our heartfelt praise and joyful service.

Reading

Luke 1:26-34

Meditation of Mary

'You've got it wrong,' I told him.
'You can't mean me,
no way!
Someone else perhaps,
more worthy, more important, but not me!'

Honestly, what did I have to commend me?
No connections or special qualities,
nothing –
just an ordinary girl from Nazareth,
so what could God see in me?

But it was academic anyway,
for I wasn't even married yet,
and there was no way I'd sleep with Joseph until I was.
So I came out with it straight, 'Sorry, but you're wrong!'

Only he wouldn't take no for an answer.
Just stood there smiling,
unruffled;
and before I knew it he was off again –
the message even more fantastic than before:
God's power overshadowing me,
a child born of the Holy Spirit,
the Son of God!

It was way over the top,
and I should have turned him out there and then,
but I was flummoxed,
too amazed to reply.
Even when I found my tongue
it wasn't much use to me –
my mind so befuddled with questions
that I ended up saying, of all things,
'Here am I, the servant of the Lord,
let it be with me according to your word.'

Oh, it sounded good, granted –
the epitome of humility –
but if you only knew what I was thinking,

you'd have a different picture then.
So what got into me, you ask?
How could I be so meek and accepting?

Well, what choice did I have, let's be honest,
for as the angel said, 'With God, nothing will be impossible.'
How could I argue with that?
There was no way out, was there?
But it's one thing to accept that in principle,
another when it turns your life upside down.

Do I believe it?
Well, I didn't at the time,
but I do now,
for I've just discovered I'm pregnant,
and I say this perfectly reverently,
God knows how!
It's astonishing and terrifying,
exciting yet mystifying,
my mind in turmoil,
not quite sure what to think any more.

But one thing is plain now,
beyond all question –
with God, quite clearly,
nothing is impossible!

Carol

The angel Gabriel from heaven came

Reading

Matthew 1:18-25

Meditation of Joseph

It was the strangest of dreams, ludicrous really,
yet I just can't get it out of my mind.
You see, I dreamt God was speaking to me.
No, not face to face, I don't mean that,
but through this angel,
claiming to be his special messenger.

And do you know what he told me?
Take Mary to be your wife, that's what.
Just when I'd decided to put her quietly aside,
hush up the scandal as best I could,
this character was telling me to think again.
And why?

Because apparently it was nothing to do with her,
the baby she's carrying not the result of some fleeting passion,
but conceived of the Holy Spirit,
ordained by God himself.

Well, I've heard a few excuses in my time
but that one really takes the biscuit!
I mean, who did the fellow think I was –
some fool born yesterday? It was laughable,
and I'd usually have dismissed it without a second thought.
Yet I didn't –
not then,
not now.

A dream it may have been,
but it's lived with me,
as vivid today as when I first dreamt it.
I can't say why exactly –
it was a mixture of things, I suppose.
There was Mary for a start,
the way she looked at me as she broke the news –
so trusting,
so innocent,
almost as though she too had met with God
and was confident I would understand.
Then there was Elizabeth and Zechariah –
heaven knows what got into them,
but they were simply delighted,
no hint of suspicion, let alone scandal, so far as they saw it –
I suppose that boy of theirs,
after so many disappointments,
was enough to turn anyone's mind.

But what really swung it was this feeling deep within
that somehow God had touched me;
that, like it or not,
life was changed for ever.

I was right in that, wasn't I? –
for we're on the road to Bethlehem as I speak,
my wife heavy with child,
wincing with pain,
praying it's not much further.

Did I do right, standing by her?
I still have my doubts, even now,
still find it hard to meet her eye,
for it takes some getting used to,
a child you had no part in.
But despite the questions, I've done my bit,
taking her for my wife, just as I was told.

Now it's God's turn, isn't it? –
over to him for the Saviour to be born,
God with us!
Was it a dream,
a figment of my imagination?
We'll soon see, won't we?

Carol

O little town of Bethlehem

Reading

Luke 2:1-7

Meditation of Mary

He looked so tiny lying there,
so vulnerable –
like a little china doll,
like thistledown swaying in the breeze –
and I wanted simply to hold him in my arms
and protect him from the world outside.
Could this be God's Son, I asked,
the one destined to be great,
the Prince of Peace,
a ruler over Israel?
Surely not!

It had been hard enough to believe at the start,
when the angel first broke the news –
to think that I, Mary, had been chosen above all others,
singled out to bear in my womb the Messiah –
but now, as I gazed down into the manger,
and saw those little arms waving,
that sweet innocent face wrinkled up in sleep,
and those eyes so tightly shut,
it seemed doubly impossible,
out of the question,
a foolish fancy of my fevered imagination.

Be sensible, I told myself,
there's no way God could take such a gamble,
no possibility,
if the fate of the world truly hung in the balance,
that he would stake it all on a helpless child,
least of all one born where we found ourselves –
a stable of all places!
And, as if to prove the point,
that very moment Jesus awoke,

tears filling his eyes,
a scream of protest on his lips,
and I realised he was hungry,
well past his usual feed.
It dawned on me then, the staggering implications –
he needed me, this child,
not just for food, or warmth, or protection,
but for everything,
his very future in my hands.
Would God allow that?
Could he ever need us as much as we need him?
No, there had to be some mistake –
it just couldn't be, could it?
Could it?

Carol

Child in the manger

Reading

Luke 2:8-14

Meditation of the shepherds

Don't talk to strange men.
Have you ever heard that expression?
I have,
dozens of times,
far more than I care to remember.

Why do I say that?
Because all too often it's me they mean by it,
me the one people look at
as, arm wrapped protectively round their child's shoulder,
they usher them away –
the look on their faces saying it all:
'Keep away, he spells trouble!'

Yes, that's how they see us – not as shepherds,
but as vermin,
the lowest of the low.
And the worst thing is
after a while it's hard not to believe it,
all one's feelings of dignity and self-respect
eaten away by the continual suspicion,
the poisonous asides,
the sly innuendoes.

I think that's what made the other night so special –
the night we saw the angels,
heard the good news,
went to Bethlehem to see for ourselves.
It wasn't simply that the Messiah was born,
amazing though that was,
but the fact we were chosen to hear the news,
given pride of place before all others!
Don't misunderstand me,
we'd have rejoiced whoever was the first,
for, despite what folk may say,
we're as God-fearing as the next person,
and we'd been looking forward to the day of the Messiah
just like them,
hoping and praying it might be in our lifetime.
But to hear the news firsthand,
to be given a personal invitation
to see the newborn Saviour for ourselves,
that was beyond all our dreams,
and it meant more to us than I can ever tell you.
Suddenly we were worth something again,
recognised and valued as individuals.
Suddenly we could hold our heads up high
and look the world full in the face,
confident we had as much right to walk this earth as anyone.
Suddenly it didn't bother us any more what others thought,
whether they loved us or loathed us,
for we were important to God,
and what else could matter?
I've no doubt some will judge even now,
just as they always have,
still pass us by with the same dismissive gesture,
the same self-righteous glance of disdain.

But I don't care any more,
for there's another saying you may have heard
which to me says it all:
'Beauty is only skin-deep'.
I know what that means now,
for God has demonstrated to me
that he looks beneath the surface,
behind the outer show,
and sees the person hidden there, deep within –
a person more precious to him
than you would ever dare imagine.

Carol
While shepherds watched their flocks by night

Reading
Luke 2:15-20

Meditation of Mary

I had mixed feelings, to tell the truth,
not just before the birth but afterwards too.
Does that surprise you?
It did me.
I thought I'd be ecstatic once the child was born,
over the moon –
isn't that how we mums are meant to feel?
He was my firstborn after all,
a beautiful bouncing boy,
so why wasn't I bursting with happiness?
Well, I was, of course,
part of me anyway,
yet there was so much I didn't understand,
and so many things to take the edge off the moment.

There was Joseph for a start.
Oh, he was supportive –
don't think I'm complaining –
once he got over the shock of the pregnancy anyway,
and you can hardly blame him
if that took a while, can you?
But, imagined or not,
I always felt there was a shadow in his eyes
when he looked at Jesus,
as if to say, 'What *really* happened?'

And then there were those visits after the birth –
first the shepherds,
then those strangers from the East
with their lavish gifts.
It was gratifying, obviously,
not every child gets that sort of attention, after all.
But what made them come? –
that's what I keep asking.
What did their homage signify?

Don't think I'm ungrateful,
but I really wish sometimes
Jesus could have been an ordinary child,
and the three of us left to enjoy our happiness –
no fuss,
no angels,
no promises,
simply the joy of being together.

But any last chance of that disappeared
after those words of Simeon,
that curious warning of his about the future.
I've tried not to let it get to me,
but it's preyed on my mind ever since,

always that fear within me of tragedy round the corner.
So, you see, I had mixed feelings,
very mixed,
and I still do have, as much now as ever.
I want to rejoice,
to enjoy my boy while I still have him.
I want to count my blessings
and thank God for all he's given.

But there's been a price to pay already,
and deep within I've a horrible feeling
that this business of being God's servant,
of accepting his will and serving his kingdom,
involves a far greater cost
than I'd ever begun to imagine,
and a price I'd rather not pay.

Carol

The virgin Mary had a baby boy

Reading

Matthew 2:1-12

Meditation of the Magi

Do you know what we gave him –
that little boy in Bethlehem?
Go on, have a guess! A rattle?
A toy?
A teddy bear?
No, nothing like that!
In fact, nothing you'd associate with a child at all,
even if he was destined to be a king.

Gold, that's what I brought!
And my companions?
Wait for it!
Frankincense and myrrh!

Yes, I thought you'd be surprised,
for, to tell the truth
we're pretty amazed ourselves looking back,
unable to imagine what on earth possessed us
to choose such exotic and unusual gifts.

It wasn't so much that they were costly,
though they were, of course –
to a family like his they were riches beyond their dreams.

But we could more than afford it –
little more than small change to men of our means.
No, it wasn't the price that troubled us afterwards,
but the associations,
the possible meaning his parents
might have read into our presents when we'd gone.

Not the gold, there was no problem there –
a gift fit for a king and designed to say as much, of course.
But frankincense?
Well, the main use his people have for that,
as we learned later,
is to sweeten their sacrifices,
to pour out on to their burnt offerings
so that the fragrance might be pleasing to their God.
Hardly the most appropriate gift for a baby.
But compared with myrrh!
Don't tell me you don't know?
It was a drug used to soothe pain,
either for that or as a spice for embalming –
more fitting for a funeral than a birth,
having more to do with suffering and death than celebration!

So what were we thinking of?
What possible significance
could gifts like those have for a little child?
Frankly, I have no idea.
Yet at the time the choice seemed as obvious to us
as following the star,
as though each were all part of some greater purpose
which would one day become clear to all.
Were we right?
Well, after all I've said, I rather hope not,
for if this king was born to die,
to be offered in sacrifice
rather than enthroned in splendour,
then his must be an unusual kingdom,
very different from most we come across –
in fact, you might almost say,
not a kingdom of this world at all!

Carol

The first Nowell

Reading

John 1:1-5, 10-14

Meditation of John the Apostle

'Where did it all start?' they ask me.
'Tell us the story again.'
And I know just what they want to hear –
about the inn and the stable,
the baby lying in a manger,
out in the fields by night,
and wise men travelling from afar.

I know why they ask, of course I do,
for which of us hasn't thrilled to those marvellous events,
that astonishing day when the Word became flesh,
dwelling here on earth amongst us?
Yet wonderful though that all is,
it's not where it started,
and if we stop there,
then we see only a fraction of the picture,
the merest glimpse of everything God has done for us in Christ.

We have got to go right back to see more –
before Bethlehem,
before the prophets
before the Law,
before time itself, would you believe? –
for that's where it started:
literally 'in the beginning'.

Yes, even there the saving purpose of God was at work,
his creating, redeeming Word
bringing light and love into the world,
shaping not just the heavens and the earth
but the lives of all,
every man, woman and child.
That's the mind-boggling wonder of it –
the fact not just that God made us,
but that through Christ
he was determined from the outset
to share our lives,
to take on our flesh,
to identify himself totally
with the joys and sorrows,
the beauty and the ugliness
of humankind.

It defies belief, doesn't it?
Yet it's true –
God wanting us to know him not as his creatures
but as his children,
not as puppets forced to dance to his tune
but as people responding freely to his love,
and to achieve that

he patiently and painstakingly prepared the way,
revealing year after year a little more of his purpose,
a glimpse more of his kingdom,
until at last,
in the fullness of time,
the Word became flesh and lived among us,
full of grace and truth.

It wasn't an afterthought, the incarnation,
a last-ditch attempt to make the best of a bad job –
it was planned from the dawn of time.

So next time you hear the story
of the stable and the manger,
of the shepherds gazing in wonder
and the magi kneeling in homage,
stop for a moment
and reflect on everything which made it all possible,
the eternal purpose
which so carefully prepared the way of Christ,
and then ask yourself this:
are you prepared to respond to his coming?

Prayer

God of Mary and Joseph,
God of the shepherds and the magi,
God of the baby lying in a manger,
God with us,
touch our hearts
with the living presence of Christ,
fill us with the love and joy
which he alone can bring,
and send us out to proclaim his kingdom, glad tidings for all.
In his name we pray.

Carol

Hark, the herald-angels sing

Blessing

Music

The Shepherds' Farewell Berlioz

Nick Fawcett

235

Christingle

The first Christingle

This service makes use of the traditional Christingle elements, but uses a short play/sketch to explore where the idea of the Christingle first came from. If used in a large building, care must be taken to ensure that all voices are sufficiently amplified to be heard throughout the church, and that, as far as possible, everyone can see what's going on. To prevent the congregation getting restless, a Christmas carol is introduced between the two scenes.

Welcome

Leader   Welcome to this Christingle service: an opportunity in the darkness of winter to remember the true meaning of Christmas as we celebrate the birth of Christ, the life and light of the world. We will explore together the meaning of the Christingle symbols and how the idea of putting them together might have started. The first Christingle service that we know of was a family occasion, just as all others have been since, including this one, so if you're a little anxious about your children being fidgety or fretful, please put your minds at rest – this occasion is designed with them in mind. It speaks simply of the light countless people have discovered in Christ across the years – light he invites you to share today.

Carol

The first Nowell

Opening prayer

For the light of each new day,
Lord of all,
we thank you.

For the light of the sun,
warming and sustaining,
Lord of all,
we thank you.

For the light of love,
gladdening and enriching our lives in so many ways,
Lord of all,
we thank you.

For the light of truth,
combating evil, injustice, falsehood and corruption,
Lord of all,
we thank you.

For the light of goodness and compassion,
deeds great and small contributing to heal and help,
restore and renew,
Lord of all,
we thank you.

For the light of wisdom,
instructing and equipping for life,
Lord of all,
we thank you.

For the light of Christ, shining across history,
across the world
and into our hearts,
Lord of all,
we thank you.

For the light we have received,
that is with us now
and that lies in store in your eternal kingdom,
Lord of all,
we thank you.

In Christ's name we pray.

Reading

Luke 2:8-20

Carol

Once in royal David's city

Background to the Christingle

Leader   What, you may be wondering, is a Christingle service all about and what does the word 'Christingle' actually mean? Nobody, in fact, is quite sure where the word stems from, but it almost certainly means 'Christ light' or 'Christ fire'. The first known service was held at a children's festival in 1747 in the castle of Marienborn in Germany, the presiding bishop distributing simple Christingles for the children to take home and display in a prominent window as a symbol of Christ's light shining in the darkness. Whether the bishop thought of the idea himself is unclear, but an old Czech tale suggests otherwise. It's a lovely story, and one perfectly suited to explaining the symbolism behind the Christingle service. We retell it here in the form of a short play in two scenes.

Cast

- Eight children and a narrator
- Pastor

Props

- Table
- Bowl containing fruit (apples, grapes, monkey nuts and a single orange)

- Vase of dried flowers, with four cocktail sticks concealed among the stems
- Manger
- Hay bales (or painted cardboard boxes)
- Empty boxes covered by Christmas wrapping paper
- Teddy bears and other toys
- Seven simple pre-prepared Christingles (made without sweets)
- A small blunt table knife, for gouging a hole in the orange

A Christingle play

SCENE ONE

Three children are sitting at a table, talking. One has a red ribbon in her hair. There is a vase of dried flowers on the table and a bowl containing some apples, grapes, nuts and a single orange.

Narrator   Our play takes place in Moravia, part of what is now the Czech Republic. The year is 1747, and it's just before Christmas. Three unkempt children are talking together.

Child 1   We're meant to take something special to church today.

Child 2   Are we? Who said so?

Child 1   The pastor. He's asked for every family to place a gift beside the manger.

Child 2   What sort of gift?

Child 1   I'm not sure really. Money perhaps.

Child 2   But we haven't got any money, not since dad was taken ill.

Child 3   Nor any toys either. I don't see what we can take.

   The children pause, disappointed.

Child 1   I've an idea. Why don't we make something?

Child 3   Like what?

Child 1   Oh, I don't know. Something pretty, I guess.

   Second child picks up an orange from the bowl.

Child 2   Maybe we could use this.

Child 3   An orange!

Child 2   Well, it's better than nothing.

Child 3   But look, it's going mouldy. We can't possibly take that.

Again they pause, dejected, before the first child looks up excitedly.

Child 1   Wait a minute! Why don't we cut out the bad bit and cover the hole with a candle?

Child 3   That's an idea! We could decorate it too – make it look really special.

Child 2   Yes, why not. We could start with this ribbon from my hair.

The children cut out the top of the orange and insert a candle, then attempt to tie the ribbon round the orange.

Child 1   The ribbon won't stay on. I can't tie it.

Child 2   We need something to hold it firm.

Child 3   But what?

The children look around.

Child 2   I've got it. We can pin the ribbon with these stems.

He/she lifts out some of the dried flowers, removes the cocktail sticks, and uses them to pin the ribbon to the orange. The children survey the results.

Child 1   Hmm, not bad, I suppose. Still doesn't look right, though.

Child 2   Tell you what. Let's add some grapes and nuts.

Child 3   Yes, that should finish it off nicely.

The children set to work attaching the grapes and nuts, and finally hold up the finished Christingle.

Child 2   What do you reckon?

Child 3   It's not wonderful, is it?

Child 1   No, but it'll have to do.

Child 2   We'll take it then, shall we?

Child 1   Yes, why not.

END OF SCENE ONE

Leader   So, then, how was the children's gift received? We'll learn more of that in a moment. But first, let's sing another carol, *during which we'll take up an offering for The Children's Society, to which we owe the introduction of the Christingle service to this country in 1968 – a link with the charity having been maintained ever since.* *
*Omit or adapt as necessary

Carol

O little town of Bethlehem

Offertory prayer

For the work of The Children's Society,
and the light it has brought into so many young lives,
Lord Jesus Christ, we thank you.
May these gifts help its ministry continue to shine –
a beacon of hope and a torch of love in our world today.
In Christ's name we pray.

Leader	And now let's get back to our play.

SCENE TWO

Narrator	The scene is a church in Moravia. The decorated orange is on display along with other gifts beside a manger, the three children who made it huddled in a corner looking embarrassed. Five other children are pointing at the orange and giggling, while a clergyman, the pastor of the church, is busy working at a table, apparently making something. One of the five children picks up the orange, and inspects it.
Child 4	What on earth's it meant to be?
Child 5	Looks like a hedgehog to me.
Child 6	Or a sea urchin!
Child 7	It's ugly, whatever it is.
Child 8	Yeah, hideous. Fancy bringing a present like that.
	The children laugh again, prompting the pastor to come across and take the orange from them.
Pastor	I don't know why you're laughing. I think it's a wonderful gift.
	The children look puzzled and snigger.
Pastor	You think I'm just saying that, don't you, but I'm not. Let me explain.
	The pastor holds up the Christingle.
Pastor	First of all, we've an orange: round like the world we live in. And stretched round it ...
	The pastor points to the ribbon.

Pastor   . . . is this ribbon. What better way of reminding us that God loves everyone, whoever they are and wherever they come from? Then there's the colour of the ribbon: bright red, just like the blood of Jesus shed on the cross. It reminds us that he died to bring us life.

The pastor points to the sticks.

Pastor   Next, these sticks. They suggest to me both the four points of the compass – North, East, South and West – and the four seasons of the year. They are signs, in other words, of God's love reaching out in every direction, and of his faithfulness, year after year.

The pastor points to the fruit and nuts.

Pastor   The fruit and nuts continue this idea, speaking of the food God daily provides and of the beauty of creation.

The pastor paints to the candle.

Pastor   Finally, and most important of all, this candle. It may not seem much, but once lit it reminds us of Jesus, the light of the world, his love, joy and peace shining in the darkness.

The pastor lights the candle.

Pastor   So, you see, it's a perfect gift, so special I've made some more. I want you all to take one home, put it in a window, and ask your parents to light it so that it reminds passers-by of what this season means – of everything God has done for us through his Son, our saviour, Jesus Christ.

THE END

Lighting the Christingle

Leader   Is that how the first Christingle was made? Who can say? But, if nothing else, that story highlights what it's all about, explaining the meaning of the symbols and service. Nowadays, along with the fruit and nuts, we usually add sweets to represent both the sweetness of knowing Christ and the way God blesses us beyond our deserving. Some also add cloves to symbolise the people of the world and the suffering of Christ on the cross.

Like the pastor in the play, a team has been busy behind the scenes making Christingles so that we too can light a candle as a reminder of Christ's love shining in the darkness. If you wish to take part please come to the front of the church where we'll be handing the Christingles out, and then move into the aisles, forming a circle around the inside of the church. Stewards will come round when everyone is ready and light your candle. Please take great care to keep the flame away from you and those around you, especially hair and clothes, and if you want to light your candles at home, please ask your mum and dad first and get them to supervise at all times.

Children come forward, receive their Christingles, and fan out round the inside of the church, after which stewards light the candles. When all are lit, the leader continues as follows:

Leader   'Lord God,' wrote the Psalmist, 'you are the one who illumines my path, bringing light into my darkness' (Psalm 18:28). That is the truth we celebrate today, remembering God's coming among us, born in a stable, laid in a manger. 'I,' said Jesus, 'am the light of the world. Instead of walking in darkness, all who follow me will enjoy the light of life' (John 8:12).

    Let us pray together, using an adaptation of a prayer used by Bishop John de Watteville in the very first Christingle service ever recorded.

Christingle prayer

Lord Jesus Christ,
come among us
and kindle a flame in your children here and everywhere,
that, by your grace, their hearts might become like yours,
to the glory of your name.

Carol

Away in a manger

Children return to their seats.

Prayer of intercession

In the darkness of sorrow and suffering,
Lord, bring light.
In the darkness of war and hatred,
Lord, bring light.
In the darkness of fear and superstition,
Lord, bring light.
In the darkness of poverty and hunger,
Lord, bring light.
In the darkness of injustice and exploitation,
Lord, bring light.
In the darkness of death and loss,
Lord, bring light.
In every place and experience of darkness,
Lord, bring light.

Carol

On Christmas night all Christians sing

Blessing

Go on your way,
light shining upon you,

pulsating within you
and shining from you,
through Jesus Christ our Lord.

Nick Fawcett

Jesus is part of everything

Christingle services occur in many churches and are part of the annual fund-raising programme for the Childrens' Society.

Reading

Christingle services usually take place around Advent or Christmas, and therefore a Christmas reading is appropriate.

Story and talk

This story and talk is combined, and is in three parts. Each should be based and told from a different area of the church. You will need the phrase CHRIST IN written up on a large sheet of paper and displayed, and the G, L and E on pieces of paper to put with it.

1. Christ in G. Stand near the crib or tree if you have one in place. Ask a child to hold up the letter G. Explain that G is for gifts. Jesus was a gift which we remember at Christmas, as God sent Jesus as the best present we could ever have. But we all have gifts to use too that come from Jesus. We can share, love, care, etc.

Key message: Christ is a gift from God, and gives us gifts.

2. Stand near a candle. Ask a child to hold up the letter L. Explain that L is for light. Jesus brought light to the world. When he had grown up he went from town to town and village to village speaking to people, healing and helping them. He also explained who he was, on one occasion saying 'I am the light of the world'. He brings light to the darkness and sad times in our lives.

Key message: Jesus is the light, and brings light to our dark times.

3. Stand amongst the congregation. Ask a child to hold up the letter E. Explain that E is for Everyone. Because Jesus was the best gift, and because he brings light to all the world, we can all have Jesus with us. Another name for Jesus is Immanuel, which means 'God is with us'. Jesus wants to be with everyone, including all of us here.

Key message: Jesus wants to be with everyone, but do we want Jesus? *Nick Harding*

An inextinguishable Christingle

This service uses a short sketch to explore the meaning of the Christingle symbols, while also focusing on the idea of light shining in the darkness, unable to be extinguished. The number of children needed can be reduced (names being changed as appropriate) if there are not enough to take all six parts.

Welcome

Leader   Welcome to this time of worship, a time set aside in the rush and bustle of Christmas to celebrate the one at its heart: God's Son, Jesus. Through this service, and particularly through the symbols of the Christingle, we will remind ourselves of what his coming meant and continues to mean today. The service is designed to be short, relaxed and easy to follow, a time that we hope you will enjoy and that will contribute towards making this Christmas a more meaningful and special occasion for you and your family.

Carol

Angels from the realms of glory

Opening prayer

Living God,
at this glad season
open our hearts and minds to what it's all about:
your coming to our world and sharing our humanity in Christ
so that we might share in your eternal kingdom,
rejoicing in the blessings you delight to shower upon us.
Speak through this simple service,
that the symbols of Christingle
and the story of the Christ-child
may help us to glimpse also the Lord of life
and Light of the world,
finding in him our Lord
and *our* Light,
with us this day and always.

Reading

John 1:1-5

Background to the Christingle

Leader   Of all the verses in the Bible, few are more appropriate for a Christingle service than those we've just heard, with their message of light shining in the darkness. No one is altogether sure what the word 'Christingle' actually means, but the most common translations are 'Christ light' or 'Christ fire'. The first service was held at a children's festival in 1747 in Germany. The presiding bishop at the closing service handed out simple Christingles for the children to take home and display in a prominent window as a symbol of Christ's light shining in the darkness. The practice has been continued ever since, and was introduced into this country by The Children's Society in 1968. The link has been maintained ever since, most churches, as part of the Christingle service, taking an offering to support the work of The Children's Society. *We will do so ourselves during our next hymn.* *Various symbols have been added but the message at its heart remains the

same: in the birth of Jesus, God has brought light into our world, light that continues to shine today despite the darkness that so often surrounds it.
Omit or adapt as necessary

Carol

The virgin Mary had a baby boy

Offertory prayer

God of all,
as we commit these gifts to you
we commit also the work of The Children's Society,
thanking you for the vision that brought it into being,
the faith that inspires it,
the lives it has helped to shape
and the light it has brought to so many.
Prosper its continuing ministry,
and provide it with faith, courage and resources
to respond, creatively and effectively,
to the pressures and challenges
faced by young people today.
In Christ's name we pray.

The inextinguishable Christingle – a fun sketch

Cast

- Teacher
- Isobel
- Kate
- Kyle
- Emily
- Robert
- Laura

Props

- A complete Christingle
- A relighting birthday cake candle (check beforehand that this relights properly; and have a couple of extra candles on standby, just in case the candle fails to re-ignite on the day. If this happens, make a joke of it and replace it with another)
- A small table, on which the Christingle should be placed
- An empty bowl (supposedly full of water)

The sketch takes place in a classroom. A Christingle is set on a small table, from which a group of children are furtively removing the candle and putting an apparently identical one in its place. They hurry back to their seats sniggering, sitting down again just before the teacher walks in. The teacher lights the Christingle, then turns to face the class.

Teacher	Now then, children, as you know we're looking today at the Christingle service. Hands up those of you who've taken part in one.

All the children eagerly put up their hands. The teacher smiles.

Teacher	I thought you might have. So, who can tell me what it's all about?

Laura puts her hand up, and calls out excitedly.

Laura	Oranges!
Teacher	Well, yes, we use oranges, Laura. But there's a bit more to it than that . . .

Kate puts her hand up.

Kate	It's about light, isn't it? The light of Jesus shining in the world.
Teacher	Excellent, Kate. Quite right.

The teacher holds up the Christingle.

Teacher	And here, of course, is what a Christingle looks like. As you can see, we use various things to make it, and this morning I want to explore what those mean, but before we do so I think perhaps, to be safe, we ought to blow the candle out first. Emily, could you do that for me?

Emily comes forward, blows the candle out and returns to her seat, grinning. The candle lights again behind her, unobserved by the teacher.

Teacher	Right, well, first the orange. Any idea what it means, Robert?
Robert	My lunch?

The children chuckle and the teacher smiles.

Teacher	Very good, Robert, but does anyone know what it really stands for?

Emily puts her hand up.

Teacher	Yes, Emily.
Emily	It's the world, isn't it?
Teacher	It is. Well done! Now, who can . . .

The teacher pauses, looking at the Christingle in surprise.

Teacher   That's strange, Emily. I thought I asked you to blow the candle out.

Emily   I *did* blow it out.

Teacher   I thought so, but it's alight again. How odd. Oh well, maybe someone else would like to blow it out instead.

All the children put their hands up.

Teacher   Kyle, you're sitting nicely; so you can do it.

Kyle comes forward, blows the candle out and returns to his seat, again grinning broadly. Once again the candle relights itself.

Teacher   Now where was I? Ah yes, the ribbon. Why do you think we tie it round the orange?

Laura puts her hand up.

Teacher   Yes, Laura.

Laura   To make it look pretty?

Teacher   That's part of it, certainly, but there's another and more important reason.

Robert puts his hand up and shouts out.

Robert   My mum says it's something to do with God caring for us.

Teacher   She's right, Robert. The ribbon stretches round the orange just as God's love reaches round the world. Some people also say that it reminds us of the blood of Jesus shed on the cross. Now then, next we . . .

Again the teacher pauses, looking at the candle in disbelief.

Teacher   Kyle, did I just ask you to blow the candle out?

Kyle   Yes, miss.

Teacher   And did you?

Kyle   Yes, miss.

Teacher   Then how come it's alight again?

Kyle   No idea, miss.

The teacher mops her brow, looking flustered.

Teacher   Oh well, not to worry. It couldn't have been quite out, I suppose. Kate, could you do it for me?

Kate comes out and gives the candle an extra hard blow, then sits down again, winking at the other children. The teacher continues, pointing to the cocktail sticks on the Christingle.

Teacher   What about these? Any idea what they represent?

Isabel puts up her hand eagerly.

Isabel   Ooh, I know!

Teacher   Yes, Isabel.

Isabel   They stand for the four seasons and the four directions: North, South, East and West.

Teacher   Very good, Isabel. Well done. And those in turn remind us not only of God's faithfulness but also once again of his love for all.

Robert puts his hand up and calls out.

Robert   And the fruit and nuts remind us of the food he provides, don't they? At least that's what they said in Sunday school.

Laura puts her hand up and blurts out.

Laura   Yes, and the sweets stand for all the extra things he gives us.

Teacher   You have learned well, haven't you. I reckon you should be teaching me! Well, there's only one thing left, and that of course is the . . .

The teacher turns to the candle and stares in astonishment.

Teacher   I don't believe it. What is going on? I'm sure that candle was out.

The children struggle to stifle their giggles, and the teacher looks at them curiously, sensing they've been up to something.

Teacher   Is there something you're not telling me, children?

The children do their best to look innocent, but their chuckles give them away.

Teacher   I get the feeling someone's been playing tricks on me.

She blows out the candle herself and watches it carefully. Sure enough, after a few moments it relights. She tries again and the same thing happens. Trying to look stern, but with a smile playing on her lips, she turns back to the children.

Teacher   As I thought, a relighting candle. So who's responsible for this?

Kate puts her hand up.

Kate   Please, miss, it was all of us. It was my birthday yesterday, and my dad put the candle on my cake for a laugh. We thought it would be fun to use it again today.

Teacher Did you now?

Robert We didn't mean any harm, miss, honest, and it wasn't just to tease you . . .

He pauses, looking sheepish.

. . . well, not completely anyway.

Laura No, that's right, miss. You see, we knew that the candle stands for light shining in the darkness, and we sort of thought a light that doesn't go out is extra special.

The teacher breaks into a smile, unable to keep up her stern expression.

Teacher Well, you're right there, Laura. Not that you should play tricks on me, but I have to say you've summed up perfectly what this candle stands for: a light that never goes out! You see, Christmas isn't just about the past but about now, about God continuing to bring light into the world today despite so much that causes darkness. We can, in fact, put this candle out by ducking it under water, but the light of Jesus can never be put out, no matter how hard people try. Now then, what time is it? . . . Ah yes, break-time. OK, then, you can go out, children, once someone's blown this candle out. Fair enough?

The children look dismayed.

Emily Oh miss, couldn't you put it out for us? Please. We won't do it again . . . promise.

Teacher All right, I will, but remember: no more tricks.

She 'douses' the candle in the empty bowl.

Teacher OK, off you go.

The children disperse and the teacher starts to walk out. Meanwhile the candle relights. The teacher spins round, looks at it, then walks off with a smile.

Lighting the Christingle

Leader A relighting Christingle, made possible, of course, with a trick candle. What we celebrate today, though, is no trick but reality: the truth of what God has done for us through his Son, Jesus Christ.
'What has come into being in him,' said our reading earlier, 'is life; life that is light for all people. That light shines in the darkness, and the darkness has been unable to extinguish it.' No matter how dark it may seem, somehow that light keeps shining, bringing strength, hope, courage and peace into even the bleakest of circumstances. As one of the Psalms puts it: 'If I say, "Surely darkness will steal over me, night will envelop me", darkness is not dark to you; the night is as bright as day; for you both dark and light are the same' (Psalm 139:11-12).
It's time, then, for us to light our own Christingles, not relighting ones but nonetheless reminding us of light that cannot be extinguished: the light of Christ shining in the darkness of our world. If you'd like to come to the front, we'll hand

them out here, after which move into the aisles and form a ring round the inside of the church. When we're ready stewards will come round and light your candle, and once that's done please take great care to keep the flame well away from you and those around you, especially hair and clothes. Remember also that the cocktail sticks are very sharp, so make sure you don't prick yourselves. One final warning: if you want to light the Christingles back at home, ask your parents first, and get them to supervise the lighting and the candle once it's lit. On no account leave a candle burning unattended.

Children come to the front of the church, receive their Christingle, and disperse as instructed. When ready, stewards light the candles, and the lights are turned out.

Leader   Let us pray together, putting our faith and trust in the light God brings us in Christ.

Christingle prayer

In the darkest places, Lord,
and the darkest moments of life,
shine your light of love and goodness,
peace and joy,
so that, whatever obscures it,
it will finally win through.
Amen.

Carol

Away in a manger

Children return to their seats.

Prayer of intercession

Lord Jesus Christ,
bring light to all whose lives are overshadowed by trouble -
all those facing the darkness of famine,
disaster,
illness,
fear,
loneliness,
hatred,
pain
and death.
Though the shadows may lengthen and the darkness deepen,
may your light finally break through and shine for evermore.

Carol

See amid the winter's snow

Blessing

The light of Christ illumine your path
and fill your days with sunshine.
The light of Christ shine in your darkness
and banish the clouds.
The light of Christ radiate to you and through you,
to the glory of his name.

Nick Fawcett

Carrying or Lighting a Candle

Many churches find that this simple act brings a sense of peace and the presence of Jesus to what can be a very busy time in the church day. As a candle is carried forward, or someone from the congregation is invited up to light it, the symbolism of the light of Christ can be very effective.

Candle responses
We welcome Jesus,
the light of the world.
As the candle shines
so your light shines for us.

Jesus is the light of the world.
Let us welcome him now.
Jesus, Light of the world,
shine in our hearts and lives.
Jesus, the light
bring light to our worship.

As we light the candle today,
light a flame in our hearts.
In our dark world
let Jesus bring light.
In our dark hearts
let Jesus bring light.

Nick Harding

Christmas Service 1

In many Churches the Christmas services are a major highlight of the calendar, with Christingles, carols by candlelight, and cribs dominating the scene. However, strong publicity, hopefully increased attendances, and not least the weight of received tradition mean that Christmas is just about the most difficult time of year to engage in ecumenical worship. The exception to this is found mostly in well-established LEPs (Local Ecumenical Projects), where the people no longer dream of a united Christmas because it has been made to happen. (Our own LEP has reached this stage, though it has taken a couple of years to merge the two traditions into a coherent programme – and we're not sure it's quite right even now!). Ironically, the mainstream Churches have more in common at Christmas than at almost any other time of year, as the carols, readings and symbolism are recognised by everyone.

Christingle and crib services come in more or less the same form in every tradition and are ideally suited to ecumenical worship, even if there are guaranteed to be a few minor differences in execution. The carol service (often entitled a 'Festival of Carols' or 'Carols by Candlelight') is also familiar to all denominations, though it may vary in style from the formal and tightly structured 'Nine Lessons and Carols' (Anglican in origin and style) through to a more lively and exuberant 'Carol Praise' (in the charismatic tradition). An ecumenical version will probably try to combine the best of both worlds.

From traditional carols to the folk ballads of the Iona Community, from Plainsong to John Rutter or John Taverner, there is a wealth of Christmas music available. What you choose will be determined as much as anything by the available resources.

The following outline suggests one way that well-known items can be integrated together by a common thread. Readings 1 and 7 frame the narrative, describing God's eternal purposes, and the rest of the readings and the carols reflect our response to God's love in Christ. A final reading and song express our commitment to what we have heard and understood. Each reading is concluded with a brief prayer, and an opening bidding in modern style is also included, together with a closing response.

Bidding

In the name of our Lord Jesus Christ we welcome you all, as we gather together once more to hear the story of his coming among us as a helpless baby, yet Lord of all. With the shepherds we run joyfully to the manger, to see for ourselves the Word made flesh. With the angels we sing 'Glory to God in the Highest', and join with the praises of all heaven as we celebrate the coming of our Saviour. With the wise men we bring to the infant Christ our own gifts and offerings, to acknowledge him as King of kings. With Mary and Joseph we ponder these things in our hearts, as we seek to understand more of God's loving purposes.

We offer to God our prayers for the world into which he sent his Son, with its conflict and chaos, its greed and selfishness, its sadness and pain, especially . . .

We offer to God our prayers for the Church throughout the world, divided and confused, yet united in our one Lord and in seeking to bring the good news of his love to all people . . . We offer to God our prayers for those whose rejoicing at this Christmas season will be overshadowed by grief, illness, anxiety or loneliness, especially . . .

We pray finally for ourselves, that we may not only hear the familiar story of Christ's birth, but may open our minds to reflect on it, our hearts to respond to it, and our lives to proclaim it, day by day. And so we worship the newborn King, together with the angels and all God's people throughout the world, rejoicing at his coming among us and praying as he taught: Our Father . . .

Carol

O come, all ye faithful

First reading

John 1:1-14

Prayer

Living Word,
who came to be the light for all people;
shine in our darkness

and help us to recognise you living among us,
that believing in your name,
we may become children of God.

Carol

Of the Father's love begotten

Second reading

Isaiah 11:1-9

Prayer

Lord God,
may your Spirit of wisdom and understanding
rest upon us,
that we may deal fairly with the needy
and act justly for the world's poor.

Carol

Who would think (God's surprise)

Third reading

Zechariah 2:10-13

Prayer

Lord Jesus,
as you once came to live among your people,
come now and dwell in our hearts,
that we may rejoice and be glad
as your presence breaks into our lives
with power.

Carol

Lord Jesus Christ

Fourth reading

Luke 1:26-38

Prayer

Lord God,
as we hear your gracious call,

make our ears open to the message you give,
and our hearts willing to obey you
as faithful servants.

Carol

For Mary, mother of our Lord

Fifth reading

Luke 2:8-14

Prayer

Lord Jesus,
we hear again the angels' song of praise
at your coming to earth as our Saviour;
rejoicing with them,
may we treasure what we see
and hear in our hearts,
that our lives may reflect
the presence of Emmanuel, God with us.

Carol

Angels from the realms of glory

Sixth reading

Matthew 2:1-12

Prayer

Lord Jesus,
recognising you as King of kings
and Lord of all,
we offer you our gifts
and ask you to use them
for the glory of your kingdom.

Carol

In the bleak mid-winter

Seventh reading

Hebrews 1:1-4 (or 9)

Prayer

Lord Jesus,
you are the radiance of your Father's glory
and through you the universe was made;
as you descended from your heavenly home
to share our life and bear our sins,
may we make room for you in our hearts
and be filled with your eternal life.

Carol

Meekness and majesty
or Thou didst leave thy throne

Final reading

Philippians 2:5-11

Carol

From heaven you came, helpless babe

Final prayer

Lord Jesus,
encouraged by our union with you
and comforted by your love,
make us one in heart and mind.

Lord Jesus,
may we do nothing out of selfish pride or ambition,
but regard others as more important than ourselves;
make us one in heart and mind.

Lord Jesus,
may we be filled with your Spirit of humility,
and give priority to the interests of others;
make us one in heart and mind.

Lord Jesus,
may we acknowledge you to be Lord of all,
both with lips which sing your praise,
and in lives dedicated to humbly serving you;
**make us one in heart and mind
that together we may confess
that Jesus Christ is Lord,
to the glory of God our Father.**

Carol

Hark, the herald angels sing

Blessing

May God, who in his Son
left heaven's glory to take the form of a servant,
make us faithful in his service.
May God, who in his Son
was obedient even to death on a cross,
make us obedient to his perfect will.
May God, who has exalted his Son
to the highest place in heaven,
give us grace to acknowledge Christ as Lord
both in word and deed.

And the blessing . . .

Stuart Thomas

Christmas Service 2

Music

Hodie Christus natus est Sweelinck

Call to worship and introduction

We have come today to celebrate an event at the very heart of our faith – the coming of Christ into our world as the Word made flesh, God identifying himself irrevocably with humankind through the birth of Jesus in Bethlehem. A story we have heard retold countless times in countless ways, and yet, however often we hear it, we cannot begin to exhaust the riches of this wonderful season. There is always more to discover, more to understand, more to give thanks for. So we come today to hear words and music familiar and not so familiar, and to consider some of those who shared in the events of that first Christmas and some whose lives were later touched by Christ. We come so that the Christmas story may speak afresh to us, and our lives may be touched by Jesus in turn.

Carol

O little town of Bethlehem

Prayer

Loving God,
we come today to remember with gratitude
the birth of your Son.
We remember how prophets foretold his coming,
and how those words were wonderfully fulfilled in Bethlehem.
We remember how you needed Mary
to bring him into the world,
and how she willingly allowed you to work through her.
We remember how shepherds heard the Good News,
and how, having seen the truth of it for themselves,

they went on their way rejoicing.
We remember how Simeon held you in his arms,
and with praise in his heart gave thanks to you.
We remember how generations since
have seen your face revealed in Christ,
and through him heard you speaking in a new way.
Lord Jesus Christ,
we come to look back
so that we may discover you in the present,
and find faith for the future.
Be born in our hearts this day
that we may be born again to eternal life.

Music

For unto us a child is born (*Messiah*) Handel, during which Luke 2:1-7 is read

Meditation of Mary

What a day it's been!
I'm shattered, exhausted,
and yet I'm over the moon!
Does that sound strange?
Well, let me tell you what happened,
then you'll understand.

It could hardly have started worse,
arriving in Bethlehem like that
to find the place packed.
My heart sank.
I knew we wouldn't find anywhere, not a chance,
but Joseph wouldn't have it.

'Next time,' he kept saying, 'you'll see.'
Next time indeed!

A stable, that's what we ended up with –
hardly the accommodation I had in mind!
It wouldn't have mattered, mind you,
not in the usual run of things,
but I was nine months pregnant
and my pains had started that morning,
getting stronger by the minute.
I was in agony by the end, you can imagine,
just about desperate by then,
not bothered where we stopped
just so long as I could rest.

That's why we accepted the innkeeper's offer,
makeshift though it was.

I lay there with cattle breathing down my neck,
straw prickling my back,
and what felt like a gale whistling beneath the door –
but I didn't care;
I didn't care about anything by then,
just wanted the baby to be born.

Poor Joseph, he was beside himself.
No idea how to cope or what to do next,
but thankfully one of the women from the inn took pity on us.
You'll never know how good it was
to see her kindly reassuring face,
her confident smile beaming down at me through the haze of pain.
It seemed like an eternity for all that,
but it wasn't long really.
And then that sound,
that wonderful exhilarating sound,
my son, Jesus, crying!
I didn't want to let go of him,
but I had to, of course, eventually.

I was exhausted, just about all in.
So I wrapped him in strips of cloth
and laid him in a manger.
Sleep came easy after that,
blissful peace at last,
but a moment ago I woke with a start,
remembering those words in that vision I had –
'And they shall name him Emmanuel,
God with us'.
My child, Emmanuel?
Can it really be true?
God come to his people?
He's everything to me, I admit that,
I could gladly worship him.
But others? I wonder.
Time alone will tell, I suppose.

Anyway, no more time for talking,
I need my sleep.
But wait, who's this knocking on the door?
Shepherds!
What on earth can they want at this time of night?
I don't know.
What a day it's been!
What a day!

Music

Pastoral Symphony (Messiah) Handel, during which Luke 2:8-20 is read

Meditation of the shepherds

It was just an ordinary day, that's what I can't get over;
nothing special about it,
nothing different,
just another ordinary day.
And we were all just ordinary people,
that's what made it even more puzzling;
not important,
not influential,
just plain ordinary shepherds out working in the fields.

Yet we apparently were the first,
singled out for special favour!
The first to know,
the first to see,
the first to celebrate, the first to tell!

I'm still not sure what happened –
one moment night drawing in,
and the next bright as day;
one moment laughing and joking together,
and the next rooted to the spot in amazement;
one moment looking forward to getting home,
and the next hurrying down to Bethlehem.

There just aren't words to express what we felt,
but we knew we had to respond,
had to go and see for ourselves.
Not that we expected to find anything mind you,
not if we were honest.
Well, you don't, do you?
I mean, it's not every day the Messiah arrives, is it?
And we'd always imagined when he finally did
it would be in a blaze of glory, to a fanfare of trumpets,
with the maximum of publicity.

Yet do you know what? When we got there
it was to find everything just as we had been told,
wonderfully special,
yet surprisingly ordinary.
Not Jerusalem but Bethlehem,
not a palace but a stable,
not a prince enthroned in splendour
but a baby lying in a manger.
We still find it hard to believe even now,
to think God chose to come
through that tiny vulnerable child.

But as the years have passed –
and we've seen not just his birth but his life,
and not just his life but his death,

and not just his death but his empty tomb,
his grave-clothes, his joyful followers –
we've slowly came to realise it really was true.

God had chosen to come to us,
and more than that, to you –
to ordinary, everyday people,
in the most ordinary, everyday of ways.
How extraordinary!

Carol

Angels from the realms of glory

Music

Saviour's Day Cliff Richard, during which Luke 2:22, 25-32 is read

Meditation of Simeon

I'd all but given up hope, truth to tell.
It had been so many years waiting and wondering,
and I'd begun to think I'd never see his coming after all.
Why should I be different, I asked myself?
Why should I see the Messiah
when so many others have been disappointed?
Yet I shouldn't have doubted, should I?
I'd kept on telling everyone he would come,
and he came, just as God had promised.
What a joy it was,
to hold him in my arms,
to gaze down on his face,
and know that God had not forgotten us.
What a relief to find I hadn't been deluding myself,
that I wasn't off my head after all,
that it hadn't been simply wishful thinking.
It made it all seem worth it, the mocking,
the sneers,
the pitying expressions.
I could hold my head up high
having clung on to faith through thick and thin.
They'd written me off as some kind of religious fanatic.
Still do, come to that,
but they were the misguided ones.
They couldn't see the truth
though it was staring them in the face,
there before their very eyes.
And the tragedy is that they're still waiting for the Messiah,
still hoping,
still praying for his coming,

when all the time he's here among them,
cradled in his mother's arms.
Well, now the joke's on them, isn't it?
I suppose I could feel smug,
even that it serves them right,
but I don't.
Quite the contrary.
It's the only fly in the ointment right now,
the one blot on my happiness.
My eyes have seen the salvation of the Lord,
and I could die quite happy this minute,
totally at peace,
if only they could see it for themselves
and know the joy that I know now!

Carol

It came upon the midnight clear

Music

Comfort ye (Messiah) Handel, during which Matthew 2:1-6 is read

Meditation of Matthew

'It has been written.'
How often have I heard those words?
On the mouth of priest, rabbi, and Pharisee –
time and time again, the same old refrain: 'It has been written.'
And it's true of course.
It's there in black and white, just as they say;
God's word to his people for us all to see –
the sacred words of the Law,
given to our fathers by God himself,
spelling out his commandments.
The history of our people,
the wisdom of the Teacher,
the poetry of the psalms,
the visions of the prophets,
all that, and so much more,
God's word to us!
Yes, it's there all right,
but though I've always believed that,
somehow it has never really touched me,
not deep down in my heart where it matters.
I've accepted it, yes,
but the words have never spoken to me in quite the way I hoped.
Now, though, it's different –
astonishingly, incredibly, different –
for I have only to think of Jesus to find myself saying,

'It has been written!'
Why?
Well just listen to this.
'You, Bethlehem,
are by no means least among the rulers of Judah,
for from you shall come a ruler
who is to shepherd my people Israel.'
'The virgin shall conceive and bear a son,
and they shall name him Emmanuel.'
'The people who sat in darkness have seen a great light,
and for those who dwelt in the region and shadow of death
light has dawned.'
'For a child has been born for us,
a son given to us;
authority rests upon his shoulders; and he is named
Wonderful Counsellor,
Mighty God,
Everlasting Father,
Prince of Peace.'
Need I go on?
I don't think so.
It's all there in the prophets,
foreshadowed in the Law,
foretold from the very beginning.
And it happened –
the prophecies fulfilled in a way I never for a moment expected,
brought to life in Jesus Christ.
And now when I read the Scriptures
I do not simply see words on a page;
I see the Word made flesh,
the one who alone makes sense of it all, God with us –
'It has been written!'

Music

Glory to God (Messiah) Handel, during which John 1:1-5, 9; 1:14, 18 is read

Meditation of John the Apostle

There's only one word for it,
one word that gets anywhere near the truth,
that sums up the wonder of it all,
and that's 'Jesus'.
Trust me, I know,
for I've spent a lifetime trying to find the right words.
Since I followed Jesus all those years ago,
since I sat with the apostles in that upper room,
since we went out teaching and preaching in the Master's name,
I've been looking for ways in which to describe my experience,

and I've used words,
masses of them,
more than I can begin to count . . .
When I stood and preached to the multitudes,
when I nurtured believers in their new-found faith,
when I prayed for the sick,
when I led times of worship,
when I reminisced with friends,
when I witnessed to strangers,
words, words, words.
But they've never been sufficient,
never begun to express what I really want to say.
And now more than ever I find that's true,
sitting here trying to record the good news as revealed to me.
I've written so much,
page after page,
my own words and his,
woven together as best I can
into a tapestry of his life.
I've told of the beginnings and the ends,
of his signs,
of his teaching,
of his actions.
I've spoken of those lesser-known characters,
the ones Matthew, Mark and Luke missed out,
and I've given details of those private moments,
when it was just us and Jesus together
as the end drew near.
I've tried,
I've really tried to get it across,
to tell you what Jesus meant to me and to so many others.
But there's so much more I could still write,
so much I've had to leave out.
I could go on to the end of time
and still not do justice to all I want to tell you.
That's why I say there's only one word,
one word that says it all,
because Jesus was the fulfilment,
the embodiment,
the personification of God's word.
The Law and the Prophets spoke of him.
The wisdom of the teachers spoke of him.
The universe in all its glory speaks of him.
And if you want to listen,
if you want to hear,
if you want to understand what life is all about,
then take my word for it,
the only way is to know him for yourself,
the word made flesh!

Prayer

Lord Jesus Christ,
you came to our world,
to your people,
yet among so many you found no welcome.
From the very beginning the majority shut you out,
and of those who did accept you
many did so only half-heartedly.
Forgive us that sometimes we do the same.
Help us to make room for you,
and to give you not just a token place,
but to put you at the very centre of our lives.

Carol

Hark, the herald-angels sing

Blessing

Music

Hodie Christus natus est Sweelinck

Nick Fawcett

Christmas Service 3

A stable, a manger, a baby wrapped in strips of cloth – from Christmas carols to Nativity plays such details are intimately associated with the birth of Jesus. Together with Mary and Joseph travelling to Bethlehem, shepherds hurrying from their fields by night and magi following a star, they are part of the magic of this season. But behind the romance of the story, what do they have to say to you and me today: about life now, the people we are and lives we lead? That's what we're going to explore today through a series of readings and reflections designed to take us back to that first Christmas over two thousand years ago. Imagine yourself in the shoes of some of those directly involved in the events of that night – Mary, shepherds, even one of the sheep! – and consider afresh the message of the Nativity and its relevance for you, here and now.

Opening prayer

Gracious God,
we have heard countless times the story of your coming,
perhaps so often that it fails to speak as it once did.
We hear the words,
sing the carols,
listen to the message,
without really taking it in,
familiarity blunting its force.

Help us to hear it again today as though for the first time,
to take ourselves back in heart and mind to Bethlehem
and to the events surrounding the birth of your Son,
so that you may speak to us afresh,
just as you spoke then,
making known the immensity of your love
and your gracious purpose for all,
through Jesus Christ our Lord.

Hymn

Christians awake! Salute the happy morn

Reading

Luke 1:26-38

Comment

The example of Mary at the annunciation is surely second to none as a source of inspiration to Christians across the years. Her humility, faith, courage and obedience are held up as a model to emulate, a paradigmatic response to the call of God. We can read the story time and again, yet still get more from it, for there are always fresh insights to be unearthed, new lessons to be learnt, unexplored angles to consider. The aim of our first meditation is to help open up just one of those possible perspectives, so that Mary's response may more fully help to shape our own.

Meditation of Mary, the mother of Jesus

Don't be afraid, he said!
As though angels popping up out of the blue are two a penny,
no cause for concern.
Well I'm sorry, but I was petrified,
caught between the urge to run and scream.
And when he started on about being favoured by God,
blessed among women,
it only made things worse.
Who was *I* to be singled out,
I to be chosen –
a nobody like me from Nazareth?
Whoever this guy was, he'd come to the wrong house,
and the sooner he was gone the better.
But he *didn't* go,
and somehow, despite myself, I listened,
my amazement growing by the second
as he talked of a child I would bear;
a saviour who would rule over the house of David
and whose kingdom would never end.
'How can this be?' I asked.

265

'For a start, I'm still a virgin!'
But he wasn't finished yet, not by a long way,
this child he spoke of to be not just *my* son,
but *God's* too,
conceived by his Spirit.
Well, if I was troubled before,
I'd more reason to be then,
for this was mind-blowing stuff,
certain to turn the world upside down
and change my life for ever.
Yet somehow I suddenly felt strangely calm,
happy to accept whatever was asked of me,
no questions asked.
Why?
Because, if God was really speaking,
and could actually use someone as ordinary as me,
then surely *nothing* was beyond him,
however impossible it might seem.
The future was in *his* hands,
not *mine*,
and what better place could there be to leave it!

Silence

Prayer

Mighty and mysterious God,
for all kinds of reasons we don't find faith easy.
We consider what is asked of us,
the scale of your challenge,
and we feel small,
incapable of rising to it.
We come up against questions of faith,
and we struggle for answers,
so much seeming to defy explanation.
And though part of us longs to serve you,
another part rebels,
preferring to serve self instead,
resisting your call and turning from your way.
Help us, despite everything that fights against you,
that deflects us from the path of faithful discipleship,
to stay true nonetheless.
Give us the courage,
confidence
and conviction we need
to understand what you want from us
and gladly to respond.

Hymn

Born in the night, Mary's child

Reading

Luke 2:1-20

Comment

The story of the shepherds hurrying to Bethlehem provides us with one of the iconic images of the nativity, recalled and re-enacted by generations since. We'll consider things from their perspective shortly, but first let us take a different and somewhat more unusual approach. Imagine if the sheep had somehow been able to reflect on their experience during that memorable night. Imagine if they could communicate what it felt like to be suddenly abandoned and left to fend for themselves, and the sense of relief they must have felt when the shepherds finally returned. Our next meditation builds on that tantalising idea.

Meditation of the sheep

1 I've never seen them move so fast –
   one moment sprawled round the camp fire,
   and the next up and off into the night –
   heading for Bethlehem I think they said.

2 Well, sheep we may be,
   but even we knew something was afoot,
   something momentous,
   truly special,
   for they've never abandoned us before,
   not even for a second,
   what with wolves and the like prowling in the darkness.

3 We were terrified –
   more even than when that strange light had appeared in the sky,
   causing the shepherds to grovel in the dust,
   then dash off like men possessed –
   for we heard howling in the distance . . .
   nearer . . .
   nearer still . . .
   until the shadows took shape . . .
   ready to pounce . . .
   anticipating their kill.

1 We waited for the end,
   hot breath upon us, slobbering jaws gaping wide,
   but suddenly . . .
   voices . . .
   laughter . . .
   and the danger gone –
   the shepherds were back at last! What relief!

2 What joy!

3 What delight!

4 We'd faced death and been saved!

2 But I tell you what,
   something very strange:
   those shepherds seemed happier still,
   beside themselves with excitement,
   almost as if they'd been saved too.

1 What was it, I wonder, they saw that night?

3 It must have been good.

Silence

Prayer

Gracious God,
help us not just to hear the message of Christ's birth
but to make it our own,
meeting him afresh,
responding to his grace
and welcoming him into our lives.
May we recognise more fully what he means for us and for all –
what you accomplished through his life,
death and resurrection,
and what you continue to accomplish in countless human hearts.
Grant that the child of Bethlehem –
the crucified saviour and risen Lord –
may be born in us today,
and that we may walk with him to our journey's end.

Hymn

Once in royal David's city

Reading

Luke 2:15-21

Comment

A baby lying in a manger wrapped in strips of cloth – it doesn't sound that exciting, does it; hardly sufficient, were we shepherds, to prompt us to forsake our flock and rush off to Bethlehem. And if that's all there had been to it, then that's perfectly true. It was a happy sight, no doubt; a heartwarming and pleasing scene to move even the hardest of hearts, but hardly one to set the pulse racing, the heart skipping a beat. But that, of course, is to miss the point, for this was no run-of-the-mill birth, no ordinary child. He was the Messiah, God's promised deliverer, come at last to his people. The years of waiting were over, patience finally rewarded. The kingdom of God was at hand. No wonder they hurried off as fast as their legs could carry them, and raced back afterwards intent on telling everyone they met just what it was they'd seen. Our next meditation explores their story.

Meditation of the shepherds

It was just as the angel had told us,
down to the very last detail:
the stable,
the manger,
even the strips of cloth,
and above all, of course, the child,
lying there so peaceful,
his exhausted mother looking on,
husband by her side.
I'll never forget that look in their eyes:
pride naturally, like every parent –
joy, relief, excitement –
but more than that,
an air of awe and reverence,
as if they couldn't quite take it in.
And as we talked with them,
sharing what we'd heard and seen,
we could understand *why*,
for *they'd* been told what *we* had –
that this boy of theirs was sent by God,
the promised Messiah,
saviour of the world!
We'd hardly dared credit it,
and neither it seems had they,
but the more we heard
and the more we listened,
the more indisputable it seemed.
We'd come, hoping,
longing to believe
yet not sure that we could.
We left, singing,
called to believe,
and quite certain that we *should*.

Silence

Prayer

Saviour Christ,
thank you for promises of old foretelling your coming,
for the testimony of the Gospels to your birth in Bethlehem,
for the witness of Scripture to your life-changing power,
for the experience of those across the ages

called to be your Church.
But, above all,
thank you that we can know you for ourselves,
believing not just *about* you but *in* you
as we joyfully respond to your love.
You have called us to an adventure of faith.
Help us to explore it with you.

Hymn

Silent night

Reading

John 1:1-18

Comment

The accounts of the Nativity, whether of Luke or Matthew, are written from the perspective of those directly involved – Mary, Joseph, shepherds, magi – and in their immediacy they capture the sense of joy and wonder that characterised the night of Christ's birth. John's Gospel approaches things from a different angle, the Evangelist – years after the event – beginning his account of the life of Christ by reflecting on the wider meaning of his coming. He does so from the context not only of his birth, but also of his death, resurrection and ascension, the child born in Bethlehem seen from the start as someone of cosmic significance. In our final meditation, we consider the insights he sought to share.

Meditation of John the Evangelist

What's it all about, they ask me?
What does Jesus bring that we didn't have before?
Well, I've thought about that over the years,
pondered what it is that makes him so special,
and if I had to sum it up in one word,
it would be this:
grace!
That's what sets him apart from all others,
what makes the difference between the old and the new.
Moses brought us the Law,
precious undoubtedly,
serving us well for centuries,
but it put the onus on us living up to it –
our observing its decrees and performing its rituals,
following its prescriptions as best we could.
The way of Christ is so very different,
for it speaks of a new covenant
written not on tablets of stone but in our hearts –
a relationship with God based on what he has done
rather than anything we might do.

Yes, we fall short of what he wants us to be.
Yes, we fail him time and again.
Yes, we are unworthy of his love and undeserving of mercy.
But none of that matters,
for God has made the running,
accomplished what we could never achieve on our own.
Don't settle for less.
Don't struggle against the odds to put yourself right with him,
striving somehow to earn his blessing.
Reach out and accept what he longs to give.
From his fullness we have all received . . .
grace upon grace.

Silence

Prayer

Loving God,
we know we fall short,
that we repeatedly fail you,
that we have no right to your love or claim on your mercy,
and such knowledge hangs heavy upon us,
filling us with frustration and remorse.
Yet we know also that you are slow to anger and swift to forgive,
your desire being to pardon rather than punish,
to redeem, renew and restore.
For your grace revealed in Christ
and the fresh start you daily make possible through him,
receive our praise.

Hymn

It came upon the midnight clear

Closing prayer

Lord Jesus Christ,
born in Bethlehem,
come afresh to our world today –
to our towns and cities,
our fractured communities,
our divided nations,
our bleeding planet.
Lord Jesus,
born in a stable,
come afresh to the poor and homeless,
the disenfranchised,
the weak and vulnerable,
the outcast, oppressed and exploited.

Lord Jesus,
born to suffer and die,
come afresh to those who are sick, those in pain,
those facing death,
those who mourn loved ones.
Lord Jesus Christ,
born in ages past,
be born in us today.

Nick Fawcett

The Lodging Keeper

Don't blame me
Matthew 1:18-2:18; Luke 2:1-22

Opening Prayer
Glory to God in the highest.
Glory to God in the highest.
Peace on earth for all people.
Glory to God in the highest.
Today is the day of joyous news.
Glory to God in the highest.
A Saviour born, the Messiah, the Lord.
Glory to God in the highest.

Hymn
Hark the herald-angels sing

Praise
Sing to the Lord a new song;
sing to the Lord, all the earth.
Sing to the Lord and bless his name;
tell out his salvation from day to day.
Great is the Lord and greatly to be praised.

Declare his glory among the nations
and his wonder among all peoples.
For great is the Lord and greatly to be praised;
he is more to be feared than all gods.
Great is the Lord and greatly to be praised.

For all the gods of the nations are but idols;
it is the Lord who made the heavens.
Honour and majesty are before him;
power and splendour are in his sanctuary.
Great is the Lord and greatly to be praised.   *Psalm 96:1-6 (Common Worship, adapted)*

(A brief time of silence)

Confessions

Through Jesus our Saviour, born in humility,
we ask for forgiveness.
Through Jesus our Saviour, proclaimed by the angels,
we ask for forgiveness.
Through Jesus our Saviour, sought by the shepherds,
we ask for forgiveness.
Through Jesus our Saviour, worshipped by magi,
we ask for forgiveness.
May God the Father in his mercy, through his Son our Saviour and in the power of the Spirit, grant you forgiveness for all your sins and the grace to live with love and peace, justice and compassion, now and always.

Reading

Micah 5:2-5

But you, O Bethlehem of Ephrathah,
who are one of the little clans of Judah,
from you shall come forth for me
one who is to rule in Israel,
whose origin is from of old,
from ancient days.
Therefore he shall give them up until the time
when she who is in labour has brought forth;
then the rest of his kindred shall return
to the people of Israel.
And he shall stand and feed his flock in the strength of the Lord,
in the majesty of the name of the Lord his God.
And they shall live secure, for now he shall be great to the ends of the earth;
and he shall be the one of peace.

Hymn

Come and join the celebration

Prayer

Heavenly Father,
we join with angels in proclaiming the good news
of the birth of your Son our Saviour.
May the light of his coming shine in our hearts,
illumine our path, and fill the earth.
In his name we pray.

Story

It's no use blaming me. I did the best I could for them. But the place was throbbing. It was a nightmare. All week people had been arriving from all over the place, staying a night, getting registered and moving on. Oh, I know it was OK for business but frankly I could have done without it. Everyone was grumbling. There was even talk among some of the hot heads of

273

rioting, as a protest against the census. They said it was against the Lord to number the people. A lot of notice the Romans took of that. It wasn't going to stop them. Orders from Rome. Anything to get more taxes out of us. Poll tax here, property tax there. The census made sure they milked us dry. A real pain.

Anyhow, back to this couple I was telling you about. Ordinarily I wouldn't have taken much notice of them, certainly wouldn't have gone out of my way for them, seeing they were northerners. But my missus took one look at the woman and that was that. We were overflowing in the house but there was the caravan lodge and the animal cave out the back and as I told them, that was the best I could do. The missus fussed over them and it must have been sometime the next afternoon the kid was born. Don't remember exactly when but I think the fellow had got back from registering by then. I had to let them stay – couldn't just throw them out.

It was after that that things got a bit strange. Never really did get to the bottom of it. Nothing like it had ever happened before – or since for that matter.

It was later that night. I'd got to bed around midnight – absolutely bushed I was – when there was this banging and calling. Well, to be honest it's never exactly quiet round here but this was out of order. I jumped out of bed, got my staff, just in case, and went out front. Just like I thought. A crowd of shepherds. They're always making trouble when they come into town. I told them to clear off. Well, they quietened down but just stood there. One of them said something but I couldn't make sense of it. 'A baby,' he shouted, 'is there a baby here?' 'No,' I said, 'my boys are all grown up.' 'A newborn,' he persisted. 'Born today.' 'What's that to you?' I asked. 'We want to see him,' another of them said. 'The way we've been told he should be all wrapped up in a manger of all places.'

So I took them out back and there it was just as they said. They just stood around like they were dumbfounded. 'It was the angels,' one of them said to me. 'They told us about him. It was amazing. Lots of lights and things. He's going to be a great leader and save us from the Romans. Honest.' Well, that's a laugh for a start – an honest shepherd. I thought it was the drink. But they didn't cause any trouble and after a while they left. I don't know what the man and woman made of it. Just talked a bit and seemed to treat it as though it was normal. I went back to bed.

I don't suppose I would have thought anything more about it – stranger things do happen. And they did. That was what made it so weird. The crowds in town had thinned out a bit and after a couple of days we had a spare room. The missus insisted we let the couple have it – after all they weren't poor, they could afford it and you couldn't just leave them outside.

Anyhow they said they would be grateful if they could have it for a week before making their journey back home. 'No more shepherds,' I said, joking. 'No,' they said.

But then there were the travellers! We get a lot of them of course. Caravans from the east, stopping by for the night before going into Jerusalem with their goods. But these were different. They were from the east right enough, but not business people, not your usual traders. Strange they were – astrologers, magicians, something like that. Very classy. They'd been to the palace apparently, looking for a newborn prince but had been turned away, directed this way. They said something about stars, as far as I could make out. Didn't make any sense to me. I told them straight – we're not exactly the sort of place you'd find a prince in. But they just insisted. And there it was – that couple from up north again and their new baby. Well, you should have seen the travellers. Down on their knees they went and showered him with gifts. I don't understand these foreigners. They've got some very strange ways. They stayed just the night and then left. It wasn't long after that the couple went – all in a bit of a hurry it was, very early one morning. And that was the last I saw of them.

We had one hell of time just after that. Terrible it was. Soldiers came, raiding the houses, assaulting people, killing children. Terrible. No reason for it. No wonder we hate them.

I sometimes get to thinking about that couple and their baby. All that fuss. What was so special about him? Couldn't see it myself. I wonder what became of him?

(Take time to reflect on/discuss the story)

Prayers

In the power of the Spirit and in union with Christ let us pray to the Father.
We give thanks for the angel's message of peace:
we pray for the peace of our world,
for the leaders of the nations,
for peace keepers and peace makers,
remembering all whose lives are torn by war and violence.

We give thanks for the angel's message of the Saviour's birth:
we pray for all who have never heard the Good News,
for all who seek to share the Good News with others,
for missionary societies and those who translate the Scriptures,
remembering our responsibility to live the Gospel life.

We give thanks for the love of Mary and Joseph:
we pray for all parents and carers,
for those who bring up children on their own,
for those couples who cannot have children,
remembering all children and young people who are abused and neglected.
We give thanks for the welcome of the shepherds and the gifts of the wise men:
we pray for all asylum seekers and refugees,
for all who lack a sense of true worth,
for all who have nowhere they can call home,
remembering all who are strangers in a strange land.
Lord, in your mercy,
hear our prayers and let our cry come unto you.

(Say The Lord's Prayer)

Hymn

Brightest and best

Blessing

May the humility of the shepherds,
the perseverance of the wise men,
the joy of the angels,
and the peace of the Christ child, be God's gift to you.
And the blessing of God almighty,
Father, Son and Holy Spirit
be upon you and remain with you,
now and always.

John Cox

SERMON IDEAS

Christmas Day

Year A (Set 3)

Thought for the day
The Word of God is made flesh. In the birth of Jesus we see God expressed in human terms.

Readings
Isaiah 52:7-10
Psalm 98
Hebrews 1:1-4 (5-12)
John 1:1-14

The well-loved reading from Isaiah resounds with hope. It is not wishful thinking, talking about impossible dreams, but rings with utter surety that God has revealed to his attentive prophet, so that the good news can be shared with all the people of Israel. There is a great sense of excitement, like the stirring in a great crowd as word gets round that the famous and adored person they have been waiting for is about to arrive. Today God has arrived in person to live with the people of his creation, sharing their humanity in order to save them.

The writer of Hebrews chooses this to introduce his whole teaching: in the past God had spoken through his prophets, but from the Incarnation onwards we are looking at an entirely new and dynamic experience, as God speaks to us in person, through Jesus, the Son of God.

The introduction to John's Gospel helps us to see the extraordinary depth of the meaning of God's 'Word', flinging us back to the emerging creation from chaos, and forward to the streams of people through the generations who choose to receive the light of God's life to transform them and the world they inhabit. Stretched out across it all is the person of Jesus, expressing God's creative and redeeming love in a way we, as humans, can understand. No darkness can ever extinguish the hope of this light.

Susan Sayers

Year B (Set 2)

Thought for the day
Jesus Christ, the world's Saviour, is here with us, born as a human baby.

Readings
Isaiah 62:6-12
Psalm 97
Titus 3:4-7
Luke 2:(1-7) 8-20

Dogs and cats will never let you forget that it's feeding time. They go on and on reminding you loudly until you do something about that empty bowl. At the same time they are voicing (and wagging) their excitement that you will definitely be feeding them because you always do.

Today's reading from the book of Isaiah has a lovely sense of God's watchmen being posted where they can see what is going on, and given clear instructions to keep shouting both their need for God to send the promised Saviour, and their faith that he will, until he acts. Christmas is the great celebration of that action – of God breaking into his creation in a new and extraordinary way in order to save us.

Like the shepherds, we have been getting on with our daily and nightly lives, and on this night we remember the splash of God's glory across the sky, and the cry of a newborn child on a heap of straw. The ordinary and the extraordinary are shaken together, the hopes and promises become fused in practical reality, and the whole world is closer to salvation than ever before.

The Incarnation – with all its risk, its glory laid aside, its daring love – speaks as clearly to us, two thousand years on, as it did to those shepherds marvelling at the angels' message as they discovered the baby in the stable. Marvelling is filled with questions as well as wonder, and most of us find that God's presence in our world as a human baby raises many questions. Such questions are to be valued, as they can lead us forward into deeper understanding.

We are told that Mary kept all these questions and pondered them in her heart. Christmas is a time for such pondering, as well as the more usual feasting and celebrating. Wrapped up in those swaddling bands is God's answer to our longing for inner peace, our need for healing and wholeness, and our recognition that we cannot save ourselves no matter what effort we put into it. The baby in Mary's arms is God hearing our hidden fears and tears, and coming in person to save us and set us free.

Susan Sayers

Year C (Set 1)

Thought for the day

Emmanuel – 'God with us' – is born at Bethlehem into the human family. Now we will be able to understand, in human terms, what God is really like.

Readings

Isaiah 9:2-7
Psalm 96
Titus 2:11-14
Luke 2:1-14 (15-20)

The rejoicing Isaiah speaks of is a deliriously abandoned relief. After years and generations of oppression and injustice, this coming day is filled with evocative images of the security of a good harvest, the elation of overcoming an enemy in battle, and the freedom of slavery yokes being triumphantly shattered.

Typically, God brings about this longed-for day amid all the noise and confusion of ordinary life, with the census crowds jostling for space in the Bethlehem streets, the usual mix of noble and base behaviour, and in the context of unsettling circumstances. It is as if God is proving a point by acting out his name 'Emmanuel'; as if he is emphasising beyond doubt that he is truly with us in the untidy and muddled world we really inhabit. Nothing special is expected to be laid on, because he is not coming to meet us on our best behaviour, but on our real behaviour.

It is only when we are ourselves before God that he can truly be born in us. And if that place is crowded and dusty, or insecure or dark or full of questions, then he will be feeling very much at home.

Susan Sayers

A Free Gift

Aim

To encourage people to wonder at the mystery of Christmas.

Reading

Romans 6:23

Illustration

I get tired of letters through the door that say you have been especially chosen – I know that everyone is getting such a letter. Then it tells me I have won £10,000 – whoopee! But the small print says, 'if my number comes up', and the real chances of that are more than a million to one.

God is not like that. God's offer is not gifts (though he does offer us them); he offers himself to us in Jesus Christ our Lord. We do not deserve this; we cannot win it. God has chosen to give himself to us. All we have to do is accept his presence and his love.

David Adam

Beyond the Margins

He has displayed strength with his arm, scattering the proud with their airs and graces. He has caused the powerful to fall from their thrones, and has exalted the lowly. He has filled the hungry with many blessings, but has sent away the rich empty . . . God chose the foolish of this world in order to shame the wise, the weak to discomfit the strong, the lowest and the despised – those considered as nothing – to quash those who consider themselves something, so that nobody may boast before him. (Luke 1:51-53; 1 Corinthians 1:27-29)

First class, second class or third class: those were the tickets available for the ill-fated maiden voyage of the Titanic on 15 April 1912, and they eloquently reflected the social status of those who bought them. In first class were the gentry, in second the well-to-do, and in third – or steerage – the poor, many having sold everything to buy their passage in the hope of escaping the class system and building a better life in the United States.

The tragedy that subsequently unfolded was to throw all the passengers together, social divisions briefly forgotten amid the crisis, but in death they re-emerged, the bodies of first-class passengers being placed in coffins and brought back to shore while those of second- and third-class passengers were typically put in canvas bags and buried at sea. It calls to mind the notorious verse from 'All things bright and beautiful', long-since excised from most hymn books:

The rich man in his castle,
the poor man at his gate,
God made them, high or lowly,
and ordered their estate.

Happily, the idea that some people are superior to others simply by dint of birth or wealth holds less sway today, but vestiges still remain, not least in the idea that a massive divide between the rich and poor is inevitable and acceptable. The events of the nativity challenge such a comfortable assumption. God chose to come into the world not through the affluent or powerful but through the poor, ordinary and looked-down-upon. He was born not in a palace but in a stable, not to an influential mother but to a young woman in the backwater of Nazareth. And the first to hear of his coming were not those at the top of the social ladder but shepherds, representative of those on the edge of society. In all this is a reminder – should any be needed – that the poor and marginalised matter to God. Do they matter also to us?

Nick Fawcett

Good News!

I am bringing you good news of great joy that is for all people: today a Saviour has been born to you in the city of David, who is Christ the Lord. (Luke 2:10b, 11)

What sort of stories make it into the news? Just occasionally an inspiring event or heart-warming action may hit the headlines, but ninety-nine times out of a hundred the latest reports are dominated by doom and gloom: another conflict, another rise in unemployment, another political scandal, another grim set of economic figures, another famine, another natural disaster, and so on. We grow so used to bad news that we come to expect it, life being seen as intrinsically negative.

Compare that with the announcement of the birth of Jesus. It wasn't simply news; it was good news, the best there could be, glad tidings of great joy for all people! Why? Because ultimately it has changed everything for ever. Yes, bad news still continues, just as real and bleak as it has always been, frequently hard to bear and testing us to the limit, but it will not be allowed to have the final word. Light will replace darkness, love will conquer hatred, good will triumph over evil, life will defeat death. That's what the gospel is all about: not any demands that God puts upon us, still less warnings of judgement and punishment if we fail to toe the line, but the glorious message of his love in Christ from which nothing on earth or in heaven will ever be able to separate us. We have something to celebrate and something to share, good news to make known to all. However things may seem, never lose sight of that truth or forget to make it known.

Nick Fawcett

Ordinary People

There were shepherds in that area, living in the fields and keeping watch over their flock during the night. Suddenly, an angel of the Lord appeared to them, and the glory of the Lord shone around them, and they were overcome with terror. (Luke 2:8, 9)

The stained-glass windows were magnificent. Each panel depicted scenes from the life of Jesus, beginning with the annunciation, his birth in the stable and the gathering of the shepherds around the manger. For me, though, one detail spoilt them completely: each of the characters had a halo around their head; not just the angels, though that was bad enough, nor simply Jesus, but Mary, Joseph, the innkeeper and the shepherds as they gazed down at the Christ-child. It turned what would have been a lifelike and hugely evocative picture into something altogether different: a depiction of the way religion is so often seen as divorced from reality, concerned instead with surreal saintly figures that have little in common with people like you and me. The gospel, it seems to say, is not for ordinary mortals but for a special breed set apart, not about life as we know it but about some ethereal existence in a world far removed from our own.

Of course, that couldn't be more wrong, for the Nativity stories, the events of the gospel and indeed the accounts of the Bible as a whole are concerned throughout with ordinary people, flesh and blood just as we are. The shepherds out watching their flocks couldn't have been more ordinary or less pious; they were simply going about the business of their daily lives. Likewise with the apostles: each of them was plucked from obscurity to follow Jesus. These were no plaster saints living in an idealised utopia. The message of Christ then, as now, was for real people in real situations in the real world. His call, his challenge, his promises, his way, relate not just to others but equally to you!

Nick Fawcett

ALL-AGE SERVICES

Carol Service

God is with us

Resources

- Music and words
- Laptop, projector and screen
- Speakers
- A DVD of the The Nativity (BBC, 2011). This is available from amazon.co.uk. You will need the following clips (DVD timings given in minutes):
  - the angel visits Mary (26:58–31:19) – the shepherds hear the news (1hr 42:13–1hr 43:29)
  - the wise men follow the star (1hr 14:45–1hr 16:25)
  - Jesus is born (1hr 49:21–1hr 52:26)
- A manger or wooden fruit box
- Some hay
- A baby Jesus doll
- Lots of rough strips of white cotton fabric
- Lots of short pieces of white ribbon
- Two bowls

Leaders

Minimum: 1
- Leader

Optimum: 6
- Leader *(Introduction and Conclusion)*
- Activity Leader
- Storyteller/IT technician
- Music Leader
- Explorer
- Prayer Leader

Suggestions for additional music

- Ding dong, merrily on high!
- O little town of Bethlehem
- See him lying on a bed of straw

Service

Welcome/Activity

As people arrive, invite children to prepare the manger by filling it with hay. Then give them the baby Jesus doll and lots of strips of white cloth. Explain what 'swaddling' is and invite them to have a go.

Introduction

Happy Christmas! Welcome to our joyful celebration today. This morning, some of you have been helping to recreate the most important part of our Christmas story: the baby Jesus, wrapped in swaddling clothes, lying in the manger. (Show the manger and child.) Every Christmas, schools put on Nativity plays to tell the wonderful story of Jesus' birth. Today we are going to enjoy a fresh version of the Nativity story, which was made by the BBC. Let's begin at the beginning, with Mary. She is about to meet an angel.

Storytelling 1

Show the first clip: the angel visits Mary.

Music

The angel Gabriel from heaven came

Storytelling 2

Show the second clip: the shepherds hear the news.

Music

While shepherds watched

Storytelling 3

Show the third clip: the wise men follow the star.

Music

We three kings

Storytelling 4

Show the fourth clip: Jesus is born.

Music

Silent night

Exploring

The final moments of *The Nativity* showed us the scene which sums up Christmas: the baby in the manger, watched over by Mary and Joseph, worshipped by shepherds and kings. During this version of the story, we learned why all those people were there. Mary and Joseph had been rejected by the people of Bethlehem, who thought Mary's pregnancy was shameful. They were in the stable with the animals because it was the only houseroom anyone would give them. Joseph was by his fiancee's side, even though he had been so angry about her pregnancy that he had come close to leaving her.

The shepherds were there because an angel had promised a Saviour who would care for poor people like them. They wondered if such a thing could really be true. The wise men were there because their study of the stars showed that an old prophecy was about to be fulfilled: the king of the Jews, the Messiah, was to be born in Bethlehem.

When Jesus was born, all these people came to know the truth. Mary knew that God had kept his promise to her. Joseph looked around at the strangers worshipping Jesus and knew that the child in the manger was indeed God's Son – and his beloved Mary had told him the truth. The shepherds knew that God had not forgotten them, because he had sent his own Son to save them. The wise men knew that God's ancient promises had been fulfilled: this baby was the long-awaited Messiah.

We celebrate Christmas because it is the moment when we, too, know the truth. God became a human being and lived among us. As the angel in our first clip put it, Jesus formed 'a bridge between heaven and earth for all time'. Through Jesus, we can know God. We know that he loves us and is always with us. What news could be better than that?

Prayer action

In our prayers today, we give thanks that God is with us. We remember the reality of the baby in the manger. As a focus for our prayers, please take a piece of this white ribbon to remind you of the swaddling clothes that Mary wrapped around her child.

Hand round the bowls of ribbons and encourage everyone to take one.

Let us pray.

Heavenly Father,
thank you for the gift of your Son.
The body that Mary swaddled with such love
was the same body he sacrificed with such love
for our sake on the cross.
We give thanks today for the birth of Jesus,
our Saviour and friend,
the Light of the world.

Please take home your ribbon – your piece of swaddling cloth. Keep it in your purse or wallet as a reminder of Jesus' birth.

Music

O come, all ye faithful

Conclusion

May the love of God and the peace of Christ
fill our hearts and homes this Christmas.

Claire Benton-Evans

Christmas Eve

Circle of light

Lots of tubes of glow-sticks.*

Leader

Jesus said that he is the light of the world. But he also said that each one of us is the light of the world, too. That light is like this glow-stick. *(Show the inactive glow stick in your hand.)* The light in this stick is hidden – just as some of the goodness in us is hidden. We could do something kind, or helpful, or caring – but sometimes we choose not to, or we just can't be bothered. But when we do make the effort to be kind or helpful *(bend the glow-stick until the stuff inside it cracks, activating the light)*, then the goodness in us breaks out, like this light, and shines around us. Today, we are going to use these glow-sticks to help make our prayers.

Prayer action

Invite everyone to form a circle and take a glow-stick, then turn out the lights.

Make this glow-stick your prayer: it is your promise to God to do something loving, kind or helpful for someone else. Make your promise, then crack your glow-stick to let the light break out. Let there be light!

Allow some time for people to make their prayers, then invite everyone to join the sticks up in a huge circle, either by laying them end-to-end on the floor, or by using the connectors supplied. A connected circle of sticks can be held in people's hands.

Let's take a moment to look at this circle of light, made up of our prayers which represent the light that shines in each of us.

Closing words

God of all goodness,
we offer you this circle of light.
May you bless our good intentions
and help us to do good.
May this light of love shine in the world
wherever there is darkness.

Claire Benton-Evans

---

* These are thin plastic sticks which contain a coloured chemical which becomes fluorescent when the stick is flexed. They are available from toyshops, pound shops and many newsagents. Each pack also contains a number of small plastic connectors which can be used to join sticks together to form chains and circles. See also www.glowsticks.co.uk

Can I Have a Word?

Joseph describes how he saw the events of Christmas

Introduction

This drama was written to use in a carol service. It looks at the challenges that Joseph faced, in an attempt to get away from the way in which the Nativity is so often seen as a kind of fairy tale. As it is quite long, an optional break is given. In the original version Gabriel wore a magnificent halo made of Christmas tree lights, which was very popular with the congregation. However, Gabriel has the key speech at the end of the drama, and it will lose its impact if he looks too ridiculous. If you would like Gabriel to dress up, an optional extra section is included to explain the removal of the halo for his second appearance.

Scripture reference
Matthew 1:18–2:14

This is how the birth of Jesus Christ came about: His mother Mary was pledged to be married to Joseph, but before they came together, she was found to be with child through the Holy Spirit.

Matthew 1:18

Characters

Joseph
Mary, *his fiancée/wife*
Anna, *his mother-in-law*
Gabriel, *an archangel*

Joseph stands on one side. Mary, Anna and Gabriel should preferably be out of sight and only appear to hold their part of the conversation.

Joseph	I'd just like to point out, I didn't ask for any of this. Quite the contrary in fact. I had my life sorted just as I wanted it. I had a good home, family and friends close by and a nice little business. I liked my life. I trusted God and was at peace with the universe. It seemed to me, in those long ago days that now seem like they happened to someone else, that all I really lacked was a family of my own. And I was quite sure that Mary was the partner I needed. So when she said . . .
Mary	Joseph, can I have a word?
Joseph	*(still addressing the congregation)* . . . how was I to know how much life was going to change? It just doesn't occur to you, does it? . . .
Mary	*(interrupting)* Joseph, I really do need a word.
Joseph	*(turning to Mary)* Of course, Mary, my love.
Mary	Joseph, you might want to sit down for this.

Joseph   It's all right, Mary, you can't shock me. Overspent on the wedding plans have you?

Mary   Not quite.

Joseph   Want to invite a few more relatives?

Mary   No, it's not about the wedding.

Joseph   What's your mother done now?

Mary   It's not my mother, it's me. I'm pregnant.

Joseph   I think I need to sit down.

Mary   Yes, Joseph.

Joseph   Pregnant, how can you be pregnant? No don't answer that – I know how you can be pregnant.

Mary   It's not what you think.

Joseph   It's exactly what I think. There's only one way for a woman to get pregnant!

Mary   Don't you be so sure!

         Exit Mary.

Joseph   *(addressing congregation)* I really hadn't asked for that, had I? You have no idea what it was like. Half my friends assumed I was the father and thought I was a fool for not being more careful when I was with my fiancée. The other half assumed I wasn't the father and thought I was a fool for not being more careful in my choice of fiancée. I didn't want to hurt Mary, but why should I get landed with a baby that wasn't mine? So I started to make my plans to quietly cancel the wedding. You can understand, I'm sure, that I really wasn't ready for an angel to say . . .

Gabriel   Joseph, can I have a word?

Joseph   *(addressing congregation)* I mean this is not the sort of thing that happens to normal people, is it? One minute there I was comfortably in the land of nod and the next thing I know I'm face to face with this, this vision. You should have seen his wings, they were . . .

Gabriel   *(interrupting)* Joseph, I really do need a word.

Joseph   *(turning to Gabriel)* Of course, um . . . Gabriel. Archangel Gabriel. Very glad to meet you, Mr Archangel, Sir.

Gabriel   Joseph, you might want to sit down for this.

Joseph   Oh that's all right. There's nothing left can shock me now.

Gabriel   You're to marry Mary.

Joseph	I think I need to sit down.
Gabriel	Yes, Joseph.
Joseph	You do know that she's um …
Gabriel	She's um?
Joseph	You know, how does the King James Bible put it, 'great with child'?
Gabriel	I hear she's not bad with teenagers as well.
Joseph	No, no, that's not what I mean. I mean, she's pregnant.
Gabriel	Yes, we know all about that.
Joseph	And it's not mine.
Gabriel	Yes, we know that too, You're still to marry her. The child is God's and we want you to be the father.
	Exit Gabriel.
Joseph	*(addressing congregation)* Well, I really hadn't asked for that, had I? But you don't argue with angels *(uncertainly)*, do you? So I reorganised the wedding and began to look forward to a nice quiet life with Mary and the baby. If only I had known.

BREAK

Joseph	It was a bit of a rush, organising the wedding so suddenly. I'm sure you'll understand that afterwards I was ready for a bit of space, just me and Mary and time to get ready for the baby to come. I really wasn't ready for my mother-in-law to say …
Anna	Joseph, can I have a word?
Joseph	You do expect to be left alone after you get married, don't you …
Anna	*(interrupting)* Joseph, I really do need a word.
Joseph	Certainly, how can I help?
Anna	You might want to sit down for this.
Joseph	Trust me, after what I've gone through in the last few months, nothing could shock me any more.
Anna	There's going to be a census.
Joseph	A whatus?

Anna   A census. The Romans want to count everyone.

Joseph   Oh well, if it keeps them happy.

Anna   They want to count everyone in their home town. We all have to go back to where our family came from – in the next two months.

Joseph   But, but, my family's from Bethlehem; that's miles away.

Anna   There's lots of people will have to travel further than that.

Joseph   The baby's due at the end of next month. I wanted to be there for the birth.

Anna   Oh, I think we can guarantee you will be.

Joseph   What do you mean?

Anna   We've checked the rules, Mary has to go with you.

Joseph   But Mary doesn't come from Bethlehem!

Anna   What can I say, it's the first century, it's a very sexist time.

Joseph   What stupid idiot thought this up?

Anna   I believe the stupid idiot's name is Caesar Augustus.

Joseph   I think I need to sit down.

Anna   I'll see you when you get back.

            Exit Anna.

Joseph   *(addressing congregation)* So I made some new plans. What else could I do? Eighty miles and no public transport. I cannot tell you how difficult it was, and when we got there we discovered someone had forgotten to book the room. So there I was with a new wife and a new baby, contemplating another 80 mile trip to get home. I really didn't need any more bad news.

Gabriel Joseph, can I have a word?

Joseph   *(addressing Gabriel)* That depends, will I have to sit down?

Gabriel Probably.

Joseph   OK, so tell me, how are things going to get worse? There must be a way, though I can't see it. I've got a new baby, I'm miles from home, oh and by the way, who should I thank for the shepherds?

Gabriel Me, I'm afraid.

Joseph   I don't want to complain Gabriel, but they did arrive just as we got the baby off to sleep. There were rather a lot of them and they were very excited, and it's a very small stable.

Gabriel   Sorry.

Joseph   I wouldn't have minded, but they had to explain why they had come. Which involved their own special rendition of the song of the heavenly host. It's a great pity none of them could actually sing. Still, at least they were better than the next lot who showed up.

Gabriel   The wise men? What possible objection could you have to visitors from the east?

Joseph   It would have been nice if one of them could have spoken English.

Gabriel   Joseph, you're a first-century, Middle-Eastern Jew – you can't speak English!

Joseph   All right, Aramaic. All I'm saying is that a little mutual understanding would have helped. I don't think they had the least idea what was happening – do you know what they brought as presents for the baby?

Gabriel   Well, as I was saying, I really do need a word.

Joseph   Of course, things are going to get worse, aren't they? You have some other visitors up your sleeve, haven't you?

Gabriel   No.

Joseph   Caesar Augustus had another bright idea?

Gabriel   No.

Joseph   Don't tell me, Mary has another little surprise for me.

Gabriel   No.

Joseph   So what is it then?

Gabriel   Herod wants to kill the baby.

Joseph   I think I need to sit down!

Gabriel   It's a bit of a shock, I know.

Joseph   No, no hang on a minute. It's going to be all right. How could I have forgotten, little Jesus is God's son, right?

Gabriel   That's right.

Joseph   So, obviously God is going to keep him safe.

Gabriel   Well...

Joseph   So Heaven must have a plan. What is it? Are you going to drop in on Herod and get him to change his mind?

Gabriel   Herod doesn't listen to us, I'm afraid.

Joseph   OK, then, so perhaps you've got an army of angels stationed outside the stable.

Gabriel   No.

Joseph   I know, you're going to spirit us away in the night; in the blink of an eye we'll be somewhere else, right?

Gabriel   Not exactly.

Joseph   So, come on then. What is the great plan? Run like hell for Egypt.

   Silence.

Joseph   Is that it?

Gabriel   Pretty well, yes.

Joseph   I definitely need to sit down.

Gabriel   I can give you some directions if you like. *(produces large map with Bethlehem and Egypt marked, a large arrow showing the way from one to the other)*

Joseph   Gabriel, can I have a word?

Gabriel   Yes?

Joseph   *(calmly)* I have a small complaint. *(louder)* You've ruined my life!

Gabriel   We have?

Joseph   I was happy, you know. I thought that faith was about a bit of peace in a busy world. A sense of purpose and meaning in life. I didn't think faith would mean ending up as the father of someone else's baby, 80 miles from home, running for the border pursued by a psychotic tyrant!

Gabriel   Didn't you?

Joseph   No. I thought God would keep me safe. Instead, I'm scared, Gabriel. I thought God cared about me. Why has this happened?

Gabriel   Who said faith means being kept safe?

Joseph   Um, I don't know. I just assumed.

Gabriel   Joseph, that little baby we're asking you to look after, he is going to show people what faith really means. His life is never going to be safe, easy or comfortable, He's going to turn the world upside down and have enemies as well as friends, And he's going to show people that God doesn't sit safe in his heaven, immune from all the suffering down here. God has a human face and you and Mary are going to hold him in your arms and watch him grow. Your life will never be easy and comfortable, but it will be full of love and touched by the beauty of God himself.

Joseph   I see, well, I guess there's only one thing left to ask then, really.

Gabriel   Oh, yes. What's that then?

Joseph   Which way did you say to Egypt?

Judith Rossall

A Child is Born

Resources

- Advent wreath and matches
- Postcard-sized pieces of a large picture of an angel *(see note)*
- Board and sticky tack
- Basic angel costume *(white sheet/tunic, tinsel halo)*
- Two large cardboard speech bubbles: *Do not be afraid* and *This is Love*
- Music and words
- The Paschal candle *(already lit)* and as many candlesticks and candelabra as your altar will hold. Next to the altar, place stands for votive candles and on the floor in front of it, lie a piece of board on which tea-lights may safely stand
- Lots of *(unlit)* candles and tea-lights, plus matches and tapers

Leaders

Minimum: 2
- Leader
- Oriel

Optimum: 7
- Leader
- Activity Leader
- Storyteller
- Music Leader

- Explorer
- Oriel, in a suit and carrying a briefcase
- Prayer Leader

Suggestions for additional music

- Mary had a baby
- Little Jesus, sweetly sleep
- Angels from the realms of glory

Service

Welcome

Light all the candles on the Advent wreath.

Introduction

Happy Christmas! Let's begin this joyful day by singing.

Music

O little town of Bethlehem

Activity

Now I want to get you out of your seats and moving around. Hidden all around the church are pieces of a picture. Here is one of them *(show a piece)*: can you find the rest? I wonder whether you can help me fit them together like a jigsaw, so we can see what picture they make?

Invite all volunteers to hunt around the church for the pieces and bring them to the front, where you can assemble them on the board. Encourage general participation in fitting together the jigsaw. When it is finished, invite comments:

What is this a picture of? Do you think this is what angels look like?

Storytelling

Today's story is full of angels. Why don't you close your eyes and imagine yourself in the story as I tell it to you? Imagine you are a shepherd, sitting on the rocky hills with your sheep. You are wearing long, rough robes and sheepskins to keep out the cold. It is dark and you are sleepily trying to keep an eye on your flock. The sheep are munching loudly. There are other shepherds around you, and you can hear some of them chatting quietly. Some of the younger boys have dozed off, even though the ground is hard and frosty. It is a cold, still night; the sky is vast and inky-black and the stars twinkle brightly.

Suddenly – whoosh! – an enormous explosion of bright, white light tears open the sky. It looks like the end of the world – as if the sun has exploded. You have never seen anything like it, and the hillside around you erupts in noise and panic: the sheep scatter in every direction, bleating madly at the sky; the other shepherds yell and the boys run, screaming, to hide in the caves. The explosion becomes a column of fierce brilliance, and rays of light fan out like wings, spanning the sky.

As you stay rooted to the spot in terror, an unearthly voice rings out above all the racket: 'Do not be afraid! I bring good news! Today a Saviour, the Messiah, has been born! You will find him in the city of David: a child wrapped in bands of cloth, lying in a manger.'

Your ears are ringing with the voice when the whole sky becomes filled with light, as if it were the middle of a summer's day. But instead of sun and blue sky, there is a shimmering whiteness from east to west; beams of light spread and dazzle, pulsing like the beating of wings. You stand with your mouth open as the angel-song fills the air: 'Glory to God in the highest! Peace on earth and goodwill to all!'

Music

While shepherds watched

Exploring

Today we will be thinking about the angels in our story and the message that they bring. Now, no Nativity play is complete without angels. Who can tell me what angels wear?

(As people say 'A white sheet!', 'A tinsel halo!' and so on, invite a volunteer to dress up in these items.)

So this is the kind of angel we all recognise – the kind of angel who decorates our Christmas cards. But think about the angels in our story. How did those shepherds feel, surrounded by angels on that cold hillside? How did you feel as I was telling the story? *(Invite responses.)* Who can remember the very first thing the angel said? *(Invite responses.)* It was the first thing that angels in the Bible always say to people: 'DO NOT BE AFRAID!' Our angel here is very beautiful, but I don't think we are frightened of her, do you? Angels are out of this world: they are God's servants and messengers and they give us a glimpse of his almighty power. No wonder they are awe-inspiring!

Angel holds up a speech bubble saying, 'Do not be afraid'.

Here is another kind of angel. He is the Archangel Oriel and he and his diary were imagined by the writer, Robert Harrison. Oriel is an important manager in heaven: he organises things for God, and in particular makes the arrangements for Jesus' birth. In his diary, Oriel confesses that he cannot understand why almighty God should want to become a human being at all. This is what he says:

Oriel   And now, the One who held every atom in his grasp is no more than a clutch of watery cells in the midst of a teenage girl, in an obscure village, in a defeated nation, on one of the smaller planets that orbit an ordinary star, in an uneventful galaxy that turns on its little axis in that gassy cloud that is the Universe, which the Son himself made. Such smallness I can barely begin to imagine. This is Love.*

Oriel holds up a speech bubble saying, 'This is Love'.

Explorer   Instead of remaining in power and glory with all his angels, God made himself human in the form of his Son, Jesus, and he came to live among us. This is the message of the angels: the baby lying in the manger is Love – God's love for each and every one of us.

---

*   Robert Harrison, *Oriel's Diary*, Scripture Union, 2002, p.11.

Music

It came upon the midnight clear

Prayer Action

Arrange for two volunteers to light all the candles on the altar and turn off the lights in church as you introduce this prayer.

In the beginning, God said, 'Let there be light'; and there was light. On that first Christmas Day, there was the light of a new star and the promise that Jesus had come to be a light for all people – a light which would shine in the world's darkness and never be extinguished. Today we will each light a candle as a prayer in the darkness and a sign of our faith.

Pause until all the altar candles are lit.

Each person comes up and lights a candle to add to the lights around the altar.

You are invited to join in the words of a very ancient song of praise by saying simply, 'Holy, holy, holy Lord'. Let us pray together with the words of the angels:

> **Holy, holy, holy Lord,**
> The whole earth is full of your glory,
> the world blazes with your light.
> **Holy, holy, holy Lord.**

Music

O come, all ye faithful

Conclusion

Living Lord,
may the good news
which the angels brought
be shared by us today,
and may your love live
in our hearts and homes
this Christmas.

Note

Angel

Posters of classical paintings are a useful source (try shops in big art galleries), as are children's books, for example: *This is the star* by Joyce Dunbar, illustrated by Gary Blythe (Doubleday, 1996). Shops attached to religious houses often have postcards and prints by monastic artists: I have seen some startling interpretations of the familiar 'angel and shepherds' scene. For this activity, you will probably need to produce a large, colour copy of the picture you choose. This may involve some expense, but if you cut the picture into large pieces which can then be laminated, you will have a durable resource.

Claire Benton-Evans

God's Glory

Resources

- Advent wreath, matches and tapers
- Hand-held votive candles, given to each person as they arrive
- Felt pens for every pew or row of seats
- A selection of stickers: gold and silver stars, moons and planets if possible
- A sealed envelope under every seat, (including the Leaders') containing the printed Christmas card *(see note)*
- Whiteboard or flip chart and pens
- Music and words

Leaders

Minimum: 1
- Leader

Optimum: 6
- Leader (Introduction and Conclusion)
- Activity Leader
- Explorer
- Storyteller
- Music Leader
- Prayer Leader

Suggestions for additional music

- The Virgin Mary had a baby boy
- Infant holy, infant lowly

Service

Welcome

Light all the candles on the Advent wreath.

Introduction

Merry Christmas! Who has opened some presents already today?

Invite responses. If the church is bristling with children carrying new toys, you may like to invite some to show the congregation what they have received.

Now we begin our celebration today by singing.

Music

Once in royal David's city

Activity

Christmas is a time for thinking big – and I don't just mean presents and turkey. In our familiar Christmas carols, we sing 'Joy to the world' and 'Unto us a boy is born! King of all creation', but do we ever stop to think about what huge things we are describing? Joy to the world: all 6.8 billion people and 197 million square miles of it. And what about 'King of all creation'? How big is creation? Today's Bible reading describes it as 'all things that have come into being' – in other words, 'life, the universe and everything'.

Our activity today is going to help us think big. Under your seats you will find an envelope. It is yours to keep, but don't open it yet – it is waiting for an address. Your address. Start right at the top and write your address on the envelope.

Allow time for people to do this, and fill in your own envelope, using your church's address.

You have probably finished your address with your county or postcode – but now let's see how long you can make your address. Which country do you live in? Which continent? Which hemisphere? Which planet? Which part of the solar system? Use all your knowledge of geography and space to address your letter so that it could reach you from the other end of the universe! You may need to carry on writing on the back of the envelope.

When you have finished the address, you may like to decorate the envelope with stars and planets for its journey through space.

Allow plenty of time for people to complete their envelopes. Complete your own address (see Exploring, below).

Music

Ding dong, merrily on high!

Exploring

Let's hear some of your universal addresses. Don't read out the first bit – start from the country and go on from there.

Hear some addresses and then read out your own example:

> (Your name),
> (Your church),
> (Your town),
> (Your county),
> (Your country),
> (Your continent),
> Planet Earth,
> 3rd Planet in the Solar System,
> Orion Arm,
> The Milky Way Galaxy,

The Local Group,
The Local Supercluster,
The Known Universe,
The Unknown Universe.

There's a lot of universe out there! A science fiction writer summed it up like this: 'Space is big. Really big. You just won't believe how vastly, hugely, mind-bogglingly big it is. I mean, you may think it's a long way down the road to the chemist's, but that's just peanuts to space.' (Douglas Adams, *The Hitchhiker's Guide to the Galaxy*). And all of this – the known and unknown reaches of space – are part of God's creation, just as we are part of it, too.

Now here's a big question for you. Imagine you were God, the Creator of EVERYTHING. You don't want to stay in the background: you want to reach out to the individual people on earth. You want to say to them, 'I am your God!' and show them your glory and power. What would you do? Would you send them each a letter, like this? *(Show your envelope.)* Would you do something big with weather, such as making a rainbow? Would you show them a miracle? If you were God, what would you do to show people that you loved them?

Invite suggestions, valuing all contributions by writing them on the whiteboard or flip chart.

Let's see what God actually did to show us who he is and to let us know that he loves us. Your envelopes are addressed to you: open them and see what's inside.

Everyone opens their envelopes, including you.

This is what God did to show that he loves us *(read the words on the card)*: 'God became a human being and lived among us.' Although he created the whole universe, he didn't terrify us with some earth-shattering display of power, or dazzle us with his glory. He was born as the little baby, Jesus, so that we might know him and could say, 'We have seen his glory.' That is what our carols, cards and presents are all about, and that is why we celebrate Christmas. Although we are a tiny part of his creation, God gave himself to us today. Joy to the world!

Storytelling
Read John 1:1-14.

Music
Joy to the world

Prayer action
Turn out the lights.

Today's Gospel says this about Jesus: 'In him was life, and the life was the light of all people. The light shines in the darkness, and the darkness did not overcome it.' For our prayers today, we wait in the dark and remember all those known to us who need the light of life, especially in this Christmas season.

Pause. Light your own votive candle from the central candle of the Advent wreath.

In Jesus was life, and the life was the light of all people.

Pass the light among the people. When all the candles are lit, say the closing words.

Jesus, Light of the world,
shine among us this Christmas Day
and for evermore.

Music

O come, all ye faithful

Conclusion

Heavenly Father,
We thank you for the gift of your Son.
In him we have seen your glory.
As we celebrate his birth,
may our hearts be open to receive him.

Note

Christmas card

Make double-sided copies onto coloured A4
paper or card. Cut out, fold and put into
envelopes which should then be sealed.

Claire Benton-Evans

More Than Just Fancy Dress

Text

Hebrews 1:1-12

What's the point

The Bible tells us that God's glory, which is also Christ's glory, is part of his eternal being,
not just something he wears. By the same token, when Christ took on our humanity he wasn't
just wearing it like a jacket – just the outward appearance – but he actually *became* fully human!

Preparation

You will need:

- children dressed up as Nativity characters – make sure that they've got suitable clothes
  on underneath, though, because you're going to ask them to take their costumes off!
- a carrier bag (the scruffier the better, to make the point) for each child's costume to be
  rolled up and carried away in

Activity

Call the dressed-up children to the front to form a Nativity tableau, and ask the congregation if they think they 'look the part'. Ask each child to say which role they're playing, and then say something like, 'But, now, let's see who they really are!' One by one the children then remove the costumes, revealing their ordinary clothes underneath. You can then make the point that we can't do that with Jesus! When God became human, he didn't just put on the outward appearance, but actually became fully human. There's no pretence with God – what you see is what you get. Similarly, the glory of God that Christ now shares isn't something temporary and superficial like an old bit of clothing. It's permanent – eternal.

Ask the children to roll up their clothes, put them in the carrier bags and return to their seats.

Reading
Hebrews 1:1-12

Now, when it comes to God speaking: he did that long ago, in, oh, all kinds of different ways, through the prophets; but now, finally, he's spoken to us through his Son, his Son whom he's made his heir in everything – in fact, it was through him that God created the universe. And he's the very reflection of God's own glory, the perfect image of God's very self – and it's by the power of his word that everything continues to exist. When he'd finished clearing up the mess of our sin, he took his place seated at the right hand of the throne of God himself. And why not? – after all, he'd become just as much superior to the angels as his title is to theirs.
Look: was there ever an angel to whom God said,
'You're my son – I've begotten you'?
Or, there again,
'I'm going to be his Father,
and he's going to be my Son?'
And then, when he brings the Son and Heir into the world, he says,
'Worship him, all you angels!'
And what does he say about those angels?
'He makes his angels as winds,
his servants as fiery flames.'
But when it comes to the Son, well, that's different altogether:
'God, your throne is seriously permanent – like for ever and ever –
and the only sceptre you need is the justice of your own rule.
I mean, you've really loved truth and justice,
and all those things, and you've hated everything unjust and evil,
and therefore God – your God – well, he's really anointed you
with the oil of pure happiness, way beyond all your comrades.'
And what about this:
'Right from the beginning, God, it was you who created the earth,
everything in the heavens is your handiwork;
that'll all die, but you'll still be here;
they'll wear out like so many old clothes!
You'll roll them up like a worn-out jacket,
change them like yesterday's underwear!
But you – you're always the same,
your life is never going to end.'

Michael Forster

Christmas Lights

Bible Reading

For you were once darkness, but now you are light in the Lord. Live as children of light (for the fruit of the light consists in all goodness, righteousness and truth) and find out what pleases the Lord. Have nothing to do with the fruitless deeds of darkness, but rather expose them.

But everything exposed by the light becomes visible, for it is light that makes everything visible.

Ephesians 5:8-11, 13, 14

Staging

Staging is simple – all that is needed is some kind of rostrum or raised platform. The performers face out over their audience.

Characters

Councillor Bundle, a fussy town councillor
Michael Cane, the town mayor
Thompson, a hard-working, yet slightly dim council worker

The Sketch

Councillor Bundle	Right then, before his worship the mayor actually throws the switch that will turn on our Christmas illuminations, may I just say how pleased I am to see so many of you here. Granted, we had hoped for a crowd of double figures, it being such an important part of our Christmas celebrations, but I do appreciate that it is a cold night and scheduling the illuminations ceremony on the same night and time as Coronation Street was perhaps, with hindsight, a bit of a mistake. Anyway, without further ado, may I hand over to his worship, the mayor.
Mayor	Well … well, thank you for your warm applause, much needed on a cold night like this.
Councillor Bundle	*(forced)* Ha, ha! Very good, Your Worship.
Mayor	Oh, not at all. Well it is, indeed, a great honour to be here … but before we move on I must just say that I hope that no one has been brought here under false pretences due to the advertising of the event which, as you may recall, proclaimed who was going to switch on the lights this year. Well, my name really is Michael Cane … actually it's without the I in the surname but there was a bit of a mix up at the printers and it was too late to change them once they'd gone out. Ha ha … so, as I said, I hope there was no confusion there. Anyway, let's turn our attention now to the job in hand . . . turning on the Christmas illuminations to really start the festivities of the season. Shall we all count down together?
Councillor Bundle	Aye … a good idea, Your Worship.

Councillor Bundle and Mayor	Five . . . four . . . three . . . two . . . one.

(The lights are turned on.)

(They both look up and around.) Oh, that looks lovely . . . wonderful!

Mayor	Look at them all, sparkling and pretty. They make everything look so attractive, don't they?
Councillor Bundle	Ah, well yes, you're right there, Your Worship. I mean you'd never guess that that string of lights flashing there *(points)* was hung up on the back of the abattoir. Makes it look like a veritable fairy-tale castle it does, a real winter wonderland. See the way the lights glisten on the back of the gasworks there? *(points)* Beautiful! Yes, and look at them shops down there *(points)*. Don't they look festive, glinting and shining? You'd hardly know they'd been empty and derelict for the past five years. The way the light glints on their broken windows, it's like a fairy palace. And, you may also have also noticed, Your Worship, that no expense has been spared this year – we actually have some words written up there in lights . . . a traditional Christmas greeting as you can see.
Mayor	Oh really. And where is that?
Councillor Bundle	Over there, Your Worship, *(points higher and in the near distance)* over there, hanging between the off licence and the betting shop.
Mayor	Oh yes . . . oh yes . . . *(sounding out the letters)* N . . . O . . . E . . . um, N . . . O . . . E . . . What's that?
Councillor Bundle	*(a little confused to start with)* No, um, I don't think so, have another look. *(he looks too)* Oh, no . . . I don't believe it. You're right, there it is, N . . . O . . . E . . . *(angrily)* Whatever's going on? Who's responsible? Thompson, come here!

(Enter Thompson.)

Thompson	Yes, guv'nor.
Councillor Bundle	Now, Thompson, you set these lights up . . . what's going on? Are you responsible for this fiasco?
Thompson	No, no fiasco sir, mine's a Ford Fiesta . . . *(points offstage)* that red one over there . . . bit rusty on the side, but looks quite nice with these lights mind you. Why, is it in the way? Do you want me to move it?
Councillor Bundle	*(impatiently)* Not 'Fiesta', 'Fiasco' . . . the lights Thompson, the lights . . . look over there. N . . . O . . . E, N . . . O . . . E . . . What's that? Didn't you get the message?
Thompson	*(defensively)* Don't go blaming me! I got the message loud and clear down the phone and I wrote it down there and then. They said, do the

Christmas message, Thompson and don't you forget, 'no L'. Now, sir, you look up there and tell me if you can see an L? Can you see an L, sir? No, sir, you can't, and I'll tell you why, sir . . . 'cause I never put one up there, that's why . . . because that's what my instructions was . . . no L. No L is what you wanted and no L is what you've got.

Councillor Bundle   *(dawning realisation and then sarcastically)* Aye, Thompson, thanks . . . thanks very much!

And the point is . . . ?

Yes, it is amazing how attractive Christmas lights can make things look. They make things sparkle, make things look pretty. But they can be used to cover up what things are really like. What a very different idea to the one expressed in the passage from Ephesians. How different to the light that Jesus brings and is. His light doesn't disguise things – it doesn't hide things, but shows things for what they are. And if we live in that light it shows us for who we are and exposes the motives behind the things we do. That's why his light can be so challenging. But then it is important that we are prepared every now and then to be challenged. Perhaps Christmas is as good a time as any.

Michael Catchpool and Pat Lunt

The Light Audition

Ideal for a Christmas family service, informal carol service, Christingle service or pre-Christmas assembly, this is a fun sketch with plenty of humour but a reverential ending focusing on Jesus as the centre of Christmas and the true Light of the World. Inviting a new mother and baby to make the final entrance will add warmth and realism.

Bible source

John 1:1-18

Performance time

Six minutes

Characters

A1 and A2	angels of the host
Sylvia Sun	an actress of the old school
Sid Sparkler	a stand-up comedian
Torch and Battery	a double act
Mandy Moon	a sultry charmer
Olympic Flame	an American athlete
Mary and baby	the real thing

Bare acting area with two director-type canvas chairs with ANGEL 1 and ANGEL 2 printed on the backs. A1 and A2 wear halos – preferably up-ended sports eye-shields. A1 is obviously in charge; rather correct, a stickler for detail, a bossy lady. A2 is a more down-to-earth chap; casual and happy-go-lucky. A1 enters busily Left, checking through a clipboard of names, looks out Right, checks watch, consults list again. She has a second clipboard and a paper scroll. After a few moments A2 casually saunters across from Right.

A2   Morning A1.

A1   What time do you call this, A2?

A2   Sorry A1. The old halo's playing up something shocking today.

A1   Well, now you've arrived we can start.

A2   Start what?

A1   The audition of course. Don't you *ever* read King's Regulations? We're auditioning for the light.

A2   Oh yes. Er – what light?

A1   *The* Light. The Light of the World. You know – John's Gospel.

A2   Oh yes. Good book that. How's it selling?

A1   *(heavy sarcasm)* He hasn't written it yet.

A2   Oh, well. There's plenty of time then.

A1   *(briskly, checking watch and bustling about)* There's no time at all. Here. *(gives A2 a clipboard)* He's going to talk about the Light and we don't know what it is. *(picks up scroll)* Listen, this is what he's going to say. *(reads from scroll)* The true light that gives light to everyone was coming into the world.

A2   And that's all?

A1   Yes. The rest is very unclear. But we need to know, so we're holding an audition.

A2   Fine. I like auditions. Gives me a sense of power. *(sits in his chair in film director fashion and reverses halo over his eyes)*

A1   Careful! Remember what happened to You Know Who. *(tetchy)*

A2   All right, all right. Let's get on with it.

A1   *(using A2's arms as a clapperboard)* Audition for the Light of the World. Take one. *(slaps arms together)*

A2   *(rubbing arms)* Ow! No need to overdo it. I'm not as young as I will be. O – er . . . *(Sun has taken her place)* . . . Name please.

Sun   *(synthetic smile)* Dame Sylvia Sun.

A1   *(catty)* Aren't you – well, a little old for this job?

Sun   True, I have been around for ages, but no one has ever complained about my performances – except, perhaps, in the British holiday season.

A2   And what exactly do you do, Dame Sylvia?

Sun   *(indignant)* What do I do? I beam, dear boy. Beam, beam, beam. *(she beams to all corners)*

A2   Is that it?

A1   Well, thank you Dame Sylvia. We'll let you know. *(Sun exits)*

A1   What do you think?

A2   Bit past it if you ask me.

A1   *(pleased)* I agree. Next please.

Sid Sparkler takes the stage. He wears a check jacket, party hat and red nose and carries a hooter.

Sparkler   Hallo, hallo, hallo. You're in luck this morning and no mistake. What did the Roman Candle say to the Catherine Wheel? *(hooter)* I'm sure I don't know. What did the Roman Candle say to the Catherine Wheel?

(silence)

A2   Well, what *did* the Roman Candle say to the Catherine Wheel?

Sparkler   Er – I've forgotten.

A1   *(to A2)* Another of these stand-up comedians. *(to Sparkler)* We'll let you know Mr er . . .

Sparkler   Sparkler, squire. Sid Sparkler. Every joke a winner. Children's parties a speciality. *(to himself)* I must get that right . . . What did the Roman Candle say to the Catherine Wheel? *(exits repeating patter)*

A2   Sparkler! More like a damp squib.

A1   No stamina. That's what we need A2. An unchanging light.

A2   Exactly A1. Perhaps these will be better.

Torch and Battery take the stage. A little mirror action business can be introduced here; walking close together, raising arms at the same time etc.

A1	Names please.
Torch	Torch . . .
Battery	. . . and Battery.
Torch	The ever-ready . . .
Battery	double act.
A1	Carry on.
Torch	A recitation. I wandered lonely as a cloud . . .
Battery	I say, I say, I say. A funny thing happened to me on my way to this audition.
Torch	I don't wish to know that. Kindly leave the stage.
	Battery runs off and Torch slumps to the ground.
Torch	Well that's all very nice, but Battery's run out.
A2	Can't have that A1. This light has to be permanent, doesn't it?
A1	It certainly does A2. Thank you Torch and Battery. We'll let you know.
	Battery returns to help Torch off.
A1	Next!
	Moon takes the stage; seductive, glittering.
Moon	*(to A2)* Hallo, handsome.
A2	Oh – er – halloo Who are you? *(he is moonstruck)*
Moon	I'm Mandy Moon. People go crazy about me.
A1	Yes, I'm sure they do. *(to A2)* That'll be quite enough of that A2. *(to Moon)* What's your act, Miss Moon?
Moon	Rather more than an act sweetie. I gleam, I glisten, I am glimpsed palely over a silvery sea. I inspire poets. I rhyme with spoon and June.
A1	Maybe. But you don't give very much light, do you, sweetie? And that's what we really need – light. Don't call us, we'll call you.
Moon	Well, really! *(exits in a huff)*
A2	Pity about that. I thought she was rather nice.

A1	*(extra brisk)* Time's getting on A2. We're just not going to find the light.
A2	Don't be so pessimistic A1. *(consults list)* There's a good one next. I seem to remember his performance on television.

Flame rushes on; shades, running kit, flashy.

Flame	Hi folks! Here I am. Can't stop long. Schedules you know. Timetables man. Athens today. London tomorrow.
A1	And you are?
Flame	O. Lympic Flame at your service lady, but just call me Olly. You've heard of me. Flame is the name of the game. I've been everywhere man – Atlanta, Montreal, Berlin, Paris, Barcelona, Sydney – even Wembley. Far out, man, far out.
A1	How are you at lighting, Mr Flame?
Flame	Are you kidding, lady? I'm always alight. Rushing here, rushing there. Non-stop activity. Just feel my muscles, lady.
A1	Er – no thank you, Mr Flame.
Flame	Well, I must be sprinting along. Next stop Rio de Janeiro. I've got a few national anthems to learn. Always running, baby; always running. *(he runs off)*
A2	Phew!
A1	Exactly A2. Impossible. He'd never stay still long enough to be the light.
A2	That's it then. The true light may be coming into the world but we don't know who it is.
A1	Just a minute. There's a late addition here. Must be a relative of the producer's. Just a scribbled name – looks like a Mr E. Manuel.
A2	Someone's coming.

Mary walks quietly on with the baby in her arms. She stands looking down at the baby while music or a carol is played. One by one each of the other lights comes forward and kneels in front of her.

A2	Well, A1, I think we've seen the light.
A1	You know, A2, I do believe you're right.

They kneel. Blackout.

Peter Jackson

Christmas – The Real Thing

Aim

- To have fun and celebrate the birthday of Jesus, God's gift to the world, who is just what we need and just what the world needs.

- To encourage the children to respond by giving thanks to Jesus for being born into this world and by praying for others who need him.

You will need

For the Opener

The game

- Two identical selections of four to six parcels wrapped in Christmas paper at the front of the room.

- A chair at the side to mark the end of the course.

The sketch

- Six actors to be a family – grandma, mum, dad, teenager Kev, Tom aged 9, and baby Susie. The presence of additional people for your session will add to the sense of occasion.

- Wrapped presents: a cricket bat and ball, a pair of earrings, a bottle of after-shave, woolly hat and gloves (adult size), Bob the Builder CD (or current children's favourite), skateboard.

For the Memory verse

- Four large cards each with a part of the verse written in large letters – 'God loved the world so much that he gave his only Son' (John 3:16).

For the Project time

- Scissors – safety scissors are preferred, otherwise supervision will be needed.
- Thin gift ribbon.

Preparation

Even though the Christmas story is so familiar to us, it may not be so well known to our children. Surveys show us that despite the number of Nativity plays, many children are still largely ignorant of the truth about Christmas. Some believe it was Santa Claus who was born in Bethlehem, and find no real relevance to their experience of Christmas.

Admittedly, it is likely that many of the misinformed children are those who do not attend a children's group like yours but, nevertheless, we cannot take things for granted. Schools (and some churches) stage Nativity plays that continue to merge the visit of the wise men (and the Bible says there were three kinds of gifts, not three wise men) with the visit of the shepherds, when it is most likely they came on a quite separate occasion. (Matthew tells us they 'went to the house', not the stable – Matthew 2:13.)

Even worse, in an effort to involve as many children as possible, the story is elaborated with animals and other characters to the degree that it is clearly 'just a story'.

The commercial Christmas tends to leave out Jesus altogether. It is a gigantic marketing exercise, when parents are coerced into spending huge sums on the latest 'must-haves'. Fewer cards have Nativity scenes. Films make more of the 'spirit of Christmas', and/or Santa Claus. No wonder children are confused.

But this is not the time for a crusade against the secular celebration. This session is not about the story itself, rather it is focused on the Christian reason for the birth of Jesus. God sent his Son because the world needed salvation, and that time was right. 'I tell you that the "right time" is now. The "day of salvation" is now.' (2 Corinthians 6:2, New Century Version, International Children's Bible).

It is always 'now' – we need salvation 'now'. It is a process that will continue to the end of life on earth, as we surrender more of our lives to the God who reveals himself more and more to us. This Christmas, we need Jesus.

Look through the session notes, and prayerfully consider how each part will apply to the children in your group. Pray for them and for yourself, that the Christ of Christmas will, in the words of the carol, 'be born in us today'.

Worship time

It is always good to include a time of worship. While this should be something which your children should be comfortable with, it is always worth trying to push the boundaries or your group and explore with imaginative worship. In this session, worship time comes after the opening activities.

Pastoral time

Spend time with the group, building relationships, not only with you as a leader, but amongst the young people, some of whom might not attend the same school and who might be meeting each other only at Sunday school. Encourage the development of friendships.

The group may be excited about Christmas. Talk about what they are doing at school or at home. What do they least like about Christmas? What are they looking forward to?

Opening activities

Piles of parcels relay

The children need to be split into two large groups and from each of these you need to select a pair of children to play the game. The remainder of the children can cheer their team on.

One player in each team stands by the parcels at the front of the room. The other player has to have one hand behind their back and the other stretched out in front to hold the parcels. It is important that only one hand is ever used by player two. Play begins when player one places the first parcel on player two's outstretched hand. Player two then has to walk as quickly as possible round the chair and back to the front where player one balances the second parcel on top of the first and player two walks round the course again.

Play continues in this manner with an ever-increasing pile of parcels. The game is won by the first team to complete the course with all their parcels. A dropped parcel disqualifies that team and the other team wins by default.

If you have time you could split your group into two large teams and give more pairs the opportunity to play by having several heats. The overall winners would then be the team with the most wins.

Christmas sketch

Scene: A Christmas tree with a pile of presents underneath. A family – grandma, mum, dad, teenager Kev, Tom aged 9, and baby Susie sitting around opening presents.

Tom	*(searching through presents)* Here's a present for you, Grandma.
Grandma	O thank you, Tom. I wonder what it could be. *(unwraps present, everyone is eager to see what she's got)* Ah, a cricket bat and ball– *(G smiles but looks rather puzzled)* Ermm. How different, it's years since I've played . . . ermm . . . Thank you.
Tom	*(searching through presents again)* Here you are, Dad. Here's one with your name on.
Dad	About time, come on let's see what it is. *(rips off paper)* A pair of earrings, eh? Very fetching, I'm sure. *(aside)* I can't imagine what the blokes at work would make of this. *(to the family)* Erm – thank you very much everyone. Is there a present here for your mum, Tom?
Tom	Yep. Here you are, Mum.
Mum	Oooh, I love getting presents; it's so exciting. Er . . . *(face changes as she opens the present)* Oh, Lynx aftershave for men. That's different; I've never been given any of that before. *(trying to hide her disappointment)* Thank you very much.
Tom	O look, Susie, there's a present here for you. *(Susie plays with parcel, giggles and gurgles)*
Mum	Aren't you going to open it then? Shall Mummy help? Let's see what's inside the pretty paper shall we? Oooh, look. A lovely woolly hat to keep you warm in the winter and some pretty gloves too. *(Mum fits hat on child)* Oh dear, it is a bit big, isn't it?
Kev	I'm sure there must be one for me somewhere. I haven't had anything yet.
Tom	All right, keep your hair on, I'm doing my best. Here you go.
Kev	Great, a CD. Who's it going to be I wonder? Limp Bizkit? Daft Punk? *(rips off paper)* WHAT??? Bob the Builder? Someone's gotta be joking. I mean I'm gonna look really cool, aren't I? Telling me mates I got a Bob the Builder CD for Christmas. Bob the flippin' Builder. Huh! Here you are, Susie, look who it is. Bob the Builder!
	(Susie gurgles and giggles happily to the tune of Bob the Builder.)
Dad	You know, Kev, I think you've got something there. I think the labels must have got put on the wrong parcels and so we've all ended up with the wrong presents. Here you are, darling *(giving the earrings to Mum)* I think these are for you.

309

Mum Oh wonderful! I lost one of my favourite earrings last week and now I don't have any. They're just what I need.

Grandma And Tom, I think this cricket set would get used much more by you than me.

Tom Thanks, Gran, my old set is getting a bit small for me now. This set is bigger. It's just what I need!

Mum Susie, dear, give Grandma the hat and gloves, they'll fit her much better than you.

Grandma Oh thank you, dear. Such a pretty colour, too. They'll look lovely with my new coat and they'll keep me ever so warm when I'm waiting at the bus stop. They're just what I need.

Mum *(gives aftershave to Dad)* Here, this must be meant for you. I'll enjoy the scent much more on you than me.

Dad Thanks. My old aftershave ran out only this morning. It's just what I need.

Kev Oh great. Now everyone's got a present except me. That's typical.

Dad Well, there is just one more hidden round the back there. Your mum and I have seen you wobbling about on three wheels and so we thought it was time you had . . .

Kev A new skateboard! It's just what I need!

Worship time

Choose one or two from these suggested songs or others your group enjoys:
- Christmas, It's Christmas
- Lord, I lift your name on high
- I'm special
- Light of the world you stepped down into darkness
- O come, all ye faithful

Presentation

In the sketch we saw earlier we saw different people of different ages who, once they got things sorted out, each had just what they needed. In the same way all sorts of people in the world today have things they really need; but sometimes we need different things at different times of our lives.

The good news of Christmas is that whoever we are and whatever our situation, Jesus is just what we need. Let's have a look at some of the Bible passages which talk about Jesus' birth and see some of the ways in which he is just what people really need.

Look up each verse in turn and ask the following two questions:
- What does this say about Jesus?
- Who really needs this?

You might find it helpful to ask the children to work in pairs looking at one verse each and then to report their findings back to the whole group.

- **Matthew 1:21 – Jesus will save his people from their sins**
  The wrong things we have said and done cause us to feel guilty and bad about ourselves. They also separate us from God. Jesus came to set us free from guilt and shame and to make us right with God again.

Those who need Jesus in this way are people who have done wrong and feel weighed down with guilt about it.

- **Matthew 1:23 – Jesus is Emmanuel, which means 'God with us'**
  Jesus left the glory of heaven and became like one of us, and he promised that he would be with us, even to the end of the world. This means that wherever we are and whatever we are doing, God is always present with us. Sometimes we are very aware of Jesus being with us and sometimes we are not, but he is always there.

People who feel lonely and afraid need to know Jesus as Emmanuel, God with us.

- **Luke 1:32-33 – Jesus is the King**
  It is very easy for human beings to become self-important and think only of themselves. Jesus is the King who rules over everyone and everything. It is good for us to have someone who is bigger and stronger than us and to have a king who will act for the good of everyone.

Those who especially need to know Jesus as King are people who are selfish and who think too much of themselves, or people who feel that the circumstances of life are against them or beyond their control. Jesus is in charge!

- **Luke 1:52-53 – Jesus will deal with injustice and unfairness**
  Most of us will have felt that we have been treated unfairly by others at some time or another. Jesus came to put things right, so that those who have had a difficult life can receive good things from him, and those who have used their power to harm others will be punished.

People who have been treated unfairly by others need to know that Jesus will deal with it.

- **Matthew 2:6 – Jesus will lead and care for his people like a shepherd**
  A shepherd takes care of the sheep. He guides them along the right paths, he finds pasture with good food for them, he protects them from wild animals and other dangers and he takes care of them when they get ill or hurt. In another part of the Bible, Jesus calls himself the Good Shepherd. He takes loving care of all his people.

Those who need to know Jesus as their shepherd are people who are sick and ill, people who don't know the way ahead and people who need to be protected from danger.

- **Luke 1:33 – Jesus will reign for ever**
  As we have seen already, Jesus will bring in a new way of living: he will be in charge and will set all wrongs right. The good news is that this will not be for a lifetime as in the case of earthly kings and rulers: his reign will go on and on – it will last for ever!

People living without hope for the future, people who have been let down by others and had their hopes dashed, need to know that Jesus' reign will last for ever.

The things we have looked at this morning are just the things that were said about Jesus around the time of his birth. If you look through the rest of the New Testament you'll find many, many more!

Response

Choose at least one of these – more if time allows and if your group will cope at this stage of their development.

- Look back at the things we've said Jesus came to be. What is there about Jesus that you really need right now? Spend a few moments in silence talking to Jesus about this. It could be helpful to have some quiet, ambient music playing on a CD while you do this.
- You may want to end this time by using this responsive prayer. Tell the children that when they hear the words:

  'Thank you, Lord Jesus', they need to say: 'You are just what I need'.

It is helpful to practise the response a couple of times before you start the prayer.

When I know I've done wrong and I need to be forgiven:
Thank you, Lord Jesus;
You are just what I need.

Lord God, when I feel lonely and in need of a friend:
Thank you, Lord Jesus;
You are just what I need.

When I get too self-centred and need reminding that I need to serve others:
Thank you, Lord Jesus;
You are just what I need.

When people treat me unfairly and accuse me of things I haven't done:
Thank you, Lord Jesus;
You are just what I need.

When I have choices to make and I need someone to guide me:
Thank you, Lord Jesus;
You are just what I need.

When I am sick and ill and I need to be made well again:
Thank you, Lord Jesus;
You are just what I need.

When I am scared about what's going to happen in the future and I need to know that you will reign for ever:
Thank you, Lord Jesus;
You are just what I need.

- You could encourage the children to add their own lines, finishing each time with: 'Thank you, Lord Jesus'. Everyone can then join in with: You are just what I need.

We could develop the prayer time by thinking more widely, focusing on others rather than just ourselves. Do you know people who really need Jesus, even though they might not realise it? Pray that this Christmas they will discover that Jesus is just what they need.

Memory verse
God loved the world so much that he gave his only Son. *John 3:16*

As part of your celebrations you could have fun by learning this verse together as a Mexican wave.

Split the group into four smaller groups. Allocate each group one part of the verse.

Produce the four cards each with a part of the verse and have one child per group stand at the front and hold the card up for their group to read.

Say the whole verse with each group contributing their part. When it is time for a group to say their part they stand and throw back their arms in the air as they shout their words then quickly sit down again as the next group takes over. Repeat several times, and see how smoothly the children can move through the verse. You could change the words the groups are shouting and take the cards away altogether when you think the children have learned the verse.

Project time

World poster
The group could produce a poster which sums up what you have been thinking about today; it could be displayed, perhaps on a wall in church, to form a focal point for the church's intercessions over the Christmas season.

Conclusion
An appropriate way to end the session could be to return to praising God for sending Jesus by singing together. You could either return to a song you have already used or choose a different one.

The Big Ones

Christmas Day

For pre-school age to 5 years – Years A, B and C

Thought for the day
A. The Word of God is made flesh. In the birth of Jesus we see God expressed in human terms.

B. Jesus Christ, the world's Saviour, is here with us, born as a human baby.

C. Emmanuel – 'God with us' – is born at Bethlehem into the human family. Now we will be able to understand, in human terms, what God is really like.

Readings

Year A
Isaiah 52:7-10
Psalm 98
Hebrews 1:1-4 (5-12)
John 1:1-14

Year B
Isaiah 62:6-12
Psalm 97
Titus 3:4-7
Luke 2:(1-7) 8-20

Year C
Isaiah 9:2-7
Psalm 96
Titus 2:11-14
Luke 2:1-14 (15-20)

Activities

Christmas Day is very much a time for all God's children to worship together.

Involve all the children in the singing and playing of carols, decorating the church, and in the other ministries of welcoming, serving, collection of gifts and so on. Have Nativity toys for the very young to play with, such as knitted Mary, Joseph and Jesus, sheep and shepherds.

Included is a drawing and colouring activity for today so that children in church can work at this during the sermon.

Susan Sayers

For 6 to 10 years – Year A, B and C

Thought for the day

A. The Word of God is made flesh. In the birth of Jesus we see God expressed in human terms.

B. Jesus Christ, the world's Saviour, is here with us, born as a human baby.

C. Emmanuel – 'God with us' – is born at Bethlehem into the human family. Now we will be able to understand, in human terms, what God is really like.

Readings

Year A
Isaiah 52:7-10
Psalm 98
Hebrews 1:1-4 (5-12)
John 1:1-14

Year B
Isaiah 62:6-12
Psalm 97
Titus 3:-7
Luke 2:(1-7) 8-20

Year C
Isaiah 9:2-7
Psalm 96
Titus 2:11-14
Luke 2:1-14 (15-20)

Activities

Christmas Day is very much a time for all God's children to worship together.

Involve all the children in the singing and playing of carols, decorating the church, and in the other ministries of welcoming, serving, collection of gifts and so on.

Included is a drawing and colouring activity for today so that children in church can work at this during the sermon.

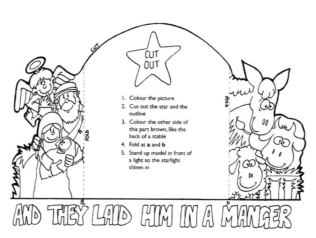

Susan Sayers

Prayer Action

Newborn

If you are introducing your church to a more active, creative way of praying, then this is a good place to start. Your congregation on Christmas Day will probably be more varied than usual, and this prayer is designed as a gentle, step-by-step introduction to all-sorts prayer.

Resources

- Small pieces of paper with the outline of a new baby (see CD-ROM for photocopiable sheet)
- Pens and pencils.

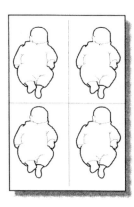

Leader

When God became one of us on that first Christmas day, he didn't make sure he had a specially built palace. He was born as an ordinary baby and made do with what there was: he slept in an animals' feeding trough instead of a cradle. When we say our prayers, they don't have to be especially fine and grand, either. We can make our prayers out of everyday things. Today we are going to use paper and pens.

Hold up blank outline of a new baby.

This is a newborn baby. This child could grow up to be or do anything – but at the moment of birth, everything is an unexplored possibility, like a blank sheet of paper.

Hand out outlines and pens, or have piles at the end of pews.

Take an outline of a new baby and as you look at it, think about fresh starts and new beginnings. Perhaps you would like to say thank you for the fresh start which Jesus gave us all when he was born and lived and died among us. Perhaps you know a new baby; perhaps you know someone older who is trying to make a fresh start. Perhaps you are beginning something new, or perhaps there are things in your life that you'd like to put behind you, so that you can start afresh. Whoever or whatever it is, write or draw it on this picture of a newborn baby and offer it to God as your prayer for a new beginning.

Prayer action

Allow enough time for people to complete their prayers. You may like to have some music playing during this time – perhaps a carol which focuses on the child in the manger, such as 'Away in a Manger' or 'In the Bleak Midwinter'. Then invite people to come and lay their prayers on the altar, or perhaps at the foot of the crib if your church has a large Nativity scene. When all the prayers have been offered, call for a moment of quiet in which to bring them before God.

Closing words

Lord Jesus,
you came here as a new baby and grew up among us;
you brought us the gift of new life.
We offer these – our own prayers for new beginnings –
in your name.

Claire Benton-Evans

Light of the world

Resources

- Advent wreath, matches and tapers
- Hand-held votive candles, given to each person as they arrive

Leader

Turn out the lights.

John's Gospel says this about Jesus: 'What has come into being in him was life, and the life was the light of all people. The light shines in the darkness, and the darkness did not overcome it.' (John 1:4-5.) For our prayers today, we wait in the dark and remember all those known to us who need the light of Christ, especially in this Christmas season.

Prayer action

Pause. Light your own votive candle from the central candle of the Advent wreath.

In Jesus was life, and the life was the light of all people.

Pass the light among the people. Pause once all the candles are lit.

Closing words

Jesus, Light of the world,
shine on those for whom we pray
and give them new life.
May your inextinguishable light
burn in our hearts
this Christmas and every day.

Claire Benton-Evans

RESOURCES

Christmas

Christmas (literally, 'Christ's Mass') is the annual celebration of the birth of Jesus Christ. Most of the worldwide Church observes 25 December, although the actual date of Jesus' birth is unknown.

Christians generally regard Jesus' death and resurrection to be of greater significance to the gospel message than his birth, which may explain why no fixed observation of Christmas emerged until the fourth century. A number of dates throughout the year had been suggested before then, but 25 December was adopted, in Rome at least, by 354. Various theories have been offered to account for this choice of date. Some point out that the date corresponds with the day nine months after the Annunciation (traditionally 25 March), when the Virgin Mary was told that she would give birth to Jesus. A more widely held explanation is that 25 December coincided with the festivities of the pagan winter solstice. The Church was thus able to communicate the gospel using symbols that would be familiar and engaging in the surrounding culture. This meant that while the people of Rome were celebrating *Natalis Solis Invicti*, the festival of the Invincible Sun, Christians were afforded an opportunity to meaningfully proclaim Christ as 'the sun of righteousness' (Malachi 4:2).

Although both Western and Eastern churches observe 25 December as Christmas Day, the original date in the East was 6 January, in connection with Epiphany. Some churches still maintain this tradition. The situation is complicated further because of differences between the internationally used Gregorian calendar and the older but less-used Julian calendar. In practice, this means that many who recognise 25 December as Christmas Day actually celebrate on 7 January because of discrepancies between calendars. Most Christians would maintain that it is not the date itself that is of primary importance, but the recognition that 'the Word became flesh and lived among us' (John 1:14).

Over the centuries, many traditions have emerged around the celebration of Christmas. The giving and receiving of gifts has become central. This practice may have been inherited from the Roman celebration of Saturnalia, which took place in late December. For Christians, sharing gifts is a reminder of the gold, incense and myrrh brought by the Magi to the infant Jesus. The sending of Christmas greetings cards, usually in the weeks before Christmas itself, is also very popular. The first commercial cards were produced in London in 1843. Today, many cards are sold to raise money for charity.

Christmas gifts can also be linked to the tradition of St Nicholas, which has gradually evolved into 'Santa Claus' (a derivation of the Dutch *Sinterklaas*, meaning 'St Nicholas'). St Nicholas was a fourth-century bishop of Myra, renowned for generosity to the poor. He is noted for saving three poverty-stricken girls from prostitution by throwing purses of money into their rooms for their dowries so that they could marry. The tradition of St Nicholas Day on 6 December has become fused with Christmas to the extent that, under the influence of western commercialism, the figure of Santa Claus often now eclipses the biblical story in popular culture.

Another popular custom is the decoration of Christmas trees. This can be traced to sixteenth-century Germany, where trees in guildhalls would be adorned with sweets to be enjoyed by the apprentices and children. The custom may derive from medieval mystery plays telling the story of Adam and Eve, where trees were decorated with apples to represent the forbidden fruit, and wafers to symbolise the Eucharist.

As a cultural event, Christmas is arguably the most widely celebrated holiday in the Western world. Though exploited commercially, Christians continue to strive to make use of its cultural symbols to retell the biblical story today.

Russell Herbert

Christingle

Although the exact meaning of the word 'Christingle' is unclear, it is generally understood to mean 'Christ light' or 'Christ fire'. It refers to a candle, symbolising Christ the light of the world, mounted in an orange, which represents the globe. A red ribbon stands for the blood of Jesus shed on the cross, and this is tied round the orange to symbolise that God's love embraces everyone. Four cocktail sticks inserted around the orange denote the four points of the compass as well as the seasons of the year. This is to emphasise God's omnipresence, faithfulness and provision of our daily needs. Dried fruit and nuts represent the fruits of the earth, and these, along with sweets signifying the additional blessings over and above our needs, are skewered onto the cocktail sticks. Sometimes cloves are pushed into the orange, to represent the world's people.

According to tradition, the first Christingle was created by three poor children wanting to present a gift at church one Christmas. All they could find was a mouldy orange. The eldest cut the mould off and inserted a candle. The youngest took the best red ribbon from her hair and attached it to the orange with toothpicks. Dried fruits were added by the middle child. They took their creation to church, where the priest used it as a visual aid.

That story may or may not be true, but in December 1747 it was recorded that Bishop John de Watteville of the Moravian Church distributed candles with red ribbons to help him present the Christmas story to children. The idea developed, with the gradual addition of the other symbols. Churches started to hold special Christingle services just before Christmas.

In 1968, The Children's Society introduced the Christingle service to the Church of England. Such services are now enormously popular and are held each year at Christmas time by many denominations. Carols are sung, Christingles are lit and offerings are often taken for the work of The Children's Society.

Russell Herbert

Carols and Carol Services

Early Christmas hymns can be dated from around the fourth century. However, Christmas carols, which are more distinctively rhythmic and originally written specifically with dancing in mind, emerged in the twelfth century. The word 'carol' derives from the old French *carole* which referred to a festive circle dance, not necessarily associated with Christian worship.

Christmas carols gradually evolved from folk songs produced by minstrels to an art form developed by ecclesiastics during the fifteenth century. Following the Reformation, carols went into decline. Interest was revived from the 1820s onwards with the publication of several printed collections.

Today, many local churches find carol services to be among the most well attended of the year. Such services are often held by candlelight, symbolising Christ the 'light of the world'. Alongside the carols are included various Bible readings which present the story of the fall of humankind, the prophecy of the Messiah and the events surrounding the birth of Jesus.

The modern-day carol service stems from the 'Festival of Nine Lessons and Carols', first introduced in 1880 by Edward White Benson, then Bishop of Truro. The service was held in a temporary wooden shed while Truro Cathedral was under construction. Tradition claims that it was held at 10pm on Christmas Eve as a way of trying to keep men out of the pubs. The format of the service became popularised following its introduction as an annual event at King's College, Cambridge in 1918. It was broadcast from this venue in 1928 by the British Broadcasting Corporation, and has continued to be broadcast every year since, except 1930.

Carol services, which celebrate Christmas, are different from Advent services, which focus on the promise of the coming Christ. Thus there is an argument that carols should be reserved for the end of the Advent season in order to allow a proper emphasis on the theme of preparing in hope during Advent.

Russell Herbert

Cribs and Crib Services

At Christmas time, many churches and Christian homes will display a crib – that is, a nativity scene, which depicts the birth of Jesus as described in the Gospels of Matthew and Luke. Figures are used to represent the baby Jesus with his mother Mary, and Joseph. Also often included are shepherds, angels, Magi, and various animals such as a donkey and an ox.

The purpose of a crib is to present the story of Jesus' birth. Saint Francis of Assisi is often credited as the first to create a nativity scene in 1223, following a visit to the Holy Land. Pope Honorius III gave it his blessing, and within 100 years the idea had become popular throughout Christendom.

Saint Francis' creation used real people and animals. 'Live nativities' such as this are still popular today, although for practical reasons real animals tend not to be used in most situations. It is a very common practice for children to act out the various characters in services running up to Christmas.

'Crib services', traditionally held on Christmas Eve, retell the Christmas story, gradually building up the nativity scene as the story is unpacked. Such services will often include the Magi, although it is not uncommon to leave that part of the story out until Epiphany (generally celebrated on 6 January, or the Sunday nearest to that date), on the grounds that this reflects a truer sense of the chronological unfolding of the story. Others maintain that it is right and proper to integrate the Magi into the nativity scene as it expresses a harmonisation of the narratives of Matthew and Luke. Either way, crib services, often incorporated with Christingle services, are enormously popular, and many local churches find they are among the most well attended of the year.

Russell Herbert

Preparing a Christingle

In advance or during the service?

Churches vary in practice when it comes to making Christingles. Some prepare them beforehand and distribute them at a set point in the service. Others prefer to get children present to make their Christingle as part of the proceedings. There are pros and cons to both methods:

- Making the Christingles in advance is certainly safer and cleaner than children making them themselves. It gives less chance of pricking their fingers on the cocktail sticks, or of sticky hands making a mess. If this method is preferred, it is worth snapping the ends off the exposed sticks, so as to minimise the risk of accident and injury.

- Making Christingles in advance has the added advantage of ensuring that no child ends up with an incomplete Christingle. They are fiddly to put together, and it is easy for children to drop the sweets, raisins, etc., while attempting to impale them on the cocktail sticks.

- A further advantage of making Christingles in advance is that it gives more time for plays/sketches, etc. during the service and increases the likelihood of people listening to what's going on rather than being absorbed in putting the various Christingle items together.

- A disadvantage of making Christingles in advance is that it gives less direct contact with the various Christingle symbols, and fails to involve children. Putting them together as part of the service holds their attention throughout, even if the proceedings can become somewhat riotous in the process!

- Another disadvantage of making the Christingles in advance is the amount of work involved. Putting a hundred or so together can take a considerable time, especially if volunteers to help in this are thin on the ground. Remember though, that if you go for the option of making the Christingles during the service you need to be fully prepared. Most churches distribute bags to the children containing the various items needed so that they can make their Christingle in their seat/pew (don't forget something to fasten the ribbon on to the orange – some use a pin, though a piece of sticky tape is probably safer).

- A final disadvantage of making Christingles in advance is that you may end up with insufficient to go round, or indeed far too many. If children are making them themselves, you can have spare supplies ready for use as necessary, and items not used can be taken back home by donors afterwards or distributed locally.

Key items needed for each Christingle

- One orange/satsuma
- One length of thin red ribbon or red sticky tape (sufficient to be fastened around the orange)
- Four cocktail sticks
- Four raisins/sultanas
- A handful of cloves
- Four monkey nuts, with shells (for safety reasons you may choose to use an alternative)
- Four soft sweets (dolly mixtures, jelly beans or similar)
- One white candle (a small birthday cake candle in a plastic holder, or small white candle with the base wrapped in foil)

If you are providing these items in individual bags so that children can make their own Christingle as part of the service, it may be worth including one extra of each, apart from the orange, candle and ribbon, in case items are dropped during the process of assembly. In order to make a visual impact while explaining the symbolism of the service, the leader ideally needs large-scale props.

Putting it together

The key stages in assembling a Christingle are as follows:

- Take an orange and slice a small sliver off the top and bottom. This means the final Christingle can stand up without toppling over, and allows for a candle to be pushed into the top. If a party candle and holder is used, there is no need to slice off the top, and if a loose-skinned satsuma is used rather than an orange there is no need to slice off the base either.

- Place and fasten a length of red ribbon or red sticky tape round the orange. Ribbon is more aesthetically pleasing but is harder to fasten round the orange, needing to be pinned or tied.

- Push a cocktail stick into the orange an inch or so away from the top centre, so that it protrudes upwards at about a 45 degree angle. Push in a second stick opposite, a third halfway between the two, and a fourth opposite the third.

- Impale a raisin/sultana on each of the sticks, pushing it an inch or so down.

- Impale a monkey nut on to each of the sticks, pushing it down next to the raisin/sultana.

- Impale a sweet, on to each of the sticks, pushing it down next to the monkey nut.

- Push cloves liberally into the orange at random.

- Wrap foil round the base of a small candle, and push this into the soft flesh of the orange. Alternatively use a small party candle and holder, which can easily be pushed through the skin of the orange.

Nick Fawcett

Running a Christmas Workshop

The Christmas present

STAGE 1 Pray

Invite everyone in the church to pray, either through the weekly handout or through prayer and Bible study groups, It is important that the whole community is involved, Get in touch with God's agenda and concerns before you start organising anything, as he is in a far better position to know the needs of those who will eventually be coming. Invite some people (the elderly and housebound, perhaps) to volunteer prayer support for the entire time the workshop and service will be running.

STAGE 2 Browse

Read through the script in God's company, bearing in mind the families in your area, and make a note of any adaptations that may spring to mind.

STAGE 3 Leaders' planning

Make copies of the script for everyone and read through them together. Decide who is going to take responsibility for what.

- Checklist
- Teaching the acting

- Teaching the music
- Special effects
- Advertising and registration
- Copying and OHP
- Budget
- Costumes
- Art and craft
- Refreshments
- Furniture arranging
- First Aid
- Young leaders

It's quite a long list, but the key to running a workshop and staying sane is making sure you delegate, so that no one person has too much to do.

STAGE 4 Advertising

You could design your own posters. If your church sends a Christmas card, have the workshop included on that.

Ask if you can display details of the event at the local school, or mention it at an assembly. Contact any clubs which use the church hall and ask if you could come and tell the children about the workshop. Give out leaflets so the messages reach home.

STAGE 5 Timetable

Plan a detailed timetable which is realistic, allowing time for the hidden extras, such as visits to the toilet, moving from one area to another, and putting on outdoor clothes.

Here is a possible timetable, to be adapted to your own needs.

1.00pm Registration

1.15pm Introduction and singing

1.30pm First run through

2.15pm Refreshments

2.25pm Costumes and props making

2.45pm Practice of particular sections/art and craft

3.00pm Second run through

3.30pm Refreshments, toilets and quiet game

3.45pm Dressing up and action stations

4.00pm Service and presentation begin

The Christmas Present

Setting

Two children are about to go to bed on Christmas Eve when they notice a huge Christmas present in the corner of the room. When they look into it, they begin to realise it is, quite literally, a Christmas present, as it has Christmas inside it.

No end of characters magically pour out from it, and through each of them the children start to see beyond the materialism and traditions of Christmas to what it is really about.

A narrator and two children read the script, and all the other children mime the different parts. CDs of music and sounds are used during the production.

Cast List

Narrator Andrew (reader)
Jane (reader)
Andrew (miming)
Jane (miming)
Group of carol singers
Group of shoppers
Postman (or several)
Flock of sheep
Group of shepherds
Angels
Cherub
Mary
Joseph
Jesus

Production guidelines

1 Readers

Have an adult voice for the narrator, to contrast with the children's voices. These three readers need to have a script before the workshop, so as to be familiar with it.

Try the reading out with the microphone they will be using, to check for volume and speed, and emphasise the need to speak quite slowly, so that people have time to take in what they are hearing. Since the other children will be taking all their cues from the readers it is essential that they can be heard clearly.

2 Music

Whenever the Christmas present is about to produce something, this is heralded by some music or sound effect. All these can be gathered together in order beforehand, to make things easier for the operator.

You can, of course, vary the sounds to suit your situation, but here are some suggestions:

Introduction
Short piece of 'opening-up music' – perhaps from a musical box.

Track 1 – Carol singers
Record a group of people singing and playing a familiar carol. Or go upmarket and use a track from a cathedral choir.

Track 2 – Shopping
Go to the checkout of a busy local store and ask if you can make a recording. Make sure your tape recorder is close enough to pick up the sound of coins, the till, and the usual checkout conversations.

Track 3 – The postman
Use the Postman Pat theme song.

Track 4 – The sheep
If you live in the country you might want to record some real sheep. Or you may prefer to give people the hint of sheep country with the James Herriot theme music. This track needs to be long enough for the sheep to climb out of the present, and the children to try and catch them, so that it ends with the shepherds climbing out of the box.

Track 5 – The angels
Use a cathedral choir rendering of *Ding dong! merrily on high*.

Track 6 – The cherub
Silent night, holy night.
This can either be a recording of your church choir, or you could use a track from a cathedral choir carols collection. Or you may prefer to have this last track accompanied 'live', using such instruments as keyboard, guitar, xylophone, chime bars or recorders.

3 Other music

Clap hands Gloria
God has put his angels
Jesus, Jesus
Shine, Jesus, shine

4 Props and special effects

The Christmas present
For this you will need a very large, firm packing carton, such as a washing machine box, as it has to be big enough for children to climb out of. If you prefer, this could be made from wood.

The back of the box is cut away, a step or stool is placed inside the box, and another step outside, so that the children can creep in from behind when their turn comes, climb on to the step and out into the 'sitting-room'. The children who are acting as Andrew and Jane steady them as they climb out.

If the basic shape is completed beforehand, the children can decorate it with Christmas wrapping paper, ribbon and tinsel during the workshop.

A screen or curtain backdrop is hung, or stands immediately behind the Christmas present, so that all the children can sit behind it until they climb out into the 'sitting-room'. If the design for this is drawn on in advance, one group of children can do the painting during the workshop. Sponge painting covers large areas effectively and quickly.

Thunder
A sheet of card, or a metal tray is shaken and rattled.

5 Costumes

If you have a set of traditional nativity costumes, these can be used for Mary, Joseph and the baby, the shepherds and the angels. You may be able to use a family with a real baby.

If you are making costumes just for the day, cut out tabards from sheets and curtains and fasten round the waist with cord or string. Have a selection of teacloths and scarves for head coverings. Borrow dressing gowns and lengths of cloth for cloaks.

Andrew and Jane can wear nightclothes over their clothes.

The carol singers wear their outdoor clothes and carry the lanterns made in the workshop.

The shoppers carry carrier bags from well-known shops, filled out with crumpled newspaper.

Your local sorting office may be willing to lend you a real Royal Mail bag if you ask them nicely and invite them along! Failing that, use a brightly coloured satchel, full of old Christmas cards and used envelopes. Traditional hats are available from toy shops.

For the sheep, ask the children to bring white clothes, and make masks.

6 Action

There is no need for all the children to be sitting behind the Christmas present all the time. They can sit and watch what is going on, provided they are sitting in the right order, until someone ushers them up just before they are due to emerge from the present.

Andrew and Jane listen to what the readers are saying, and mime what they hear, going over to look inside the Christmas present, and helping out whoever starts to emerge. When the sheep come out they can chase them all over the building. Provide two chairs in the 'sitting-room' so they can sit down when they are not involved in the action.

The carol singers climb out of the box and gather as a group, walking about the church during the singing of *We wish you a merry Christmas*. Then they can sit on the floor to watch the rest until they gather round the family at the end.

The shoppers climb out of the box with their bags, or pick them up from the box as they come out. The actions and words for their chant are as follows:

Christmas shopping here
(rush to one side of the aisle)
Christmas shopping there
(rush to the other side)
Only 5 more shopping days to Christmas!
(hold up 5 fingers)
Long queues here
(make a line on one side)
Long queues there
(make a line on the other side)
Only 4 more shopping days to Christmas!
(hold up 4 fingers)
Heavy parcels here
(look weighed down by left side bag)
Heavy parcels there
(look weighed down on right side)
Only 3 more shopping days to Christmas!
(hold up 3 fingers)
Grumpy children here
(stamp feet and look cross)
Grumpy grown-ups there

(all shout 'because I say so!')
Only 2 more shopping day to Christmas!
(hold up 2 fingers)
Sore feet here
(hobble about on one side of the aisle)
Sore feet there
(hobble about on other side)
Only 1 more shopping day to Christmas!
(hold up 1 finger)

AND WE'RE EXHAUSTED!
(Flop in a heap on the floor.)

The postman/postlady climbs out of the box and walks around the church delivering Christmas cards. Then he/she sits down to watch until it is time to gather round Mary, Joseph and Jesus.

The sheep climb out of the box and run all over the church, bleating. The children try to catch them, but the sheep keep escaping. When the shepherds get out of the box and whistle, all the sheep run to form a flock in front of the shepherds. When the shepherds leave to run down the aisle to the back of the church, the angels take over from the shepherds and lead the sheep to sit down at the side. They can watch the rest of the action until they gather round Mary, Joseph and Jesus at the end.

The angels get out of the box and walk towards the shepherds where they sing the 'Gloria'. Then they go and sit down until it is time to gather round at the end.

The cherub climbs out and runs down to the back, where Mary and Joseph are sitting with Jesus. The cherub leads them up the aisle to the front, and everyone gathers round to make a tableau.

7 Crowd control

Have some freezer labels marked with initials for different parts and, as children arrive to register, work through the labels in rotation, ensuring that all essential parts are allocated, and the group sizes are well-balanced.

Choose someone to demonstrate the magic of the bottomless Christmas present, so they can see how clever it will look to the congregation, but then make this a 'no go' area for everyone, apart from those who will be decorating it. Sit the children in order before the first run through, so the action can flow more easily.

Susan Sayers

Sketches

While shepherds watched

Many carols, traditional and modern, lend themselves to dramatisation and often provide a familiar peg on which to hang all or part of the Christmas story.

The 17th-century carol 'While shepherds watched their flocks' used to be familiar to many children – mainly because of the alternative words involving dirty washing and a bar of Sunlight soap! Today, when school assemblies and Christmas concerts are often multi-faith events, this sketch uses the story in this carol to serve the more important role of putting across the basic facts of the birth of Jesus Christ.

Please note: tea towel headdresses, striped dressing gowns and Persil-white toy lambs should be avoided! Palestinian shepherds, despite the qualities of care, bravery and leadership given to them throughout the Bible, were looked down on by polite society: their anti-social working hours prevented their attendance at the synagogues and they were generally thought of as an isolated and wild bunch of men. So if costumes are to be provided, think rough and ready rather than neat and tidy.

As to speaking, if the children have natural accents then encourage their use but avoid fake 'Mummerset' at all costs – it's fine for humour but destroys any serious message.

Bible source

Luke 2:8-20

Performance time

Five minutes

Characters

Four groups of shepherds – any number in each group. Groups One and Two are older and more experienced. Group Three are younger. Group Four are the comedians – although they become more serious as the story unfolds.

Scene setter

A bare acting area with a glowing campfire. The first verse of 'While shepherds watched' is sung offstage. The shepherds enter from both sides of the stage, having just penned their flocks for the night. They greet each other and settle down around the fire to keep watch, some standing, some sitting. Some have sticks or crooks and leather slings, others something to eat or drink. A repeat of the carol tune, played on a recorder or flute, and some recorded (genuine) sheep bleating would help to set the scene.

Group one	What a long day we've had, feeding our flocks.
Group two	First finding grass for the creatures to eat.
Group three	Then having hills to climb – oh our poor feet!
Group four	*(to audience)* Please turn your backs while we take off our socks.

Group one	People look down on us, dirty and rough.
Group two	It's a difficult job. We must work night and day
Group three	And never abandon our sheep on the way.
Group four	Whenever there's danger we have to act tough.

Group one	Gripping our crooks if a wolf should come near.
Group two	Raising our slingshots and fearing the worst.
Group three	Rubbing our stomachs and dying of thirst.
Group four	Just cut the cackle and pass round the beer!

(General laughter and relaxation as they eat and drink.)

Group one	*(looking up)* Oh, look at those stars. They're so shiny and bright.
Group two	Just like the time when that angel chap came.
Group three	Angel! What angel? You must be insane?
Group four	Don't ask them questions – they'll go on all night!
Group one	You saw an angel! Is that really true?
Group two	That's right. We were sitting like now on the ground
Group three	When he just appeared, hardly making a sound.
Group four	Stop all your gabbing and pass round the brew!
Group one	Weren't you all scared? Did you shake in your shoes?
Group two	Scared's not the word – they were frozen with fright.
Group three	Not so. We were dazed by that great golden light.
Group four	'Fear not,' he said, 'for I bring you good news.'
Group one	'Jesus the Saviour is born' – fancy that!
Group two	'Wrapped in cloth strips with a trough for his bed.'
Group three	Goodness! Poor baby! Was that all he said?
Group four	No. When they come, angels like a good chat.
Group one	He said we would find him in Bethlehem town.
Group two	Bringing joy to all men – such good tidings he spoke.
Group three	You've spun us some stories but this one's a joke!
Group four	It's best to believe when an angel comes down.
Group one	Everything's truthful – though strange it must seem.
Group two	Then after he'd finished a great choir sang.
Group three	Such praises to God that the whole heavens rang!
Group four	Amazing! Perhaps it was really a dream?
Group one	Not on your life! There was no time to waste.
Group two	Our sheep were forgotten – we hurried away.
Group three	And found the new baby asleep on the hay.
Group four	Seeing him smile was worth all our haste.
Group one	His lodgings were simple; no hint of a fuss.
Group two	A bare, draughty stable; an ox by the door.
Group three	If he was the Saviour why was he born poor?
Group four	So God could send him to people like us.
Group one	We took him a fleece – it was such a cold night.
Group two	Then as we journeyed we told all we knew.
Group three	We'd seen that the words of the angel were true.
Group four	Good heavens! You've witnessed a wonderful sight.
Group one	And we won't forget it – such memories live on.
Group two	Neither will you now; so trust what we say.
Group three	We certainly will. Look – the first sign of day.
Group four	Get on your feet, shepherds! It's time we were gone.

(All the shepherds quietly gather their possessions and exit left and right while the last verse of the carol is sung offstage.)

Peter Jackson

Away in a manger

Characters

Innkeeper
Wife
Deborah (villager)
Rubin (villager)

Innkeeper walks on carrying a lantern. His Wife walks across to meet him.

Wife   Well? Did you find out what all that commotion was?

Innkeeper   Yes I did.

Wife   And? *(Innkeeper scratches his head and seems a bit lost for words)* Herschal? What's going on?

Innkeeper   Sorry, dear?

Wife   What was making all that noise?

Innkeeper   It was singing.

Wife   Singing? I might have known! A group of drunken rowdies no doubt. Typical! I hope you didn't join in with them? I know what you're like!

Innkeeper   No . . . Well, it wasn't . . . I, it sounded like a choir.

Wife   A choir?

Innkeeper   They were very good.

Wife   Did you tell them to move on? That there are people in here trying to get a decent night's sleep? Who were they?

Innkeeper   I'm not sure, I didn't exactly get a look at them, but anyway, you know that couple earlier who came looking for a room and all we could offer them was the stable?

Wife   You mean that man from Nazareth and the pregnant girl on the mule?

Innkeeper   Yes, them.

Wife   Oh, I did feel sorry for her. It won't be very comfortable in that barn, and she looked like she was going to have her baby at any moment. By the way, you didn't charge them, did you?

Innkeeper   Well, I gave them a discount.

Wife   Herschal!

Innkeeper	Oh, come on Sofia. We've got to make a living like everybody else, and the town won't be busy again like this for a good long while, if ever.
Wife	I suppose so. It just seems a shame, and they looked so worn out. Anyhow, what about them?
Innkeeper	Oh yes, well, they've had their baby.
Wife	No? Really? I shouldn't be surprised, but ooh, what a place to be born.
Innkeeper	I heard the singing, which seemed weird to me, although I had no idea where it was coming from, so I knocked on the door to see if they knew anything about it. You won't believe this but they'd put the little baby in the manger, and there were these chaps from the hills, you know, who look after sheep, kneeling in front of him.
Wife	Good heavens! Why on earth did they allow such rough and uncouth men to get so near? Those shepherds don't wash, you know, and they smell of mouldy old blankets . . . so I've heard.
Innkeeper	It was a strange scene and there was something . . . something different about this birth. I can't explain it, but I felt in such awe.
Wife	What's the matter with you? You've gone all misty-eyed!
Innkeeper	It was a puzzle, Sofia. I even knelt down as well. I was overcome.
Wife	Hmmm. I'm wondering if they offered you a little cup of wine or two?
Innkeeper	Of course not! You had to be there.
Wife	Anyway, go and shut the door and let's turn in. I've been working hard all day and I'm shattered.
Innkeeper	*(lost in thought)* Yes . . . I suppose so . . .
	Two villagers, Deborah and Rubin, suddenly appear.
Deborah	Hello!
Rubin	Have we come to the right place?
Wife	Who on earth are you?
Innkeeper	We're fully booked, we've no room left. I feel like I'm repeating myself a lot tonight.
Wife	We don't even have a cupboard for you to squeeze into, I'm afraid.
Innkeeper	Although, saying that, if you're not at all fussy . . .

Wife	Herschal! I'm sorry, my husband is mistaken. All my cupboards are spoken for, not to mention unsuitable.
Deborah	Er, well that's all right. We're not really looking for a room.
Rubin	We live in the village. We already have a house.
Deborah	With a very nice shack and goat pen attached.
Wife	Sorry, we thought you were visitors.
Rubin	An understandable mistake. We only moved here last month.
Wife	I see.
Rubin	*(initiating the shaking of hands. Innkeeper and his Wife aren't particularly keen)* It's very lovely to meet you.
Wife	Oh er, yes, thanks.
Deborah	We wanted to get to know our neighbours.
	There's an awkward silence then Wife digs her husband in the ribs. He jumps slightly.
Innkeeper	Um, welcome to Bethlehem.
Deborah	That's very hospitable of you. We appreciate it.
Wife	Thanks for dropping by to introduce yourselves.
Rubin	Oh dear, this is embarrassing.
Wife	What is?
Innkeeper	Don't worry, you're not that bad.
Rubin	No, it's just that we were told to come here to see the new baby.
Innkeeper	Sofia?
Wife	Don't look at me!
Deborah	They said that he's been born here . . . in this very place . . . tonight, would you believe?
Wife	What are you talking about?
Rubin	The Messiah.
Innkeeper	Who told you that?

Wife	There's been no Messiah child born here this evening. We would have known about it if there was.
Innkeeper	Yes, we would have charged the parents extra!
Wife	Someone's been having you on, I'm afraid.
Deborah	Oh really? They seemed genuine enough, didn't they Rubin?
Rubin	Yes, seemed like very reliable chaps – for shepherds, that is.
Wife	You've been talking to shepherds?
Innkeeper	You must be hard up for social contact.
Deborah	If you ignore the almost overpowering odour, they make quite good company really.
Wife	So these shepherds sent you to us?
Rubin	Yes, they were very excited.
Innkeeper	You know what, Sofia, this must be about that couple we let stay in the old . . . *(Wife coughs)* I mean, in our open-plan rustic extension with complimentary livestock.
Deborah	Have they had a new baby arrive tonight?
Wife	Yes, I believe so.
Deborah	I don't understand. You said that no baby had been born . . .
Wife	Well, they're just a poor couple from Galilee. I wasn't including them.
Innkeeper	They've travelled all the way from Nazareth. It seems they only just made it here in time.
Wife	And I don't think their mule could have taken another step!
Rubin	We'd really like to see this baby, though. *(to Deborah)* Wouldn't we, dear?
Deborah	If it's not too much trouble, that is?
Wife	No it's no trouble . . . Er, you mentioned earlier something about the Messiah? What did you mean?
Rubin	The shepherds we bumped into as we were taking a stroll around the village . . .
Deborah	*(interjecting)* We'd had rather a large supper.
Rubin	They told us that some angels had appeared to them in the fields and instructed them to come into the village to find a newborn baby who is, well, I know it sounds a bit far-fetched . . . but the Saviour, or so it seems. Christ our Lord.

Wife   Really?

Deborah   Yes, according to them, the angels sang wonderful songs of praise to God and proclaimed good news of great joy to all humankind.

Innkeeper   *(to his Wife)* See, I told you I heard singing!

Wife   And they told you to come here?

Rubin   Apparently an angel told them they'd find him wrapped in cloth and lying in a manger. So they rushed into the village and found him.

Deborah   They were so excited.

Rubin   And they kept urging us to go and see him too.

Deborah   And hugging us.

Wife   Urghh! How awful!

Deborah   To think, the Messiah has been born amongst us, after all this time.

Innkeeper   I knew there was something special going on there.

Wife   What do you mean?

Innkeeper   In the stable, tonight, the shepherds were there. *(to Rubin and Deborah)* They must have been the same fellows you spoke to.

Wife   They were probably drunk!

Deborah   That's what I thought at first, from their behaviour, but after talking to them I don't believe that's true.

Wife   But they're shepherds, they're unreliable and not the kind of people to be chatting to, or to be seen with, come to that.

Rubin   Well yes, I know, and normally we wouldn't associate ourselves with any of their kind socially . . .

Deborah   But if you'd heard them talk about what happened out there tonight, you'd be as intrigued as we are.

Wife   It does sound incredible.

Rubin   So if you could just show us through to see the holy child we'd be very grateful.

Deborah   We're simply dying to see him. The newly born king. We don't want to miss out.

Wife   But why would a king be born in such a place as . . . well, our rundown donkey shed?

Innkeeper	Hang on a minute, it's not that bad.
Wife	Yes it is! I feel so embarrassed. Why didn't they say they were giving birth to royalty? Surely a king should be born in a fine palace?
Innkeeper	OK, it's not the finest accommodation around, I grant you, but it does have its good points.
Wife	What good points? It's shameful, so grubby and untidy, and you should see the size of some of the spiders in there – you wouldn't believe it.
Innkeeper	I kept meaning to fix the door and mend the roof, but you know how it is . . .
Wife	Didn't I ask you to sort those out ages ago? Honestly, you've completely shown me up!
Innkeeper	All right, all right! I never saw you in there with a duster!
Rubin	*(coughing awkwardly)* Yes well, if you could just direct us . . .
Deborah	It's getting quite late and we don't want to keep you up.
Innkeeper	Go outside again, walk down the alley and it's around the back.
Rubin	Thank you.
Deborah	Thank you so much!
	They all shake hands again and Rubin and Deborah exit quickly.
Innkeeper	They seem like unusual neighbours!
Wife	Do you think it can be true?
Innkeeper	What?
Wife	That the Saviour has been born here tonight?
Innkeeper	Maybe we should go and see?
Wife	Yes. Why not?
Innkeeper	I only had a glimpse earlier but I think perhaps I need to take a closer look.
Wife	I feel a bit nervous now.
Innkeeper	Why?
Wife	I'm sure I look such a mess.
Innkeeper	Don't worry about that. Come on.

Wife   I don't feel good enough to come before a king.

Innkeeper Nobody will notice, I'm sure. They'll all be looking at the baby.

     Innkeeper begins to exit.

Wife   Wait, I'll just go and fix my hair, have a wash and change my clothes. Oh dear, it'll take ages. I wonder if I should try and borrow some different shoes?

Innkeeper *(shouting over to her)* Sofia!

Wife   Yes, Herschal?

Innkeeper Come just as you are!

Penny Garret

Celtic Thoughts

Christmas

Psalm 96; Isaiah 54:1-10; Luke 1:39-45

> Christ always had the nature of God . . . but of his own free will he gave up all he had and took the nature of a servant. He became like a man and appeared in human likeness.

Philippians 2:6-7

The Gaelic race see the hand of God in every place, in every time and in every thing.

Douglas Hyde

He was imprisoned by his Jewish flesh and bones
within the confines of his country
but he gave them as living planks to be nailed
and raised from the grave, despite the guarding, a catholic body by his Father.
And now Cardiff is as near as Calvary,
Bangor every inch as Bethlehem.
The storms in Cardigan bay are stilled
and on each street the deranged
can obtain salvation at the edge of his hem.
He did not hide his Gospel among the clouds of Judea,
beyond the eye and tongue of man.
But he gives the life that will last for ever
in a drop of wine and a morsel of bread,
and the Spirit's gift in drops of water.

Gwenallt *translated by C. Davies*

Let the rumble of traffic diminish
and the song of the birds grow clear,
and may the Son of God come striding towards you
walking on these stones.

St Aidan's Chapel, Bradford Cathedral

Ray Simpson

Child of humanity

Psalm 89:1-14; Isaiah 11:1-5; John 1:1-14

> The Word of God became a human being and, full of grace and truth, lived among us.
> We saw his glory, the glory which he received as the Father's only Son.
>
> *John 1:14*

On the face of the world
there was not born
his equal.
Three-person God,
Trinity's only Son
gentle and strong.
Son of the Godhead,
Son of humanity,
only Son of wonder.
The Son of God is a refuge, Mary's Son a blessed sanctuary,
a noble child was seen.
Great is his splendour,
great Lord and God
in the place of glory.
From the line of Adam
we were born. From David's line
the fulfilment of prophecy,
the host was born again.
By his word he saved the blind and the deaf
from all suffering.
The ragged,
foolish sinners
and those of impure mind.

12th or 13th century Welsh

Child of glory, Child of Mary,
born in the stable, King of all.
You came to our wasteland, in our place suffered.
Happy we are counted who to you are near.
Strengthen our hope, enliven our joy,
keep us valiant, faithful and near.

Carmina Gadelica (adapted)

Ray Simpson

Mary nurtures a life

Psalm 89:46-52; Proverbs 23:15-25; Galatians 4:1-7

> This was how the birth of Jesus Christ took place. His mother Mary was engaged to Joseph, but before they were married, she found out that she was going to have a baby by the Holy Spirit.
>
> *Matthew 1:18*

Mary nurtures the Son of tenderness,
God, supreme ruler of every nation:
her father, her strengthener, her brother.
Mary nurtures a Son on whom dignity rests:
none can violate his boundaries
whose words are beauty, who is neither young
nor grows old.
The unwise can never perceive
how Mary is related to God:
her Son, her Father, her Lord.
But I know, though I be but frail and earthly,
how Mary is bonded in the Spirit to the Trinity:
her Son and brother in the flesh,
her Father, her Lord, blessed almighty.

Early or Middle Welsh, trans. Paul Quinn

Medical experts tell us that getting fit to have a baby takes time. If a mother's body is full of addictive substances from smoking, alcohol or drugs, or if it is lacking in vitamins, three to six months are needed for it to provide a healthy womb. Research now also confirms that stress, or lack of harmony, harms the unborn baby. Parents who pray for the child in their womb, who sing to it, feel it, and love it, are following in the path of Mary. Celtic Christians often imagined that they were present when Mary gave birth to Jesus, and they made beautiful prayers for the children they themselves bore.

> Help me to nurture your life in myself.
> Help me to nurture your life in others.
>
> *Ray Simpson*

Love's furnace in a little room

Psalm 138; Isaiah 9:2-7; Matthew 1:1-17

> The angel said to Mary, 'Do not be afraid, God has been gracious to you. You will become pregnant and give birth to a son, and you will name him Jesus. He will be great and will be called the Son of the Most High God.'
>
> *Luke 1:30-32*

Forget not, Trinity, holy and glorious
that heaven's bright prince came down to bestow on us
his love, as babe, into Mary's fair womb.

For nine months he who is angels' Lord
was hidden, love's furnace, in a little room
humbler than all, whom all adored.
A pure lamb, he stole down to earth
to free us from our sin so blind.
No city home will shield his birth,
his mother a stable for bed must find;
there poorest of the poor she lay
nor wine nor meat for hunger's sting
in the rude confines of the cattle bay
where God was born, apostles' King.
Cold and exile he did not scorn
in the donkey's manger, that holy morn.

Tadg Gaelach O Suilleabhain, medieval Irish

May the trust of Mary troubled by her strange call
and Joseph's encouragement beside her through all
be God's gift to us.
May the radiant brightness and light of the Star,
the hope and longing of searchers travelling from afar,
be God's gift to us.
May the wonder of shepherds surprised by God's love,
the joy of the angels who came from above,
be God's gift to us.
May the peace of the Christ-child in carved trough of stone
sounding the word 'Saviour' fashioned by Grace alone
be God's gift to us.

Crawford Murrey

Ray Simpson

Born for us – the Healing Man

Psalm 98; Isaiah 62:1-5; Luke 2:1-7

> Mary gave birth to her first son . . . and laid him in a manger – there
> was no room for them to stay in the inn.

Luke 2:7

The night the star shone
was born the Shepherd of our flock
of the Virgin of the hundred charms,
the Mother Mary.

The Trinity eternal by her side
in the manger cold and lowly.
Come and give tithes of your means
to the Healing Man,
the foam-white breastling beloved
without one home in the world,
the tender holy Babe driven forth,
Immanuel!

The three angels of power,
come you, come you down
to the Christ of the people,
give salutation.

Kiss his hands,
dry his feet
with the hair of your heads.
And O! you world-pervading God,
and you, Jesus, Michael, Mary,
do not forsake us.

Carmina Gadelica

Your gift to us this day is more than we could ask or think – your very life. This day may my gift to you be nothing less than my very life.

Hail King! hail King!
blessed is he! blessed is he!
Hail King! hail King!
blessed is he! blessed is he!
Hail King! hail King!
blessed is he
the King of whom we sing.
All hail! let there be joy!

Carmina Gadelica

Ray Simpson

Reflections

Mystery

When it comes,
after all the preparation
and the long, long lists of things to do,
Christmas is pure poetry.

It has inspired
more painting, music, writing,
than any other event in human history.
Even more than Crucifixion
or Resurrection.

Its stories
are not in the language
of everyday experience
or logical argument:
it touches mystery.

We are so obsessed with facts;
we want to measure everything
with our narrow materialism.

But Christmas
cannot be packaged or tied down,
labelled,
filed,
or analysed.

Scientific accuracy hardly matters
for we are in the realm
of greater truth and reality.

And in its mystery
we may touch eternity . . .

Ken Taylor

Incarnation

I know it was not December 25th –
even in 7BC! –
but there was one specific day
in human history
when it really happened –
this 'great step forward for humankind'
that we call Incarnation.

Like all the great facts of life –
birth, death, pain, love –
Incarnation confronts you with mystery:

Incarnation faith claims
that somehow
God –
the eternal source
and ground of being,
who is beyond us,
and anything we can understand –

somehow
God
was in Christ,
in that child,
in the man he grew to be –
that man was God
and God that man,

Don't try to understand it
or explain it:
no one can-
it's *mystery*.

If you do try
you'll get yourself in a tangle.

It's not God
with the appearance of a man
or a man with the mind of God –
but really a man (with all the limitations)
and really God at the same time!

See what I mean
about a tangle?

This is truth so deep
we can never fathom it,
so different we can never grasp it –
all we can do
is believe it or reject it.

That man was God –
eternal love
incarnate
on our doorstep,
in flesh-and-blood terms
that we can understand,
so that we might begin to learn
all it is humanly possible
to grasp
about God.

That man was God –
so committed to us
that he makes himself in our image,
puts himself in our hands,
at our disposal
for us to use as we will.

Incarnation is beyond me,
beyond anything
you or I can understand:
all we can do
is believe it or reject it.

Reject it –
and nothing has changed:
little hope and less help.
Believe it –
and a new world begins,
a new lease of life
a miracle of love.

Ken Taylor

What a way to have a baby!

She travelled on a donkey,
at night they both slept rough.
In the last stage of pregnancy
a journey's really tough.

No car ride to the hospital,
no ante-natal care,
no hygienic labour ward –
germs simply everywhere!

Nowhere to go in labour,
nothing to help the pain,
not even a bed to lie on –
just straw where beasts had lain.

No modern central heating,
just the cold night air,
no curtains at the windows,
stone walls, cold and bare.
No white-coated doctors
with sterile clothes to wear,
just Joseph and some animals
and smelly stable air.

What a way to have a baby!
where are the cards and flowers?
Just shepherds to share their gladness
in the midnight hours.

'Before she married Joseph
she was in the family way.
She said an angel told her . . .
What a thing to say!'

But Mary had her baby
before the light of dawn.
This was how it happened,
how the son of God was born.

Mary Hathaway

Title deeds

Isaiah 9:2-7

Wonderful Counsellor

Wonderful, for a start, that words spoken by Isaiah
seven hundred years before
should travel safely through so many ages,
and arrive expectant, at that stable door,

recognising in that backroom baby
the child with an insatiable thirst
for wisdom; who would linger in the temple,
putting his heavenly Father's business first,

recognising in that eager child
the carpenter whose hammer blows
would bring the old religion crashing down,
the sacrificial system to a close

saying – 'And now for something completely different!'
and the wise men, those who had eyes
to see, laid down their swords and pens,
recognised in him the wisest of the wise.

Received wisdom, though,
is rarely flavour of the month today;
old wineskins can't contain heady new wine
says 'No thanks: I'll do it my way!'
Strange, then, that we have so many counsellors,
think-tanks and therapists, quality controls,
consultancies, advisers, mentoring
life coaches and opinion polls . . .

Do we secretly still doubt ourselves?
How am I doing? Have I got it right?
What is it all about? Who do I ask,
whose answer can I trust? Where is the true light?

Truly, there is only one most Wonderful Counsellor:
Jesus Christ, son and heir to all the wisdom of God.

Mighty God

The fact that the world keeps turning
with seeming indifference in the face of so much grief
has made it hard for us to think of God as mighty:
surely his power or his love must be beyond belief?

Why doesn't God just do something
to make this world a happier, more peaceful place?
I wonder what, exactly, we'd suggest –
short of simply airbrushing the human race.

Even those who don't buy into God
look at the power lines and wonder whether,
among those multi-nationals, media moguls,
Mafiosi, might and right will ever come together?

And would we ever in a million years
have guessed at a divine solution
that countered human power with – meekness?
Astonishing, subversive revolution:

Jesus – meek, but mighty in word, proclaiming the truth of God;
Jesus – meek, but mighty in thought, discerning the wisdom of God;
Jesus – meek, but mighty in deed, serving the purpose of God;
Jesus – meek, but mighty in love, expressing the heart of God;

mighty because he was free from fear and pride,
mighty because he was free from the need to be driven,
mighty because in the end he had nothing to lose except for his life:
and that he had already given.

The might of our mighty God
is not military might, or media might, or monetary might;
not force of character, force of will or force of circumstance;
it is not force at all.

The true might of our mighty God
is life-giving
sacrificial
love.

Truly, there is only one Mighty God:
Jesus, our Saviour by the power of the cross.

Everlasting Father

It should be such a wonderful thought,
the fatherhood of God; but we have moved so far;
with paternity disputes and all mum's boyfriends,
so many of us wonder who our fathers are

or even if we want to know, if he's the one
who left us in the lurch, chased by the CSA,
who turns up, looking wretched and distraught
to take us out, while mother looks the other way ...

What's in our mind, then, as we come to pray
'Our Father'? How can we reclaim
the guiding hand, example, warmth, security,
that should be part and parcel of that name?

Jesus said: 'He who has seen me has seen the Father.'
'Let the children come to me.'
'I will never, ever leave you.'
'I am the truth, and I will set you free.'

If you never knew that safe place behind a father's coat,
that awe at his wisdom and skill,
that excitement when he said 'Come on, let's go!'
being carried up a hill;

if you never knew that love,
and awe at his voice,
that strong arm around you
that look of sheer delight
that his child was lost,
but he found you –

never too late
our Father God has signed the adoption papers
and is waiting to bring us home.

Truly, there is only one Everlasting Father
who, in Jesus, invites us into his kingdom as the children we are . . .

Prince of Peace

Whatever did he mean – saying
'I come not to bring peace but a sword.'
Yet at the same time 'Peace I leave with you,
a peace not of this world . . .'?

Ah, there perhaps is the clue:
not as the world gives, Jesus said . . .
So when the angels sang of peace on earth
as the baby slept in his makeshift bed

they sang, it says, of goodwill to men
not goodwill between men. Ah,
goodwill, then, from God to men:
no way a promise of an end to war.

For outward conflict cannot cease
until the conflicts of the heart and mind,
the insecurity, the greed, the lust for power
cease to be the curse of all mankind.

And this, even this, is the great gift of Christmas
Gold – the promise of peace in my soul
setting me free to love
Frankincense – the promise of peace in my spirit
setting me free to worship
Myrrh – the promise of peace in my heart
setting me free even to suffer with joy.

Truly, the peace of God,
passing all human understanding,
keeps our hearts and minds
as they hush their demanding,
consent to be still
and accept from his hand
that in spite of apparent ill,
all is for good in all he has planned.

In this world, we will have trouble:
that is a promise;
but in our hearts, we can have peace:
that is a greater promise.

Truly, there is only one Prince of Peace:
Jesus, who gives us, this Christmas, his hard-won peace to rule in our hearts.

Sheila Walker

Please do not adjust

Luke 2:8-14; John 1:10-11

While people watched their sets one night,
all seated round the screen,
the angel of the Lord appeared
where evening news had been.

'Fear not,' said he (for flashing light
had altered the transmission;
this strange, celestial visitor
had interfered with vision).

'I bring good news of peace on earth
for all mankind,' he said;
but crackling sparks zigzagged the screen
and every set went dead.

So angry viewers growled and cursed
and electricians fumed,
until as soon as possible
normal service was resumed.

Peter Dainty

The secret

I carry a secret,
a wonderful secret,
it lives and moves and stirs in me.
We created a person,
a new human being,
it grows in my body so silently.

Christ grew in secret,
the world's greatest secret,
part of his mother, hidden inside.
Then born as a baby,
a perfect little baby,
helpless, dependant, he fed and cried.

But while still in the womb
this tiny baby's fingers
reached out in love and touched every land.
He was creation,
not just one of its creatures,
and he held the world in his unborn hand.

Mary Hathaway

Meditation

Luke 2:1-20

When the angels had left them and gone into heaven, the shepherds said to one another, 'Let us go now to Bethlehem and see this thing that has taken place, which the Lord has made known to us.' So they went with haste and found Mary and Joseph, and the child lying in the manger.

Luke 2:15, 16

Meditation of one of the shepherds

Surprised?
I should say so!
It's not every day, after all, that God comes calling,
announcing the birth of the Messiah –
and for us to be the first to hear of it,
the first to respond,
well, quite simply, the very thought still takes my breath away.
But it wasn't only surprise we felt –
it was also fear, awe, amazement,
none of us quite knowing what to expect or do next.
You see, one moment there we were, going about our usual business –
another uneventful night's work –
and the next, everything was different,
an incredible light filling the sky
brighter than the brightest day,
seeming somehow to shine deep within,
searching, yet full of promise,
probing into the deepest corners of our minds,
yet at the same time speaking of joy, peace, love and hope.
Yes, I know that sounds odd,
fanciful, you might say,
but it's the best I can do,
that experience of ours unlike anything we'd known before:
out of this world, yet very much within it,
terrifying but thrilling,
mysterious but marvellous.
And after the light had faded, and we'd hurried off to Bethlehem,
eager to see the truth of what we'd heard,
then the full wonder of it all became clear,

for in a ramshackle stable,
there among the hay,
watched over lovingly by his mum and dad,
was a child,
lying in a manger and wrapped in swaddling clothes,
just as the angel had said –
and in his parents' eyes a light glowed,
as real and vibrant as out in the fields earlier.
We'd glimpsed God's glory,
not once but twice.
He was enthroned on high –
breathtaking,
stunning,
overwhelming,
yet there by my side –
and I know now that this awesome God we serve
is greater than I'd begun to imagine,
but closer than I'd dared to dream,
his radiant love filling the heavens,
yet touching every part of life.

Prayer

Thank you, Lord, for the wonder of your love,
always able to surprise us with joy
and with yet more reason to praise.
Thank you that you are higher than our highest thoughts,
greater than we can ever comprehend,
the Lord and redeemer of all.
Help us,
this and every day,
to glimpse more of who and what you are,
to your praise and glory.

Nick Fawcett

PRAYERS

Seeking

Matthew 2:1-12

Lord Jesus Christ,
we celebrate today how wise men were prepared to seek,
and keep on seeking,
persevering despite setbacks and disappointments
until they found you.
We remember how you promised that all who seek will find,
that those who ask will receive,
that to those who knock the door will be opened,
and so we come now,
asking for your guidance and seeking to know you better,
so that, drawing ever closer to you,
we may offer our love and our lives in glad response,
to the glory of your name.

Nick Fawcett

Epiphany praise

Loving God,
we remember today that
from the beginning
the good news of Jesus Christ
was not just for a few,
but for all.
Receive our praise.

You made it known to shepherds
tending their flocks by night,
ordinary, everyday people
pursuing their daily life and work,
unlikely yet special representatives
of your chosen nation.
Receive our praise.

But you made it known also
to wise men from the East,
strangers living far away,
with no knowledge of you,
and regarded by many at the time

as having no part in your promises.
Receive our praise.

Loving God,
for the truth this symbolises –
that there is no one outside your love,
that the message of the Gospel
transcends all barriers,
that you want to bring light
to all corners of the world –
Receive our praise.

For the fact that we are part of your great purpose –
heirs of the promise made to Abraham,
members of the great company of your people,
called to proclaim the gospel to those around us –
Receive our praise.

For the knowledge that your light continues to shine –
despite opposition,
persecution,
and rejection by so many –
Receive our praise.

For the way so many have followed the example of Jesus
and responded to your call –
through the waters of baptism,
through commitment to your Church,
through a life of faith and witness –
Receive our praise.

Loving God,
you have made your light shine in our hearts.
Help us to show our gratitude
by walking in the path it illuminates,
and shedding that light on those around us,
to the glory of your name.
Receive our praise,
through Jesus Christ our Lord.

Nick Fawcett

Confession

Footsteps of the wise men

Lord Jesus Christ,
this is a day which reminds us
of the journey of the wise men –
their determination to greet you
which inspired them to persevere

despite difficulties and disappointments along the way.
Forgive us that we lack their sense of vision,
their willingness to undertake a pilgrimage into the unknown
in the confidence that you will lead.
Forgive us if our response to you has lost its initial sparkle,
the flame which once burned so brightly within us
now grown cold
and our hearts no longer stirred
by the prospect of one day seeing you face to face.
Lord, in your mercy,
hear our prayer.

This is a day which reminds us
of how you led the magi on their journey,
your light always with them –
a guiding star,
a sign of your presence,
a call to follow until they came to the place where the child lay.
Forgive us that we are so often closed to your guidance,
unable or unwilling to see your hand,
more concerned with our own way than yours,
reluctant to commit ourselves to anything
when the final goal is not clear.
Forgive us for talking of faith as a journey
but turning it instead into a comfortable destination.
Lord, in your mercy,
hear our prayer.

This is a day which reminds us of the magi's worship –
their falling to their knees before you,
their bowing in homage,
their mood of joy and exultation, wonder and privilege.
Forgive us for losing such feelings –
for being casual,
complacent,
even blasé when we come into your presence,
taking it all for granted.
Forgive us for offering our worship out of habit or duty,
outwardly correct but inwardly empty.
Lord, in your mercy,
hear our prayer.

This is a day which reminds us of the magi's gifts,
their presents of gold, frankincense and myrrh,
each one an expression of love,
a token of esteem,
a symbol of all you meant to them.
Forgive us that, though we have received so much,
we give so little,
our thoughts more for ourselves than for you,
our offering made out of routine

rather than as a sacred act of consecration.
Forgive us that we give what we feel we can afford
rather than what your great love and goodness deserves.
Lord, in your mercy,
hear our prayer.

Lord Jesus Christ,
we come to recommit ourselves to the journey of faith,
to follow where you would lead,
to bring you our worship
and to offer ourselves in joyful service.
Receive us in all our weakness
and go with us on our way,
that we may live and work for your kingdom.
Lord, in your mercy,
hear our prayer.
For we ask it in your name.

Nick Fawcett

Petition

God of love,
we remember today,
on this Epiphany Sunday,
how wise men from the east
came seeking the newborn king,
how finally they reached the end of their journey,
and how they knelt in worship
before the infant Jesus.
Help us to learn from their example.
Guide our footsteps,
and lead us closer to Christ.

Teach us to continue faithfully
on the path you set before us,
remembering that true faith
involves a journey of discovery
as well as arrival at a destination.
Guide our footsteps,
and lead us closer to Christ.

Teach us to seek your will resolutely,
even when the way ahead is not clear.
Guide our footsteps,
and lead us closer to Christ.

Teach us to look at the world around us,
and to recognise the signs
through which you might be speaking to us.
Guide our footsteps,
and lead us closer to Christ.

Teach us to keep on trusting in your purpose,
even when the response of others
may give us cause for doubt.
Guide our footsteps,
and lead us closer to Christ.

Teach us to offer to Jesus
our wholehearted devotion –
not simply our gifts but our whole lives,
given to him in joyful worship and grateful praise.
Guide our footsteps,
and lead us closer to Christ,
for in his name we ask it.

Nick Fawcett

Intercessions

Blessed are you, Lord our God,
for you have called us to seek you,
to know and to love you.
You have revealed yourself in Jesus Christ,
our Saviour and our God.
We come to worship you.
Blessed are you, Father, Son and Holy Spirit.

We give thanks for the wise men
and the leading of a star.
We ask your blessing upon all who are seekers
and all who dedicate their lives to you.
We remember all those who lead worship
and teach of your love and salvation.
We pray today especially for the Churches of the Far East.

Silence

Lord, we seek you and call upon you:
hear us and help us.

As the wise men sought a king,
we rejoice that you are the King of kings and Lord of lords.
May your love and your will rule in our hearts.
We ask your blessing upon all leaders of people
and all who make important decisions for our world.
We pray today for all research scientists.

Silence

Lord, we seek you and call upon you:
hear us and help us.

As the Holy Family shared in an ordinary home,
we ask your blessing upon our homes.
May our homes reveal your presence
and our relationships increase our love for you.
We remember all homeless peoples,
all refugees and those who belong to homes
where there is violence or lack of love.

Silence

Lord, we seek you and call upon you:
hear us and help us.

With the gift of myrrh
there was an offering of the sorrows of our world.
We remember all who long for freedom and redemption.
We pray for all suffering people,
all who are distressed
and all who feel that no one cares for them.
We pray for the work of doctors, nurses, paramedics
and all who are involved in healing.

Silence

Lord, we seek you and call upon you:
hear us and help us.

We rejoice with Mary and Joseph,
with the shepherds and the angels,
with the wise men,
with the Church in heaven and on earth.
We commend ourselves, all peoples and the whole world
to your unfailing love.

Silence

Merciful Father,
accept these prayers
for the sake of your Son,
our Saviour Jesus Christ.

David Adam

Lord of Light,
we have remembered today
the journey of the wise men –
how, inspired by what they took to be a sign,
they set off in search of a newborn king,
a king who would change not simply their lives,
nor merely the life of his people,
but the life of the world.
Come again now,
and may light shine in the darkness.

We remember how they persevered in their quest,
travelling in faith
even though they had no clear idea
of where they were heading,
or any certainty of what they would find
when they reached their destination.
Come again now,
and may light shine in the darkness.

We remember how they refused to be discouraged,
despite their reception in Jerusalem,
despite the fact that no one seemed to have any idea
that a new king had been born.
Come again now,
and may light shine in the darkness.

We remember how they kept going,
single-minded in pursuit of their goal,
until at last their determination was rewarded
and they came face to face with the infant Jesus.
Come again now,
and may light shine in the darkness.

Living God,
we pray for all who seek today,
all those who are looking for a sense of purpose in their lives,
all who are searching for spiritual fulfilment,
all who long to find you for themselves.
Come again now,
and may light shine in the darkness.

Help them to keep looking,
even when the journey is demanding
and no end seems in sight;
to keep believing,
even when others
seem oblivious to their quest
or scornful of it;
to keep on trusting,
even when those they look to for guidance
seem as confused and as lost as they are.
Come again now,
and may light shine in the darkness.

Living God,
you have promised through Jesus Christ
that those who seek shall find.
May the experience of the wise men
inspire all who seek for truth to keep on searching,
in the assurance that they too, come what may,
will one day complete their quest,

and discover you for themselves.
Come again now,
and may light shine in the darkness,
in Jesus' name.

Nick Fawcett

Merciful God,
We give thanks to you
for your love towards all peoples of the world.
You have chosen to give yourself to us all
and invite us to give ourselves to you.
Blessed are you, Lord God,
for all things come from you and of your own do we give you.
We come in our poverty to your riches,
in our foolishness to your wisdom,
in our sorrows to your healing and joy.

Silence

Light of Christ,
shine in our lives.

As we remember the wise men,
we pray for the rich and the comfortable,
all who have plenty of this world's good things.
May they know that all things come from you
and their lives are a gift from you.
May the riches of the world be put to good use.
We remember the world's poor,
the homeless and the hungry.

Silence

Light of Christ,
shine in our lives.

We pray for all who are seekers,
who search for the truth,
who look for meaning and who desire to know you.
We pray for pilgrim peoples,
especially those on their way to Bethlehem or Jerusalem.
We pray for those who are new to our church or community.

Silence

Light of Christ,
shine in our lives.

We give thanks for all who come to you in worship,
all who are aware of awe or mystery in their lives.
We pray for leaders of worship, choirs and organists,
for all who give us a sense of wonder and beauty.

Silence

Light of Christ,
shine in our lives.

We come with all who are in pain or sorrow.
We remember those whose sickness finds no cure,
those who are permanently ill
and those with a short time to live.
We pray for doctors and nurses
and all who are involved in healing.

Silence

Light of Christ,
shine in our lives.

Lord, we worship and adore you.
We offer you our joys and sorrows,
our sickness and health,
our riches and our poverty.
We remember all who have enriched our lives
by their goodness.
We pray for loved ones who are now in the fullness
of your kingdom.

Silence

Merciful Father,
**accept these prayers
for the sake of your Son,
our Saviour Jesus Christ.**   *David Adam*

May the star that brought the Magi from the east
spread its light through the ages and attract us still.
Let us take inspiration from the Magi in their journey of faith,
using their knowledge to learn more and know you better.
Create in us that wonder and the humility that goes with it, we pray.
Lord, in your mercy
hear our prayer.

Your Church became our Church
because of all that Paul was able to do
in his ministry and leadership among the Gentiles.
Let us be good stewards of that ministry
through our faithfulness to your Son's word and example.
Grant to our ministers insight and understanding
in helping our faith to grow and reach out to others.
Lord, in your mercy
hear our prayer.

We remember all those who cannot travel far
and who may be coping with fear and oppression at this time,
especially in . . .
May they know the comfort of your love in their distress
and may they know that in coming to earth in Palestine,
your Son identified with the poor, the deprived and the refugee.
May our responsibility be to travel far for you in word and deed
in order to help meet their needs.
Lord, in your mercy
hear our prayer.

In our own community we pray for . . .
Lord, in your mercy
hear our prayer.

Give to those who are ill in mind, body or spirit
the hope that lies ahead and the love that enfolds us
through your Son's unfolding ministry.
We ask especially for your support at this time for . . .
And may those who have a caring role
be strengthened in their ministry too.
Lord, in your mercy
hear our prayer.

Let the star shine on those who have reached their destination
and are now at peace with you . . .
May their lives illuminate ours
and may those who mourn give thanks in their tears.
Merciful Father,
accept these prayers
for the sake of your Son,
our Saviour Jesus Christ.

Rupert Bristow

In Jesus we see God's secret plan revealed

We pray for all who spend their lives
leading others to you,
supporting and encouraging them on their journey;
give them your ideas, their love for others,
your joy and your humility.

Silence for prayer

Father, today and every day:
lead us to yourself.
We pray for our leaders and advisers in politics
business, education and health;
for good values, integrity and compassion,
for courage to stand up for what is right.

Silence for prayer

Father, today and every day:
lead us to yourself.
We pray for our relationships with our neighbours,
colleagues and those in our family;
for the grace to forgive readily,
listen attentively and to be available
whenever you need us.

Silence for prayer

Father, today and every day:
lead us to yourself.

Susan Sayers

Star in the Night

Lord, when you were born in Bethlehem
there were armed soldiers patrolling the streets
and distrust, bitterness and conflict.
But there came
a star in the night
to lighten the darkness
and because the wise men were ready to receive its message,
it led them to find you,
a baby in a manger.
We want to be ready to receive your message.

Help us to find you.

Today, Lord,
in Bethlehem
there are still armed soldiers patrolling the streets
and distrust, bitterness
and conflict.
But each year
Christmas comes to us
like a star in the night
to lighten our darkness
and if we too are ready
to receive its message,
it still leads us to find you,
not just in Bethlehem
but wherever people truly seek you,
for you came to be the light of the whole world.
We want to receive your message.

Help us to find you.

Mary Hathaway

God, who by the leading of a star
brought the wise men to the Christ child,
guide our journey and our seeking,
until we glimpse his glory,
and rejoice in his presence.

David Adam

Blessed are you, Lord our God,
who by the leading of a star
brought seekers from other nations
to bow before the Christ child.
As they offered their gifts and their lives,
may we offer ourselves to you in love and adoration,
for you are the giver of life and life eternal.

David Adam

Journeying

God, lighten our journey and direct our way.
As we seek your presence and long for you,
lead us until we come before the Child of Mary:
guide us until we bow in love and adoration.
As we remember the journeying of the wise men,
and the offering of their gifts,
help us to give our hearts to Christ,
and to spend our lives in his service.

David Adam

Sovereign God,
we are reminded today of the journey of the magi:
of how they stepped out into the unknown,
persevering despite adversity,
searching diligently until their quest was rewarded.
We come today, seeking in our turn:
looking to learn from their experience,
to worship the one before whom they knelt in homage,
to understand what his birth,
life, death and resurrection mean for us.
Help us to discover each day a little more of your love,
and to discern more of your gracious purpose,
so that we may offer our lives to you,
in joyful praise
and glad thanksgiving
through Jesus Christ our Lord.

Nick Fawcett

Lord Jesus Christ,
like the wise men following your birth,
teach us to search for you until we come to faith,
and then to go on searching just as eagerly and whole-heartedly

to discover more of your will and purpose for our lives.
Continue to surprise us with the wonder of your love
and the awesomeness of your grace,
so that we may know you and love you better each day,
to the glory of your name.

Nick Fawcett

Light of the World

Lord Jesus Christ, Light of the World,
you shine in our hearts,
banishing all that obscures your goodness
and darkens our lives.
Illuminate this time of worship,
so that in every part it will draw us closer to you,
revealing more of your purpose
and unfolding more of your grace.
Come to us
as we come now to you,
and flood our lives with the radiance of your love
so that it may shine not just in us
but also through us –
a light set upon a hill.

Nick Fawcett

Thank you, Lord, for your light,
guiding to Bethlehem, shining on the mountain,
pouring from the empty tomb and sparkling in our hearts.
Thank you for the knowledge that,
whatever life brings,
you will give light to our path,
this and every day.

Nick Fawcett

We pray that the light of God
will shine in all the dark corners of the Church,
and set us free from prejudice,
small-mindedness and hypocrisy;
that as members of the Body of Christ
we can move freely through the power of God
wherever we are called to go,
available and active in God's service.

Susan Sayers

Lord of light
we pray that our world may be lit
by your light in the darkness
to bring us freedom and hope, recognition and respect,
and in all conflicts positive ways forward.

Susan Sayers

Gold
The wise men brought gold to Jesus.
Jesus, we bring you the gold of our obedience.
Help us to live as you want us to.

Frankincense
The wise men brought frankincense to Jesus.
Jesus, we bring you the incense of our worship.
You are God and we worship you.

Myrrh
The wise men brought myrrh to Jesus.
Jesus, we bring you the myrrh of the world's sadness.
Help us to look after one another better.   *Susan Sayers*

We welcome your light that glints in the rising sun.
We welcome the light that dawns through your only Son.
We welcome your light that gleams through growing earth.
We welcome the light that you kindle in our souls.   *Ray Simpson*

Great God,
in creation you commanded the light
to shine out of darkness.
As the season of darkness recedes
may the incoming light be to us the true Light
in whose presence no unworthy thought,
no deed of shame,
may stubbornly remain.   *Ray Simpson*

Gifts

The magi searched for an infant king;
Christ, lead us into your presence.
They offered incense as their prayer;
Christ, we bow in awe before you.
Myrrh they gave to mourn your death;
Christ, to you we pour out our suffering love.   *Ray Simpson*

Purify our lives like gold
that we may be royal priests to you.
Sanctify our hearts like incense
that we may be adorers of your presence.
Beautify our hearts like myrrh
that we may be your fragrance on Earth.   *Ray Simpson*

Anna and Simeon

Living God,
like Anna and Simeon before us,
may our hearts leap for joy
as we celebrate your coming
in Christ,
the one anticipated for so long
and on whom the hopes of so many rested.
Help us to recognise in him
the fulfilment of your promises
and the answer to our needs;
the one who brings unsettling challenge yet also offers peace;
who brings light and life
not only to us but also to all the world.
Teach us to respond faithfully,
offering our grateful praise,
and witnessing in word and deed
to everything you have done through him.
In his name we pray.

Nick Fawcett

Thank you for the prophetess Anna who,
honed in daily attunement to you in the offering of praise,
discerned your presence
in an ordinary but significant moment.
Take our senses, hone our intuition,
steep us in the disciplines of the Spirit,
that we may see your hand at work
in the events of today and tomorrow.

Ray Simpson

SERVICES

Epiphany 1

Music

Sie Werden aus Saba alle kommen (Cantata No. 65, Epiphany) J. S. Bach

Introduction

After Christmas, Epiphany; after shepherds, wise men – the end of a marathon journey and an arrival long after the events of Bethlehem. But one thing was unchanged – the light which had begun to shine then was shining still, as strongly and brightly as that first day; a light which nothing, not even death itself, would ever be able to extinguish. We come to remember that journey of the magi, and to consider the meaning both of their pilgrimage and the gifts they brought. We come to give our homage to the one at the centre of it all, Jesus Christ, the light of the nations, the Saviour of the world.

Hymn

As with gladness men of old
Let all mortal flesh keep silence

Prayer

Light of the world,
shine in our darkness today.
Where there is pain and sorrow
may the brilliance of your love bring joy.
Where there is sickness and suffering,
may sunshine come after the storm.
Where there is greed and corruption,
may your radiance scatter the shadows.
Where there is hatred and bitterness,
may your brightness dispel the clouds.
Lord Jesus Christ, light of the world,
rise again upon us we pray,
and illuminate the darkness of this world
through your life-giving grace.
In your name we ask it.

Music

Earl of Salisbury Byrd (arranged Graves) during which Luke 2:21-24, 39-40 is read

Meditation of a priest at the Temple

There was something about that couple,
something that caught my attention the moment I saw them.
Happiness, I suppose it was,
the joy of sharing a new-born baby.
Only it was more than that,
for I've seen a multitude of parents over the years,
each coming bubbling with excitement,
skipping with delight,
and yet none had that look of wide-eyed wonder which these had.
It was as though they thought their child different from any other,
a unique gift from God to be handled with infinite care,
treasured beyond all price.
Oh, I know all parents feel their baby's special –
in their eyes the most beautiful thing ever born –
yet with these two it was more than that.
It was almost as if they were in awe of the child,
elated yet terrified at the responsibility of parenthood.
You think I'm exaggerating,
reading too much into an innocent moment?
Well, possibly.
She was very young after all,
and this was their first child –
everything new,
unknown,
unexplored.
Yet I still say I've never seen a look quite like they had.
Probably it will always remain a mystery,
for though no doubt they'll come back
for the occasional festival or ceremony,
I'm not sure I'll recognise them when they do.
Perhaps, though, I may find the answer despite that,
for when his mother handed me the child,
and announced his name – Jesus –
she did so as if it should mean something to me,
as if I would understand straightaway
why the child was so important,
as if he was a gift not just to *them*, but to *me*,
to *you*,
and to *everyone*.

Silence

Music

Sleep, holy babe Carol, during which Luke 2:25-35 is read

Meditation of Simeon

It was as though a wave of peace engulfed me,
a great surge of tranquillity flooding my soul
with a quietness beyond expression –
for I held him in my arms,
God's promised Messiah –
there, in that little wrinkled face,
that tiny, vulnerable child staring up at me,
the fulfilment of God's eternal purpose.
I just can't tell you what that meant to me,
not only the joy but the relief I felt,
for there had been times when my faith had begun to waver.
No, I don't just mean my conviction
that I'd see the Messiah's coming,
though I did question that sometimes, it's true.
It went deeper than that,
to the very heart of my faith,
to those words of the prophet
about us being a light to the Gentiles,
bringing glory to God through our life and witness.
I'd always believed that implicitly,
the vision stirring my imagination and firing my faith,
but over the years the flame had begun to splutter,
doused by the harsh realities which surrounded me.
The fact is we'd turned inwards rather than outwards,
our concern more for ourselves than the world beyond,
and, if anything, our horizons were growing narrower by the day.
It was understandable, of course,
the oppression we'd suffered across the centuries
enough to dampen anyone's fervour,
but that didn't make it any easier to stomach,
still less offer any grounds for hope.
Could things change, I wondered?
Was there really any chance we might recapture that old spark,
that sense of sharing in the divine purpose, testifying to his glory,
or was that dream destined to die for ever?
It was impossible not to ask it.
But that day, there in the temple, suddenly it all changed –
faith vindicated,
hope realised –
for I knew then beyond all doubt
that God had been faithful to his purpose,
his chosen servant there in my arms,
the one who would bring light to the world,
salvation to all.
I saw him with my own eyes,
touched him with my own hands,
and after that I could die happy,
my joy complete,
my faith rekindled,
my soul at peace.

Silence

I lift my eyes to the quiet hills
Peace, perfect peace
Infant holy, infant lowly

Music

The Three Kings Carol, during which Matthew 2:1-12 is read

Meditation of the Magi

Well, we made it at last.
After all the setbacks,
all the frustration,
we finally found the one we were looking for –
our journey over,
the quest completed.
And I can't tell you how relieved we were.
You see, we'd begun to fear we'd be too late,
the time for celebration long since past
by the time we eventually arrived.
It was that business in Jerusalem which caused the delay,
all the waiting
while Herod and his entourage rummaged around
trying to discover what we were on about.
They were unsettled for some reason,
taken aback, it seemed, by the news we brought,
apparently unaware a king had been born among them.
A rival claimant, they must have thought,
and who could tell what trouble that might stir up?
Anyway, they pointed us in the right direction if nothing else,
but we'd wasted time there we could ill afford,
and although the star reappeared to lead us again
we were almost falling over ourselves with haste
by the time we reached Bethlehem.
It was all quiet, just as we feared –
no crowds,
no family bustling around offering their congratulations,
no throng of excited visitors,
just an ordinary house –
so ordinary we thought we'd gone to the wrong place.
But we went in anyway,
and the moment we saw the child,
we knew he was the one –
not just the King of the Jews,
but a prince among princes,
a ruler among rulers,
a King of kings!
We were late,
much later than intended,

the journey far more difficult than we ever expected,
but it was worth the effort,
worth struggling on,
for, like they say, 'Better late than never!'

Silence

Prayer

Loving God,
inspire us, as you inspired the magi,
to journey in faith,
following where you would lead
until we reach our goal.
Though we do not know the way ahead,
and though the path may be hard,
keep us walking in the light,
travelling steadfastly to our journey's end.
Teach us to live as a pilgrim people,
fixing our eyes on Jesus,
and running the race with perseverance
for the joy set before us,
until that day when we kneel
before the throne of grace,
and offer our homage to Christ our Lord.

Hymn

Brightest and best of the sons of the morning
The light of the morning is breaking

Blessing

Music

Sie Werden aus Saba alle kommen (*Epiphany*) J. S. Bach

Nick Fawcett

Epiphany 2

Epiphany rarely feels as celebratory as the rest of Christmas. It marks fairly closely the end of an old year, the end of holidays from school and work, and the end of decorations and celebrations for another eleven months. Perhaps this comes as a relief, but it can also seem a bit of a let-down after all the excitement. For the western Church, Epiphany celebrates the visit of the magi to the infant Christ, and his revelation to the Gentiles. In other Christian traditions the emphasis is on his baptism and the start of his earthly ministry – the Revised Common Lectionary identifies the first Sunday of Epiphany as the feast day for the Baptism of the Lord. Church calendars may make it more practical to use one of the other Sundays of Epiphany for ecumenical activity (Epiphany-tide lasts until Candlemas on 2 February), and Christian Unity is a now major theme of this season, since it contains the Week of Prayer for Christian Unity, which is recognised and marked by most mainstream Churches.

On an ecumenical level, Epiphany is a great opportunity for a fresh expression of commitment to working more closely together in mission. In many areas the local Churches now unite every few years expressly to bring the good news of Jesus Christ to their community. Since planning for such events invariably takes many months, Epiphany is the ideal point at which to launch a year of mission and evangelism, even though the focal point will probably lie some way ahead.

At this time of year Methodist congregations hold their annual 'Covenant Service', and in some places like to invite members of other Churches and Christian traditions to share in this act of commitment with them, though the Covenant itself could be used in any service which emphasises discipleship and devotion.

Epiphany carol services and processions are the traditional liturgies for this season, though a major ecumenical celebration in addition to whatever is done during the Week of Prayer for Christian Unity may prove impractical. *The Promise of His Glory** also provides a liturgy for Anglicans to renew their own baptismal promises, though this would be difficult to extend to other traditions with a different view of the sacrament of baptism.

The following outline picks up the themes of revelation and personal commitment to provide a liturgy which can be used by Churches worshipping together at the start of any year, though especially one looking forward to a time of mission and evangelism.

Opening response

The whole earth is covered
with the darkness of sin and despair.
Arise, shine, for our light has come;
the Lord's glory is rising upon us.

The people of the earth are wandering
in deep darkness and confusion.
Arise, shine, for our light has come;
the Lord's glory is rising upon us.

The nations of the earth will come
to the light of Christ,
their leaders as they see the brightness of his dawn.
Arise, shine, for our light has come;
the Lord's glory is rising upon us.

Carol

O worship the Lord in the beauty of holiness

---

* Published by Church House Publishing. Also available on CD: *Visual Liturgy.*

Confession

Lord Jesus Christ,
you reveal your truth to us,
but we fail to understand
or obey your will for our lives.
Forgive our stubbornness;
help us to see your glory.

Lord Jesus Christ,
you reveal your compassion to us,
but we fail to show it to others.
Forgive our selfishness;
help us to see your glory.

Lord Jesus Christ,
you reveal your power to us,
but we prefer to trust our own strength.
Forgive our wilfulness;
help us to see your glory.

Lord Jesus Christ,
you reveal God to us
as Father, Son and Holy Spirit,
perfect in unity,
but we persist in our divisions
and maintain our differences.
Forgive our disunity;
help us to see your glory,
the glory of the Father's only Son,
and to bear witness to the Word
who became flesh and lived among us,
for his name's sake.

Absolution

May God in his mercy draw you to himself,
forgive all your sins
and pardon your wrongdoing,
and grant you a vision of his glory,
that through you Christ
may be revealed to all the world,
in whose name we pray.

Hymn

Faithful vigil ended

Old Testament reading

Isaiah 49: 6b-13

Psalm

May God be gracious to us and bless us;
Lord, make your face shine upon us.

May God's power be known on the earth;
Lord, show the nations your saving power.

May God be praised by all people;
Lord, let all the peoples praise you.

May the nations be glad and sing for joy;
**Lord, guide them in their ways
and judge them with your righteousness.**

May God bless us
with the riches of his creation;
**Lord, continue to bless us,
that the ends of the earth may honour name.**

Let all the peoples praise you, O God,
Let all the peoples praise you.   *(from Psalm 67)*

Hymn

God of mercy, God of grace

New Testament reading

1 Peter 2:4-10

Response

How beautiful on the mountains
are the feet of him who brings good news,
proclaiming peace and salvation;
say to the people: 'Your God reigns'.

Burst into songs of joy together,
for the Lord has brought comfort to his people;
say to the people: 'Your God reigns'.

All the ends of the earth will see
the salvation of our God;
say to the people: 'Your God reigns'.

Hymn

How lovely on the mountains

Gospel reading

Matthew 2:1-12

Sermon/Meditation

Procession

The gifts offered could be either twenty-first century equivalents of those offered by the magi, or those which members of the congregation are offering to assist in the mission project which the Churches are launching. If the former, representatives of three Churches should bring to the Communion table symbolic gold, incense and myrrh. If the latter, invite all members of the congregation to write on a slip of paper what help they might offer to an overall mission event.

If each seat has a slip of paper on it when people arrive, these can be collected up by a number of representatives and presented in the same way, or if necessary incorporated into the offering. Quiet music could be played while this happens, or a hymn sung – for example 'At this time of giving'.

As gifts are offered, the following response could be used:

> Whoever sows generously
> will also reap generously.
> **Thanks be to God for his indescribable gift.**

Intercession

With the wise men
we follow the guiding star to Bethlehem,
bringing gifts to offer to Christ our King.
Lord, receive this offering,
and hear our prayers.

Gold speaks of wealth and power,
kingship and government.
We bring to God the nations of the world
and their leaderships.
those who hold high office
in our nation and local community,
those with responsibility for money,
and those in the public eye, especially . . .
May they place in your hands
the influence and resources at their disposal,
to bring relief to the poor and justice to all.
Lord, receive this offering,
and hear our prayers.

Incense speaks of prayer and devotion,
worship and praise.
We bring to God our Churches

both in this local community
and throughout the world,
that Christians may put aside their differences
and through worshipping
and serving God together
demonstrate the unity which Christ has won for his people.
We pray especially for . . .
May all Christians proclaim your truth
with one voice
and show your love with one heart.
Lord, receive this offering,
and hear our prayers.

Myrrh speaks of suffering and death,
pain and distress.
We bring to God all who are suffering
through ill-health or depression,
anxiety or grief, ill-treatment or exploitation,
mentioning by name . . .
May they know the peace and comfort of your presence
in their current distress
and the healing touch of your hand.
Lord, receive this offering,
and hear our prayers.

All of our gifts, all of our life
we offer to the infant king.
As he ministers to us
so may we with our gifts minister his love
and compassion to our world.
This we ask in his name and for his glory.

Alternatively, each bidding can end with '. . . and hear our prayers', the congregation responding by using a well-known Taizé chant, e.g. 'In the Lord I'll be ever thankful' or 'Ubi caritas'.

Our Father . . .

Song

Let there be love

Final response

We offer to God the worship of our lips and our lives:
Lord, you have given us this world and its resources;
make us good stewards
of all you have entrusted to us,
and keep us faithful to our calling.

Lord, you have placed us in families
and communities;
make us good neighbours to those around,
and keep us faithful to our calling.
Lord, in Christ you have forgiven all our sins
of thought and speech, action and inaction;
make us willing to forgive those
who wrong us,
and keep us faithful to our calling.

Lord, you have given us eternal life
and the hope of heaven;
make us faithful witnesses
to the joy of your kingdom,
and keep us faithful to our calling.

Lord, you have called us
to show your limitless love
in acts of service and compassion;
make us worthy servants,
and keep us faithful to our calling.

**Accept the worship of our lips and lives,
strengthen us in faith,
and make us one as you are one,
through Jesus Christ our Lord.**

Hymn
From the sun's rising

Blessing
God our Father has called us
from darkness into his wonderful light;
may he shine on our path
and guide our footsteps.

Jesus Christ his Son is the Light of the World;
may he bring light to our lives
and banish all darkness.

God the Holy Spirit enlightens our minds
and fills us with his love;
may he shine through our lives
and draw others to the love of God.

The blessing of God Almighty,
Father, Son and Holy Spirit,
be among us and remain with us today and always.

or

The grace of our Lord Jesus Christ,
the love of God,
and the fellowship of the Holy Spirit
be with us all evermore.

Stuart Thomas

Epiphany 3

Melchior, the wise man

We thought we knew
Matthew 2:1-12

Opening Prayer
Arise, shine; for your light has come,
and the glory of the Lord has risen upon you.
Your light has come.
The Lord will arise upon you
and his glory will appear over you.
Your light has come.
Nations shall come to your light
and kings to the brightness of your dawn.
Your light has come.
They shall bring gold and frankincense
and shall proclaim the praise of the Lord.
Your light has come.

From Isaiah 60

Hymn
We three kings of Orient are

Praise
Give the king your justice, O God,
and your righteousness to the king's son.
That he may rule your people righteously
and the poor with justice.
That the mountains may bring prosperity to the people,
and the little hills bring righteousness.
Kings bow down before him;
all the nations do him service.

He shall defend the needy among the people;
he shall rescue the poor and crush the oppressor.
He shall live as long as the sun and moon endure,
from one generation to another.
Kings bow down before him;
all the nations do him service.

The kings of Tarshish and of the isles shall pay tribute,
and the kings of Arabia and Saba offer gifts.
Kings shall bow down before him;
and all nations do him service.
Kings bow down before him;
all the nations do him service.

For he shall deliver the poor who cries out in distress,
and the oppressed who has no helper.
He shall have pity on the lowly and poor;
he shall preserve the lives of the needy.
He shall redeem their lives from oppression and violence,
and dear shall be their blood in his sight.
Kings bow down before him;
all the nations do him service.

Psalm 72:1-5, 10-14
(NRSV adapted, Revised Common Lectionary)

Confession

(A brief time of silence)

Lord Jesus, the Light of the world,
illumine our hearts and forgive our blindness.
Lord, have mercy.
Lord, have mercy.

Lord Jesus, king of all, and child of Mary,
grant us understanding and forgive our dullness.
Christ, have mercy.
Christ, have mercy.

Lord Jesus, Word of Salvation
and bringer of Good News, forgive our deafness.
Lord, have mercy.
Lord, have mercy.

Reading

Proverbs 3:13-22

Happy are those who find wisdom,
and those who get understanding,
for her income is better than silver,
and her revenue better than gold.
She is more precious than jewels,
and nothing you desire can compare with her.
Long life is in her right hand;
in her left hand are riches and honour.
Her ways are ways of pleasantness,
and all her paths are peace.
She is a tree of life to those who lay hold of her;

those who hold her fast are called happy.
The Lord by wisdom founded the earth;
by understanding he established the heavens;
by his knowledge the deeps broke open,
and the clouds drop down the dew.
My child, do not let these escape from your sight:
keep sound wisdom and prudence,
and they will be life for your soul
and adornment for your neck.

Hymn

The Virgin Mary had a baby boy

Prayer

Heavenly Father, source of all wisdom and insight,
give us eyes to see and grace to understand
the revelation of yourself in the world around us,
through the pages of Scripture,
and in the life of your Son.
In his name we ask it.

Story

Pray, forgive my keeping you waiting. I have been to the bazaar and was unusually delayed. I hope my servants have welcomed you and offered you some mint tea. As I say, I was in the bazaar when out of nowhere I was confronted by a question of great profundity. An urchin ran from behind a carpet stall, stood right there in front of me and stared at me. 'Who are you?' he asked and without waiting for an answer ran off again. Not *What* but *Who* are you? I've been repeating that question to myself all the way home. I am Melchior I might have said – but my name is no more than a label on the market stall of humanity. A man? Yes. A son, a father, an uncle, a neighbour? Yes.

Perhaps then I am the sum of my relationships. But I am also a Magus, a so-called wise man. An observer of events in nature and the world. A watcher and waiter who sees, but more than that, interprets what he sees. If you wish to have knowledge you must seek more than mere data. It is the meaning within and behind and between the facts that makes for wisdom. Interpretations and meanings are discovered after much searching. They reveal themselves to the true seeker. But even then I have no guarantees they are right. There are surprises in the search that can merely lead to more questions. Let me explain with a story – a true one.

Many years ago some friends and I were particularly interested in the message given to us in the stars. Their regularity tells much but it was the disjunction of that regularity that was of particular interest. We had noticed the way in which the path of the stars you would know as Venus and Saturn was being crossed by Jupiter, accompanied by the appearance of a different very bright, evanescent star. It presented us with a puzzle. All that we had learnt indicated that this was herald to a birth. Not just an ordinary birth but one of great significance, somewhere to the west. A king, we thought. I was intrigued and we decided to test our theory, for that is the way the quest for knowledge works.

We prepared for a long journey with both camels and donkeys and each of us, myself and my two companions, had a couple of servants for both our comfort and our protection. We set out with no precise knowledge of where we would end up. Our guides were the stars and we made careful observations each night so as to determine the direction for the following day.

We went via Babylonia, followed the Euphrates and entered Palestine from the north east. The general direction was clearly towards Jerusalem, and that of course made great sense since it was there that Herod had his palace. All the signs indicated that the birth we had seen heralded in the star formation was that of a new king of the Jews. So it was to Herod's palace that we made our way, convinced both of the accuracy of our observations and of their meaning.

We were given a polite, though not particularly warm welcome. As our custom dictates, we had gifts to present both to the king and to the newborn child. The latter we wished to present in person and so we asked if we could see the infant king. The response was guarded and we were kept waiting for a considerable time – way beyond the point of courtesy. We were also puzzled for there were no signs of celebration that we had expected at the birth of an heir. But we had had little contact previously with the Jews and we put it down to local custom. After what must have been several hours we were told that no birth had occurred at the palace but that we should go to a town to the south east, called Bethlehem. Apparently their own wise men in the past had predicted a king would be born there. These things are possible of course and we had, perhaps unwisely, made assumptions in directing our path to the palace.

We set off again and soon came to this rather unpromising little town. We found the caravan lodge and, having left the camels and donkeys along with the other camel trains, set off to the nearby resting house to enquire of news of the royal baby. It was there we found this young couple and their child.

There are times when despite the careful observations, the calculations and hypotheses, the weighing of the evidence and reference to the manuals, it's not your head that gets the answer but your heart. You just know that the answer you sought is there in front of you. Not at all as you expected. Not at all in the place you were looking for it. The answer finds you. In a tatty little lodging-house in downtown Bethelehem, amidst the traders and travellers was this ordinary family with an extraordinary son. It didn't make sense. It turned all we had expected upside down. We were certain yet unsure, all at the same time. Certain enough to pay him homage and present our gifts, but uncertain where it left our science. We had made our observations. We were sure of our interpretation, but what in fact we had come to, who in fact we had seen, we were never sure.

We never did return to the palace to give them the news. Caspar had a dream of warning and we left next morning by a different route.

(Take time to reflect on/discuss the story)

Prayers

Let us come to our Saviour with joy and wonder,
offering our prayers to our heavenly Father.

We give thanks for wisdom and knowledge,
for the insights of past ages and for the discoveries of today.
We pray for scientists and investigators,
for researchers and technicians,
that the results of their work may be used for the benefit of all.
Lord of glory,
hear our prayer.

We give thanks for artists and novelists,
for poets and musicians,
whose works shine in our imagination

and dance through our feelings.
May we value their insights and listen to the voice of our hearts.
Lord of glory,
hear our prayer.

We give thanks for all who help us in our quest for knowledge,
for those who have taught us and inspired us to learn.
We pray for teachers and lecturers
and all who work in schools and colleges,
that they may work with integrity and passion
to lead others to wisdom.
Lord of glory,
hear our prayer.

We give thanks for the generosity of others:
for all who share their time, their possessions and themselves.
We pray for a generous spirit,
that we might offer the gifts you have given to us
for the well-being of those in need.
Lord of glory,
hear our prayer.

(Say The Lord's Prayer)

Hymn

O little town of Bethlehem

Blessing

May Christ our Lord,
the Babe of Bethlehem and King of all,
to whom wise men came and bowed in worship,
reveal to you the glory of his presence;
and the blessing of God,
the Father, the Son and the Holy Spirit,
rest upon you and surround you,
today and always.

John Cox

SERMON IDEAS

A Mixed Response

Herod secretly summoned the wise men and ascertained from them exactly when the star had appeared. Then he sent them to Bethlehem, saying, 'Go and search carefully for the child; and when you have found him, bring word to me, so that I, in turn, may go and offer homage.' (Matthew 2:7, 8)

One person's meat, it's said, is another's poison. In other words, we react to things in very different ways. That truth is graphically illustrated in the journey of the magi, for we see there how, from the beginning, Jesus met with hugely contrasting responses: acceptance by some, rejection by others – a curious mixture of love and hatred, welcome and opposition that was to continue throughout his ministry.

The magi, on the one hand, set off on a journey into the unknown to meet the Christ-child. And when they found him, they knelt down and offered their gifts in joyful worship. In stark contrast stands the figure of Herod, greeting the idea of a newborn king with consternation and swiftly resolving to do away with him. For him, Jesus was a threat, a potential challenge to his authority, or so at least he imagined. His thirst for power and prestige closed his eyes to the fact that this child was as much good news for him as for anyone.

The pattern continues to this day, some being for Jesus, others against; some worshipping him as Lord, others being indifferent or hostile to his claims. Why the divergence? Who can say? The reasons are many and varied. We can no more account for why strangers from the East were irresistibly drawn to Jesus than for why those schooled in expecting the Messiah should have failed to recognise him when he came. But it's not what others think or do that matters. It's what we think, what we do, how we respond. What's your answer to that?

Nick Fawcett

Never Too Late

Following the birth of Jesus in Bethlehem of Judea during the reign of King Herod, magi arrived in Jerusalem from the East, saying, 'Where is the one born king of the Jews, for we saw his star rising in the East and have come to pay our respects.' (Matthew 2:1, 2)

When did the magi visit the Christ-child? They're typically portrayed as arriving shortly after the shepherds, but they almost certainly came considerably later, maybe over a year after Jesus' birth. How do we know this? Because they arrived not at a stable but at a house, and when Herod resolved to kill his newborn 'rival' he ordered that all boys aged two and under should be put to the sword. In other words, a considerable time had elapsed from when the magi first saw the star to the completion of their journey, in no small part due to the delay they encountered in Jerusalem. We can only imagine the frustration they must have endured as the days passed with no end in sight, matched only by their joy and relief when they finally made it to their destination. Late perhaps, but better late than never.

We can learn much from their epic pilgrimage, not least that it's never too late to respond. We may have put off facing the challenge of Christ, not wanting to make a firm act of commitment despite being attracted by his message. We may have made that commitment but then lost our way, our faith being a shadow of what it once was. We may still be committed but feel we have failed somehow and that there's no way back for us. Or it may be that we're resisting some avenue of service to which God is calling us, hesitant as to what it may involve. Whatever it is and however long it may have been, it's never too late to put things right. Jesus is always ready to welcome us, eager to receive those who truly seek him. It may have taken you longer than it should to make your response, but don't let that stop you. It's not when you do, but whether you do that matters.

Nick Fawcett

Year A

Thought for the day

Jesus, the hope of the nations, is shown to the world.

Readings

Isaiah 60:1-6
Psalm 72:(1-9) 10-15
Ephesians 3:1-12
Matthew 2:1-12

Beginning with one person (Abraham) and developing to embrace one family and eventually one nation, God has painstakingly planted the seed of salvation and nurtured it until the whole earth is involved. Isaiah had sensed that day in terms of a sunrise dawning with the light of day on a world of darkness, with all the hope and joy and relief that a new day can bring after a long, dark night. Probably this was one of the prophecies these magi had read as they studied the signs of the sky and wondered about life's meaning. And perhaps it was then that they felt stirring in them a profound calling to be, in person, those visitors who could symbolise the light dawning on the wider world. Certainly they must have been inspired by a powerful sense of urgency and necessity to make such a journey. And as they travelled, both physically and spiritually, towards Bethlehem, bearing the gifts laid down in those ancient scriptures, perhaps they were drawn by much more than a star. Jesus later proclaimed that anyone who sets out to search always finds.

Paul also knows himself to be commissioned to explain God's nature to the Gentiles. He is overwhelmed by the extraordinary way that the Christ has enabled us to approach the great and awesome God with freedom and confidence – as one of the family. And for all of us who are Gentiles, the feast of the Epiphany is particularly one to celebrate, since it marks the truth that we too are part of God's salvation and can share the light of dawn.

Susan Sayers

Year B

Thought for the day

Jesus, the promised Messiah, is shown to the Gentile world.

Readings

Isaiah 60:1-6
Psalm 72:(1-9) 10-15
Ephesians 3:1-12
Matthew 2:1-12

We are well used to thinking of the Church's call as outreach. Partly this is because of the empty chairs we have got used to seeing around us each Sunday and on weekdays. Partly it is a growing awareness of the deep spiritual hunger of many who have not been brought up to go to church and do not see it as a viable answer to their need. So there is almost a daydream quality for us, as well as the dispirited people of Israel, when we are asked to imagine crowds and crowds of people from all walks of life, actively seeking us out, in order to find God and spiritual fulfilment.

I wonder how the Church would cope with such a situation? Would we be able to help them with their search? Would we understand their questions? Would we be overjoyed to see them pouring through the doors, or would they pose a threat to our traditional way of doing things?

When we recognise that being 'a light to lighten the Gentiles' can actually be quite disturbing, we can start to understand something of the hesitation the Jewish people had about welcoming the early Christians, many of them totally 'unsynagogued'. We can also thrill to the hope of a new direction – of a Church on the grow at last. The signs are there, and the tide is turning.

Epiphany has therefore particular significance for us at the moment. The light of the world is for everyone – all groups and nations, all cultures and ages, not just those we are familiar with or approve of, or who know 'how we do it' in our own church. Since most of us are Gentiles ourselves, the significance of Christ being shown to the Gentile 'outsiders' tends to pass us by unnoticed, unless we ask ourselves another question. Which 'outsiders' might those wise men represent today? To enter into the spirit of Epiphany we need to alter our vision until we understand that God has no outsiders, and no person or group is excluded. It was God's delight to reveal his baby Son to searching pagan foreigners.

As we hear once again the story of these outsiders, travelling many miles over difficult terrain in order to find for themselves the world's enlightenment, we could do well to bear in mind all those in our own times who are spiritually awake and searching, many travelling over difficult terrain, and make sure that we light the lamps, ready to welcome them.

Susan Sayers

Year C

Thought for the day

Jesus, the hope of the nations, is shown to the world.

Readings

Isaiah 60:1-6
Psalm 72:(1-9) 10-15
Ephesians 3:1-12
Matthew 2:1-12

Beginning with one person (Abraham) and developing to embrace one family and eventually one nation, God has painstakingly planted the seed of salvation and nurtured it until the whole earth is involved. Isaiah had sensed that day in terms of a sunrise dawning with the light of day on a world of darkness, with all the hope and joy and relief that a new day can bring after a long, dark night. Probably this was one of the prophecies these magi had read as they studied the signs of the sky and wondered about life's meaning. And perhaps it was then that they felt stirring in them a profound calling to be, in person, those visitors who could symbolise the light dawning on the wider world. Certainly they must have been inspired by a powerful sense of urgency and necessity to make such a journey. And as they travelled, both physically and spiritually, towards Bethlehem, bearing the gifts laid down in those ancient scriptures, perhaps they were drawn by much more than a star. Jesus later proclaimed that anyone who sets out to search always finds.

Paul also knows himself to be commissioned to explain God's nature to the Gentiles. He is overwhelmed by the extraordinary way that the Christ has enabled us to approach the great and awesome God with freedom and confidence – as one of the family. And for all of us who are Gentiles, the feast of the Epiphany is particularly one to celebrate, since it marks the truth that we too are part of God's salvation and can share the light of dawn.

Susan Sayers

Wise Men

Aim

To show how the Christ was revealed to all nations.

Reading

Matthew 2:1-12

Illustration

The wise men were not all that wise because they went to the wrong place and the wrong person. They went to the capital, Jerusalem, and to King Herod. Fancy asking him, 'Where is he who is to be born King of the Jews?' Herod hadn't a clue but he knew who would know about the Messiah, about the Christ. He asked the chief priests and scribes. They told him, 'In Bethlehem in the land of Judah.' Lucky for the wise men it was only about seven miles away. Herod sent them off and told them to search diligently for the child and to tell him when they had found him. Fortunately, the wise men did not trust Herod or his interest in the Christ child.

We assume there were three because we are told of three gifts. We know that they were rich, foreign and wise, but we do not know that they were kings. The shepherds were ordinary Jews smelling of sheep and probably not able to read or write. These men were different indeed, almost in total contrast. It helps us to see God calls all peoples to come to him – rich and poor, the known and the stranger, simple and wise; all are invited to come to God.

David Adam

ALL-AGE SERVICES

Talk Material

God's secret plan is revealed in Jesus

Readings
Psalms 2, 8
Isaiah 42:1-9
John 1:29-34

Aim
For the children to look at different ways God leads us in our spiritual journey.

Beforehand set up the secret worship place, which is where the trail will end. It might be a large cupboard or under-stair area, a small vestry or even a tent. Whatever you decide, it needs to be out of sight when the children start their trail. Set the children off in groups on a trail, either inside or out, depending on the weather. Each group follows their own colour of stars, which are placed far enough apart for there to be times when the direction is uncertain until they look more carefully (rather like cairns on mountains).

Every group's journey eventually leads to the same finishing point. This worship area is beautiful. It may have flowers placed on a mirror, lights or candles (great care!) an open Bible and a cross. Have a rug or blanket down on the floor and quiet music playing, and make the entrance low, so that they have to stoop to go in. The idea is to make it a secret place of wonder which they are led to find. Have a SILENCE notice outside, and make sure the children come in quietly. When everyone is crowded in, tell them quietly and simply how God led the wise men to find him; how he led John the Baptist to recognise him, and he leads us to find him as well. But we don't all come by the same route. God uses all the different events of our lives, and the different people we meet; he can use sad times as well as happy times.

Sing a worship song together that the children know well, and then pray for people who are going through different bits of their journey at the moment. Have music playing again as the children file out and colour this star prayer to hang up at home.

Susan Sayers

Ideas for Activities

A long journey

Take the children on a long journey to different parts of the room, with the star always leading them. Different children can take it in turns to carry the star. As you all trail along you can chant:

Leader	We're going on a journey,
All	we're going on a journey,
Leader	We're following a star.
All	We're following a star.
Leader	We're going to find Jesus,
All	we're going to find Jesus,
Leader	Hope it's not far.
All	Hope it's not far.

Susan Sayers

Presents

Matthew 2:1-12

When people buy presents for us they usually have a good idea of our likes and dislikes, favourite music, clothes and current rave chocolate bar. The choice of present isn't just a random 'pick anything off the shelf and hope it's OK' type of thing. Presents are given with the hope that the recipient will appreciate (and possibly really like) the choice of gift which will earn the buyer a heartfelt 'thank you'. More often than not, we can even guess what certain people will buy or give us as a present. You know, Gran always buys you a book token equivalent to the price of a book in 1920 while Uncle Arthur never fails to give you a crumpled paper bag containing a selection of boiled sweets. And, on a good year, Great Aunt Dot will give you a box of patterned handkerchiefs which she received for Christmas two years ago.

Often the selection of a present has been given lots of thought and chosen to 'fit' the recipient. Usually a present means something, even if it is only a 'Look, I remembered!'

The wise men didn't just happen to be passing the stable where the infant Jesus was. Neither did they hear about his birth and rush down to the nearest shop and pull any old thing off the shelf. Each present was given for a reason, to mean something, to reflect something of the character of the recipient.

Gold has always, and still does, represent royalty. In Old Testament times it was also a sign of holiness.

Frankincense was a very desirable perfume. It was used by the Jewish priests in the Temple who acted as the 'middle-men' between God and the people.

Myrrh was another perfume used to relieve pain and to anoint the dead prior to burial.

Each of the wise men's gifts represented something of the character of Jesus. He was a Holy King who would act as the bridge-builder between God and the people and would eventually suffer and die as a sacrifice.

The wise men had travelled a great distance to bring their gifts. They knew something of the character of the infant and each gift had a particular significance.

For each of us, Jesus himself became a gift. He became the once and for all sacrifice that would enable us to form an eternal relationship with God. Now, that's a gift that really means something!

Pete Townsend

Where is he?

Reading
Matthew 2:1-11

Aim
To demonstrate that Christmas isn't simply about celebrating the coming of Jesus long ago, but more importantly about our personal response to him, now.

Preparation
Fold in half eight A4 pieces of stiff paper to make A5 cards. On the front of these write the following words in bold letters:

JUDEA

BETHLEHEM

MANGER

STABLE

HOUSE

NAZARETH

JERUSALEM

EGYPT

On the inside of each card, again in bold letters, write 'NOT HERE!' Place the cards prominently around the front of the church so that the word on the front of each can be seen.

Also prepare eight pieces of A4 paper with one of the following written in large, bold letters: E, I, H, H, S, R, E, E.

You will also need a question mark sign and an exclamation mark sign.

Talk
Ask the congregation if anyone can remember what the wise men asked Herod when they came to Jerusalem? (Where is the one born King of the Jews?) Explain that you want to ask this question again today, and that to do so you need eight helpers. Invite volunteers to come to the front, and pin one of the single letters (E, I, H, H, S, R, E, E) on the front of each.

Invite each volunteer in turn to look behind one of the cards to discover where 'the King of the Jews' has been born. After each unsuccessful attempt ask the volunteer to display the words inside – NOT HERE! – and to stand at the front of the church until all eight volunteers are standing side by side in a line.

Observe that, despite the volunteers' help, your question remains unanswered. Ask the congregation to look again very carefully, and see whether they might have missed something. Allow time for people to think, then line the volunteers up so that the letters pinned to their fronts spell 'HE IS HERE'.

That's the answer to our question. Or is it? Well, not quite, for it all depends on what comes after these words. (Position yourself at the end of the line.) Is it a question mark (hold up '?'), or is it an exclamation mark (hold up '!')?

We all know Jesus was born in Bethlehem of Judea; we all know he was born in a stable and laid in a manger because there was no room in the inn; we all know his parents came from

Nazareth, and that they took Jesus later to Jerusalem; and we probably know that after Jesus' birth they fled to Egypt to escape Herod.

All that is part of the wonderful Christmas story we know and love so well. But unless there's another chapter in that story, then all the rest doesn't finally mean anything. It is only when Jesus can also be found here in our hearts, in our lives, in each one of us, that Christmas truly comes alive.

Where is the one born King of the Jews? Is he simply here (point to one of the cards), or here (point to one of the volunteers), or here (point to the congregation)? Or can we point to ourselves and say, honestly and without hesitation, 'He is here!'

That's the question we need to ask this Christmas, and the answer we need to give.

Nick Fawcett

God is awesome

Have seven large cards available. On each card write one letter from the word 'awesome'. Place the first card on the flipchart and ask the group to think about their dreams and ambitions. While they are thinking, turn the card over to reveal the word: 'Almighty'. Do this with each of the other cards.

A: Almighty

W: Wonderful

E: Everlasting

S: Saviour

O: Omnipotent

M: Majestic

E: Everywhere

After you have revealed each word and the group have recognised each one as telling us a little bit about God's character, finish with the following prayer:

God, you are
Almighty, creator of all things seen and unseen.
You are Wonderful, absolutely amazing, totally astounding.
You are Everlasting in your love for each one of us.
You are our Saviour, our rescuer from everything
    that would try and put a barrier between us.
You are Omnipotent, powerful, able to do
    the impossible, able to love me.
You are Majestic, royalty above all royalty.
You are Everywhere, all around, with us in everything we do
    and watching out for us every step of the way.
God, you are AWESOME.

Pete Townsend

Services

Gold, frankincense and myrrh

Resources

- A sheet of lining paper and felt-tip pens, in front of the altar
- Basic Nativity costumes:
  - Brown fabric for Joseph
  - Blue fabric for Mary
  - A manger/wooden crate with hay
  - A baby Jesus doll
  - Shiny or velvety cloaks for kings
  - Three cardboard crowns
- Large piece of brown felt in the shape of a cross
- The gifts: *(see note 1)*
  - 'Gold' (a small box covered in gold foil), wrapped in a stiff rectangular piece of gold paper
  - A box of frankincense granules, wrapped in white crepe paper cut in a cross shape, smaller than the brown cross
  - A bottle of myrrh oil, wrapped in three red ribbons
- Music and words
- Four 'prayer stations' around the church, with the following:
  - A frameless mirror or mirror tile (to reflect and intensify the glitter of the gold)
  - A small thurible or charcoal burner for the frankincense
  - A small dish for the myrrh oil
  - A space for the media pieces which will be produced during the Exploring
- A sign for each station:
  - *GOLD* for the King
  - *FRANKINCENSE* for God
  - *MYRRH* for the body
  - *JESUS* for us
- Several copies of each of the four media sheets, spread out on some tables *(see note 2)*
- Pens and pencils

Leaders

Minimum: 2
- Leader/Storyteller
- Storyteller

Optimum: 7
- Leader
- Activity Leader
- Storytellers x 2
- Music Leader
- Explorer
- Prayer Leader

Suggestions for additional music

- He's got the whole world in his hands
- Lord Jesus Christ
- Glorious light

Service

Welcome

Invite people to come up to the altar and draw round their feet or hands on the sheet of lining paper as a way of saying, 'Here I am, Lord'.

Introduction

Today is called Epiphany. It is the day when we remember the wise men who visited Jesus. I wonder if we could recreate the scene in the stable today? Who would like to dress up as a king?

Dress up volunteers as Mary, Joseph and three wise men. Place Mary and Joseph around the manger with the baby in it. Ask each wise man to process down the aisle in turn with the gold, frankincense and myrrh, and then remain kneeling by the manger. By the end, you should have a living Epiphany tableau.

Encourage children to gather around you and the tableau for the storytelling. You will need one storyteller to tell the story and another to take the gifts from the tableau in turn and unwrap them as described below.

This is a scene we all recognise. But our story today is about the three gifts given to the baby Jesus. Mary and Joseph unwrapped these presents on the stable floor *(lay out brown cross)*. The first was heavy and bright: it was gold. *(Hold up the gold then unwrap it, unfolding the gold wrapping.)* Gold was a present fit for a king. *(Spread out the wrapping at the top of the cross, in the position of the sign at the crucifixion which read, 'The King of the Jews'.)*

The next present smelled wonderful. It was frankincense, made from the sap of an exotic tree. *(Unwrap the frankincense and pour out some grains into the palm of your hand for people to look at.)* When these hard little grains are sprinkled on burning wood or charcoal, they release a heavenly smell and pure white smoke. *(Hold up the long white wrapping.)* Frankincense suggests holiness, so it is a gift which people offer to God. *(Unfold the white wrapping in the middle of the brown cross, forming a smaller cross like the figure of Christ.)*

The last present was myrrh. It was a sticky resin with a sweet, earthy smell which made people sad because it reminded them of death. A dead body was rubbed with myrrh to sweeten and preserve it. So the last present brought with it the shadow of a death which would come in the future. *(On the white cross where Christ's hands and feet would be, drop each red ribbon in a little pool and let it trail down.)*

Mary and Joseph looked at all these precious, important gifts. The gold for a king, *(place gold and the sign on one prayer station)* the holy white smoke of frankincense for God *(place frankincense and the sign on another prayer station)* and the myrrh for a dead body *(place myrrh and the sign on another prayer station)*. They kept them safe and treasured them through the years which followed, as their baby son grew into a man and went out into the world.

Music

We three kings

During this hymn, the tableau actors can remove their costumes and return to their seats.

Exploring

Today is called Epiphany: it means 'showing' or 'revealing'. The wise men came from different parts of the world and so their visit is seen as the moment when God showed himself to the world in the body of the baby Jesus. As we have seen in our story, their gifts reveal who he is in a clear and beautiful way. But what happened once the wise men left? What happened once they started to spread the news, and the truth of Jesus' birth was shown to the world?

We are going to explore this in a different way today – by making an imaginative leap from Israel, two thousand or so years ago, to the present day. I invite you to imagine what would happen if Jesus were born not in a stable, but in a garage behind a dilapidated hotel, somewhere in the modern Middle East. When important foreign visitors come to see him, how would they spread the news today? Where do we get our news from?

Elicit the answers and introduce the four media sheets: TV, the internet and newspapers.

If Jesus were born today, I wonder what we might see, hear and read about him in the media? For example, would there be paparazzi photographs of the garage? Would the wise men hold a press conference? Use your imagination as you look through these media sheets. Write or draw any ideas you have about how the Epiphany would be announced – how God would go public – in our modern world.

Allow plenty of time for people to circulate and generate ideas, then share some of the responses.

The Epiphany today would be big news. It would attract frenzied media attention of all kinds, from the most serious BBC reports to the silliest bloggers. That is the thing about publicity and exposure today – you don't get to choose how people treat you or your story. This was true of Jesus, too. As soon as news of his birth spread, then people like the shepherds and the wise men came to worship him – but King Herod also sent soldiers to kill him. This is the reality of the Epiphany: it is when God exposes himself to all the riskiness and unpredictability of life. And he did it for us.

Music

What child is this

During this hymn, light the charcoal burner and add some incense; then pour a little myrrh oil into the dish.

Prayer action

In our prayers today, we will use four prayer stations. At each one there is an Epiphany gift which helps us to understand something about who Jesus is. As we learnt in our story, gold is a gift for the King of the Jews – but Jesus was born in a stable and spent his life serving whoever needed him, regardless of what they believed. Frankincense reminds us that Jesus is God – but he came into our world as one of us. Myrrh reminds us that Jesus died a real death – and yet he rose again. The fourth station uses our imaginary twenty-first century Epiphany to remind us that above all, Jesus gave himself to us by exposing himself to the best and the worst that life could offer. In a time of quiet, come forward and explore these gifts with all your senses: rest in God's presence and listen to what these things tell us about his Son.

In turn, the people look at the glow of the gold, smell some of the burning frankincense, rub a little myrrh oil on their palms and read the media pieces.

Let us pray.
Here is gold for a King born in a stable,
frankincense for God who became flesh and blood,
myrrh for the man who died but rose again.
Lord Jesus, Embracer of contradictions,
these gifts were given to you
but you gave yourself to us
so that we might have the gift
of everlasting life.
Open our hearts and minds
to receive you today.

Music

The first Nowell

Conclusion

Turn the sheet of lining paper with footprints on it so that the footprints are facing towards the door of the church, or heading down the aisle.

Lord Jesus,
send us out into the world
to walk in your footsteps
and to follow your star wherever it may lead us.

Notes

1. Gifts

Frankincense

Frankincense is available from church suppliers and, often, gift shops connected to religious houses and cathedrals. Make sure that you buy incense in granular form, not the oils, sticks or cones found in shops specialising in Eastern produce. Also check websites such as www.incense-man.co.uk. There is also useful advice here about lighting charcoal and using incense.

Myrrh

Myrrh is sold as an essential oil: it can be found with aromatherapy oils in health food shops.

2. Media sheets
Print out and make several copies of each one on A4 paper.

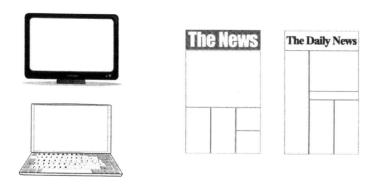

Claire Benton-Evans

Follow the star

Resources

- A large piece of black card with a silver Star of Bethlehem in the centre
- Lots of gold and silver star stickers
- Music and words
- Props:
    - 3 telescopes (decorated cardboard tubes will do)
    - a large scroll
    - a rolled-up rug, placed at back of church
    - a manger/wooden crate with some hay, placed before the altar
    - a swaddled baby Jesus doll
    - three wrapped gifts for the wise men
- Materials for the Star/Comet Activity *(see note)*:
    - A large cardboard star (at least 1m long and wide)
    - Shiny or glittery gold and silver paper to decorate the star, front and back
    - Glue
    - Scissors
    - Fabric for the tail. This should be long and light: a few metres of cheap white polyester would be ideal, or plain net curtain fabric
    - Streamers to run either side of the tail, for example: gold or silver tinsel, strips of white or yellow crepe paper, long ribbons
    - A long-arm stapler and staples (or strong silver duck tape) to attach the tail and streamers

Leaders

Minimum: 4
- Leader
- Cast x 3

Optimum: 9+
- Leader (Introduction and Conclusion)
- Storyteller
- Cast x 3:
  The Persian, Arabian and Babylonian wise men, wearing tunics and shiny or velvety cloaks
- Music Leader
- Activity Leader(s)
- Explorer
- Prayer Leader

Suggestions for additional music
- Lord, the light of your love
- You are the King of Glory

Service

Welcome
Invite people to add a star to the Bethlehem sky picture as a sign of their prayer.

Introduction
Today is the feast of Epiphany. It is the day when we remember the visit of the wise men who came from the east, bringing gifts of gold, frankincense and myrrh. Let's tell their story.

Storytelling
The wise men take up visible positions around the church. They scan the skies with their telescopes. The Arabian wise man mimes making notes on his scroll.

Long ago in the lands of the Middle East there were experts who studied the mysteries of the stars and planets. In Persia, a wise man read patterns in the stars and interpreted their meanings. In Arabia, a wise man made detailed drawings of the night skies and mapped every change he observed. And in Babylonia, a wise man looked to the stars for news and prophecies of great events. One night, they all spotted something new.

Persian wise man	A new star! It's separate from the other constellations, and brighter than them all. This can only mean one thing: the birth of a king.
Arabian wise man	It first appeared above the eastern horizon and it seems to be moving slowly across the skies, getting brighter all the time. It draws me towards itself like a magnet.
Babylonian wise man	I have never seen a star like this before. This must mark an extraordinary event. Only the birth of a king would be heralded like this – but such a star! He must be a king unlike any other.

Carrying their gifts, the wise men walk from their different places and meet at the back of church. One picks up the rolled-up rug. They walk together down the aisle during the following speech.

Storyteller	And so they came, wondering and amazed but sure-footed, following the bright star which moved slowly across the skies towards Bethlehem. The journey took weeks, so they camped out in the desert and slept in the starlight.

The wise men unroll the rug and lie down on it briefly, before standing up and rolling it up again. They carry on walking to the front of the church.

They carried gifts for the king they expected to meet. They may have been surprised by the stable, the animals and the shy young couple holding the baby, but they recognised the king whose birth had been announced by the star. They were overwhelmed with joy to have found him at last. They laid their precious gifts on the dirty straw and they bowed down and worshipped him.

The wise men place their gifts before the manger. They kneel down and remain like this during the next hymn.

Music
We three kings

Activity
What was this strange, bright star which travelled slowly across the sky from the east and stood still over Bethlehem? Astronomers suggest that what the Bible describes as a 'star' may have been a comet. Chinese astronomers in 5 BC recorded a long-tailed comet which blazed across the skies for 70 days. Perhaps it was this comet which led the wise men to Jesus.

Imagine them following a comet with its fiery tail like a highway of stars! We are going to explore this idea in our activity today.

Invite everyone to gather round the craft tables. People can decorate the star itself or create the fiery tail, which should be as long as possible. The finished comet should be held like a Chinese dragon, with two people supporting the star at the head and everyone else following in a line, supporting the tail over their heads. It's now time for the comet conga! Process around the church like this, perhaps accompanied by the music of one of the hymns.

Music
From the eastern mountains

Exploring
The story of the wise men is very familiar to us. All the different elements of the story are like old friends: the wise men who spotted the star *(hold up the telescope)*; their long journey through the desert *(hold up the rolled rug)*; the precious gifts *(hold up one of the gifts)*; and the baby in the manger *(hold up the manger)*. But if we look more closely at each of these things, they may help us think about what this story means for us. The wise men followed the star which led them to Jesus: how might we follow the light of Jesus in our lives?

(Hold up the telescope.) First of all, the wise men didn't spot the star by accident. They had spent a lifetime studying the skies and paying close attention to what they saw. We need to pay attention to God if we are to follow where he wants to lead us. We don't need a telescope for this, but we do need to pray and to study the Bible. This is the first thing we can learn from the wise men: we need to pay attention to God in our lives.

(Hold up the rolled rug.) For the wise men, following the star meant undertaking a long journey. We may live in the same place all our lives, or we may move across the world, but wherever we live Jesus calls us on a spiritual journey of growth and change. He said, 'I am the way', not 'I am the destination': following him means leaving some of our old ways behind and being open to new experiences which may change us. This is the second thing we can learn from the wise men: we are called to go on a journey of faith.

(Hold up one of the gifts.) The wise men did not go to Jesus empty-handed. The Bible tells us that they 'opened their treasure-chests and offered him gifts of gold, frankincense and myrrh'. We, too, need to be prepared to give generously of our time, our energy, our resources and ourselves. Following Jesus is not without cost, and this is the third thing we can learn from the wise men: we need to be generous.

As the wise men followed the special star, they must have wondered where they would find the newborn king. Would he be in a palace, surrounded by royal guards? Would he be lying on silk and velvet? When the star stopped over Bethlehem, the Bible tells us they were 'overwhelmed with joy'. *(Hold up the manger.)* But they found him lying on straw in an animals' feeding trough. This is the most important thing we can learn from the wise men: we can meet Jesus in surprising and unexpected places. Let's hope that we recognise him, so that we too might be overwhelmed with joy.

Prayer action

Lean the star up against the altar and spread the tail out down the aisle like a bridal train.

The star's bright trail streaked across the skies, and the wise men followed it like bridesmaids after a bride's long, white train. As we remember their journey which led to Jesus, our prayers today will help us reflect on how we follow his light in our lives. Let's rest in his presence now.

Pause for a short time before singing a few repetitions of the Taizé chant, 'The Lord is my light', growing louder and then quieter. Pause.

Lord, you are our light.
May we follow you faithfully,
trusting that you will lead us.

Conclusion

Jesus, Light of the world,
your love shines like a bright star.
May you draw us closer to you.

Note

Star/comet activity

The aim is to make something that looks like this, which can be carried around the church rather like a Chinese dragon. There are streamers on both sides of the tail. Remember that both sides of the star should be decorated.

Claire Benton-Evans

Prayer Action

Bethlehem sky

Resources

- A large piece of black card with a silver Star of Bethlehem in the centre
- Lots of gold and silver star stickers

Leader

The wise men followed the star that led them to Jesus, but they can't have been the only people who were drawn to that strange, bright light in the sky. Ordinary people must have looked at it and wondered, hoped that it was a sign of their Saviour's coming. Our prayers today will focus on that bright Bethlehem star. Whatever it is you would like to bring before God, whoever you would like to pray for, come and add a little star to this sky as a sign of your prayer.

Prayer action

Encourage people to come forward and add a star to the Bethlehem sky picture.

Closing words

God of everything,
the prayers of your people are more
than all the stars in the sky,
but your love is wider, longer, higher and deeper
than space itself.
May each prayer hold its place in your heart,
in Jesus' name.

Claire Benton-Evans

Gold, frankincense and myrrh

Resources

Three 'prayer stations': gold (any gold or shiny brass objects you have in the church*); frankincense** (burning in a small thurible or charcoal-burner) and a small dish of light olive oil infused with a few drops of myrrh oil.*** Place a sign at each station: 'GOLD for the King', 'FRANKINCENSE for God', 'MYRRH for the body'.

---

*   If you stand these objects on a frameless mirror or mirror tile, the glitter is reflected and intensified.

**   Frankincense is available from church suppliers and, often, gift shops connected to religious houses and cathedrals. Make sure that you buy incense in granular form, not the oils, sticks or cones found in shops specialising in Eastern produce. Also check websites such as www.incense-man.co.uk. There is useful advice here about lighting charcoal and using incense.

*** Myrrh is sold as an essential oil: it can be found with aromatherapy oils in health food shops.

Leader

In our prayers today, we will use the three gifts given to Jesus at Epiphany. Each of these gifts helps us to understand something about who Jesus is. Gold is a gift fit for a king, and Jesus was the King of the Jews – but he was born in a stable and spent his life serving whoever needed him, regardless of what they believed. Frankincense is hardened tree sap which produces pure white smoke and a beautiful smell when it burns, so it has become a symbol of holiness. Frankincense reminds us that Jesus is God – but he came into our world as one of us. Finally, myrrh has a sweet, earthy smell. In Jesus' time it was rubbed on dead bodies to sweeten and preserve them, and it reminds us that Jesus died a real death – and yet he rose again.

In a time of quiet, move around the station and explore these three gifts: rest in God's presence and listen to what these things tell us about his Son.

Prayer action

In turn, the people look at the glow of the gold, smell some of the burning frankincense and rub a little myrrh-infused oil on their palms. Gather everyone together for the closing words.

Closing words

Here is gold for a King born in a stable,
frankincense for God who became flesh and blood,
myrrh for the man who died but rose again.
Lord Jesus, Embracer of contradictions,
these gifts were given to you
but you gave yourself to us
so that we might have the gift
of everlasting life.
Open our hearts and minds
to receive you today.

Claire Benton-Evans

Sketch

Ships of the desert

Characters

Melchior
Balthasar
Caspar

The Three Wise Men have just visited Jesus in Bethlehem.

Caspar   Right then, I suppose we'd better get going. Now that we've seen him. It was worth the long journey.

Balthasar   The trek across the hot sweltering wilderness.

Caspar   Sitting on a camel for hours upon hours.

Balthasar Oh I know, don't remind me. I felt seasick most of the way. Well, they are called the 'ships of the desert', you know.

Caspar Is that the reason why?

Balthasar I don't know. Maybe.

Melchior Actually, we'd better go and find where we left them.

Caspar Don't you mean 'docked' them?

Melchior Hey?

Caspar Never mind.

Balthasar Yes, they were difficult travelling conditions, what with the constant stops for you to throw up and having to find our way by following a star in the sky.

Melchior There are so many.

Caspar My neck really hurts from looking up all the time, plus it's hard to steer like that.

Balthasar How many trees did you crash into?

Caspar All right, don't mock me. You fell down a well!

Balthasar That wasn't my fault. It was a stupid place to put it!

Caspar *(sarcastic)* Oh yes, in a desert, over an underground water source, how silly.

Balthasar It's not funny. I hurt myself, and my camel was dazed and confused for hours.

Melchior But everything we went through was forgotten when we found him.

Balthasar Yes. For the privilege of worshipping the new king, I'd do it all again.

Caspar Me too.

Melchior Who'd have thought that we'd be led to a place like that, so humble and poor.

Caspar I know. We expected him to be born in Jerusalem, the holy city.

Melchior How wrong we were!

Balthasar OK then, let's saddle up and report back to King Herod on our way home.

Melchior Actually, I think we should take a different route.

Balthasar Why, what do you mean?

Melchior We should avoid Jerusalem, and especially Herod.

THE BUMPER BOOK OF RESOURCES: ADVENT, CHRISTMAS AND EPIPHANY

Caspar   But he asked us to return and tell him where to find the child. I know he wasn't the most charming of people but it would seem rude if we didn't.

Melchior   It doesn't matter.

Balthasar   Also, he seemed very keen to worship the new king himself.

Melchior   Look, I think we'd be making a big mistake.

Caspar   Really? But we could dine at the palace again and be waited on.

Balthasar   Yes, prepare for the long journey ahead of us.

Caspar   A little bit of comfort and luxury before we set off. Is that too much to ask?

Melchior   I had a dream last night.

Balthasar   So did I.

Melchior   What was it about?

Balthasar   Well, I dreamt that I was eating an enormous piece of . . .

Melchior   *(interrupting)* Excuse me!

Balthasar   Sorry?

Melchior   I think my dream is a little bit more significant.

Caspar   How do you know?

Melchior   Listen and you'll find out.

Balthasar   All right. You go first and then we'll all listen to my dream.

Melchior   *(sighs)* OK, I suppose so.

Caspar   *(to Balthasar)* I did like the sound of yours.

Balthasar   I can tell you about some others I've had as well, if you like? I can write them down for you to read . . .

Caspar   Oh er, thanks, but there's no need to go to any trouble.

Melchior   Anyway, about my dream!

Balthasar   Yes, well tell us then.

Caspar   Stop dithering and get on with it!

Melchior   In my dream God warned me, or should I say 'us', that we shouldn't return to Herod.

Caspar   Really?

Melchior   So I think we should definitely go home another way.

Balthasar   Hmm. I suppose you're right, that is more significant than my dream.

Caspar   Why do you think God doesn't want us to go back to the king?

Melchior   I can't be sure exactly, but come on, you met him. Did he strike you as being totally sincere?

Balthasar   He struck me as the sort of monarch who would be less than pleased to hear of a Messiah, a new King of the Jews, coming on the scene.

Caspar   Yes, come to think of it, that does make sense.

Balthasar   You mean, when we told him why we'd come to Jerusalem and he smiled, that grinding sound coming from his teeth wasn't an expression of politely controlled happiness?

Melchior   I think not.

Caspar   So when he said that he wanted to go and 'worship' him too, he really meant something else? Something less friendly?

Melchior   Let me put it this way – I don't think he intends to take him any presents.

Balthasar   Just one thing, though. How did he know where to send us to find the child?

Caspar   Yes, I mean, he directed us there, didn't he?

Melchior   I believe his chief priests and religious teachers told him the details.

Balthasar   How?

Melchior   By consulting their holy writings which prophesy their Messiah's birthplace.

Caspar   There's another thing I don't get.

Melchior   What's that?

Caspar   Why didn't he go himself, if he knew where to find him? Why send us?

Melchior   I assume he didn't know the precise location – which house he'd be found in or which parents he'd been born to. We had our star, remember?

Balthasar   Oh yes, it showed up again just when we needed it.

Melchior   Also, he couldn't waltz into Bethlehem and inquire in person where to find the baby, could he? For one thing, he doesn't seem to be that popular.

Caspar   That's true.

Balthasar   And I'm not sure he has the personality to relate to small children.

Melchior   So are we agreed? We won't go back and tell him what we've seen? And where?

Caspar/   *(together)* Agreed!
Balthasar

Melchior   It was amazing, wasn't it? Finding him like that?

Caspar   I know. Just one look brought me to my knees.

Balthasar   Even though he was just a little child. He could have been anyone, if we hadn't known better.

Melchior   But with a holy presence to command the stars themselves.

Balthasar   You can be quite poetic at times, can't you?

Melchior   Yes, I have a way with words, and I like to bring a sense of grandeur to such events. So what?

Balthasar   I'm not saying there's anything wrong with it, just that you can be a bit flowery when describing the most humdrum of scenes.

Melchior   You're just jealous of my ability.

Balthasar   *(rolling his eyes)* That must be it.

Caspar   Do you think our gifts were all right?

Balthasar   Yes, I think so.

Melchior   Gold for a king, that was very fitting.

Balthasar   And frankincense, that's good because there's something quite spiritual about that.

Melchior   Smells nice.

Balthasar   That, too, of course.

Caspar   And myrrh. Er, that's quite useful as well.

Balthasar   Especially as an embalming oil.

Caspar   OK, but it can come in handy for all sorts of other things too.

Melchior   Yes, true, it has many uses. That was a thoughtful gift.

Caspar   Yes, thanks, I reckon so.

Balthasar   It's good for treating wounds.

Caspar   Is it?

Balthasar   I heard you can use it as a cure for baldness.

Caspar   That's what they said about pigeon droppings, but it wasn't true!

Balthasar   Yes, I'm glad you've given up on that idea.

Melchior   We all are!

Caspar   Yeah, yeah, very funny.

Melchior   Right then, I think we should be off. We've done enough talking.

Caspar   You're right!

Balthasar   Come on, let's get back!

Melchior   Er, does anyone know the way?

Caspar   Yes of course, *(points to sky)* all we have to do is just follow the . . . Oh, wait.

Balthasar   *(sighs)* I think it's going to be a very long journey home.

Penny Garret

Based on the Lectionary

For pre-school age to 5 years – Years A and C

Thought for the day

Jesus, the hope of the nations, is shown to the world.

Readings

Isaiah 60:1-6
Psalm 72:(1-9) 10-15
Ephesians 3:1-12
Matthew 2:1-12

Aim

To become familiar with the story of the wise men finding Jesus.

Starter

Play pass the parcel. At the different layers have old bus and train tickets. The prize at the end is a star-shaped biscuit.

Teaching

Tell the children that today we are going to hear about a journey. It isn't a bus journey or a car journey or a train journey. This is a camel journey. (All pack your bags and get on your camels.) We are very wise people, but we don't know where we are going. We are looking for a baby king. And we are packing presents for him. (Pack gold, frankincense and myrrh.) Produce a star on a stick as you explain how a special star has started shining in the sky and we are sure it will lead us to the baby king. Lead off behind the star, riding your camels, and pretending to go over high mountains, through water, stopping for the night, and going to sleep and so on. At last you reach the town of Bethlehem (stick up a sign) where you find the baby king with his mum and dad. (Have a large picture, or one of the cribs made before Christmas.) We all get off our camels and give the baby our presents. The baby's name is Jesus and we have found him at last!

Praying

This is a prayer the wise men might have said. We have all been invited to find Jesus as well, so we can say it with them.

Thank you, Jesus,
for inviting me
to come and look for you.
I am glad I have found you!

Activities

To emphasise that the journey of the wise men was probably a hard one, there is a maze to help the wise men find their way to Bethlehem. The star-making activity will need star templates, and ready-cut card for the younger children.

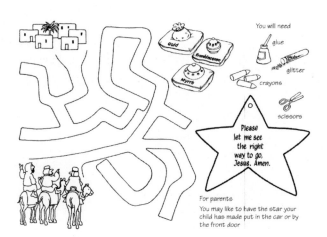

Susan Sayers

For pre-school age to 5 years – Year B

Thought for the day

Jesus, the promised Messiah, is shown to the Gentile world.

Readings

Isaiah 60:1-6
Psalm 72:(1-9) 10-15
Ephesians 3:1-12
Matthew 2:1-12

Aim

To know that the wise men brought presents to Jesus.

Starter

Fix a star on to a stick and give it to one of the children. Wherever this child goes with the star, the others follow. If the star stops, everyone stops. Swap the star around until everyone who wants to lead has had a go.

Teaching

On a long strip of lining paper or wallpaper draw some hills and a starry sky, based on the picture below. Lay the sheet out in front of the children, and have at the ready a shiny star and a cut-out picture of the wise men. The smaller you make these the longer the journey will look.

Who do we know who followed a star? Yes, it was the wise men from many miles away. They followed a great bright star in the sky which was moving, night by night. (Move the star as you speak, and then make the wise men walk after it to catch it up.) The star went on like this for nights and nights, until at last it stopped. (Stop the star over the town of Bethlehem.) And the wise men followed it all the way to a town called Bethlehem. Who did they find at Bethlehem? They found Jesus there. (Place a Christmas card of Joseph, Mary and Jesus on the city of Bethlehem.)

What did they do when they found Jesus? (Swap the Christmas card for one showing the wise men giving their presents.) They treated Jesus as if he was a little king. They bowed and knelt in front of him, and gave him the presents they had brought.

What were the presents? There was gold (lay down something gold – preferably real gold if practical! If you are wearing a gold ring you can take it off and place it down, which says a lot about real giving without a word spoken) . . . frankincense (again the real thing is ideal, so they can smell what it's like) . . . and myrrh (the Body Shop sells it, or use any spicy ointment and let them rub a bit into their skin if they want to).

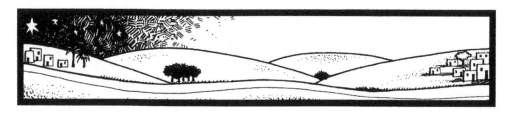

Praying

Jesus, can you guess
> (*pretend to hide a present behind your back*)

what I have brought to give you?

It's ME!
> (*bring hands out and hold them up and out, as you jump forward*)

Activities

There is an activity to match objects with their silhouettes, and a picture to colour of the wise men giving their presents.

Susan Sayers

For 6 to 10 years – Year A

Aim

To encourage the children to tell the story of the wise men.

Readings

Isaiah 60:1-6
Psalm 72:(1-7) 10-14
Ephesians 3:1-12
Matthew 2:1-12

Teaching

Use a set of crib figures, including a star and the wise men, if possible. Alternatively, you can use cut-out figures from Christmas cards. Get various children to pick up a figure until all the figures are gone. A new group of children could do this after it has been done once.

Who has the figure of the baby? Can you tell me who this baby is? Do you remember who came to see the baby? The shepherds came to see Jesus because the angels told them he is the Saviour. Can anyone tell me what it means to be the Saviour?

Now, who has the baby's mother? Can you tell me her name? Yes, she is called Mary. Can you remember where her baby was born? He was born in a stable, because there was no room at the inn.

Who has Mary's husband? Do you know his name? Yes, it is Joseph and he is a carpenter. What sort of work does a carpenter do?

Now, who has the star? Why do you think there is a star here? It is to guide people in the darkness. The star is to show them the way. How many people were to follow this star? Let the three wise men follow the star. *(Get the star to go round the room with three children following – the rest might like to follow behind them.)*

Now let us look at the presents the wise men brought to Jesus. Can anyone find them on their card? Who knows what they are? What do you think these strange presents mean? *(If possible, try and have some gold, incense and myrrh to show the children.)*

Why do you think a wise man gave gold to Jesus?

Gold is a sign of power and wealth, and it is a good gift for a king.

Incense *(at this stage it would be good to burn a little incense – an incense stick would do)* is used by people who want to pray to God. Incense smoke rises upwards, as do our prayers. Incense says God is near. Why do you think one of the wise men offered the gift of incense? This gift tells us Jesus is the Son of God.

Myrrh is used like a painkiller. If you are in pain, what are you given to take the pain away? Myrrh is used to take away pain. Why do you think a wise man gave this gift to Jesus? Myrrh was given as a gift to show that Jesus would suffer pain for us. Do you know when he did this? Jesus would also bring us freedom from many troubles and sorrow.

Activity

Have a golden crown, a stick of incense, a small white box for myrrh. Make sure the children know what each is. Then play 'pass the parcels'. When the music stops, the one with gold puts the crown on their head and stands up tall; the one with the incense puts his or her hands together in prayer; the one with the myrrh pretends to cry in pain. Let the music start again and continue as before.

Prayer

Lord Jesus, we thank you
for the wise men and their gifts.
We love you as our King,
our God and our Saviour.

Song

The Virgin Mary had a baby boy

See if you can find the letters to make the gifts the wise men are carrying. You have been given the first letter.

Draw in the star an offering you could give to Jesus.

PRAY

Lord Jesus, we come to you. We offer you our lives and our love. AMEN

David Adam

411

For 6 to 10 years – Year B

Aim

To encourage the children to offer a gift to Jesus.

Readings

Isaiah 60:1-6
Psalm 72:(1-9) 10-15
Ephesians 3:1-12
Matthew 2:1-12

Teaching

Talk about stars, planets and shooting stars. Do they know the names of any stars? Let us draw a star – a five-pointed star. It is actually quite hard to draw a five-pointed star. The star of King David is easier to draw or to make; it can be done by using two triangles *(demonstrate)*.

The wise men decided to follow a bright star because they believed it would bring them to a very special baby, and they decided to bring special gifts with them. What were these special gifts? Produce each of the gifts and talk about them. Gold and frankincense are easy to understand; myrrh is more difficult. See if you can get ideas from the children, using the carol 'We three kings' as an aid. You could ask, 'What sort of people would have such gifts to offer?' If you could offer the most precious thing you have, what would it be? Talk about the offering of our self.

Activity

Give children gifts of gold, frankincense and myrrh to offer to Jesus. Let each of them say why they have brought this gift. Give others a piece of paper on which they write the gift they would like to bring to Jesus.

Prayer

God, we thank you
for the gift of Jesus to the whole world.
He shows us your love and care.
We offer you our lives and our love today.

Song

The wise may bring their learning

David Adam

For 6 to 10 years – Year C

Aim

To encourage the children to see themselves as seekers who are able to offer themselves to God.

Readings

Isaiah 60:1-6
Psalm 72:(1-9) 10-15
Ephesians 3:1-12
Matthew 2:1-12

Teaching

Once there were three very clever men. One was very rich, one was a priest and the third, though clever, was often poorly. Each of them wanted to know God better.

The rich man could buy anything he wanted. He could order it or have it made. All around him were beautiful and expensive things. But there are some things money cannot buy. Can you think of any? Health, love, life – and you cannot buy God. The rich man felt a great emptiness in his life and knew he could not fill it with anything – only God could do that. So he decided he would look for God until he found him. When he found him, the rich man would offer a gift and himself to God.

The next man was a priest and he worked in a church. Every day he offered prayers to God and with them offered frankincense (incense). Does anyone know what it is? It is the gum from a tree. When it is burnt it produces smoke and a nice smell. (If possible, give a demonstration using incense or a joss stick.) The smoke as it swirled was an offering to God and it was a sign that we believe God is very near. The priest burnt the incense and prayed that he would be more aware of God's presence. He decided to seek for God until he knew him better and then he would offer incense and himself to God.

The third man was very clever but he was also often very poorly. He knew all about medicines and sometimes used myrrh to take his pain away. He prayed that one day his pain would be taken away and that he would enjoy life more. He knew the closer he got to God, the less his pain would bother him and one day God would take it away. He decided that he would go and seek for a better awareness of God and when he came to him he would offer himself and his myrrh.

God sent a star to guide each of the seekers. As it was the same star they followed, they soon joined together in their seeking. They journeyed a long way until at last they came to Bethlehem and to Jesus. Here they bowed before him and offered their gifts of gold, frankincense and myrrh. They gave thanks that they saw God in the face of Jesus.

Activity

Play 'pass the parcel'. Let there be three boxes – one gold, one silver and one plain white. Tell the children that when the music stops, whoever is holding the parcel is out. When the group is down to six or less, tell them that the people holding the parcels when the music stops will become the three seekers.

Then, remembering the story, they have to say why they are seeking Jesus.

After this encourage the children to talk about why they come to seek Jesus.

Prayer

O God, we seek you until we find you.
When we find you, help us to know you
for when we know you, then we can love you.
Help us to come before you
through Jesus Christ our Lord.

Song

We are marching in the light of God

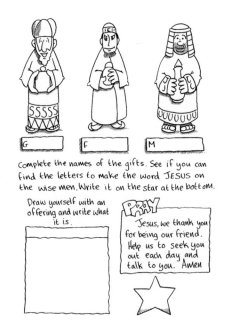

Complete the names of the gifts. See if you can find the letters to make the word JESUS on the wise men. Write it on the star at the bottom.

Draw yourself with an offering and write what it is.

Jesus, we thank you for being our friend. Help us to seek you out each day and talk to you. Amen

David Adam

RESOURCES

Epiphany

A transliteration of the Greek *epiphaneia* (meaning 'manifestation' or 'appearance'), 'Epiphany' is the name used in the Western Church for the celebration of the visit of the Magi to the infant Jesus Christ (Matthew 2:1-12). The annual celebration takes place on 6 January or, in some churches, such as the Church of England or the Methodist Church, on the Sunday nearest to that date.

The theological essence of Epiphany, or in the Eastern Church, the synonymous Theophany (meaning 'divine manifestation'), is Christ as the appearance of God incarnate. As such, the early origins of the festival lie not only in the celebration of the Magi's visit but also in all the events leading up to and including the baptism of Jesus, as well as the turning of water into wine at the wedding in Cana, identified as the first miraculous manifestation of Jesus' glory (John 2:11). The development of Epiphany or Theophany and its relation to Christmas is historically complex and at times unclear, but in the Eastern Church the traditional focus is the baptism of Jesus, while in the Western Church it is the visit of the Magi.

According to Matthew 2, Magi (Zoroastrian priests who practised astrology) were guided from the East by a star. They presented the infant Jesus with gifts of gold, frankincense and myrrh. Traditionally the gold symbolised Jesus' kingship. The frankincense, associated with priestly worship, pointed to Jesus as the great High Priest. Myrrh, which was used for embalming corpses, foretold Jesus' death on the cross.

The Bible neither names nor numbers the Magi. The traditional assumption that there were three is probably attributable to the number of gifts. Western tradition names them Caspar, Melchior and Balthasar, identifying them as kings. Such status has little biblical basis beyond rather speculative references to Old Testament prophecies such as Isaiah 60:3, Psalm 68:29 and 72:10-11, which describe the Messiah being worshipped by kings.

Russell Herbert

Celtic Thoughts

Wise kings of the long journey

Psalm 106:24–end; Joshua 4; Matthew 2:1-11

The three magi rejoiced when they saw the star. They entered the house and saw the child with Mary his mother, and they knelt and worshipped him. They offered him gifts of gold, frankincense and myrrh.

Matthew 2:10-11

At a new year we step out afresh on virgin ground. Let us learn from the wise kings of the long journey how our journey should be.

The first king stands for gold, something we all want, something good in itself. It stands for prosperity, and all the things money can buy. Hopefully many of us will have times of prosperity. But gold cannot buy love, truth, eternity; it cannot fill the heart. The wisdom of this king was that he knew this, and he came to find that which would fill his heart, that for which he could give his life. In this wise person money was put in perspective, and he was willing to kneel and offer it as a gift.

The second king brings incense; he is at home with the routines of religion, of scholarship. These things, too, can be good. But, just as the pocket cannot satisfy the heart, neither can the brain. Perhaps this man came to realise that. He was drawn onwards by a sense of mystery. As he knelt, he was filled with a sense of wonder that no amount of theory could have produced. When the heart is right, we have a sense of wonder at the smallest thing, and all life becomes a sign of God's Presence.

The third king is a sad person; it is unusual for an adult to talk about death in front of a newborn baby. This wise man had an intuitive understanding of the suffering and early death that was to mark Jesus' life. He shows us how to accept and be dignified in the times of loss, disappointment or downturn.

High King of the universe,
we offer you our possessions,
make them all your own.
We offer you our mindsets
and we place them at your feet.
May we be filled with your Presence
as incense fills a holy place.
We offer you the shadows of our lives,
the things that are crushed;
our little deaths and our final death.
May these be like the straw in the out-stable.
May something beautiful for you be born in all this straw.

Ray Simpson

Another way

Psalm 2; Numbers 22:1-35; Matthew 2:12-23

Being warned in a dream not to return to King Herod, the visitors who studied the stars returned home another way.

Matthew 2:12

After the star, the dim day.
After the gifts, the empty hands.
And now we take our secret way back to far lands.
After the cave, the bleak plain.
After the joy, the weary ride.
But journey we, three new-made men, side by side.
Came we by old paths by the sands.
Go we by new ones this new day,
homewards to rule our lives and lands by another way.

Author unknown

I beg assistance, God of my journey,
to accept that all of life is only on loan to me, to believe beyond this moment,
to accept your courage when mine fails,
to recognise the pilgrim of my heart,
to hold all of life in open hands.   *Joyce Rupp, OSM, A Pilgrim at Glendalough*

Be a smooth way before me, be a guiding star above me, be a keen eye behind me, this day,
this year, for ever.

                                                                            Ray Simpson

Reflections

Magi

The way that Matthew wrote it
is so very different
from the story of three kings,
of Caspar, Melchior, and Balthazar,
which we've received.

Matthew did not give their rank,
their number
or their names,

nor were they led to a stable
but a house!

Nor did he suggest their origins:
what mattered most to him
was where they did not come from,
and they did not come from Palestine.

They were not Jews
but foreigners –
and the Christ child was for them.

That's the point:
Christ is for everyone –
and none is specially chosen,
no barriers of race or gender:
God has no favourites.

The magi also witness
to that important truth
that God is no respecter of persons:

God reveals himself
not to Herodic politicians,
intent to keep their power
or to be re-elected,

nor to religious leaders,
sure in their blinkered truth
that they have grasp of God,

but God reveals himself
to secular men,
astrologers,
who seek the future in the stars.

He starts where they are –
and leads them . . .
. . . by an unexpected path
to an unexpected place
and at their journey's end
a most surprising King.

Call them astrologers
or kings
or what you will

but make sure you ask
where you can find the Christ;

be prepared to look
in unexpected places
and unexpected people;

. . . and don't be surprised
to find God revealing himself
to secular people who think
that they can find their future in the stars!

There are many stars
but only one to follow;
there are many gods
but only one to serve.

He will start just where you are
and lead if you will trust him;

however dark the way
his light will always guide;
he may take you

by a different road
than you expected

but at your journey's end
you will find Christ.   *Ken Taylor*

Following stars

Isaiah 60:1-6; Psalm 72:(1-9), 10-15; Ephesians 3:1-12; Matthew 2:1-12

Like surfers we stand
poised, trying to anticipate the next big wave

we all do it,
businesses looking for the untapped market
that will see them nicely through the next decade;
publishers hunting the next Booker prize winner
with several sequels up their sleeve;
clubbers spying out the next cool venue
where anyone who is anyone will go to be seen.

Whose star is in the ascendancy?
Keep up! or miss out . . .

we all do it,
head hunters second-guessing the skills of the future
capturing creativity;
media bosses plotting the rise and fall
of the market's idols;
politicians predicting what will save the nation
and win them the next election.

Whose star is in the ascendancy?
Keep up! or miss out . . .

But who is setting the pace? Who is calling the shots?
Do things simply happen, evolve, because life's like that
and we poor mortals just do our best to see round the next corner?
Or is someone, somewhere, pulling the strings,
playing with us like puppets, making us jump, and jumpy
as they move the goalposts, just for the hell of it?

Who says
that every High St fashion store will stock only minis and crop tops this year?
Designers' whim? Or hand in glove with the porn trade?
Who says
that the next thing to dominate the political agenda is the war on terror?
Necessity? Or cynical smokescreen, displacement tactics?
Who says
that there's no place for creation theory on the school curriculum?
True educationalists? Or a secular lobby?

Who says
that I must watch out for whose star is in the ascendancy,
that I must keep up, or miss out?

When the focus of the world's attention
is shifting, always shifting:
from the White House to Black Africa
from gold mines to oil wells
from priest to scientist
from Western Bloc to Pacific Rim
from kings and presidents to multi-nationals
from economic growth to climate change:

How am I to know,
how to read the signs, if I'm not to miss out?

How am I to know
on whom the mantle will next alight?

And how am I to know
whose star will still be shining when the final curtain falls?

But this I do know,
this: that when the planets cease to spin
and the tides of all the affairs of men recede
and the heavens stand, for a moment,
still: that the star will stand, there,
where it stood before: over the house of Israel
and over its most famous Son,
locus from which all life came
and to which all life must again come . . .

The opposite of a *black hole*:
dazzling wholeness
drawing all things, all men and women to itself – himself:
from east and west nations,
kings, sons and daughters,
herds of camels, fleets of ships and flights
of birds and planes;
wise men of every kind and gender,
those who knew, and those who thought
they didn't want to know,
mountains, trees and all creation –
not to swallow them up, use and discard them,
a passing craze, as is the way of the world –
no, but to welcome them, one and all,
inviting them to make their true,
their final home in the place of praise.

And this I also know
this: that we, the house of Israel, we, who follow the Son,
we are to hold our course:
we are to shine like stars over a storm-tossed sea
until that defining hour when the earth slows
and the world sees whose star is for ever in the ascendancy.

Sheila Walker

Gone?

And when it's all over . . .
Baby Jesus, goodbye,
baby Jesus, goodbye!

We've put him away with the Christmas tree,
get him out again next year, maybe,
baby Jesus, goodbye!

But Jesus grew to a man,
Jesus grew to a man.
He lived and he loved us so much that he died,
that is why God was crucified,
Jesus grew to a man.

Baby Jesus is dead,
baby Jesus is dead.
In fact he was never there at all,
just a plastic doll in a cattle stall,
baby Jesus is dead.

But Jesus rose again,
Jesus rose again.
He's alive and he cares about you,
he wants you to have eternal life too,
Jesus rose again.

Baby Jesus is gone,
baby Jesus is gone.
He goes away with the Christmas cheer,
and then it's all over – till next year,
baby Jesus is gone.

But Jesus is coming as King,
Jesus is coming as King.
He waits for you to invite him in,
he wants so much your love to win,
Jesus is coming as King.

Mary Hathaway

Meditation

Ride that camel! Follow that star!

(Based on Matthew 2:1-12)

Narrator   Melchior, Caspar and Balthazar were three wise men. They used to meet together often to talk about important things, and to look at the stars. They would sit around, very late at night (long after well-behaved children were asleep!) discussing whatever new star they had most recently seen. One evening, Melchior got very excited.

Melchior   Look over there! There's a great big star that I've never seen before. I wonder what it means.

Balthazar   I'll look it up. Let me see, 'Star – extra bright . . .' Hey, it says here that it means a special king has been born, and the star will lead us to him.

Melchior   Then what are we waiting for? Let's go and follow it.

Narrator   Everybody suddenly got very busy, packing the things they would need, and by the next night, when the star appeared again, they were ready to go.

How do you think they travelled?

- Would they *ride* on donkeys?
- Would they *drive* in a car?
- Would they *ride* on bicycles?

Of course, they would ride on camels, wouldn't they?

Balthazar   Come on everyone, let's get moving! The three of us will ride ahead and the servants follow behind with all the food and water and camping kit – and I hope you've remembered to pack the kettle.

Narrator   They travelled through the desert for many weeks, moving at night when they could see the star, and sleeping in their tents during the day. Eventually, they saw a big city ahead.

Melchior   Where are we?

Caspar   According to my reckoning that should be Jerusalem.

Balthazar   Good, that's a capital city. Let's find the palace.

Narrator   Now this was definitely a bad idea. The king in Jerusalem was the wicked king Herod – and he got a bit worried when he heard what the wise men wanted.

Herod   *(Aside, to audience)* I'm the king! There's not room for another one. I'd better find him and get rid of him.

Narrator   So Herod did a bit of checking up, and then went back to the wise men.

Herod   I think the king you're looking for is in Bethlehem. When you've found him, would you let me know, so that I can go to see him, as well?

Narrator   So off went the wise men, and Herod turned to his courtiers and started making plans.

Herod   Right! When those silly men come back and tell me where this so-called king is, I'll have him killed. King indeed!

Narrator   The wise men went to Bethlehem, and found Mary and Joseph with Jesus. They had some presents for the baby.

Gold, for a king

Frankincense, for God's special king

Myrrh, for his suffering

Narrator Then they went to their tents to sleep. And next morning they got ready to leave for home.

Balthazar We mustn't forget to stop and tell that nice King Herod where Jesus is.

Melchior I don't think so. I've found out that 'nice King Herod' as you call him is bad news.

Caspar I knew it! Shifty character! Don't trust him a millimetre' I vote we give him a miss.

Melchior Good idea! Let's go home the pretty way.

Michael Forster

Matthew 2:1-12

Then Herod secretly called for the wise men and learned from them the exact time when the star had appeared. Then he sent them to Bethlehem, saying, 'Go and search diligently for the child; and when you have found him, bring me word so that I may also go and pay him homage.'

Matthew 2:7, 8

Meditation of the magi

(Three parts)

1 He seemed very interested, that king of theirs.

2 Almost *too* interested, we thought.

3 He'd every reason to be concerned, mind you.

2 After all, a newborn king represented a threat,

3 a rival,

1 a possible challenge to his rule.

3 Unless, of course, the child was his.

2 That's what we'd assumed –

1 well you would, wouldn't you:

2 we'd fully expected to find the child there in the palace.

1 But no, Herod hadn't the first idea what we were talking about, not when we first arrived,

3 just stood there, looking at us blankly, trying to hide his bewilderment,

2 until his priests rooted around in their scriptures and turned up something about a child being born in Bethlehem.

1   That's when Herod became all ears, all attention, urging us to hurry off and look carefully for the boy.

2   He wanted to pay him homage, so he said, but do you believe that?

1   *We* didn't.

3   Not having seen the expression in his eyes as he sent us off.

1   Honestly, if looks could kill!

2   It was strange,

3   very strange . . .

2   for we'd come all that way expecting to find rejoicing,

1   celebrations,

3   a people gathering to welcome their king,

1   and instead we found them unprepared,

3   taken by surprise,

2   and if I'm not mistaken, actually unwilling to receive him.

3   An event of cosmic significance was taking place among them, and they didn't want to know.

3   Amazing.

2   *You* wouldn't make that mistake, *would* you.

All   *Would you?*

Prayer

Lord Jesus Christ,
for our failure to welcome you as we should, our keeping you at arm's length,
our resistance to your will,
forgive us.
Overcome our disobedience,
our apathy and weakness,
and help us to give you the place you deserve, at the centre of our lives.   *Nick Fawcett*

ABOUT THE CONTRIBUTORS

DAVID ADAM was the Vicar of Lindisfarne, off the Northumbrian coast, for thirteen years until he retired in March 2003. His work involved ministering to thousands of pilgrims and other visitors. He is the author of many inspiring books on spirituality and prayer, and his Celtic writings have rekindled a keen interest in our Christian heritage.

CLAIRE BENTON-EVANS writes exclusively for Kevin Mayhew. She is the author of many resource books for church leaders working with children, including two popular series, *Allsorts Worship* and *All-sorts Prayer*. She studied English at Oxford before teaching English and Drama in London, Devon and Cornwall. Her writing for schools includes *What's the Story?* – a collection of Bible assemblies – and the *Beastly Bible Stories* series. Claire regularly trains clergy, head teachers and school governors in children's spirituality; she also enjoys leading *Beastly Bible Stories* school events. She lives with her family in the Scottish Borders, where she works as the Youth and Children Officer for the Diocese of Edinburgh.

RUPERT BRISTOW, a Reader in Trinity Benefice, Folkestone, is the author of seven books of prayers for Kevin Mayhew and was Director of Education for Canterbury Diocese from 1995 until his retirement in 2008. He has taught on VSO in Rwanda, was the second Director of the UK Council for Overseas Student Affairs, and then Dean of Student Services at London South Bank University. He has also been a specialist adviser to a House of Commons select committee, edited and written for various educational publications and chaired Kent SACRE (Standing Advisory Council for Religious Education). He is an Honorary Fellow of Canterbury Christ Church University and is currently a governor of East Kent College and a member of the Discipleship and Spirituality Resource Group in Canterbury Diocese.

MICHAEL CATCHPOOL and PAT LUNT are the authors of several popular books in the Kevin Mayhew catalogue, including the very popular assembly resources *Kings and Monkeys, Ugly Bugs and Apple Trees* and *Cooks and Ogres*. They have co-written a musical adaptation of the medieval mystery plays and have performed sketches on local BBC radio stations.

JOHN COX was ordained to a curacy in the diocese of Liverpool in 1968. He spent a second curacy in an inner-city ex-slum parish in Birmingham and became rector in the same parish. After a five-year period at Church House, Westminster where he was Senior Selection Secretary, helping to select ordinands, he was made Canon Treasurer at Southwark Cathedral and Diocesan Director of Ordinands and Post-ordination training. Following four years as Vicar of Roehampton he moved to become Archdeacon of Sudbury in the Diocese of St Edmundsbury and Ipswich in 1995. When he retired in 2006 he was asked to be the part-time Diocesan Director of Education, a job he did for nearly four and a half years before retiring for a second time. It has been during these retirement years that John has been writing for Kevin Mayhew.

PETER DAINTY was ordained in 1963 after studying church history whilst training for the Methodist ministry, and ministered in two circuits (Brigg and Pontefract). He moved to Bury St Edmunds in 1971 to teach at Culford School (an independent Methodist co-educational boarding and day school) where he stayed until his retirement in 2001. From 1973 – 1993 he was a non-stipendiary minister at a small church in Bury St Edmunds. Peter has worked part-time as an editor for Kevin Mayhew and has published many books and anthologies, as well as six gift books for special occasions, all of which include his own prayers.

NICK FAWCETT was brought up in Southend-on-Sea, Essex and trained for the Baptist ministry at Bristol and Oxford, before serving churches in Lancashire and Cheltenham. He subsequently spent three years as a chaplain with the Christian movement Toc H, before focusing on writing and editing, which he continues with today, despite wrestling with myeloma, a currently incurable cancer of the bone marrow. He lives with his wife, Deborah, and two children – Samuel and Kate – in Wellington, Somerset, worshipping, when able, at the local Anglican church. A keen walker, he delights in the beauty of the Somerset and Devon countryside around his home, his numerous books owing much to the inspiration he unfailingly finds there. Nick has had over 130 books published by Kevin Mayhew.

MICHAEL FORSTER grew up in an Anglican vicarage, trained for the Baptist ministry at Regent's Park College, Oxford, and later transferred to the United Reformed Church. He has served a variety of churches as minister, and as a whole-time chaplain in a mental health and learning disability NHS Trust. During his training, Michael became attracted to the work of the psychologist Carl Rogers and later gained a post-graduate diploma in counselling and psychotherapy. Michael is perhaps best known in the churches as a writer of hymns and other worship material. Now retired, his main activities are writing and cabinetmaking. The rest of his time he is busy doing nothing – a duty sadly neglected for far too long.

PENNY GARRET attended a three-year acting course at a performing arts school in London. After graduating, Penny decided against a glittering, highly acclaimed and award-winning career on the stage and screen, and instead devoted herself tirelessly to the work of selling programmes and ice-cream in various West End theatres, including a number of years with the Royal Shakespeare Company at the Barbican. She then began to develop her interest in writing drama and her first play 'Under the Kitchen Sink' was produced on the London Fringe at a venue in Clapham, followed by the public reading of a subsequent work, at Battersea Arts Centre. She has also written comedy sketches for the Theatre Royal, Stratford East for their variety nights.

NICK HARDING is currently Children's Ministry Adviser for the Church of England in Nottinghamshire, as well as being a magistrate, a member of General Synod, and he speaks at conferences throughout Britain and Ireland. Nick has written a range of resource books for those who work with children and has a particular interest in how all ages can work together. He has led all-age worship and seminars at Spring Harvest for many years, is married to Clare, a headteacher, and has two grown-up sons.

MARY HATHAWAY is the author of *A Word for All Seasons: Reflections, Meditations and Prayers for the Church Year* published by Kevin Mayhew, for use in public worship, house groups and other small gatherings, but also suitable for individual use.

REVD DR RUSSELL HERBERT is a Methodist Superintendent minister, with a background in both youth work and theological research. He currently serves on the team at Christchurch, Clevedon, a vibrant and fast-growing ecumenical church in North Somerset. He is also the author of two books for Kevin Mayhew: *Growing through the Church: A practical and theological vision for all-age worship* and *Living Hope*.

SIMON HILL is presently the incumbent of St John's, Copthorne, having moved to Sussex from Suffolk where he was rector of six churches. Whilst in Suffolk he completed a Doctorate in Ministry with King's College, London. His thesis focused on how those on the threshold of communities of faith use story to express their faith and the implications this has for practising ministry; an interest that continues to inform and shape his work today. Simon was ordained at Canterbury Cathedral in 1983 and worked overseas in agricultural management as a non-stipendiary minister before taking up a full-time parochial appointment in 2002.

PETER JACKSON is a writer, editor and lay preacher. A published author of business communication books, he has also written plays and sketches for schools and church groups. Several of his books of sketches have been published by Kevin Mayhew, including *The Star and the Stable, Acts of Faith, The Coming King* and *Footsteps to Glory*.

GERALD O'MAHONY was born in Wigan, Lancashire, and at the age of 18 joined the Society of Jesus (the Jesuits). He was ordained priest at the age of 30 and since then has worked in two main areas: ten years as an adviser to teachers of religious education in the Archdiocese of Liverpool, and thirty years as a retreat director and writer at Loyola Hall Jesuit spirituality centre.

JUDITH ROSSALL is a Methodist Presbyter who has also held positions as a hospital and university chaplain. She is the author of *Living the Story*, published by Kevin Mayhew, a book of drama scripts and meditations that aim to bring the Bible alive and which were first tried and tested in services that Judith led at Guildford Methodist Church.

SUSAN SAYERS is a teacher by profession, was later ordained a priest in the Anglican Church and, before retirement her work was divided between the parish of Southend-on-Sea, the local women's prison, writing, training days and retreats. Susan is the author of many popular resource books for the church including our ever-popular *Living Stones* and *Confirmation Experience* ranges. Her most recent publication for Kevin Mayhew is *The Holy Ground Around You, Reflective Services for taking the church outside*. Through the conferences and workshops she is invited to lead, she has been privileged to share in the worship of many different traditions and cultures.

KEN TAYLOR is a retired Methodist minister from Yorkshire. He is the author of *Sunday by Sunday (Volumes 1 and 2): Meditations and resources for all appointed Gospel readings Years A, B and C, Cradle of Hope* and *Tried and Tested Talks for Children*, all published by Kevin Mayhew.

STUART THOMAS was ordained in 1987 and has served in Guildford Diocese for the whole of his ministerial career. After a curacy in Guildford and a first incumbency in Churt, he spent almost 20 years in Ewell, where the ecumenical Ruxley Church was opened in 2013. In 2014 he moved to become Rector of Frimley (still in Surrey!). He has been Diocesan Ecumenical Officer and Rural Dean of Epsom, and is an Honorary Canon of Guildford Cathedral. Stuart has been involved in liturgy and training for most of his ordained life, with a particular focus on liturgical music, on which he recently completed a thesis. As well as his books for Kevin Mayhew, has also written a number of hymns.

PETE TOWNSEND's literary career began as a furniture salesman. After three years of University, he began teaching at a local Further Education College. With a brief sojourn as Head of Department in a Secondary school, and studying for a post-graduate diploma, a decision was made to indulge his passion for writing and playing music. He has written two novels, in excess of twenty educational books and contributed to numerous revision guides and magazines.

SHEILA WALKER is an assistant curate, working with four village churches in East Devon, and in addition, she is a part-time librarian. She has also worked as a French teacher, editor and careers adviser. For Kevin Mayhew, Sheila has written the successful resource book *Contemporary Reflections for Praying and Preaching* which covers Church Years A to C.